Love and You Shall Live

Love and You Shall Live

Christian Soteriology
in the Light of Interreligious
Dialogue and the Biblical
Notion of Agape

LEANDRO LUIS BEDIN FONTANA

A Herder & Herder Book
THE CROSSROAD PUBLISHING COMPANY
NEW YORK

A Herder & Herder Book
The Crossroad Publishing Company
www.crossroadpublishing.com

© 2019 by Leandro Luis Bedin Fontana

Crossroad, Herder & Herder, and the crossed C logo/colophon are registered trademarks of The Crossroad Publishing Company.

All rights reserved. No part of this book may be copied, scanned, reproduced in any way, or stored in a retrieval system, or transmitted, in any form or by any means, electronic, mechanical, photocopying, recording, or otherwise, without the written permission of The Crossroad Publishing Company. For permission please write to rights@crossroadpublishing.com.

In continuation of our 200-year tradition of independent publishing, The Crossroad Publishing Company proudly offers a variety of books with strong, original voices and diverse perspectives. The viewpoints expressed in our books are not necessarily those of The Crossroad Publishing Company, any of its imprints or of its employees, executives, owners. Although the author and publisher have made every effort to ensure that the information in this book was correct at press time, the author and publisher do not assume and hereby disclaim any liability to any party for any loss, damage, or disruption caused by errors or omissions, whether such errors or omissions result from negligence, accident, or any other cause. No claims are made or responsibility assumed for any health or other benefits.

The text of this book is set in 11/14 Sabon LT Pro.

Composition by Sophie Appel
Cover design by Sophie Appel

Library of Congress Cataloging-in-Publication Data
available upon request from the Library of Congress.

ISBN 978-0-8245-9950-8 paperback
ISBN 978-0-8245-9951-5 cloth
ISBN 978-0-8245-9952-2 ePub
ISBN 978-0-8245-9953-9 mobi

Books published by The Crossroad Publishing Company may be purchased at special quantity discount rates for classes and institutional use. For information, please e-mail sales@crossroadpublishing.com.

CONTENTS

Foreword   ix

PART I. FUNDAMENTAL QUESTIONS

1. Reducing Dialog to the Issue of Salvation:	
An Introduction	3
A Typology and Its Alternatives	5
The Element of Recognition	7
Revisiting Christian Salvation	10
A Western Soteriological Fixation?	11
Towards a Biblical Approach	14
Nostra aetate: The Christian *habitudo*	16
The Conceptual Framework	18
Setting the Focus	18
The Gospel of Luke	20
On the Feasibility of Translation	21
The Outline	22
2. Searching for Jesus' Original Message	24
The Life of Jesus as a Source of Knowledge of Theology	25
The Interweaving between Revelation	
and Human Experience	28
How Normative Is Jesus' Message to Christians?	30
Searching for a Reliable Method to Approach Jesus' Message	32
Orthodoxy and Heresy within the New Testament	32
The Valuable Help of Exegesis:	
Clarity Rather Than Certainty	36
Outcome	38

PART II. BIBLICAL FOUNDATIONS

3. The Intricacy of the Question of Salvation	
in Jesus' Context	41
Competing Discourses on Salvation	41
The Immediacy of God's Implacable Judgment	
in the Preaching of John the Baptist	44

The Apocalyptic Genre and Its Basic Features	45
Apocalyptic Influences on Early Christianity	46
The Controversial Locus of History in God's Salvation	48
Jesus' Optimistic Anthropology	50
John's Anthropological Premise	50
Pessimistic Anthropologies in Christian Tradition	54
Metanoia: A Key to Human Change	57
What Comprises the Difference between John and Jesus?	60
Was Jesus' Message on Salvation a Rupture with Judaism?	65
Can God in His Anger Annihilate His Beloved People?	68
Outcome	69

**4. The Soteriological Potential of the Praxis
of Love in the Light of Lk 10:25-37**   71

The Parable of the Good Samaritan (Lk 10:25-37)	73
The Core Message and the Main Concerns	
of Luke's Special Material	77
The Source(s) of Lukan Special Material	78
The Composition of Lukan Special Material:	
A Jewish Christian Writing?	80
A Possible Theology and a Few Apparent	
Concerns of the Texts	83
Open Questions concerning Jewish Christianity	87
Consequences of the Study on Lukan Special Material	89
Luke's Primary Concerns in His Twofold Work	95
The Poor and the Rich	95
Particular Concern with the Question of Salvation	97
The Model of Solidarity	99
Other Similar Approaches in the Synoptic Tradition	100
Mt 25:31-46: The Unity between Love of God	
and Love of Neighbor Made Concrete	100
Mk 7:24-30: Jesus Learns from a Pagan Woman	104
Outcome	107

**5. The Close Relation between Salvation
and the Twofold Commandment of Love**   110

The Twofold Commandment of Love in the Gospel of Mark	112
The Twofold Commandment of Love	
in the Gospel of Matthew	115

The Twofold Commandment of Love in the Gospel of Luke	118
Summarizing the Whole Torah in One Single Commandment	119
The Linkage between Love and Salvation	121
The Controversies around the Idea of Neighbor	123
Luke's Emphasis on the Practice of Love	127
Agape as a Key Theological Concept of the Johannine Literature	128
Paul's Understanding of the Commandment to Love	135
Outcome	144

6. The Notion of Love as a Corrective Ideal to the Concept of Salvation? — 147

Salvation in the Context of God's Threatening Judgment	148
Love Alone Can Break the Cycle of Violence	153
The New Testament Notion of Agape	155
Beyond Ethics	157
No Love without Justice	160
Outcome	165

PART III. THEOLOGICAL IMPLICATIONS

7. Agape: A Valuable Concept for the World — 169

Agape's Theological Relevance	170
Love as Universal Power	172
The Social "Function" of Love	177
Luhmann's Systems Theory: A Brief Overview	178
Love as a Social Code	182
Agape as a Competence to Reach States of Peace	189
The Potential of Love for Cognition	192
Love and the Edification of Reality	199
Atheistic Love?	205
Love as Relationship	209
Outcome	212

8. When Christian Faith and Human Agency Become One — 214

Embedding Love in the Modern Discourse on Freedom	215
The Modern Age and the Idea of Freedom	216
The Practice of Agape as a Possibility of Real Freedom	219

The Unity between Love of God and Love of Neighbor	225
The Secular World: A Conducive Environment to the Praxis of Love	228
The Complex Relation between Religion and Identity in a Secularized World	231
Unconditional Recognition	234
The Motif of the Likeness of God	243
Sacramental Love	247
Does Love Ensure Salvation?	253
Outcome	258
9. By Way of Conclusion	**261**
Rethinking Universal Salvation in the Light of Agape	262
Agape, Truth and Justice	268
Bibliography	271
Index of Names	307

FOREWORD

"Love, and you shall live" is the answer given by Jesus in Lk 10:28 to the question, "Master, what must I do to inherit eternal life?" Notwithstanding the fact that this text literally reads "*Do this*, and you will live," the formulation presented in this book's title certainly conveys its intended meaning, particularly because this is the concluding verse of Luke's account of the twofold commandment to love. Given the enormous significance that this verse assumed throughout this work, in combination with both its preceding (Lk 10:25-27) and its following (Lk 10:30-37) texts, this book could not bear a more appropriate title. More importantly, it brings to a close a long journey in search of adequate answers to the complex issues of religious identity, the feasibility of an earnest dialogue between religions, and, in particular, the possibility of unconditional recognition of other believers and religions which, in the Christian theological tradition, is inextricably connected to the question of salvation of non-Christians.

The research avails itself of both practical experience and intellectual reflection on those predicaments. Most of my experience related to those matters draws on a three-year sojourn in Nagpur, India (2005-2007), where I was given the opportunity to work together with Christians, Hindus, Buddhists, and Muslims. In addition, as my academic research on the topic of interreligious dialogue began (2011), in Germany, my participation in both the International Graduate Study Program "Religion in Dialogue" and the Research Training Group "*Theologie als Wissenschaft*" provided me with an excellent opportunity for exchange with people from different countries, cultures, and religions on this subject. Furthermore, the confrontation of my own experience and knowledge with the German philosophic-theological tradition of thought at the Goethe University as well as at the *Philosophisch-Theologische Hochschule Sankt Georgen*, both in Frankfurt am Main, offered me the most favorable conditions to carry out this research project academically.

Therefore, I would like to express my heartfelt gratitude to my supervisors, Prof. Dr. Knut Wenzel, Prof. Dr. Dirk Ansorge, and Prof. Dr. Heiko Schulz for their extensive expertise, critical remarks, insightful suggestions, and gentle guidance throughout these years of study. In particular, I thank Prof. Dr. Wenzel, my first supervisor, who has accompanied me on this journey since the beginning and constantly fostered my theological reflection on the topics of this research project. Besides, I am greatly indebted to the *Deutsche Forschungsgemeinschaft* (DFG) which has financed both the Research Training Group *"Theologie als Wissenschaft"* and my scholarship during this time, thereby contributing enormously to the conduct of this project.

I extend my gratitude to the other professors and colleagues of the aforementioned programs and institutions as well, with whom I have learned so much at different levels over the last years and from whom I have received precious feedback for the work. In particular, I would like to mention a few of them with whom I had a more intensive theological exchange: Alessandro Aprile, Ana Honnacker, Daniel Rothe, Eva Bucher, Fatma Aydınlı, Johnson Srigiri, Matthias Ruf, Mukadder Hendek, and Sarah Rosenhauer.

I also want to extend a very particular word of thanks to Dr. Susan Durst for having revised my manuscript with such diligence and devotion as to ensure not only the linguistic quality of the entire work but also a more fluent reading and the avoidance of unclear and ambiguous formulations.

Although the origins of this volume can be traced to a doctoral dissertation, which was submitted and defended in 2016 at the *Philosophisch-Theologische Hochschule Sankt Georgen*, before becoming a book, the manuscript obviously underwent extensive modifications, especially at a formal level. During this process, Christopher Myers' guidance was certainly indispensable for the successful completion of this work, and I thank him very much, too.

Finally, I would like to express my profound gratitude to my wife, Claudia, without whose patience, unconditional love, and wholehearted support I could never have accomplished this project in the fashion I did. This sincere word of thanks extends to our both families, that constantly supported me/us in various manners.

Leandro Luis Bedin Fontana
March 2018

PART I

Fundamental Questions

1

Reducing Dialog to the Issue of Salvation: An Introduction

The whole debate around interreligious dialogue, as understood today, is fairly recent both in theological discourses and in Christian practices, especially if contrasted with Christianity's millenary tradition. However, in the last decades, this issue has gained more and more relevance. The first reason which accounts for such a development is, undoubtedly, the enormous mobility of people and access to information media. Thus, intercultural as well as interreligious encounters have become essential components of the globalized world and part of daily life, that is, a concrete situation which Christians – and every other citizen – must be able to cope with. The fallacious belief inherited from the times of Roman domination, and reinforced at the Peace of Augsburg of 1555, according to which a state would only be strong and successful to the extent that it could assure religious homogeneity (*cuius regio, eius religio*), has been proven false.[1] To be sure, more direct contact with members of other religions does not necessarily mean that people know and understand better one another[2] nor that there is an interest in dialogue. But no one can ignore this reality any longer. Besides, the challenges

---

1 Werner G. Jeanrond, "Interkulturalität und Interreligiosität: Die Notwendigkeit einer Hermeneutik der Liebe," in *Kontextualität und Universalität: Die Vielfalt der Glaubenskontexte und der Universalitätsanspruch des Evangeliums*, ed. Thomas Schreijäck and Knut Wenzel (Kohlhammer, 2012), 156.
2 Karl Lehmann, "Kriterien des interreligiösen Dialogs," *Stimmen der Zeit* 227, no. 9 (2009): 582.

of peaceful coexistence in plural societies have been aggravated even more, in recent days, by the so-called refugee crisis, particularly in European countries.

In addition, secularized citizens, based on the modern conceptions of person, society, politics, democracy, equal rights, religious freedom, etc., expect from all religions the ability to overcome any claim of superiority or absoluteness and recognize one another as equals and bearers of the same dignity. Even at a theological level, there are scholars who have identified Christian hegemony or Christian hegemonic thinking as being the real problem to be addressed in any Theology of Religions, including pluralistic theologies.[3] Furthermore, in consequence of such an attitude, and because of their self-centeredness and inability to dialogue, religions have often been alleged to be responsible for war and violence in the world.[4]

In the face of this scenario, Christians are caught up in this dilemma and do struggle to combine their Christian faith and identity with the new challenges of the present world, with particular attention being paid to religious plurality. I am thinking here of very concrete, sometimes even dramatic encounters, rather than theoretic or ideal scenarios. After all, welcoming and approving of religious pluralism seems to imply, at first glance, that one is expected to give up, for the sake of tolerance, the character of absoluteness of one's religion alongside most of its fundamental beliefs.

---

3 See, among others, Marianne Moyaert, "Christianity as the Measure of Religion? Materializing the Theology of Religions," in *Twenty-First-Century Theologies of Religions: Retrospection and Future Prospects*, ed. Elizabeth J. Harris, Paul Hedges, and Shanthikumar Hettiarachchi, Currents of Encounter 54 (Leiden; Boston: Brill; Rodopi, 2016), 241–44.

4 That is one of the claims of the Project "*Weltethos*": "No world peace without peace among religions" (Hans Küng, *Projekt Weltethos* [München: Piper, 1990], 97f.). See also, for that matter, the controversial book by Samuel P. Huntington, *The Clash of Civilizations and the Remaking of World Order* (New York: Simon & Schuster, 1996). For a critical, objective, and insightful analysis of Huntington's thesis, see Amartya Kumar Sen, *Identity and Violence: The Illusion of Destiny* (New York: W.W. Norton & Co., 2006).

A Typology and Its Alternatives

The issue of religious pluralism constitutes a predicament not only for Christian believers from different walks of life in their struggle to combine their faith with modern life. It has increasingly challenged theology, too. In Western theologies, most of the debate over interreligious dialogue has taken place within a theological discipline called Theology of Religions, and has basically revolved around the issue of salvation of non-Christians, with particular attention being directed to the role of Jesus Christ in universal salvation as its exclusive mediator. Thus, the most established model in academic research to approach the issue of religious plurality has been the one proposed by the Anglican theologian Alan Race, which operates with the well-known typology exclusivism, inclusivism, and pluralism.[5]

Basically, exclusivism is an ecclesiocentric view, insofar as it affirms that the fullness of truth and salvation is found but in one single religion or church, whereas all others are excluded from it unless they convert. Inclusivism, by contrast, identifies in Jesus Christ the truth and salvation of all nations, even though "the rays of his truth" may be present in other religious traditions, too, albeit not in its fullness. This makes of inclusivism a Christ-centered approach and asserts that his presence saves all peoples, no matter if it is even hidden or unknown, at times. Finally, pluralism represents a theocentric or, more precisely, a Reality-centered view that conceives each religion as an equally legitimate interpreter of the one Reality, which is so transcendent as to restrain every particular religion from making absolute claims about it.

Needless to say, this typology is fully informed by the Western, Christian tradition of thought. As a matter of fact, it has been particularly helpful in offering a sort of systematization of the contrasting

---

5 Alan Race, *Christians and Religious Pluralism: Patterns in the Christian Theology of Religions* (Maryknoll, N.Y.: Orbis Books, 1983). In this book, Race sets out to systematically "co-ordinate" the myriad of emerging approaches that could be gathered "under the umbrella heading of a Christian theology of religions. (p. 6)" By introducing the typology inclusivism, exclusivism, and pluralism, his was a pioneering attempt at systematizing the diverse opinions in that regard.

approaches to tackle the predicament of religious plurality, just as it was designed. On the other hand, it has faced, in the last years, strong criticism in various regards.[6] Some of its limits will be seen below.

Particularism certainly was a new approach to Theology of Religions. It emerged in the mid 1990s, especially influenced by George Lindbeck's postliberal theology.[7] This stance is sustained by the understanding that the fundamental differences between religious systems cannot be reduced to a common denominator or a common ground. Rather, the peculiar differences among the partners involved in the dialogue have to be discovered, accepted, and tolerated.[8] However, the recognition of the differences is so radical as to deem the need for a dialogue superfluous and even impossible. Indeed, Lindbeck does not hesitate to say: "Not only do they [religions] no longer share a common theme such as salvation, but the shared universe of discourse forged to discuss that theme disintegrates. [...] Those for whom conversation is the key to solving interreligious problems are likely to be disappointed."[9] In his opinion, such impossibility of dialogue is accounted for by the fact that each religious system is so radically diverse for the other that any endeavor towards either translation or understanding is condemned to failure from the outset.

A later and quite recent development is Comparative Theology, which in the USA might be associated with scholars like Francis X.

---

6 A comprehensive account of the reception and development of Race's typology is provided in Elizabeth J. Harris, Paul Hedges, and Shanthikumar Hettiarachchi, eds., *Twenty-First-Century Theologies of Religions: Retrospection and Future Prospects*, Currents of Encounter 54 (Leiden; Boston: Brill; Rodopi, 2016).

7 Paul Hedges, "Particularities," in *Christian Approaches to Other Faiths*, ed. Paul Hedges and Alan Race (London: SCM Press, 2008), 112–35. Hedges provides, in this text, a brief, yet detailed, overview of particularism(s).

8 Cf. Didier Pollefeyt, "Interreligious Dialogue beyond Absolutism, Relativism and Particularism: A Catholic Approach to Religious Diversity," in *Encountering the Stranger: A Jewish-Christian-Muslim Trialogue*, ed. Leonard Grob and John K. Roth (Seattle: University of Washington Press, 2012), 245–59.

9 George Lindbeck, "The Gospel's Uniqueness: Election and Untranslatability," *Modern Theology* 13, no. 4 (1997): 429.

Clooney, Catherine Cornille, and James L. Fredericks, and in Germany especially with Klaus von Stosch. The central concerns in this perspective are the feasibility and the conditions of possibility of interreligious dialogue. Accordingly, an optimistic, liberal, purely theoretical view of this issue must give way to a more realistic, phenomenological one. Towards that end, Cornille tries to work out, in her "The Im-possibility of Interreligious Dialogue," a few essential attitudes that could make such an encounter at all possible. They are humility toward truth, commitment to truth, recognition of interconnection with others and shared common ground, genuine empathy, and hospitality toward truth.[10] On that basis, actual dialogue can only take place as exchange of testimonies, in an attitude of profound empathy,[11] and an atmosphere of great, mutual esteem.

The Element of Recognition

A further question to reflect on is to which degree the element of recognition plays a role in the approaches briefly presented above, given its enormous significance for dialogue. In his article "The Politics of Recognition," Charles Taylor observes that the very fact of being either recognized or "*mis*recognized" as a person in one's integrity exerts a profound impact on the formation of one's own identity. This can be verified especially in minority groups, which are normally regarded with contempt, no matter in which society. Consequently,

---

10 Cf. Catherine Cornille, *The Im-Possibility of Interreligious Dialogue* (New York: Crossroad, 2008); for a brief overview, see Catherine Cornille, "Conditions for Inter-Religious Dialogue," in *The Wiley-Blackwell Companion to Inter-Religious Dialogue*, ed. Catherine Cornille, The Wiley-Blackwell Companions to Religion (Chichester: Wiley-Blackwell, 2013), 20–33; Klaus von Stosch, "Komparative Theologie als Hauptaufgabe der Theologie der Zukunft," in *Komparative Theologie: Interreligiöse Vergleiche als Weg der Religionstheologie*, ed. Reinhold Bernhardt and Klaus von Stosch, Beiträge zu einer Theologie der Religionen 7 (Zürich: Theologischer Verlag Zürich, 2009), 15–33.
11 Catherine Cornille, "Empathy and Inter-Religious Imagination," *Religion and the Arts* 12, no. 1 (2008): 102–17.

members of such scorned groups may internalize those feelings of disdain and, in fact, end up believing that they are thus.[12]

Now, this remark draws the attention to two important issues: Firstly, the necessity that all interlocutors of the dialogue be recognized and accepted in their overall identity. For in any interreligious dialogue, one meets another person, whose identity comprises, on the one hand, much more than one's religious affiliation, and yet, on the other hand, a person who represents a religious group and has chosen to be or become thus. This choice has its own reasons and deserves one's utmost respect. Secondly, the hegemonic group, or religion, in any given society, is called upon to be all the more attentive towards such minority groups, lest the circle of disrespect and violence may begin or even escalate to higher levels. In the case of dialogue, it is observable that whenever one is "misrecognized" in his/her (religious) identity, either the focus of discussion tends to be shifted to other "personal" issues or religious matters may be misused for other interests of that particular group. This fact is often underestimated, at times even ignored. However, as will be seen below, lack of recognition is one of the most frequent causes for conflicts and even violence among religious groups (pp. 234–236). Being so, most religious conflicts could be analyzed from this perspective.

The question arises whether the aforementioned typology – including particularism, as several authors have included it in the classical tripartite typology – somehow incorporates the element of recognition. Considering that exclusivist approaches refuse categorically to recognize the possibility of truth and salvation in other religious traditions, the choice is narrowed down to inclusivism, pluralism, and particularism. In inclusivism, one can perceive a strong desire to recognize others, and particularly what is holy, and sacred, and true in them. However, the overemphasis on Jesus' soteriological work seems to be more of a hindrance than an impetus to genuine recognition of others and dialogue. Being so, the recognition of the other seems to be far too selective and, what is more, based on one's

---

12 Charles Taylor, "The Politics of Recognition," in *Multiculturalism: Examining the Politics of Recognition*, ed. Amy Gutmann (Princeton: Princeton University Press, 1992), 25 (emphasis in original).

own criteria, which unquestionably impedes a real encounter.[13] The pluralist approach, by contrast, appears to fully recognize all religious paths by according them equal value. But the crucial question is whether this approach really takes each one of them seriously, or whether this promise, instead, falls into a void platitude, similar to the abstract universalism of modern liberalism described by Taylor, which assures equal dignity to all the groups belonging to its society, but is, at the same time, so indifferent and blind to their differences and their irreducible particularities, that this promise may never come true.[14] Moreover, non-pluralist perspectives are usually not tolerated by pluralists, which provides evidence to confirm D'Costa's thesis that pluralism, in its most radical form, ends up becoming a differentiated form of exclusivism.[15] Consequently, the only possibility of unconditional recognition seems to be guaranteed by particularism, as it truly pays heed to the differences and peculiarities of the other, taking them seriously. However, this approach neither sees the need for interreligious dialogue nor can it conceive of the conditions of possibilities for such interaction, given that the differences among religious systems are thought to be substantial insomuch that it appears to be impossible and meaningless to enter into any exchange or to achieve any significant result.

Therefore, if (mutual) recognition is to be regarded as a decisive condition for interreligious dialogue, it has to be acknowledged

---

13 Following this line of thought, and based on Levinasian philosophy, Burggraeve affirms that "dialogue starts by resisting the inclination to exclude the other ('exclusivism') or by reducing the other to ourselves ('inclusivism')." Roger Burggraeve, "Alterity Makes the Difference: Ethical and Metaphysical Conditions for an Authentic Interreligious Dialogue and Learning," in *Interreligious Learning*, ed. Didier Pollefeyt (Leuven: Peeters, 2007), 237; see also Pollefeyt, "Interreligious Dialogue Beyond Absolutism, Relativism and Particularism."

14 Taylor, "The Politics of Recognition," 43.

15 In fact, the Catholic theologian Gavin D'Costa has become, in the last decades, one of the most known critics of religious pluralism. He argues resolutely that *"pluralism must always logically be a form of exclusivism and that nothing called pluralism really exists"* (Gavin D'Costa, "The Impossibility of a Pluralist View of Religions," *Religious Studies* 32, no. 2 [1996]: 225, italics in original).

that this element cannot be said to be essential to the classical typology mentioned above. This state of affairs gives rise to the need to develop new models that could respond to the challenges and requirements of the present time in a better way. In view of this task, the recent development referred to as Comparative Theology certainly points towards such direction. If the five virtues proposed by Cornille are observed,[16] the otherness of other religions and their respective believers can be indeed recognized. However, even though those virtues may be justified on the basis of Christian tradition, the issue with them is that they are neither compelling enough to motivate a uniquely *Christian* attitude towards other religions nor do their foundations appear to be sufficiently solid to be worked out theologically. Also, it is questionable whether a dialogue between religions can be reduced to the analysis of and conversation about their sacred texts, however important this may be.[17] Beyond doubt, this limits enormously the rich universe of religious life and, broadly speaking, reduces the vast field of religious experience to textual exegesis.

Revisiting Christian Salvation

In addition to what has been said so far, thinking about interreligious encounters informed by the categories of exclusivism, inclusivism, and pluralism appears to be potentially misleading, as, in this typology, everything basically revolves around the role of Jesus Christ for the salvation of non-Christians. Moreover, in conventional models, the mediation of personal salvation has been primarily conceived of in terms of either religious affiliation or belief in the atoning sacrifice of Jesus Christ on the cross. While, in the case of the former, salvation is said to be conveyed through baptism, along with further sacraments, and one's bond with the Church, in the latter, Christ's

---

16 Humility toward truth, commitment to truth, recognition of interconnection with others and shared common ground, genuine empathy, and hospitality toward truth.

17 This pertinent criticism raised by Moyaert was termed by her "textual bias" and may be found in her "Christianity as the Measure of Religion?," 256–58.

atoning sacrifice is believed to reach and save all people, even irrespective of their consent or awareness. As I see it, though, this mode of thinking conveys an all too hypostatized understanding of salvation, as though it was "a thing" that, given some circumstances, can be granted to some and refused to others.

A Western Soteriological Fixation?
The state of affairs described above concerns what I would call "automaticity of salvation," rendered possible in consequence of one's religious affiliation. As a matter of fact, in the literature, one frequently comes across indiscriminate groupings like Christians and non-Christians, whereby all members of Christian denominations are lumped together in the group of the "automatically saved," or "saved by default," on account of both their affiliation and their supposed faith in Jesus Christ, whereas all non-Christians fall into the group of those whose possibility of being saved may even be conceived, albeit through several theological detours. But again, this development can certainly be put down to what the already quoted Lutheran theologian George Lindbeck terms "soteriological fixation." As he sees it, the theological discourse has been determined to a great extent by an obsessive preoccupation with salvation, which, besides restraining interreligious dialogue from taking other directions, also seeks to set the agenda and to maintain Christianity's hegemony.[18]

As contrasted with a view of salvation as something which can be taken for granted (automaticity) or something reserved to just a few, who feel certain about it, the evangelist Luke recommends, in 13:22-30, a much more modest attitude towards it. The metaphor of "the narrow door" brings any certainty as to entering the Kingdom of God into question and shifts the criteriology from one's provenience, religious affiliation, and even "religious practice" to one's commitment to living out concretely in one's own life – the text juxtaposes good deeds with evil doers – that which one believes. It should be noted that this passage is, for Christians, not an arbitrary, but a normative text, inasmuch as it belongs to its canonical corpus. Because of its relevance for the issue in question, it is worth quoting it in its full length.

---

18 Cf. Lindbeck, "The Gospel's Uniqueness," 425.

Through towns and villages he went teaching, making his way to Jerusalem. Someone said to him, "Sir, will there be only a few saved?" He said to them, "Try your hardest to enter by the narrow door, because, I tell you, many will try to enter and will not succeed. Once the master of the house has got up and locked the door, you may find yourself standing outside knocking on the door, saying, 'Lord, open to us,' but he will answer, 'I do not know where you come from.' Then you will start saying, 'We once ate and drank in your company; you taught in our streets,' but he will reply, 'I do not know where you come from; away from me, all evil doers!' Then there will be weeping and grinding of teeth, when you see Abraham and Isaac and Jacob and all the prophets in the kingdom of God, and yourselves thrown out. And people from east and west, from north and south, will come and sit down at the feast in the kingdom of God. Look, there are those now last who will be first, and those now first who will be last."
(Lk 13:22-30)

What a text like this does is to break with any thinking pattern which, given determined circumstances, takes salvation for granted without due differentiation. Hence, categories such as Christians and non-Christians are, in my view, not only problematic for the topic of salvation, but they also do injustice to reality. For the taken-for-granted pattern is not so far from thinking about salvation as a merit, in its broadest sense, which squares in no way with Christianity. And reality, by contrast, does not reflect the theological classification of Christians and non-Christians. Plurality determines reality insomuch that even among the group of Christians there is such a plurality as to not allow generalization of this kind.

Therefore, conceiving the salvation of Christians just in consequence of their being baptized is as problematic as coupling it with determined practices or groupings of people. Even if it is assumed that conversion to Christ "involves an ontological change at some level of the human being" or that the Christian is viewed "as ontologically different to the pre-Christian or the non-Christian," as Whitehead does,[19] based on Paul's theology, it is highly difficult

---

19 Philip Whitehead, "Rethinking the Typology from a Biblical Perspective: Paul, Adam, and the Theology of Religions," in *Twenty-First-Century Theologies of Re-*

to demonstrate why such ontological change cannot occur among "non-Christians," considering that it depends not exclusively on the individual, but primarily on God's grace. The question is even more pertinent, if assumed that there are, for Whitehead, and supposedly for Paul, just two groups of people: those who live "in Adam" and those who live "in Christ."[20] In my understanding, the gospels criticize, in their accounts, precisely such an ontological view of human beings which pays little or no heed to the fundamental unity that has to exist between faith and human action. This applies especially to Luke, despite his having been educated in a Hellenistic milieu (cf. below, p. 95). By contrast, most of the Theology-of-Religions discourse operates with an ontological stance of reality, which is particularly problematic for interreligious dialogues.

By saying that, I do not intend to overcome the alluded soteriological fixation by evading this matter. Conversely, the aim of this investigation is to reflect precisely on this issue in the face of the challenges posed by interreligious-dialogue-related issues. For, in my view, the interreligious-dialogue debate brings up different questions than those of conventional Theology of Religions, such as the element of recognition, for instance, as seen above (pp. 7–10). I do not intend to completely separate the interreligious-dialogue from the Theology-of-Religions discourse as though they were two distinct fields of study. Yet, I do think that the practice of interreligious encounters has developed, over the years, a different awareness of the topic, not to mention the character of urgency that it took on more recently owing to greater mobility, the so-called refugee crisis, and fundamentalisms of all kinds. Provoked as I was by such questions, I will, in fact, engage a very significant one, besides salvation, which is the theological legitimation of interreligious dialogues within Christianity alongside their conditions of possibility.

Now, returning to Christian soteriology, the real challenge in setting out to think about salvation in a post-metaphysical age consists,

---

ligions: Retrospection and Future Prospects, ed. Elizabeth J. Harris, Paul Hedges, and Shanthikumar Hettiarachchi, Currents of Encounter 54 (Leiden; Boston: Brill; Rodopi, 2016), 104.

20 Ibid., 103.

as I see it, in paying due heed to the interplay between God's unmerited grace and human agency, an effort that is rarely seen across Theology-of-Religions discourses. And to my knowledge, there is no source, in Christian tradition, in which this interplay is better brought to the fore than biblical thinking. Indeed, by shifting the focus from the "logos of cosmos" onto the "meaning of history," biblical thinking breaks with Greek metaphysical philosophy and frees God's as well as human action from fate.[21] Ultimately, it frees God and man from cosmological order, which, in Paul's language, is referred to as νόμος (law). This suggests, in turn, the need to focus special attention on the Scripture for that matter.

Towards a Biblical Approach
The predicaments of the soteriology underlying the typology in question were identified and faced, in analogous manner, by the Dutch theologian Marianne Moyaert as well.[22] Based on the critique of particularist approaches, she suggested a shift from soteriological openness, which is aimed at in the typology, towards hermeneutic openness, as she terms it, which could be reached, in her opinion, through Comparative Theology. Albeit not disagreeing with her on the need to encourage such a move, I suggest, however, dwelling for a while more on the very concept of Christian salvation before engaging in hermeneutics. Hermeneutical openness will, in fact, be another topic to be dealt with, but only in a second moment, and as a consequence of the reflection on Christian soteriology.

Now, considering that such issues, far from being marginal, pertain to the very foundations and self-understanding of Christianity, the method I suggest to set about them is a close examination of Christianity's primary sources with the purpose of exploring the

---

21 Karl Löwith, *Weltgeschichte und Heilsgeschehen: die theologischen Voraussetzungen der Geschichtsphilosophie*, Urban-Bücher 2 (Stuttgart: Kohlhammer, 1953), 14; Franz Schupp, *Auf dem Weg zu einer kritischen Theologie* (Freiburg im Breisgau; Basel; Wien: Herder, 1974), 14. Cf. also below p. 48–50.
22 Marianne Moyaert, "Recent Developments in the Theology of Interreligious Dialogue: From Soteriological Openness to Hermeneutical Openness," *Modern Theology* 28, no. 1 (2012): 25–52.

person and message of its founder, Jesus of Nazareth, in the quest of new forms of understanding the questions at stake and tackling the challenges which this topic is faced with (cf. chapter 2). The passage from the Gospel of Luke (Lk 13:22-30) quoted above (p. 12) could serve as an example of the reflection I would like to engage in. Admittedly, these issues could just as well be handled from a philosophical or even an ethical perspective. However, it seems impossible to reconceive some essential elements of Christianity such as salvation without referring back to that very foundational moment of Christianity, namely, the person and life of Jesus Christ, just in the form as it was mediated by the sacred authors. After all, the canonical corpus of the New Testament represents for Christians the normative[23] source for both Christian practice and theological reflection.

Obviously, such an approach is nothing completely new in Christian theology. One needs only think of endeavors to combine "Christian original faith" and "Christian practice" such as Pietism. On the other hand, one cannot deny that the historical person and the contents of the message of Jesus have been largely neglected in systematic theology, which is even more so in recent Theologies of Religions. Therein, Jesus is either Christologically presented as the only mediator of universal salvation, no matter whether in inclusivistic or exclusivistic approaches, or left aside, as in the case of rather pluralistic approaches, lest he constitute a hindrance in interreligious encounters. Therefore, the Catholic theologian Andreas Batlogg, by recalling one of Karl Rahner's demands, argues for the liberation of the person of Jesus Christ from the "exile of spirituality history" and the "captivity of personal piety" so as to recover, in theology, the *locus* of the mysteries of his life and the liberating power of his message.[24]

---

23 Normative is employed here not so much in a legal sense as in the sense of a binding commitment to something or someone. Such an understanding, nevertheless, neither undervalues the importance of a certain "legal liability" to Christian tradition nor does it leave room for arbitrariness. It just lays more emphasis on one's own free choice.

24 Cf. Andreas R. Batlogg, "Wieviel Jesus braucht die Fundamentaltheologie: Zur

Nostra aetate: The Christian *habitudo*

Besides the whole discussion about the concept of salvation, there is, in my view, a second issue to be necessarily addressed. It concerns our very attitude towards religious otherness, as interreligious dialogue goes far beyond an intellectual debate. It involves one's overall attitude and performative actions towards difference as well. In Catholic Tradition, a great landmark in that respect certainly was the Second Vatican Council, and, most particularly, its declaration *Nostra aetate*.

Nostra aetate takes a step further than *Dignitatis Humanae*, as it holds in high regard not only the "sacred rights" of individuals (*Dignitatis Humanae* 6) – to which religious freedom belongs – or their religious experiences, but also, and especially, religions as such.[25] For, in *Nostra aetate*, the question concerning the possibility of salvation outside the Church could already be presupposed as settled.[26] The innovative aspect of this document is that such "sincere reverence" for other religions (*Nostra aetate* 2) "[...] already includes the recognition of the access to the true and holy, to divine salvation, just as Christianity understands it, in and through other religions, too."[27] It follows also that other religions can be paths to salvation and bring people to God's presence and closeness.

To affirm this does not mean in any way relativizing all paths to salvation or even making the need for evangelization superfluous.

Relevanz des (unterschätzten) Lebens Jesu – eine Problemanzeige," in *Was den Glauben in Bewegung bringt: Fundamentaltheologie in der Spur Jesu Christi*, ed. Andreas R. Batlogg, Mariano Delgado, and Roman A. Siebenrock, Festschrift für Karl H. Neufeld (Freiburg im Breisgau; Basel; Wien: Herder, 2004), 416. This matter will be developed in chapter 2 (pp. 25–28).

25 Knut Wenzel, *Kleine Geschichte des Zweiten Vatikanischen Konzils* (Freiburg im Breisgau: Herder, 2005), 137.

26 Cf. Roman A. Siebenrock, "Theologischer Kommentar zur Erklärung über die Haltung der Kirche zu den nichtchristlichen Religionen (Nostra aetate)," in *Herders theologischer Kommentar zum Zweiten Vatikanischen Konzil*, ed. Peter Hünermann and Bernd Jochen Hilberath, vol. 3 (Freiburg im Breisgau: Herder, 2005), 649.

27 Wenzel, *Kleine Geschichte des Zweiten Vatikanischen Konzils*, 137.

Instead, its primary purpose, according to an expert on this document, is to define the intended dialogue precisely as "[...] the realization of the nature and mission of the Church in the present time."[28] This being the case, *Nostra aetate* is to be understood as a normative statement of the very nature of the Church, i.e., as its most genuine *modus essendi et operandi* in the world, particularly in the encounter with other religions. As a consequence, far from offering an accurate definition of concepts present in the document such as religion, salvation, truth, etc. or even guidelines for the dialogue, this declaration is rather meant as an official, normative statement as regards the attitude (*habitudo*) of the Church towards other religions.[29]

As can be noticed especially in *Nostra aetate* 5, the effort made by the Council Fathers consisted in justifying the attitude of recognition, respect, and love towards other religions by means of the most normative source of Christianity, perhaps the only normative source common to all Christians, namely, the Scripture, which was a new strategy. By declaring God as father of all, by recognizing the dignity of every person for being an image of God, and by declaring the love of neighbor as the criterion for true knowledge of God, the Council Fathers lay a firm foundation both for a consensus among Christians, as no one would dare to contest the normativity of those statements, and for a self-commitment to dialogue.

Therefore, according to Siebenrock, the choice of the term *habitudo* in the very title has two major implications. First, the Council Fathers dispensed with any description of reality, be it of the past, present or future time. By limiting themselves to a normative statement, as they did, they provide Christians with an objective criterion to evaluate the past and to shape the future. What they could and did not do, however, in the absence of the other interlocutors, was to determine what the future of dialogue was to look like. The Fathers could solely recognize others as equal subjects of dialogue. Second, the document cannot be regarded as "merely pastoral," insofar as it presupposes the theological, normative definitions of the other Council constitutions and represents the self-commitment of the

---

28 Siebenrock, "Theologischer Kommentar," 646.
29 See, especially, *Nostra aetate* 5. For further details, cf. ibid., 645–49.

institutional Church, including all her members, to the practice of dialogue as a form of her own "self-fulfillment." However, if a dialogic attitude in the terms of the document is the criterion to assess the authenticity of the Church, in conformity with her very nature, other religions are recognized, for Siebenrock, not only as equal subjects, but also as her "inspection bodies," as it were.[30] This amounts to saying that the manner in which the Church relates with other religions can be inspected by others, so to speak, in order to validate (or not) the consistency of her *habitudo* with her very nature. Beyond doubt, according other religions such a status is something unique and original in the history of the Church.

All these aspects regarding the "attitude" of Christians in relation to otherness, implicit in *Nostra aetate,* will be worked out, from a hermeneutic perspective.

The Conceptual Framework

Setting the Focus

It corresponds with the very nature of religions to make absolute claims, which normally "make sense" exclusively within the semantic world of that particular system. To the extent that such a "right" is socially conceded to religious traditions, religions exist, in reality, as closed, self-contained units. Strictly speaking, neither do religions "need" each other, nor do they need to engage in dialogue with each other, nor can they understand each other, inasmuch as their claims are incompatible with the world and the language code of others.

As a matter of fact, however, religions do meet with each other, be it through their representatives, be it through their adherents, or even academically. Out of this observation three questions arise: what could be the motives for such an interest in the other, is there a theological legitimation for that fact, and, finally, what could be a proper attitude with which to meet the other, lest these encounters

---

30 Cf. Siebenrock, "Theologischer Kommentar," 647. The original German word is *Prüfungsinstanz*.

turn out to be a traumatic or disastrous experience for both the subject itself and its dialogue partner?

Now, given the character of absoluteness claimed by religions, the answer to those questions cannot be found in "worldly sources" such as civil law, for instance. It follows that no religion can be forced by external coercion to become open to or to seek dialogue with others. Neither can it be enforced by rules and regulations, nor can values such as democracy, respect, esteem, equality, etc. be the primary and sole motivation for that. The true and normative inspiration for such an act and attitude, the courage to take on this challenge, the vigor for endurance in such an undertaking can be found nowhere but in the individuals themselves or in the very sources of each particular tradition. This justifies once more the laborious detour through the sources of the New Testament. From a Christian perspective, as it seems to me, the answer to those questions can, in fact, be found in the New Testament idea of love, understood as agape. For in Christianity this rich concept can be conceived of both as an early-Christian regulative principle for encounters (cf. below, pp. 155–157) and as that which lies at the very root of interreligious encounters, inasmuch as love indicates the primary act of "taking an interest" in others (cf. below, p. 195), which is prior to every other act.

This being so, the answer to whether or not other religions are to be recognized as such and ascribed a positive role in God's plan of salvation lies, primarily, in Christianity's most normative sources, that is, in the New Testament. Now, since in this work the New Testament is not simply regarded as a set of documents containing infallible truth statements, but a collection of testimonies to the historical encounter with the person of Jesus Christ, thereafter handed down in the early Church, and then written down by different authors, at different points of time, in different contexts, to different addressees, and by using different rhetorical means, paramount importance shall be attached to theology's hermeneutic efforts. Such a careful investigation, as intended here, has to be carried out, in turn, in a sort of joint work between exegesis and systematic theology, as far as the former concerns itself with the interpretation of the texts of the New Testament and the latter with both the transmission of faith contents down the centuries and their translation in a comprehensible, contemporary language.

The Gospel of Luke

Obviously, a work of this nature cannot have the whole New Testament as its primary source. Hence the need for a clear delimitation of the source(s) to be examined. As will be seen below (chapter 4), in consequence of our search for any relevant statements, practices, or even images which could shed new light on the topics of salvation and interreligious encounters alike, the parable of the Good Samaritan is considered one of the most important pieces of Jesus' message regarding those subjects. Alongside the exegetical analysis of this parable and its inextricable connection to the double commandment to love, particular attention shall be devoted to the peculiar fashion in which the evangelist Luke conceives of and conveys the idea of salvation in his gospel, not least because his addressees were supposedly Christians spread out over various plural contexts, rather than a single community, as in the case of the evangelists Matthew, Mark, and John. According to the exegete Michael Wolter, although there is no consensus yet in this regard, there are good reasons to assume that Luke conceived his work in the awareness of such plurality of communities and contexts.[31] Considering the plural as well as secular character of our present context, the need to conduct a careful study on the Gospel of Luke from this aspect seems self-evident.

As far as the specific connection to the topics in question are concerned, Luke's soteriological concern is, beyond doubt, a notable feature of his double work. He employs the verb σῴζειν (to save) and its derivatives (σωτήρ, σωτηρία, σωτήριον, respectively, savior and salvation) with great frequency.[32] The source and the subject of salvation is God and the place where it takes place is human history, in fulfillment of "his promises to our fathers" (Lk 1:72). According to Schupp, it is precisely this historical perspective

---

31 Cf. Michael Wolter, *Das Lukasevangelium*, Handbuch zum Neuen Testament 5 (Tübingen: Mohr Siebeck, 2008), 23–25.

32 This word group appears 47 times in Lk/Acts (25x in the Gospel and 22x in Acts). Cf. Gert J. Steyn, "Soteriological Perspectives in Luke's Gospel," in *Salvation in the New Testament: Perspectives on Soteriology*, ed. Jan Gabriel van der Watt, Supplements to Novum Testamentum 121 (Leiden: Brill, 2005), 69.

that frees the human being from the Greek notion of necessity and paves the way for true human as well as divine freedom.[33] Therefore, it seems appropriate to recall once more Drury's remark on the overall conception of the Gospel of Luke: "History is no longer, as in Paul, the anvil on which God hammers out salvation at white heat, but the medium in which he is made known in its rhythm of prophecy and fulfillment."[34] Luke thinks already in terms of a universal salvific plan whereby salvation is presented as the encounter of human beings with the Lord, the God of Israel, who "has visited his people" (cf. Lk 1:68) in and through the person of Jesus of Nazareth.

On the Feasibility of Translation
As the topic in question concerns the possibility of communication between essentially distinct religious systems, the results of the dogmatic-exegetical survey are expected to be translated in a language that may be comprehensible not only by contemporary Christian believers, but also by members of other religions, and even atheists, which makes the challenge even more intriguing.

Nevertheless, I believe it is worth venturing. After all, is not theology itself a hermeneutic undertaking? For it involves a complex labor of translation in order to bridge the gaps between time, languages, meanings, contexts, etc. and to render the Word of God understandable to all times, cultures, and peoples, just as it was revealed in the person, message, and fate of Jesus Christ.

A quite refreshing view on such a challenging endeavor is offered by the French philosopher Paul Ricoeur in one of his essays on this topic not long before his death. He remarks, for instance, that translation is not simply accomplished out of need or on account of its usefulness. For it is out of the question that the work of translation is useful. What Ricoeur wants to point out, instead, is that, beyond the pragmatic task of mediating between words and worlds, the translator is also inhabited by a *desire* to translate, which is "more tenacious,

---
33   Schupp, *Auf dem Weg zu einer kritischen Theologie*, 43.
34   John Drury, *Tradition and Design in Luke's Gospel: A Study in Early Christian Historiography* (Atlanta: John Knox Press, 1976), 9.

more profound, more hidden" than the usefulness of translations itself.[35] The desire to translate emerges out of a drive to convey what one has understood. Yes, because "'to understand is to translate,'" to decipher.[36] Therefore, one needs first to translate into one's innermost language system in order to find an equivalence of meanings. Only then can one look for equivalent meanings in another language system and translate them into it.[37]

On that account, the image of translation, comprising both inner and outer translation, is the best "activity" to visualize what such a hermeneutic journey is all about and entails. Similarly, translation may be said to be an element intrinsic to the exercise of theology, understood as *intellectus fidei*. Peukert goes so far as to say that the very future of religions depends very much on how successful they will be in translating their precious treasure, in getting it across, in rendering it understood. Of course, what religions are in need of, as he specifies, is not so much a syntactic-lexical translation as it is a semantic one and, particularly, a "pragmatic equivalence" of assertions.[38] One might then ask, which discipline is in a better position to accomplish such a task for religions than (fundamental and dogmatic) theology? Bearing all this in mind and in awareness of the vital importance of this task as much for theology as for interreligious encounters, I would like to take on this challenge and thereby make a modest contribution to both of them.

The Outline
This book is basically divided into three parts, and this structure reveals also its method. Part I represents Fundamental Theology's

---

35 Cf. Paul Ricoeur, *On Translation*, trans. Eileen Brennan (London: Routledge, 2006), 21.
36 Ibid., 24. Ricoeur draws here on George Steiner, *After Babel: Aspects of Language and Translation* (Oxford; New York: Oxford University Press, 1998), chap. 1, and quotes him.
37 Cf. Ricoeur, *On Translation*, 24f.
38 Helmut Peukert, *Wissenschaftstheorie – Handlungstheorie – fundamentale Theologie: Analysen zu Ansatz und Status theologischer Theoriebildung* (Frankfurt am Main: Suhrkamp, 2009), 357 (Nachwort).

efforts to seek dialogue with the world, conceived here in its broadest and richest sense. The problem is briefly presented, and the object of investigation is narrowed down to two key issues: (a) a few problematic aspects of the Christian concept of salvation predominant in conventional Theology-of-Religions discourses and, as a consequence, in the classical typology; (b) the theological legitimation of a positive attitude of openness towards other religions or radical otherness.

In Part II, a detailed study into biblical sources will identify those flaws in conventional Christian soteriology and shed light on both predicaments mentioned above. Whereas question (a) will be dealt with in chapters 3, 4, 5 and 6, question (b) will come to the fore particularly in chapter 4. The significant discovery of Part II is the concept of agape (love).

The consequences drawn from Part II are worked out theologically in Part III. Therein, the notion of love, understood as *agape*, plays a central role, too. Whilst chapter 7 concerns the relevance of this concept in the present context, in chapter 8 I make a deliberate attempt to translate, for the sake of interreligious dialogue, into a more concrete language what the complex Christian concept of salvation is intended to convey, together with its consequences for both Christian faith and interreligious encounters.

All translations, especially from German sources, are my own, unless I have specified otherwise. Other translations are indicated by referring to the source and translator's name. All biblical passages quoted in English are taken from the translation of the *New Jerusalem Bible* and those quoted in Greek from the 28th edition of the *Novum Testamentum Graece*.[39]

---

39 *The New Jerusalem Bible* (London: Darton, Longman and Todd, 1985); Eberhard Nestle et al., eds., *Novum Testamentum Graece: Greek-English New Testament*, 28th ed. (Stuttgart: Deutsche Bibelgesellschaft, 2013).

2

Searching for Jesus' Original Message

This chapter marks the transition from the fundamental-theological to the biblical part of the work. This part is sustained by two convictions. Firstly, a Christian theology of interreligious dialogue must build on the solid and normative foundation of its primary source, that is, on the person and message of Jesus Christ as they were transmitted in the New Testament and, particularly, in the gospels. Secondly, the inconsistencies of the problematic and, to some extent, biased understanding of some concepts such as salvation and mediation that has been conveyed through the typology exclusivism, inclusivism, and pluralism can best be demonstrated and overcome by contrasting them with Jesus' message.

However, as will be seen in the following sections, this is neither a simple task, nor can the line of argumentation pursued in this research just be taken for granted. On the one hand, the trend of Western theology, profoundly influenced by early modernity, was to increasingly distance itself from the contents of Jesus' life and message for the systematic reflection of theological doctrines. On the other, the amazing amount of information provided in the last centuries by research on the New Testament and early Christianity has rendered a reliable access to Jesus' "original" message almost impossible. Therefore, the aim of this chapter is to explore the feasibility of such an attempt, as it is intended in this work.

The Life of Jesus as a Source of Knowledge of Theology

Confronted with the question whether anything would change in Christianity if Christians no longer believed in the facticity of Jesus' historical life, Rahner replies emphatically: "Catholic faith and dogmatics [...] remain inextricably bound up not only to the historical existence of Jesus of Nazareth, but also to the historical events of this peculiar existence."[1] Far from just repeating a platitude, what Rahner mainly wants to address in this text are two issues. Firstly, he calls attention once more to the relation between dogmatic reflection and exegetical findings. Secondly, he warns against a sort of neglect with regard to the life of Jesus both in dogmatics and exegesis. Such an approach runs the risk of confining Jesus to a philosophic-theological system of apparently valid statements, yet one that loses its grasp on the reality of the living Word of God that was disclosed through the life, attitude, message, and fate of Jesus.

Batlogg appreciates Rahner's enterprise in recovering the *locus* of the mysteries of the life of Jesus in theology, which was lost in "the exile of the history of spirituality and in the captivity of personal piety."[2] In his opinion, Jesus' entire life seems to have been "absorbed" into two poles, namely, his birth and his death. The former was the source for the incarnation theology of the East and the latter for the staurocentric soteriology of the West.[3] Since early modernity, the *topos* of the mysteries of the life of Jesus had been banished from theology especially on account of their contingency.

---

1 Karl Rahner, "Bemerkungen zur Bedeutung der Geschichte Jesu für die katholische Dogmatik," in *Schriften zur Theologie*, vol. 10 (Zürich; Einsiedeln; Köln: Benziger, 1972), 215.
2 Andreas R. Batlogg, "Wieviel Jesus braucht die Fundamentaltheologie: Zur Relevanz des (unterschätzten) Lebens Jesu – eine Problemanzeige," in *Was den Glauben in Bewegung bringt: Fundamentaltheologie in der Spur Jesu Christi*, ed. Andreas R. Batlogg, Mariano Delgado, and Roman A. Siebenrock, Festschrift für Karl H. Neufeld (Freiburg im Breisgau; Basel; Wien: Herder, 2004), 416.
3 Cf. ibid., 412; Andreas R. Batlogg, *Die Mysterien des Lebens Jesu bei Karl Rahner: Zugang zum Christusglauben*, Innsbrucker theologische Studien 58 (Innsbruck: Tyrolia, 2001), 408.

But, for Rahner, it is precisely in that contingency that one can see a theophany. This *topos* is, for Rahner, the source of knowledge of theology, that is, "the place where he [Jesus] is discovered as the Christ of God."[4]

What seems to be at stake here is the question how one arrives at the profession of faith in Christ. Is it alone through subjection to faith formulations, just as they have been handed down through the Church, that is, alone from a Christology "from above"? Or can one also attain to faith by means of an intensive human experience of shaping one's life in accordance with that of the human being Jesus of Nazareth, which is to say, through the experience of the following, of discipleship, "from below," so to speak? An appropriate answer would be: ideally, through a combination of both. Yet, if one begins and remains only on the level of doctrine, the former, the probability that one must profess a "schizophrenic faith," i.e. dissociated from one's concrete life, is higher than in the case of the latter. In 1518, the Humanist Erasmus of Rotterdam put it this way: "*Quamquam nulla doctrina efficacior quam ipsius vita*" (Nevertheless, no doctrine is more effective than his life).[5] Indeed, in the view of Batlogg, Rahner, Schillebeeckx, and others, this seems to be the more consistent way to attain to faith, while being aware that faith is, ultimately, a gift of God and, for that reason, it reaches us rather than we reach it.

To place the life of Jesus at the center of theological reflection does not mean, though, reconstructing a biography of him. This is no longer possible after J. Wellhausen, W. Wrede, and particularly K. L. Schmidt "burst the 'biographic framework' of the Gospel of Mark" which had been for a long time generally recognized as a reliable historical source of the life of Jesus.[6] Nor can it consist in the effort to reconstruct "the true life of Jesus" over against the distorted

---

4   Batlogg, "Wieviel Jesus braucht die Fundamentaltheologie," 418.

5   Desiderius Erasmus von Rotterdam, "Ratio seu methodus compendio perveniendi ad veram theologiam," in *Opera omnia*, ed. Johannes Clericus, vol. 5 (Orig. edition: Leiden, 1704; Repr. Hildesheim, 1972), 102, apud Batlogg, "Wieviel Jesus braucht die Fundamentaltheologie," 411.

6   Cf. Martin Hengel and Anna Maria Schwemer, *Geschichte des frühen Christentums*, vol. 1 (Tübingen: Mohr Siebeck, 2007), 343.

images of dogma and tradition, given that it has become a consensus in contemporary scholarship that one can only reach a certain unity between Jesus and the kerygma *through* the witnesses of the early communities.[7] For it is a commonplace nowadays that most likely the primary concern of the gospels was not to portray Jesus' historical life or to furnish early Christians with facts and evidences. However, it cannot be denied that there is a "historical kernel" to which the gospels bear witness. Even if some of the stories told by the gospels may be said to be fictive, this does not mean that they are just lies or inventions. They are rather the response of the first witnesses to an original experience made with the person of Jesus. It is exactly to this experience, which alone can render the unity between Jesus and Christ possible and plausible, that one has to arrive.[8]

Now, rediscovering that original event of Jesus' public life is beneficial not only to Christians (*ad intra*), but also to the dialogue with other religions and believers (*ad extra*), provided, of course, that such an account of Jesus is methodically mediated and justified. Particularly as far as the bilateral dialogue with Judaism is concerned, for example, the Catholic exegete Thomas Söding is convinced, just as a great number of theologians are, that the New Testament in fact offers the best basis for a conversation. For him, the hostility towards Jews and several misinterpretations of New Testament affirmations with regard to the Jewish people, as some theologians still see it today, can only be overcome once and for all if those biblical issues are settled and common misinterpretations are clarified and disproved.[9] That concerns

---

7 Hansjürgen Verweyen, *Gottes letztes Wort: Grundriß der Fundamentaltheologie*, 3rd ed. (Regensburg: Pustet, 2000), 286.

8 Cf. especially Edward Schillebeeckx, *Jesus, an Experiment in Christology*, The Collected Works of Edward Schillebeeckx 6 (London: Bloomsbury, 2014). Cf. also below pp. 28–30.

9 Cf. Thomas Söding, "'… die Wurzel trägt dich' (Röm 11,18): Methodische und hermeneutische Konsequenzen des jüdisch-christlichen Dialoges in der neutestamentlichen Exegese," in *Methodische Erneuerung der Theologie: Konsequenzen der wiederentdeckten jüdisch-christlichen Gemeinsamkeiten*, ed. Peter Hünermann and Thomas Söding, Quaestiones disputatae 200 (Freiburg im Breisgau; Basel; Wien: Herder, 2003), 38.

especially a couple of Christological issues. But the answer he gives to the question whether "[...] Christology necessarily leads to a theological marginalization of Israel, to an absorption of the Old Testament, and to the supplantation of God's people of Israel" is that "Christology is not *in itself* anti-Jewish."[10] According to him, New Testamental Christology is not as exclusivistic as it is often assumed, either relative to Jews or to the Gentiles, provided that a few criteria are fulfilled.[11]

As a consequence, the unity between Jesus' life and message and doctrinal definitions must be more elucidated by dogmatics, in order to become more plausible for Christians and non-Christians alike and to bridge the gulf between divine revelation and human life.

The Interweaving between Revelation and Human Experience
The hermeneutic task of theology can only be appropriately carried out if the intricate relation between human experience and revelation is clearly understood and handled. For Schillebeeckx, there can be no revelation dissociated from human life and experience, inasmuch as "[r]evelation is *experience* expressed in language; it is God's saving action as experienced and communicated *by men*."[12] Secondly, the experience of partial, contingent, limited salvation and meaning can only be made in terms of human practice. As he sees it, "[...] there is no question of a theory of salvation detached from any practice." If the contrary is the case, the act of faith can, with good reasons, be qualified as irrational, as a mere "decisionism," but not as an act of salvation.[13]

---

10 Ibid., 65 (emphasis in original).

11 He suggests seven criteria: a) Christology must be theocentric; b) Jesus' Jewish identity must be recognized in Christology as central; c) Jesus universal salvation cannot be anti-Jewish; d) Christology must be according to the Scripture; e) Christology must be conceived from the perspective of the Kingdom of God; f) Ecclesiologically, the Jewish people can neither be excluded from salvation nor absorbed in the Church, but their election must be reaffirmed; g) Christology must be conceived of in accordance with the commandment to love (Lev 19:18f.).

12 Edward Schillebeeckx, *Christ: The Christian Experience in the Modern World*, ed. Robert J. Schreiter, The Collected Works of Edward Schillebeeckx 7 (London: Bloomsbury, 2014), 31 (emphasis in original).

13 Ibid., 33.

On the other hand, no one would deny that the origin, the foundational moment of any human experience, particularly of revelatory ones, cannot be traced back to the causal agency of the subject who experiences it. It always lies outside the realm of one's thinking, planning, influence, control, etc. In other words, in order to experience something utterly new, illuminating, revelatory, one has to *come up against reality*, one has to be confronted with a new aspect of the real, which can be neither planned nor anticipated nor foreseen by the subject. It should be clear that Schillebeeckx is not concerned, here, with experience in terms of piety, feelings or emotions, however important these aspects may be. His focus of interest is rather the cognitive feature of experience, associated with the subject's cognitive openness and search for meaning.

Having made that fundamental distinction, the theologian must be clear about the essential constituent of revelation in order to interpret it today in such a fashion as to remain a "significant" revelation. On the one hand, such a central constituent cannot be its form, the written text, the remnants of that original experience, although one cannot have access to it by dispensing with the interpretation given by the witnesses handed down through the text. On the other, it cannot be simply a word coming "from above," foreign to human life, even though revelation, just as any other experience, has a negative, a dialectical element. The answer, for Schillebeeckx, resides in the *"responsive affirmation"* made by human beings of the transcendent manifestation of God in history. If that original experience of the first followers of Jesus could not have been generated solely by their own efforts, the primary element of revelation must necessarily be regarded as a response to something greater than or beyond them. "The transcendent lies *in* human experience and its expression in the language of faith, but as *an inner reference* to what this experience and this language of faith have called to life."[14] By holding that the transcendent lies *in* human experience, far from reducing God's action to human activity, Schillebeeckx points to the original as well as necessary relatedness between God's offer and the human response, which can only be conceived of as being horizontal instead

---

14   Ibid., 34 (emphasis in original).

of vertical. Rather than being revealed either "from above" or "from below," God's word and deeds are revealed in relationships within human history. To find forms of retrieving the original significance of that first-hand experience made with the person, the message, and the deeds of Jesus is, therefore, one of the unavoidable tasks to be accomplished by hermeneutic theology, to which attention shall be devoted in the present and the following chapters.

How Normative Is Jesus' Message to Christians?
If what has been said so far is correct, primary importance should be attached to the existential impact of Jesus' life and message in the life of early Christians, insofar as they provide the key to understanding God's eschatological revelation. Thus, there should be no doubts for Christians as to the significance of those testimonies for their own faith experience, for the reliability of their knowledge of God, and for the fulfillment of their yearning for meaning. Furthermore, as this biblical experience is at the core of what has later been referred to as Christianity, it furnishes the essential elements to define what it means to be genuinely Christian or what makes up the identity of a Christian person, community or church.

Accordingly, the aforementioned arguments appear to give sufficient reasons to attribute "absolute" normativity to the kerygma of the New Testament. From experience, however, one knows that this is not the case in the landscape of contemporary Christendom. As far as the relation between current Christianity and its past origin is concerned, there are, according to Schillebeeckx, different stances, a great number of which are problematic. To certain Christians, for instance, humanity has evolved, past forms of religious life have become obsolete and may not be deemed compatible with modern times. In a sense, they consider themselves emancipated from their origins. By contrast, there is, in other groups, a certain romanticism regarding the origins which is equally difficult. They idealize this origin in such a way as to regard the present time with contempt and despise any attempts of renewal. In Schillebeeckx's opinion, both stances fail to notice that the supposed gulf or disruption between present, past, and future actually does not exist in the way it is believed to.

In reality, the message of the New Testament and our present experiences do not stand over against each other and alongside each other as two things. They already touch each other. [...] As long as we regard the past as something that has to be sought somewhere in the distance, far away from our present culture and our present insights, we are at an abstract theoretical level which allows only formal analyses of the hermeneutical structure of our experience. The pattern of present-past already evaluates the gulf between present and past in a negative sense: there is a 'disruption of communication.' The starting-point is therefore that there must be communication and unity with the past.[15]

Schillebeeckx's view definitely casts new light on this issue. At the same time, though, theology's hermeneutical work becomes even more complex. For the illusion that one can reach through exegesis or textual analysis the intended original meaning of the contents of the gospels must be dispelled. Similarly, even the images, symbols, and expressions employed by the sacred authors of the New Testament may not have today as much significance or the same frame of reference as they had in the context of early Christianity, which justifies reinterpretation through new ones. For, as was seen above, the consciousness of any given historical context cannot be deemed as an external and/or foreign aspect of dogma or contents of faith, but rather as an element "pertaining to dogmatics' contents of reflection itself."[16]

Bearing all this in mind, one can therefore say that the message of Jesus and the New Testament continues to have, in a broad sense, the status of *norma normans non normata*. The more vexing question concerns the meaning of norm or normativity, especially when it comes to the reflection and elucidation of the contents of faith as they are presented in the New Testament. Viewed from the perspective of Schillebeeckx and Schupp, the concept of normativity cannot be thought of in the rigid categories of traditional approaches, as they fail to recognize the continuity and communication between past and present. At the same time, it must have a "regulative" function

---

15 Ibid., 63.
16 Franz Schupp, *Auf dem Weg zu einer kritischen Theologie* (Freiburg im Breisgau; Basel; Wien: Herder, 1974), 43.

for faith. Particularly if considered in connection with the notion of canon, the normative character of the New Testament preserves the history and person of Jesus against distortions and disfigurements.[17] This applies not only to the faithful who sometimes, because of lack of information, read the history of Jesus quite unilaterally. This applies to theology and the institutional Church as well, since they too can, at times, distort Jesus' message through narrow interpretations or faith definitions.

This section endorses, thus, in various ways, both the choice of the method of the present study and the hypothesis that an adequate approach to the issue of interreligious dialogue must be searched for in the message of Jesus and in face of the current time. Jesus' message remains normative, although it must be re-decoded in order to regain its revelatory and transforming character, so that it may be experienced today in as liberating a way as in its origins.

Searching for a Reliable Method to Approach Jesus' Message

Having become aware of the importance of the study of Jesus' message, one is confronted now with the methodical access to it within the corpus of the New Testament. To that end, one of the key issues to be resolved is whether the historical-critical method suffices to accomplish it or whether it must be complemented by any other. But even more intricate than that is the question of the integrity of the sources. For even though exegesis may do a wonderful job in interpreting critically the sources of the New Testament, what if the sources itself do not reproduce faithfully the contents of the original message?

Orthodoxy and Heresy within the New Testament
Normative as Jesus' message may be for Christians, the believer as much as the scholar is more often than not faced with the complex question of what the content of his message actually was. Besides the questions raised by the quest for the historical Jesus, as contrasted to kerygmatic formulations, which were dealt with above in the previous

---

17 Cf. Schillebeeckx, *Christ*, 52f.

sections, one is also faced with the question of orthodoxy and heresy within the New Testament. Exegetical research has made it plain in the last centuries of research that the canonical sources alone are not sufficient to grasp both the Jesus-event and the self-understanding(s) of Christianity at its very beginnings.

A pioneering work regarding the relation between orthodoxy and heresy within the New Testament as well as in Early Christianity is beyond doubt Walter Bauer's *"Rechtgläubigkeit und Ketzerei im ältesten Christentum."*[18] In his concise, elaborate, and programmatic introduction to this book, he outlines the key elements of his whole project.[19] To be sure, what concerns him most in this work are both the ethos and the method of a historian while examining the texts of the New Testament. But one of his major achievements was to call attention to the biased *(parteiisch)* character of the Texts of the Canon. For him, it is not the case that there was, from the very beginning of Christianity, a clear orthodox position and heretical ones, which deviated from it. There were, rather, competing positions that tried to prevail against each other. Accordingly, the historian – or exegete – as if he/she were a judge, ought to do justice as much to the orthodox position as to the heretical.[20] His justification for doing so is the conjecture that heresies might have not been deemed as a false

---

18   Walter Bauer, *Rechtgläubigkeit und Ketzerei im ältesten Christentum*, ed. Georg Strecker, 2nd ed., Beiträge zur historischen Theologie 10 (Tübingen: Mohr Siebeck, 1964). The page numbers remained, in this edition, the same as in the original publication of 1934. The first translation and publication of this work in English was in 1971: Walter Bauer, *Orthodoxy and Heresy in Earliest Christianity*, ed. Gerhard Krodel and Robert A. Kraft (Philadelphia: Fortress Press, 1971).

19   For a criticism of Bauer's project, see the recent publication by Andreas J. Köstenberger and Michael J. Kruger, *The Heresy of Orthodoxy: How Contemporary Culture's Fascination with Diversity Has Reshaped Our Understanding of Early Christianity* (Wheaton, Ill.: Crossway, 2010). In this book, besides countering Bauer's position as to the plurality of competing orthodoxies in early Christianity, the authors argue that such a view ought to be construed as a consequence of postmodern relativism, which would provide enough reason to cast doubt on the validity of such a thesis.

20   Cf. Bauer, *Rechtgläubigkeit und Ketzerei*, 1.

teaching right from the beginning, but that they, for some time, might have quite possibly been regarded as true and valid views. He gathers evidence for this claim outside the canonical sources and takes as examples Christianity as it was lived in Edessa (Mesopotamia) and Egypt. He argues that the predominant forms of Christianity present there were not as "orthodox" as in other places. What came to be defined later on as orthodoxy (true doctrine) was professed in those two places, if at all, by minority groups.[21]

Thus, Bauer succeeds in detaching orthodoxy and heresy from time and representation categories.[22] In his view, it is very problematic to maintain the hypothesis that at the beginning of Christianity was Jesus, the twelve apostles, and the one doctrine revealed by Jesus, and all heresy came thereafter. For him, what came to be called orthodoxy was not necessarily the original teaching, nor was it the view of the majority. The pattern of thinking "unbelief > orthodoxy > erroneous belief" is to be regarded as misleading, even though it was widely disseminated as early as in the second century, and is, according to Bauer, until today, deeply rooted in our minds.[23] To put it pointedly, it is neither fair nor academic to assume a priori that the holders of other views are possessed by malevolent intentions and perform the works of the devil. In the beginning of Christianity, there was a great plurality of (competing) views (of equal value), and plurality ought to be valued positively, rather than as a work of Satan.

This approach is shared by the exegete Klaus Berger, too, who admonishes to greater sober-mindedness when dealing with divergent views within the corpus of the New Testament, as its authors "may present the actual state of affairs quite tendentiously."[24] Rather than regarding conflicts as coming from outside the community, it

---

21 See, for example, ibid., 26; 53-55.

22 Cf. ibid., 2.

23 Cf. ibid., 3. He takes as examples Origen and Tertullian, who argue, in similar ways, that all heretics come at first from unbelief to the knowledge of faith, but then, over the course of time, deviate from it.

24 Cf. Klaus Berger, "Die impliziten Gegner: Zur Methode des Erschließens von »Gegnern« in neutestamentlichen Texten," in *Kirche*, Festschrift für Günther Bornkamm (Tübingen: Mohr Siebeck, 1980), 383.

would be more appropriate to assume that they arise within the community of faith and that the holders of other positions claimed to be just as legitimate Christians as the supporters of "orthodoxy." "It is highly unlikely that their stance was a malevolent, dishonest, and exotic distortion of the 'truth.'"[25] Therefore, Berger is convinced that the texts of the New Testament themselves, particularly when dealing with controversial positions, are to be submitted to special criticism,[26] as the diverging positions represent, in most cases, a more "archaic form of Christian tradition," instead of a sort of resistance coming from outside (Judaism, Paganism, Apocalypticism, etc.).[27]

Availing himself of Le Boulluec's critique[28] of Bauer's thesis, Boyarin also sees Bauer's conception of heresy and orthodoxy in terms of "essences" as problematic. "*Orthodoxy* and *heresy* are decidedly not things, but notions that must always be defined in each other's context."[29] On that account, it is difficult to define what comes before and what comes later. Orthodoxy and heresy come into being always together, not however as something taken for granted, but as something which has to be defined as such. It is not possible to define the one without the other. Consequently, "[...] the function of heresiology [and orthodoxy], if not its proximate cause, was to define Christian identity – not only to produce the Christian as neither Jew nor Greek but also to construct the whatness of what Christianity would be, not finally a third race or *genos* but something entirely new, a religion."[30] By taking as example Justin's text *"The Dialogue,"* it is possible to see how much this Church Father was engaged in the production of Christianity.[31] For that purpose, he needed an interlocutor, an "other," as identity always requires the

---

25 Ibid., 381f.
26 Cf. ibid., 391.
27 Cf. ibid., 393.
28 Alain Le Boulluec, *La notion d'hérésie dans la littérature grecque IIe-IIIe siècles* (Paris: études Augustiniennes, 1985).
29 Daniel Boyarin, *Border Lines: The Partition of Judaeo-Christianity* (Philadelphia: University of Pennsylvania Press, 2004), 3, italics in original.
30 Ibid., 4.
31 Cf. ibid., 37–74.

"different-from-myself," from whom one limits and defines himself.

The observations made here increase substantially the degree of complexity of the aim and tasks of this investigation. As could be noted, it is extremely difficult to get to the very core of Jesus' "original" message, as one has to break through all these different layers that seem to be insuperable. Moreover, the aforementioned studies on heresy and orthodoxy have lain bare that even if the hope of reaching Jesus' proclamation is given up and scholarship remains at the level of the textual analysis of the gospels, this alternative does not make things any easier. Being so, the endeavor to retrieve the original, pure understanding of any matter either in Jesus or in "early Christianity" seems to be an unattainable pursuit. Perhaps, the alternative would be, as Bauer suggests, to value plurality positively, rather than as a work of Satan, thereby rendering the notions of orthodoxy, normativity, canonicity, etc. much more open than they have been so far.

The Valuable Help of Exegesis: Clarity Rather Than Certainty
In view of the intricacies involving any quest for the original message of Jesus, even exegesis is overwhelmed with a pretension of that kind. On that account, many exegetes have already dismissed this possibility and prefer to concentrate on textual or philological analysis. Perhaps that hope has been entertained more by systematic theologians than by exegetes or historians. For to abandon that aspiration would mean, among other things, giving up one's desire to participate in that foundational, revelatory event of Christianity and having to content oneself with the remnants of that experience which have most likely become contaminated over the centuries through heresy. It goes without saying that such a view differs to a great extent from that which has been pursued in this work. Hence the need arises for a reconsideration of the purpose and tasks of both exegesis and systematic theology so that a mutual cooperation between both may be possible and fruitful.

To that end, the Catholic theologian Schwager points out that unless exegetical findings are not supplemented with philosophic-theological considerations, there is no progress in the theological reflection on the contents of faith. Admittedly, systematic theology is dependent upon the results of exegesis. Nevertheless, merely copying or adopting them uncritically is not sufficient to advance in research and understanding. In face of the varied history of Christianity and the variety of methods and approaches in exegesis, it has become all too manifest that "[...] anything can be projected on to Jesus."[32]

Likewise, Schillebeeckx's holds that "[...] form criticism and redaction criticism will not give us much of an insight into what *the text* means to say (the acceptance of a particular tradition and the omission of another is itself 'redaction,' so that from a literary-critical point of view, everything in a text is 'redaction')."[33] Therefore, he argues that, in order to grasp the real significance of the person of Jesus Christ to those people who continued his "movement," one has to go beyond "fragmentary" criticisms and take the texts seriously in their entirety. If one is willing to understand what the followers of Jesus really meant by words such as grace, salvation, Kingdom of God, etc., exegesis alone will not do.

This criticism of exegesis notwithstanding, no one can deny its remarkable achievements as a theological discipline and its valuable contributions to a better, more comprehensive understanding of the Jesus-event in all its nuances. For that reason, instead of simply ignoring the vastness of its findings and conjectures, just as several systematic theologians do, a more appropriate approach to exegesis appears to be possible if one is clear about the purpose of that discipline and what can be sought in it. If one, in exegesis, searches for compelling, unequivocal evidence for one's own theory, then it is really difficult to find anything useful. If, by contrast, one seeks clarity about determined states of affairs, contexts, backgrounds, usages, one will certainly be well served. Therefore, rather than certainties, what exegesis can best furnish systematic thinking with is clarification, enlightenment, and an openness to a plurality of possibilities and views.[34]

---

32 Raymund Schwager, *Jesus im Heilsdrama: Entwurf einer biblischen Erlösungslehre*, Innsbrucker theologische Studien 29 (Innsbruck; Wien: Tyrolia, 1990), 28f.
33 Schillebeeckx, *Christ*, 7 (emphasis in original).
34 As for the relation between exegesis and dogmatics, see Rahner, "Bemerkungen zur Bedeutung der Geschichte Jesu für die katholische Dogmatik," 219f.

Outcome

This chapter might have painted a general picture of the complexity that the research of Jesus' "original" message entails. At first glance, the task we have taken on appears impossible to accomplish. Nonetheless, the first section (the first section of this chapter), based predominantly on Rahner's and Batlogg's observations, has made clear that a serious reflection in dogmatic theology on the life and message of Jesus, which unfortunately became lost over the centuries, is urgently required. The tension between exegesis and dogmatics, which is natural, cannot lead to encapsulations on either side. Rather, it can produce fruitful and surprising results if there is a mutual cooperation and more openness to each other.

The ideal of reaching to the core of Jesus' message without the detour of the mediation of the post-Easter communities and the sacred authors, including their possible distortions, however biased they may be, had to be abandoned. They are a constituent element of revelation. What is required is not the pretension to reaching the uncontaminated message of Jesus, but a fruitful interplay between exegesis and dogmatic theology in order to understand more clearly which issues are really at stake when dealing with complex concepts such as salvation or, more recently, the modern notion of religious identity. In that line of thought, the delimitation of the research to the gospel of Luke, as shall be seen particularly in chapter 4, is nothing but a natural consequence of such a necessary mediation.

Whereas in chapters 3 and 6 the question of salvation will be deepened and considered in more detail, chapter 4 shall be devoted to religious identity. In that way, I hope to find a reliable touchstone with which to compare the manner in which those topics are dealt with in the typology of exclusivism, inclusivism, and pluralism.

PART II

Biblical Foundations

3

The Intricacy of the Question of Salvation in Jesus' Context

Christians believe in and hope for God's salvation in the end of both personal and universal history. God's salvation has been predominantly thought about in terms of justice (cf. Mt 25:31-46), of a final judgment. Admittedly, God's justice cannot be compared to ours. However, does the notion of justice suffice to comprehend what the Christian traditional concept of salvation intends to convey? Does it not give rise to serious misunderstandings instead?

The aim of this chapter is to survey in more detail the context in which the Christian notion of salvation acquires its special significance within the framework of comprehension of the synoptic gospels, so as to find new hermeneutic keys to understanding this complex category in the context of Jesus' proclamation.

Competing Discourses on Salvation?

In all likelihood, Jesus of Nazareth knew John the Baptist very well and might even have stood among his disciples to hear him.[1] Many are the theories that even maintain that Jesus, before his public life, might have been a disciple of his for some time.[2] On the other hand,

---

1 Cf. Helmut Merklein, *Jesu Botschaft von der Gottesherrschaft: Eine Skizze*, Stuttgarter Bibelstudien 111 (Stuttgart: Katholisches Bibelwerk, 1983), 27.

2 For Jeremias, this time was by no means a short one. But it is perfectly

it is equally beyond doubt that, at a certain point of time, both distanced themselves from each other. In the course of their account, the gospels differentiate, for instance, between the disciples of Jesus (οἱ μαθηταὶ αὐτοῦ) and the disciples of John (οἱ μαθηταὶ Ἰωάννου). Such a distance, though, was not solely a physical one, owing to John's imprisonment and death, but, above all, theological. These theological dissimilarities concern, fundamentally, their differentiated understanding of God, man, and the possibility of salvation. It is therefore worthwhile examining briefly such differences, in order to understand the most specific and central point of Jesus' message on salvation.

Such a differentiation is particularly important, as these two key figures typify, in their own manners, though not exhaustively, two possible forms of belief in God's salvation or in the way in which salvation can take place. John the Baptist would stand for an apocalyptic view, while Jesus stands for what may be called "theological-historical" one, which are just two models among others available at that time.[3] Obviously, the aim of this section is in no way to portray Jesus as "the better or cleverer one," nor is it to depict Christianity – or Jesus' message – as an improvement in relation to Judaism. Nor is the result of this section the claim that Jesus remained immune to the influences of apocalyptic theology in his thought. The intent is, instead, to perceive how intricate, controversial, and ambivalent the issue of salvation was in those days, not least on account of the

---

understandable that the evangelists concentrated the relationship between Jesus and John in the baptism account and that the early Church tried to avoid or mitigate accounts that would have conveyed the impression that Jesus was someone *like* John or, even worse, someone *subordinated* to him (cf. Joachim Jeremias, *Neutestamentliche Theologie*, 3rd ed., vol. 1 [Gütersloh: Mohn, 1979], 53).

3 What is meant by "theological-historical" will be spelled out in the course of the current chapter. Other possible models of belief could be found, for instance, in the convictions of the other groups present in the territory of Palestine at the time of Jesus, such as: a) the Zealot Movement (for whom liberation-salvation could be attained through political struggle); b) the Essenes (through withdrawal from the world and perfection of life); c) the Pharisees (through the observance of the Law); d) the Hellenistic "religion" (by trying to placate the gods in their moods and delight them through sacrifices); e) esoteric sects (through secret spiritual knowledge).

manifold claims of authentic interpretation of the Scripture. What might equally become clearer at the end of this chapter is that even for Christians, the issue of salvation is anything but unambiguous and unequivocal. Even Early Christianity was marked by struggles over its genuine understanding.

The second reason to proceed in that manner is that the core aspects of any topic, needless to say, can be best grasped through comparison and differentiation, rather than alone through expositions. This is all the more the case, if the considerable influence of apocalypticism on the New Testament literature is taken into account, or the very fact that the nuances between Jesus' message are not as clear in comparison to John's preaching as they are, for instance, in reference to other groups of his time.[4] This task, therefore, besides being necessary for the sake of clarity, certainly contributes towards the discernment of what indeed pertains to the core of Jesus' message and what, possibly, does not.

Finally, it seems necessary to find out whether the contrasts between both are exclusively theological, or whether Jesus disagreed with John's anthropological premise too, given the importance of the anthropological component in hermeneutic efforts. For just as any theological affirmation on salvation presupposes anthropological elements, every anthropological utterance on it implies an understanding of God, no matter whether one is aware of it or not.

---

4 See, among others, Martin Hengel and Anna Maria Schwemer, *Geschichte des frühen Christentums*, vol. 1 (Tübingen: Mohr Siebeck, 2007), 327. Hengel and Schwemer point out that, despite all major differences between Jesus and John the Baptist, if compared with other Jewish movements of those days, their mindset and focus seem to differ substantially from them, particularly as regards the apocalyptic and violence-oriented approach underlying the struggle for (political) liberation of those groups (except for the Sadducees, who were, in various ways, allied with the Romans). Such like-mindedness between Jesus and John, at least in that respect, could blur the differences between them.

The Immediacy of God's Implacable Judgment in the Preaching of John the Baptist

The core message of the preaching of John the Baptist was that *the entire people of Israel* broke the covenant, thereby entering into a state of sinfulness, and that God was in his right vis-a-vis Israel.[5] For John, Israel does not have any way out. Nothing can save Israel from God's anger in his judgment. John's following preaching shall give an idea of that conviction of his.

> But when he saw a number of Pharisees and Sadducees coming for baptism he said to them, 'Brood of vipers, who warned you to flee from the coming retribution? Produce fruit in keeping with repentance, and do not presume to tell yourselves, We have Abraham as our father, because, I tell you, God can raise children for Abraham from these stones. Even now the axe is being laid to the root of the trees, so that any tree failing to produce good fruit will be cut down and thrown on the fire. I baptise you in water for repentance, but the one who comes after me is more powerful than I, and I am not fit to carry his sandals; he will baptise you with the Holy Spirit and fire. His winnowing-fan is in his hand; he will clear his threshing-floor and gather his wheat into his barn; but the chaff he will burn in a fire that will never go out.' (Q: Mt 3:7-10, 11f par. Lk 3:7-9, 16f)

Indeed, in the opinion of Merklein, these words of John the Baptist can be deemed to be authentic, if not in their wording, but at least in their substance, especially on account of their difference from the Jesuanic as well as Christian teachings.[6] John's proclamation could be said to pertain to the deuteronomist tradition, "which again and again confronted [Israel] with the obvious situation of misery experienced in the exile as though it would be in a permanent court situation [before God], one that continued across time to the present

---

5 Cf. Merklein, *Jesu Botschaft von der Gottesherrschaft*, 28f. Actually, this is also Paul's point of departure in his teaching on justification (cf. Rom 3:5, 21–26). For him, however, not only have the Jews sinned, but all (as they abide by the law).
6 Cf. ibid., 28.

day."[7] But John appears to be much more radical than the previous deuteronomist preachers and goes even further. Whereas the latter saw the covenant and the filiation to Abraham – along with justice and good deeds, of course – as valid recourses of Israel to obtain salvation from God, John denies them vehemently. The only way out of the judgment, for John, is the baptism by water, as a sign of repentance. The baptism has the power to wipe out sin and to free those who receive it from God's judgment and condemnation. It can be received only once and can never be repeated. The main reason is the immediate coming of God and his judgment. There is no time left. Indeed, one can note such immediateness through the images used by him: "the axe is being laid to the root of the trees [...], his winnowing-fan is [already] in his hand."

The Apocalyptic Genre and Its Basic Features

John the Baptist's frightening image of God's final judgment was, actually, nothing completely new, but a common image within apocalyptic tradition. The beginnings of this tendency are attested as early as in Early Judaism, particularly in texts such as the book of Enoch and the second chapter of the canonical book of Daniel,[8] but it equally found adherents in the time of Jesus, thereafter, and to the present day. Among the typical features of the apocalyptic framework is the absolute "dissociation between history and salvation,"[9] especially as regards Israel's conventional accounts of its history of salvation. Instead of drawing their hope from the confidence that the Lord would continue to perform marvelous works of salvation in Israel's concrete history, as they had been doing for ages, apocalyptic preachers were utterly convinced that there was only one thing left to

---

7 Ibid., 29.
8 Karlheinz Müller, "Apokalyptik/Apokapypsen (III. Die Jüdische Apokalyptik. Anfänge und Merkmale)," *Theologische Realenzyklopädie* (Berlin; New York: Walter de Gruyter, 1995), 210–12. To have a representative picture of what this kind of literature is like, Müller refers to Dan 2:28-49.
9 Ibid., 212.

be hoped for: the end of history. At this end, God will finally put an end to the present, hopeless history, and definitely establish his Kingdom upon all other powers of this word, thereby becoming, in his might, the only ruler of the whole world.[10] As a consequence, apocalyptic theology is diametrically opposed to any view that believes that there can be, within history, a development, that is, a progress leading to redemption, as this latter "remains the prerogative of God" alone. So being, in the apocalyptic world view "[...] redemption and optimistic views of progress exclude each other reciprocally."[11]

Apocalyptic Influences on Early Christianity

Some of those traits might sound familiar to many Christians, too, as apocalyptic theology exerted strong influence on the texts of the New Testament as well. Karlheinz Müller observes that a clear differentiation is necessary between the synoptic gospels and the Pauline letters, though both contain apocalyptic accents.[12] For him, the crucial point for the integration of aspects of apocalyptic beliefs was the faith, and the theology of Jesus' resurrection.[13] What is not yet clear, however, is whether Jesus himself held an apocalyptic view of the world in his public life, and "whether or not the apocalyptic interpretation made by the most ancient early Christian witnesses and writers was already known before Easter."[14] Therefore, one of the greatest challenges of exegesis and hermeneutic theology is to differentiate between Jesus' message and the influences of apocalyptic thought, though in the awareness that this task, most likely, won't ever be fully accomplished, given the scarcity of material. Nonetheless, in case the thesis is correct that the mingling with apocalyptic elements

---

10 Cf. Karlheinz Müller, "Apokalyptik," *Lexikon für Theologie und Kirche* (Freiburg im Breisgau; Basel; Wien: Herder, 2006), 815.
11 Ibid., 815.
12 Ibid., 817.
13 The most striking text in that regard is, according to Müller (p. 817), 1Cor 15:20-28.
14 Müller, "Apokalyptik," 817.

is a later development of Christianity in the context of the theologies of the resurrection and the parousia, what this very fact attests to is that early Christians might have either approved and appreciated this world view or, at least, deemed it compatible with the message of Jesus.[15] Furthermore, it is extremely complicated to find out whether, or to which extent, early Christians might have attempted to find an answer to their harsh situation of religious persecution under the Roman in the apocalyptic world view, which, likewise, arose in the course of the persecutions to the Jew by Antiochus IV.

On the other hand, K. Müller warns against dualistic views such as Bultmann's, for whom "apocalypticism accomplished the dehistoricization of history," which, in turn, suggests that, in apocalyptic thought, there is no continuity between the present and the future aeon.[16] According to him, the great rupture brought about by the Hasidean movement[17] consisted precisely in the contrary: in breaking with the traditional view that regarded the Torah as a document proving the election of Israel and, instead, to reckon it God's norm for the final judgment at the end of history, the norm according to which the sinner will be punished and the righteous will be rewarded.[18] Besides there being a shift from collectivity to individualization of salvation, history is valued as the "venue" in which "the eschatological-critical function of the Torah" can be verified in its singular demands on the individual.[19]

---

15 Ibid.
16 Rudolf Bultmann, *Geschichte und Eschatologie*, 2nd ed. (Tübingen: Mohr, 1964), 35; Cf. Müller, "Apokalyptik/Apokapypsen," 232.
17 The Hasidean movement came into being in the course of the imposition of the Hellenistic culture on Jews carried out by Antiochus IV (175-164 BC). The Hasideans joined the Maccabees in their revolt against this king, by virtue of their strong desire to remain faithful to the law, and not to bend to this kind of oppression. They can be considered the first and most important thinkers of apocalyptic thought.
18 Cf. Müller, "Apokalyptik/Apokapypsen," 231.
19 Ibid., 232.

The Controversial Locus of History in God's Salvation

Also Christian tradition knows the teaching of a harsh judgment on the last day, usually associated with the talk of fire, weeping, and gnashing of teeth (cf. Mt 13:49-50; 25:41; Lk 16:19-31). However, as will be seen below (p. 101), rather than being a description of the thereafter, the purpose of such images was to admonish Christians and orientate them in their Christian life in the world and in their communities. The purpose of Mt 25:31-46 is to demonstrate in a very plastic way the unity and inseparability between love of God and love of neighbor. For one cannot love Christ (God) but through one's neighbor, and vice versa (cf. also 1Jn 4:20). By affirming that, the text of Mt 25:31-46 confers an enormous dignity upon the other, one that is impossible to beat through human adjectives. Equally noteworthy is the fact that, according to the text, not only are Christians vested with such "divine" dignity, but every human being.

Still, G. Lohfink is convinced that the image of the judgment is to be preserved, however "suppressed and rendered toothless" it might be today. "[...] [A]n hour must come when history's lies and manipulations, meannesses and hidden acts of violence will all be revealed [...]."[20] Moreover, when Jesus speaks of the threatening judgment, he does not mean alone the last judgment at the end of history, but also the one taking place in history here and now. "The coming judgment about which Jesus speaks extends just as much into the present as the coming reign of God."[21] Rather than equating judgment with condemnation, G. Lohfink prefers to speak of "clarification," that is to say, a time in which history will be made clear and its own meaning is going to be revealed.[22]

This thought is in accordance with Peukert's criticism of any theology that does not include history in its entirety as an essential element, such as existential or transcendental theologies

---

20 Cf. Gerhard Lohfink, *Jesus of Nazareth: What He Wanted, Who He Was* (Collegeville, Minnesota: Liturgical Press, 2012), 163.
21 Ibid., 162.
22 Cf. ibid., 163.

(Bultmann, Rahner, etc.). As he sees it, to conceive of salvation, redemption, or even faith exclusively in terms of the relation God-man "[...] entails failing to perceive the fundamental social conditionality of existence," so that the act of faith remains "worldless" and confined to the private sphere.[23] Such a perspective is undoubtedly out of line with the Judeo-Christian tradition, as it does not do justice to the victims of the past and to the openness of the future.

In the tradition of Liberation Theology, the category of history has occupied from the outset a privileged place. On the one hand, one can only see, bear witness to, and interpret God's work of salvation through human history. On the other, it is through human collaboration, inspired by God, that the Kingdom and God's universal salvific will become visible in the world and through history. For there cannot be two histories, a profane one and another of salvation. What exists is one historical reality in which both God and human beings intervene in collaboration, in spite of sin, violence, wars, etc.[24] But for Ellacuría, the problem is not only the paradox of history and transcendence as pointed out above, but rather the traditional understanding of transcendence as something separated or beyond reality, something "up there." As he understands God's activity in "biblical thought," transcendence is "[...] something which transcends *in* rather than *from*, something which pushes one *beyond* oneself instead of taking *out of* [...]."[25] Thus conceived of, salvation acquires a much more comprehensive character and takes account of all dimensions of human life. Viewed from the perspective of such collaboration between God and human beings, the Kingdom

---

23 Helmut Peukert, *Wissenschaftstheorie – Handlungstheorie – fundamentale Theologie: Analysen zu Ansatz und Status theologischer Theoriebildung* (Frankfurt am Main: Suhrkamp, 2009), 58.

24 Cf. Ignacio Ellacuría, "Historicidad de la salvación cristiana," in *Mysterium liberationis: Conceptos fundamentales de la teología de la liberación*, ed. Ignacio Ellacuría and Jon Sobrino, vol. 1 (Madrid: Editorial Trotta, 1990), 327; Edward Schillebeeckx, *Menschen: Die Geschichte von Gott* (Freiburg im Breisgau; Basel; Wien: Herder, 1990), 29.

25 Ellacuría, "Historicidad de la salvación cristiana," 328.

of God becomes the critical category for all systems of history, and above all for human agency.[26]

Jesus' Optimistic Anthropology

John's Anthropological Premise

Another open question is whether John the Baptist's "anthropological premise" that the *entire* people of Israel was condemned was shared by Jesus as well or whether Jesus had his own anthropology. In the view of Merklein, this question is to be answered in the affirmative. As argument, he puts forward especially Lk 13:1-5:[27]

> It was just about this time that some people arrived and told him about the Galileans whose blood Pilate had mingled with that of their sacrifices. At this he said to them, "Do you suppose that these Galileans were worse sinners than any others, that this should have happened to them? They were not, I tell you. No; but unless you repent you will *all* perish as they did. Or those eighteen on whom the tower at Siloam fell, killing them all? Do you suppose that they were more guilty than all the other people living in Jerusalem? They were not, I tell you. No; but unless you repent you will *all* perish as they did." (Lk 13:1-5, italics added)

Merklein argues that the word *all* (πάντες) would attest, in this context, to Jesus' closeness to John's view. For him, Jesus sees no point in trying to find out who sinned more, given that all are

---

26 Cf. Franz Schupp, *Auf dem Weg zu einer kritischen Theologie* (Freiburg im Breisgau; Basel; Wien: Herder, 1974), 15; an outstanding work about the connection between history and faith remains Eric Voegelin, *Ordnung und Geschichte*, ed. Friedhelm Hartenstein, vol. 2: *Israel und die Offenbarung: die Geburt der Geschichte*, 10 vols. (Paderborn: Fink, 2005); see also Karl Löwith, *Weltgeschichte und Heilsgeschehen: die theologischen Voraussetzungen der Geschichtsphilosophie*, Urban-Bücher 2 (Stuttgart: Kohlhammer, 1953).

27 Although Jesus' harsh words against his generation along with his call for repentance could also include Lk 12:16-20, 54-56; 16:1-8a; 10:13-15; and 11:31f. Cf. Merklein, *Jesu Botschaft von der Gottesherrschaft*, 34f.

equally sinners.[28] For Jesus, too, there are no exceptions to be made by God, as Israel, in its entirety, was to be regarded as a "collective of sinners." However, as against retribution theology, held mostly by the Pharisees, according to which the people who were killed must have been sinners punished by God, Jesus gives the idea of sin a new interpretation. The flaw of such an assumption is that Merklein does not define more specifically what sin would then mean. It is highly dubious that Jesus, on the basis of his Jewish background, would have construed sin in the sense of an *attitude* toward God, instead of specific deeds and transgressions against the law and, by extension, against God, as his interpretation seems to suggest.

In his attempt to figure out what the message of this pericopae might be in the context of the Lukan special source, Paffenroth points out that watchfulness is the key to it.[29] If that is correct, the point of these two short pericopae would be most likely the imminent aspect of eschatology, rather than Israel's sinfulness. To be sure, Jesus might have wanted to address the whole people of Israel[30] through his message of repentance. However, that one may draw here a parallel with Paul's theology, for example, according to which all indeed have sinned, seems to be misleading.[31] What is to the fore here, keeping the context of this source in mind,[32] is the urgent warning in the

---

28   Cf. ibid., 34.
29   Cf. Kim Paffenroth, *The Story of Jesus according to L*, Journal for the Study of the New Testament 147 (Sheffield: Sheffield Academic Press, 1997), 133.
30   Cf. Hengel and Schwemer, *Geschichte des frühen Christentums*, 1:326.
31   See Rom 3:23: "No distinction is made: all have sinned [πάντες γὰρ ἥμαρτον] and lack God's glory"; or Rom 5:12: "Well then; it was through one man that sin came into the world, and through sin death, and thus death has spread through the whole human race because everyone has sinned." Conceiving of sin as a state of being sinful, especially as not living in accordance to the truth (ἀλήθεια), may be also found in the Johannine literature. But these are, of course, later connotations of the term (cf. "ἁμαρτία," in Walter Bauer, *Griechisch-deutsches Wörterbuch zu den Schriften des Neuen Testaments und der frühchristlichen Literatur*, ed. Kurt Aland, 6th ed. [Berlin: de Gruyter, 1988], 84f.).
32   For more on the context of the Lukan special material, see see chapter 4, p. 77ff.

face of the imminent judgment, which seems to be conceived of "in individual rather than communal or apocalyptic terms."[33] Likewise, Fitzmyer suggests that the emphasis of these stories is laid on the "sudden death" of those victims.[34] Therefore, instead of continuing to procrastinate in making their full commitment to God, Israel should repent and begin "the reformation of [their] life" as soon as possible, right now. Time flies, this is the "last hour."

In Lk 7:31-35, Jesus also uses the deuteronomic motif of the hardness of heart in the form of a denunciation. But unlike John the Baptist, whose accusation applied to the whole people of Israel, Jesus' denunciation was addressed primarily to the Jewish authorities (cf. Lk 7:30).[35] Thus, the question of power is inherent in Jesus' criticism. In virtue of Jesus' ministry, Jewish authorities were destabilized in their theological convictions and came to lose their monopoly of determining on whom God's salvation was to be bestowed and on whom not. Or, as just seen above, who has sinned and who has not, who is to be punished and who is not. By opposing John's baptism and, by association, by rejecting this visible sign of repentance through which God was said to be in his right, the Pharisees and the lawyers were rejecting God's salvific will, too. But for these, repentance was rather "something for publicly known sinners and non-Jews." It had nothing to do with the "children of Abraham, who piously observed the Torah."[36]

The clue to spot the crucial difference between the Jewish authorities, particularly the Pharisees and the lawyers, and ordinary people appears to be contained in v. 29: "All people who heard him [John the Baptist], and the tax collectors too, *acknowledged God's saving justice* by accepting baptism from John." Owing to the rarity of this

---

33 Paffenroth, *The Story of Jesus according to L*, 157.
34 Cf. Joseph A. Fitzmyer, *The Gospel According to Luke*, vol. 2, The Anchor Bible 28A (New York: Doubleday, 1985), 1005.
35 Cf. François Bovon, *Das Evangelium nach Lukas*, vol. III/1, Evangelisch-Katholischer Kommentar zum Neuen Testament (Zürich: Benziger, 1986), 378.
36 Wilfried Eckey, *Das Lukasevangelium: unter Berücksichtigung seiner Parallelen*, vol. 1 (Neukirchen-Vluyn: Neukirchener, 2004), 354.

verb employed with this connotation,³⁷ its translation is quite complex. The verb δικαιόω (justify, make righteous, defend the cause of) is usually employed the other way round. Normally it is God who makes someone righteous. But in this case, it is the repented part of Israel, who listens to John and accepts his baptism, which justifies (ἐδικαίωσαν) God's will (βουλή).³⁸ This verse might have been influenced by v. 35, in which the same verb occurs. It means that these people were able to endorse God's plan for humankind, even though it does not correspond to the *justitia distributiva*. In the eyes of the Pharisees and lawyers, and according to the rules of the *aequitas*, however, such plan of salvation did not appear to be "just."³⁹

In addition, some of Jesus' sayings cast no doubt whatsoever on the fact that there are indeed people who belong to the Kingdom of God already. One need only think of Jesus' Beatitudes: "How blessed are you who are poor: the kingdom of God is yours" (Lk 6:20b). In this case, for instance, remarkably, there are no conditions of any kind. The sentence is written in the indicative mood, and the possessive pronoun is used. Why can they be said blessed, according to the Greek text? "[B]ecause the Kingdom of God is *yours*" (ὅτι ὑμετέρα ἐστὶν ἡ βασιλεία τοῦ θεοῦ). It is difficult to imagine that, in the view of Jesus, these people are also condemned, just as all others. Or to imagine that these people mentioned in the Beatitudes can just be put in the general category of sinners. To be more precise, they were indeed regarded thus in conventional views. However, Jesus' approach and message to the sinner and to the poor seems to diverge markedly to the views of his time, and even to John's. For, to John, the threatening, upcoming judgment was a certainty, and the only chance for the people of Israel could be repentance and its fruits.⁴⁰ Therefore, on the

---

37 Bovon, *Das Evangelium nach Lukas*, 1986, III/1:380. The verb δικαιόω appears seven times in Luke, two times in Matthew and nowhere in Mark. Except for these two occurrences in Lk 7:29, 35, its meaning refers to the justification of man, instead of God's.

38 Cf. ibid., III/1:379.

39 Cf. ibid., III/1:380.

40 Cf. Hengel and Schwemer, *Geschichte des frühen Christentums*, 1:333–35. In their opinion, it is especially Matthew, owing to his theological approach, who

evidence of other texts such as those which have been made reference to above, Merklein's anthropology does not seem to be the case.

Pessimistic Anthropologies in Christian Tradition
Merklein's anthropological approach is not an isolated case. Several other theologians, Catholics and Protestants alike, usually following the Augustinian tradition of thought, have developed similar New Testament anthropologies. On the Catholic side, one could mention, for instance, Raymond Schwager's soteriology. Building on René Girard's mimetic theory and von Balthasar's *Theodramatik*, he produces his own biblical theory of redemption[41] in which he makes a remarkable effort to reconcile both sides of the one and same God that is believed in the Christian tradition: his goodness and his wrath. What he wants to survey in this work is particularly the apparent contradiction between Jesus' proclamation of the good news of the Kingdom of God, God's goodness and closeness, and Jesus' threatening words regarding God's severe judgment.

Two are the merits of his theory: having unveiled many aspects of violence in the context of religious practices and having conceived God's judgment as one's self-judgment. This latter idea of his can be best seen in the parable of the pounds (Lk 29:11-27).[42] The servant who received the least amount of money and just kept it for himself, instead of making profit out of it, was in no way judged on account of his deed, but in accord with his own belief. He said, "Sir, here is your pound. I put it away safely wrapped up in a cloth because I was afraid of you; for you are an exacting man: you gather in what you have not laid out and reap what you have not sown" (Lk 19:20f.).

---

brings Jesus' message more into line with John's threatening Judgment and condemnation. The gospel of Luke, and especially the texts of his special material, show, by contrast, a quite different approach towards sinners.

41 Cf. Raymund Schwager, *Jesus im Heilsdrama: Entwurf einer biblischen Erlösungslehre*, Innsbrucker theologische Studien 29 (Innsbruck; Wien: Tyrolia, 1990); Schwager's soteriological theology was very much inspired by Hans Urs von Balthasar's outstanding work *Theodramatik*, 4 vols. (Einsiedeln: Johannes, 1973).

42 This parable is most known in the version in Matthew (Mt 25:14-30), i.e., the parable of the talents.

For Schwager, the key word to understanding the Lord's cruel judgment is his reply to that servant's statement: "You wicked servant! *Out of your own mouth* I condemn you (Lk 19:22)."[43] Anthropologically, and even psychologically, this seems to be a very innovative approach, insofar as it questions radically one's images of God, of life, of oneself.

On the other hand, what appears problematic in Schwager's theory is the way he solves the problem of the apparent contradiction between God's goodness and wrath mentioned above. Making use of dramaturgical strategies, he develops a story of Jesus in five acts.[44] The first act of Jesus' story is his proclamation of the good news of the Kingdom of God and the new gathering of whole Israel. According to Schwager, "[t]he aim of the Kingdom of God was to unite all wills, the will of God with those of the human beings, and these among themselves as brothers and sisters (cf. Mk 3:31-35 par). But, in reality, what took place was exactly the opposite. The will of Jesus was resolutely opposed by the will of human beings [...]."[45] In principle, Schwager's line of argument does not differ significantly from Merklein's. What he infers from the fact that *some* people in fact opposed Jesus and his message is that *all* human beings refused God's Kingdom and love. "Human beings are entangled with evil power; on the one hand, they may be held guilty; on the other, they are victims of evil, by virtue of which they also act in roles [i.e., not by themselves]."[46] It is because of this evil power, which is more often referred to as (original) sin, that human beings have a tendency towards lies and acts of violence. As they are not capable to break out of such a circle of violence on their own, Jesus Christ did it through his atoning death, which has its efficacy. He redeemed them from all

---

43 Ἐκ τοῦ στόματός σου κρίνῶ σε, πονηρὲ δοῦλε (Lk 19:22; Schwager, *Jesus im Heilsdrama*, 90).

44 1st Act: The Coming of the Kingdom of God; 2nd Act: The Refusal of the Kingdom of God and the Issue of the Judgment; 3rd Act: The Saviour is Judged Himself; 4th Act: The Resurrection of the Son as the Verdict of the heavenly Father; 5th Act: The Holy Spirit and the New Gathering.

45 Schwager, *Jesus im Heilsdrama*, 82f.

46 Ibid., 216.

sin, guilt, and violence. At this juncture, similarities to Karl Barth's soteriology may be noted as well.[47]

Even though this might have been a very common argumentation strategy among theologians, it cannot be simply taken for granted, either in contemporary approaches or even in the New Testament as a whole. As was seen above, it is rather questionable whether Jesus himself held such a view on sin, and whether his approach to the world and to the human being was as pessimistic as it is often assumed. By contrast, the incarnation theologies of the gospels and the approach of Jesus towards sinners seem to suggest that the world, just as it is, and the current life situation of every person is, at a first moment, accepted rather than condemned. Luke expresses it especially through the usage of the Greek verb ἐπισκέπτομαι (to visit, to look upon someone)[48] which appears in Lk 1:68; 1:78; and 7:16, meaning God's favorable attitude towards his people and the world. Interestingly, this is the same verb used by Matthew in Mt 25:31-46: I was sick, I was in prison, etc. and you visited me (ἐπεσκέψασθέ με). There seems to be a link between mercy and this verb. Even in the Johannine theology, however ambiguous the relation between world and church may be, one can hear in Jn 3:16 a positive attitude of God towards the world: "For God so loved the world [ἠγάπησεν ὁ Θεὸς τὸν κόσμον] that he gave his only Son [...]." From the understanding of the Gospels, therefore, it is possible to infer that God wants to bring the world and human beings to perfection, to fulfillment – expressed in the language of repentance – and not to destruction.

Metanoia: A Key to Human Change
For M. Hengel and A. M. Schwemer, the greatest commonality between Jesus and John was their call for *repentance*, which, in

---

47 Cf. Karl Barth, *Die kirchliche Dogmatik*, 4th ed. (Zürich: Theologischer Verlag, n.d.), vol. 4/1 (1953), § 58.

48 It is possible to assume that Luke's usage of the verb ἐπισκέπτομαι might have been a form considered by him appropriate to convey the liberating message of the Hebrew verb פָּקַד (*pakad*), particularly in Ex 4:31, which was translated in the LXX with ἐπισκέπτομαι. Compare Ex 4:31 with Lk 1:68. For more details on this relation, see below, in this chapter, footnote n. 73.

the gospels, is conveyed through the verb μετανοέω and the noun μετάνοια.[49] They observe, for example, that Matthew puts in John's mouth the same words as in Jesus,' as they respectively begin their ministry: "Repent, for the Kingdom of heaven is close at hand."[50] This is, in principle, a shorter version of Mark's account of Jesus' appearance (Mk 1:14) in which that is identified as the (great) good news of God (εὐαγγέλιον τοῦ θεοῦ). Now, with regard to the use of this word group (μετανοέω and μετάνοια), Hengel and Schwemer make a further interesting remark. Although Jesus' public life begins, in the Gospel of Mark, with a call for repentance, the word μετάνοια does not occur again in his gospel. When referring to Jesus, Mark prefers to speak of faith, belief (πιστεύω, πίστις). This applies to Matthew and Luke, too, though a few more occurrences may be found in their gospels.[51] But there is something which seems to be very particular to Luke. By handing down some texts of his special material, these words related to repentance enter into his gospel a few times more than in the other gospels.[52] What is more, Luke seems to be fond of its synonym ἐπιστρέφω, which is the translation adopted by the LXX for the Hebrew words שׁוּב / הֵשִׁיב (šûb/hešîb: to return, to turn away) and have a similar meaning to μετάνοια.[53] Very likely, Luke's intention might have been to do justice to the traditional, Old Testamental, prophetic call for repentance and used it in its religious sense:[54] to turn from one's sinful life in order to amend it. This might have been the connotation of John's preaching as well.

On the other hand, in light of Luke's theology, what could be pondered upon is whether his understanding of μετάνοια does not extend beyond its religious connotation. As Luke thinks of the existence of Christians especially "in ethical categories," rather than

---

49 Cf. Hengel and Schwemer, *Geschichte des frühen Christentums*, 1:325.

50 Compare Mt 3:2 (John the Baptist) with 4:17 (Jesus). Both begin their ministry with exactly the same words: "μετνοεῖτε, ἤγγικεν γὰρ ἡ βασιλεία τῶν οὐρανῶν."

51 Cf. Hengel and Schwemer, *Geschichte des frühen Christentums*, 1:326.

52 Hengel and Schwemer refer to Lk 5:32; 11:32; and 17:3.

53 Cf. Hengel and Schwemer, *Geschichte des frühen Christentums*, 1:326.

54 Cf. Joseph A. Fitzmyer, *The Gospel According to Luke*, vol. 1, The Anchor Bible 28 (New York: Doubleday, 1981), 237.

someone "possessed by the Spirit,"[55] as in the case of Paul, it might well be that he conceived of μετάνοια also in its profane sense, and connected with an irreproachable ethical life, just as, for instance, Cynic and Stoic philosophers used to do.[56] For also these used to call their hearers for self-examination through the word μετάνοια. As a matter of fact, the original and broader meaning of μετανοέω is to perceive (νοῦς) something afterwards (μετά) or too late.[57] Thus, μετάνοια denotes not exclusively regret regarding one's sins, but also regarding one's failed life, one's failing in recognizing the true values of life, one's realization that whatever has been lived so far cannot be said to have been a "true life." For the Cynic, for example, "[c]onversion means leaving the conventional forms of life. The Cynic's freedom from moral contingency is purchased by a conspicuously ascetic way of life, which stands at the same time as a radical critique of popular conventions and values."[58] In other words, they made every effort to show through their lives and speeches which values are really worth striving for.

The close connection between the Gospel of Luke and Cynic philosophy was recently worked out by N. Neumann. He comes to the conclusion that there is considerable evidence to assume that Luke was influenced by it and uses, at times, the same argumentative strategy to point towards the essentials of human existence.[59] In order to show his readers (hearers) quite plainly that richness, prestige, reputation and social esteem are not the true values to be sought, Luke uses the images of death and afterlife to the same extent as

---

55 Cf. ibid., 1:238.

56 Wayne A. Meeks, *The Origins of Christian Morality: The First Two Centuries* (New Haven, CT: Yale University Press, 1993), 23–25.

57 The word μετα-νοέω is, thus, exactly the opposite of προ-νοέω, i.e. to perceive something before, to foresee, to think of or plan beforehand, to provide. The Christian concept of πρόνοια (Providence) derives from it, too.

58 Meeks, *The Origins of Christian Morality*, 25.

59 Cf. Nils Neumann, *Armut und Reichtum im Lukasevangelium und in der kynischen Philosophie*, Stuttgarter Bibelstudien 220 (Stuttgart: Katholisches Bibelwerk, 2010), 134.

the Cynic.⁶⁰ The difference between both consists only in the orientation. For both demand that people turn away from richness, but whereas the Cynic philosophers pointed to the values of self-sufficiency (αὐτάρκεια), wisdom (σοφία) and virtue, excellence (ἀρετή), as true values and true life, Luke pointed to God (Lk 12:21), the Kingdom of God (6:20; 9:2; 18:24), to heaven (12:33; 18:22), and to eternal life (18:30). Indeed, the way Luke uses μετάνοια and ἐπιστρέφω is complementary: whilst the one refers to one's turning away from something harmful, the other refers to one's turning to something else, such as God, the Kingdom, etc.⁶¹

Therefore, one can affirm that the anthropological premises of Jesus' message of salvation are much more positive than those of John the Baptist or other apocalyptic movements. To be sure, many exegetes such as Bultmann, Schürmann, et al. are of the opinion that Jesus' world view was marked to a great degree by the apocalyptic views of his time. However, by attaching the word metanoia a more "profane" connotation, perhaps influenced by Cynic philosophers and in line with the spirit of the texts of his special material, Luke dissociates it from a purely moral connotation as well as from a direct connection with human sinfulness. As it seems, the usage of the word μετάνοια might have served the purpose of pointing to the essential in human life, to a reorientation, rather than condemnation or to the awareness of one's sinful nature. In that way, one's personal responsibility and contribution in the face of the Kingdom of God and one's following of Jesus is brought much more to the fore and generalizations such as the entire people, all men, and so forth, are abandoned. In spite of man's sinful condition, one is capable of collaborating in God's plan of salvation for humankind.

---

60   The passages Neumann refers to are: Lk 1:46-55; 4:14-21; 6:20-26; 12:13-21; 16:1-13,19-31; 18:18-30 (ibid., 134).
61   Cf. Fitzmyer, *Luke*, 1981, 1:238.

What Comprises the Difference between John and Jesus?

As pointed out above, it is not easy to perceive, at first glance, in the New Testament, all the nuances between Jesus' and the apocalyptic understanding of God's salvation towards Israel, and towards mankind. Only a few writings offer sufficient clarity in this respect. To the evangelist Luke, notwithstanding, this seems to have been an important issue, inasmuch as he devotes quite a few passages of his gospel to the person, significance, and theology of John the Baptist. The assumption that the need for clarification as well as differentiation between Jesus and John might have been indeed an issue for Luke can be particularly verified in the pericope in which Jesus is asked by two of John's disciples whether he was the one who was to come or not, which, in the apocalyptic view, ought to have meant whether or not he was the one who had been sent by God to do his justice and to carry out his final judgment (cf. Lk 3:16f.).[62]

> [...] and John, summoning two of his disciples, sent them to the Lord to ask, 'Are you the one who is to come, or are we to expect someone else?' [...] Then he gave the messengers their answer, 'Go back and tell John what you have seen and heard: the blind see again, the lame walk, those suffering from virulent skin-diseases are cleansed, and the deaf hear, the dead are raised to life, the good news is proclaimed to the poor; and blessed is anyone who does not find me a cause of falling.' (Lk 7:18b-19, 22-23; Mt 11:2-6)

It is noteworthy that Jesus replies to this yes-no question neither with a clear yes, nor does he deny it. His answer is, at first, everything

---

62 This vision is taken, above all, from the prophet Malachi (see particularly Mal 3). The word that establishes the close relationship between both texts is the verb "to come" (ὁ ἐρχόμενος in Lk 7:19 and ἔρχεται in Lk 3:16). Whereas it can be assumed that this word might have been associated with apocalyptic expectations, particularly in its connection to the image of a "refiner's fire" (Mal 3:2f.), this title has no direct relation to the messiah, nor to a savior/redeemer. Cf. Walter Radl, *Das Evangelium nach Lukas: Kommentar*, vol. 1 (Freiburg im Breisgau; Basel; Wien: Herder, 2003), 463.

but clear, particularly as John's expectations do not seem to be met.[63] In other words, "[t]here is no correspondence between the person, message, and ministry of Jesus and John's purely apocalyptic idea of the future."[64] Hence the need to look for possibilities of interpretation for this pericope within its immediate context and within Luke's overall theological project alike. As Luke places this episode in a different context than Matthew does, when quoting this text,[65] the clue to understand it is to be looked for firstly in its immediate context.[66] This text is inserted between two accounts from Luke's special material (the raising of the son of a widow at Nain in Lk 7:11-17 and the forgiving of a sinful woman at Simon's house in Lk 7:36-50) within a section that begins immediately after the sermon on the plain with the healing of a Centurion's servant (Lk 7:1-10). What is common to all of these texts is Jesus' unusual attitude towards certain people who were either taboo issues or just abandoned to their own fate in some milieus of Jewish society (a pagan, a widow, a sinner). In the belief of some Jewish groupings, persons like sinners and unbelievers were inevitably excluded from God's salvation. Bearing that in mind, Luke inserts this passage as a sort of justification for Jesus' unconventional approach, which, in many cases, was a reason for some people to become scandalized.

---

63 Radl considers the possibility of a change in John the Baptist's understanding of the one who was to come over time. He observes that, if at all this expression had a connotation in the sense of the apocalyptic idea of refiner's fire, this fades out already in 3:16 – through the announcement of both a more powerful one and the baptism of spirit – and nothing of that sort is noticeable any more in John's question. According to Radl, after hearing about Jesus' words and deeds, John might have reconsidered his expectations about the one who was to come as executor of God's revengeful judgment and might have come to the conclusion that Jesus could not but be the one to whom he had prepared the way (Cf. ibid., 1:463). Notwithstanding the plausibility of that conjecture within Luke's account, it appears extremely difficult to verify its truthfulness in reality and to maintain such a claim.
64 Eckey, *Das Lukasevangelium*, 1:348.
65 There prevails a broad consensus among exegetes that this pericope was quoted very likely from Q.
66 Cf. Eckey, *Das Lukasevangelium*, 1:345.

Now, considering the broader context of his Gospel, Luke makes a very determined effort to present Jesus in continuity with the promises of the Old Testament, whereby he is the beginner of the new era of God's kingdom and the fulfiller of those promises. "What God had promised to do in the last days was being fulfilled."[67] In Luke's understanding of the Scripture, John the Baptist was to be necessarily regarded as the messenger prefigured by the prophet Malachi to prepare the way for this new time.[68] On the other hand, notwithstanding this close relationship, there is a great gulf between them, since John is just the precursor of the new aeon of God's reign, yet does not belong to it.[69] The point of v. 28 would be missed, if understood as a denigration of John. Rather than criticizing him, Jesus wants to call the attention of his own followers to the importance of the decision that they are now facing. For entering the Kingdom of God, which has begun here and now, supersedes even the preaching of the greatest among men. Rather than marking differences in terms of individual features, the very point of this comparison (greater/lesser) is to highlight them in terms of membership (of humankind or of the Kingdom of God).[70]

The reason for John's question was, according to Luke, the spreading of Jesus' fame "throughout Judaea and all over the countryside"

---

[67] I. Howard Marshall, *The Gospel of Luke: A Commentary on the Greek Text*, The New International Greek Testament Commentary (Grand Rapids: Eerdmans, 1978), 276.

[68] Cf. Radl, *Das Evangelium nach Lukas*, 1:472; on the other hand, the question what such a preparation might have consisted in must remain open. Following the reference of Mk 1:2 and similar attempts in the rabbinic tradition, Eckey suggests Ex 23:30 as interpretation key to this image from Mal 3:1. Cf. Eckey, *Das Lukasevangelium*, 1:352.

[69] Cf. Eckey, *Das Lukasevangelium*, 1:353. This barrier becomes sufficiently evident in Lk 7:28. As against this view of Luke, see Jeremias, *Neutestamentliche Theologie*, 1:54. Jeremias argues that Matthew hands down an older tradition than Luke, which interprets the prepositions ἕως/μέχρι (until, till, up to) inclusively, thereby considering John the Baptist as belonging to the new aeon, while Luke interprets them exclusively.

[70] Cf. Bovon, *Das Evangelium nach Lukas*, 1986, III/1:378.

(Lk 7:17) and people's astonishment at his words and deeds.⁷¹ In fact, after having seen the raising of the son of the widow at Nain, "everyone was filled with awe and glorified God" (Lk 7:16). And so were John's disciples, who reported it all to him in prison (Lk 7:18). Faced with such extraordinary news, John feels compelled to inquire about.

Luke appears to be intent on clarifying possible misunderstandings, especially with respect to John's question: are you the one who comes, the one who is coming ... has come ... is (supposed) to come?⁷² This recalls, in the apocalyptic view, the figure of the son of man (Dan 7:13), that is, the one who "comes/goes to the most venerable and was led into his presence," the one on whom "was conferred rule, honour and kingship," and the one of whom "all peoples, nations and languages became servants" (cf. Dan 7:13f.).

That this passage is intended by Luke to qualify and specify more precisely God's salvific will and deeds should not be surprising, as this text is immediately preceded by a soteriological assertion of high value: ἐπεσκέψατο ὁ θεὸς τὸν λαὸν αὐτοῦ (Lk 7:16: God has visited his people).⁷³ This is a radically new theological assertion about God.

---

71 Cf. Radl, *Das Evangelium nach Lukas*, 1:459.

72 What accounts for so great an openness and flexibility in this translation is the use of this present participle (σὺ εἶ ὁ ἐρχόμενος;), which has no temporal determinations of any kind. It might as well be translated as 'going,' instead of coming. This can be also be interpreted as a futuristic use of the present tense. While it is still controversial whether ὁ ἐρχόμενος was a common or, rather, an unusual designation for the messiah, there seems to be a consensual association of this expression with the promised time of salvation. Perhaps on that account, John inquires, in Luke's formulation, neither about the Lord (ὁ κύριος, cf. Isa 40:3), nor about the messiah (ὁ Χριστός, cf. Mt 11:2), but about the one who is to come. Cf. Bovon, *Das Evangelium nach Lukas*, 1986, III/1:375; Radl, *Das Evangelium nach Lukas*, 1:462; Eckey, *Das Lukasevangelium*, 1:348.

73 The verb ἐπισκέπτομαι means: to visit, to be concerned about, to show care for, to go to help, to look after the sick (the same verb is employed, for instance, in Mt 25:36). Luke uses this verb in a similar way at the beginning of his gospel – it is again a soteriological assertion of great import – to describe God as someone who comes to visit and to help his people Εὐλογητὸς κύριος ὁ θεὸς τοῦ Ἰσραήλ, ὅτι *ἐπεσκέψατο* καὶ ἐποίησεν λύτρωσιν τῷ λαῷ αὐτοῦ (Blessed be the Lord, the God of Israel, for he

It does not only reaffirm God's faithfulness to his covenant, in that he fulfills what had been promised through the prophet Isaiah, but also the prophetic pattern "promise-fulfillment" taken up by Jesus.[74] The theological novelty of this new section in the Gospel of Luke is that God has entered history out of his love, care and compassion, in order to save his people. His words and deeds of salvation do not take place outside, but rather inside and amidst history, here and now. By looking at the person of Jesus, at his words and deeds, one knows what God himself means by salvation. Furthermore, John has to learn that there is in fact conformity between the Scriptures and the words and deeds of Jesus.

This "good news" must have sounded quite revolutionary in the ears of John the Baptist and many other Jewish groups. The close connection between verses 22 and 23 suggests that this beatitude (μακάριός) was addressed first and foremost to John, as he must have been the first one to become scandalized at those words of Jesus.[75] For Radl, the discrepancy between the image of the one who was to come, as it had been proclaimed by John, and the person of Jesus, as he actually came, was so evident, that not even a reference to Luke's omission of the verses of revenge prophesied by Isaiah in Isa 29:20; 35:4 and 61:2 appears to be needed.[76] Since the expected one does not annihilate the sinner nor the unfaithful, as predicted, it was now necessary for Luke to recognize in the person of Jesus the one who was to come in the eschatological time. However, Bovon regards the absence of any proper conclusion to this account reporting the reaction of John the Baptist to Jesus' answer as a clear indication for the fact that the disciples of John could not manage with such a "scandalous attitude" and might have increasingly distanced themselves

---

has visited his people, he has set them free, Lk 1:68). This sentence might as well be translated as "[...] for he has visited his people and redeemed/saved them" and certainly echoes God's works of salvation along Israel's history. This kind of language was part of the vocabulary of Jewish expectation (cf. Ex 4:31; Ruth 1:6) and could be presupposed by Luke. Cf. Marshall, *The Gospel of Luke*, 287.

74   Cf. Bovon, *Das Evangelium nach Lukas*, 1986, III/1:376.
75   Cf. Radl, *Das Evangelium nach Lukas*, 1:465.
76   Cf. ibid.

from Jesus' group. Consequently, the current hearers and readers of this beatitude (v. 23) were expected to attach to it even more significance.[77]

Was Jesus' Message on Salvation a Rupture with Judaism?

Where did the border between Judaism and Christianity run during the first century? Daniel Boyarin claims decidedly that there was none until the second century. For him, such clear limits between them were set "[...] some time in the second century with a group of Christian writers called 'heresiologists,' the anatomizers of heresy and heresies, and their Jewish counterparts, the Rabbis."[78] Accordingly, the "invention" of the notion of heresy is the decisive locus to look for those boundaries.

> Early Christian heresiology, whatever else it is, is largely the work of those who wished to eradicate the fuzziness of the borders, semantic and social, between Jews and Christians and thus produce Judaism and Christianity as fully separate (and opposed) entities – as religions, at least in the eyes of Christianity.[79]

Indeed, it is with good reason that G. Strecker, building on Bauer's theory on orthodoxy and heresy, urges closer attention to Jewish Christianity,[80] if one is willing to overcome the one-sidedness of heresiologists and to gain a more comprehensive picture of the efforts to interpret and hand down Jesus' legacy in early Christianity. Not only because those variants of Christianity were "vastly underrepresented, misrepresented, and undervalued in the ancient sources"[81] are

---

77 Cf. Bovon, *Das Evangelium nach Lukas*, 1986, III/1:374.
78 Daniel Boyarin, *Border Lines: The Partition of Judaeo-Christianity* (Philadelphia: University of Pennsylvania Press, 2004), 2.
79 Ibid.
80 Further details on Jewish Christianity can be found below in chapter 4 (p. 80ff).
81 Edwin K. Broadhead, *Jewish Ways of Following Jesus: Redrawing the Religious Map of Antiquity*, Wissenschaftliche Untersuchungen Zum Neuen Testament 266

scholars encouraged to do so, but particularly because it is actually they who are at the dawning of the church, not "gentile Christianity."

> According to the witness of the New Testament, Jewish Christianity stands at the beginning of the development of church history. Accordingly, it is not the "ecclesiastical doctrine" of gentile Christians that represents what is primary, but rather a Jewish Christian theology.[82]

Bauer observes this conflict between Jewish and gentile Christians not only in later stages of Christianity, but already during the apostolic time. The Letter to the Galatians delivers a few examples of it.[83] For Bauer, much more attention ought to be paid to the point that Judaists tried to make over and over again in the first controversies of early Christianity, especially in respect of Pauline theology. What they were convinced of, and firmly insisted in, was that "the Pauline gospel" would be, as such, "even for Gentile believers, insufficient."[84] In consequence of such insufficiency, people would be restricted from the access to the fullness of "messianic salvation." Beyond question, Jewish Christians thought, conceived of, and sensed otherwise. The question then arises, firstly, whether their demands were at all legitimate; secondly, how the conflict was handled, which position was privileged by whom; and finally, what might have become lost through that solution in terms of faith. This attempt towards "dislodging the traditional 'Eusebian' account of the origins of orthodoxy and heresy"[85] may even be correct and justified, at least to a certain

---

(Tübingen: Mohr Siebeck, 2010), 28.

82 Georg Strecker, "Zum Problem des Judenchristentums," in *Rechtgläubigkeit und Ketzerei im ältesten Christentum*, by Walter Bauer, 2nd ed., Beiträge zur historischen Theologie 10 (Tübingen: Mohr Siebeck, 1964), 245.

83 Cf. Walter Bauer, *Rechtgläubigkeit und Ketzerei im ältesten Christentum*, ed. Georg Strecker, 2nd ed., Beiträge zur historischen Theologie 10 (Tübingen: Mohr Siebeck, 1964), 237f.

84 Cf. ibid., 238.

85 In the version of the Church historian Eusebius, orthodoxy was nothing but the original teaching of Jesus to the apostles, which, in turn, was passed down to the bishops, and heresy the distortion of that original teaching under the influence of the

extent. The relevant question for this section is, however, whether or not Jesus himself drew a border vis-a-vis his own tradition, and, if yes, to which extent.

Martin Buber is deeply convinced that Jesus' message of salvation does not represent any rupture with the heritage of Judaism on which he drew throughout his whole lifetime. On the contrary, it was a later development of Christianity that should be held responsible for the distortion of his original message or for the contrasting juxtaposition between Judaism and Christianity that gave rise to a hostile attitude towards the former since the very beginnings of the Church.[86] According to Buber, Paul's understanding of grace, which evolved in the theologies of Augustine and Luther, reshaped anthropology substantially, as contrasted with Judaism. Firstly, rather than encouraging Christians to perform "good deeds" in accordance with God's will, thereby acting positively so that his Kingdom may become a reality on earth, it fostered an attitude of passivity, as these were supposed to wait for God's grace and action. Secondly, it contributed towards the emergence of an exclusive claim to salvation that conditioned one's relation with God and one's own salvation exclusively on faith in Jesus Christ.[87]

On the other hand, there are two things to be borne in mind. First, no one can cast doubt on the fact that, as has been seen in the previous sections, Jesus' "theology" did constitute a significant paradigm shift in many respects with regard to his religious tradition. Second, even if it is argued that his views represented those of "original" Judaism, as Buber suggests, one may ask with good reasons, in the face of the plurality of currents and groupings at Jesus' time and before, whether there has ever existed something to that effect in Judaism.

Devil. Boyarin, *Border Lines*, 3; see also Bauer, *Rechtgläubigkeit und Ketzerei*, 3.

86   Buber regards Paul as the first prominent figure in Christianity to adopt such a hostile frame of mind with respect to Judaism, which culminated with the theology of Marcion of Sinope (cf. Karl-Josef Kuschel, *Martin Buber – seine Herausforderung an das Christentum* [Gütersloh: Gütersloher Verlagshaus, 2015], 101).

87   Cf. ibid., 96.

Can God in His Anger Annihilate His Beloved People?

Jesus is neither the only nor the first one to claim that God's attitude on the day of judgment is not one of wrath, but of love. The Catholic exegete Gerhard Lohfink refers, for instance, to the prophet Hosea, whose theology stands emblematically for such a perspective in Jewish prophecy.[88] Hosea enumerates a lengthy list of accusations against Israel on account of its unfaithfulness towards the Lord (Hos 4-11). However, at the end of such a "long, wrathful discourse," the prophet is himself surprised by the words of the Lord. In the end, God's wrath turns into compassion, into salvation. God's relationship with Israel, God's love towards it appears to be stronger than anything else.

Therefore, it appears helpful to place both texts side by side, in order to notice that "theological tension" in the words of the prophet.[89]

> Israelites, hear what Yahweh says, for Yahweh indicts the citizens of the country: there is no loyalty, no faithful love, no knowledge of God in the country, only perjury and lying, murder, theft, adultery and violence, bloodshed after bloodshed. This is why the country is in mourning and all its citizens pining away, the wild animals also and birds of the sky, even the fish in the sea will disappear. [Hos 4:1-3] [...] Ephraim, how could I part with you? Israel, how could I give you up? How could I make you like Admah or treat you like Zeboiim? My heart within me is overwhelmed, fever grips my inmost being. I will not give rein to my fierce anger, I will not destroy Ephraim again, for I am God, not man, the Holy One in your midst, and I shall not come to you in anger. [Hos 11:8-9]

Also the Catholic theologian Verweyen holds the view that the book of Hosea is one of the most insightful texts to truly grasp

---

88 Lohfink, *Jesus of Nazareth*, 163f. Besides Hosea, Lohfink mentions other texts in the Old Testament such as Isa 54:6-8, in which such love on the part of God can be perceived as well.

89 Owing to its length, Hos 4-11 was shortened, and its first part was limited to its first three verses.

what the love of God is all about. For, according to him, what takes place therein is a twofold "iconoclasm." The faithful activity of the prophet is the means chosen by Yahweh to shatter "not only the images of love created by human beings, but also the caricatures of him."[90] This was a long way which the prophet himself had to go in order to understand what God's love towards his people Israel really means. Otherwise, he could never have come up with a reaction to his spouse's unfaithfulness such as that contained in Hos 2:16: "But look, I am going to seduce her and lead her into the desert and speak to her heart." In the book of Hosea, it becomes clear that the response to refused or not corresponded love does not have to be unavoidably punishment. Insofar as God decides to build up a relationship with human beings, he becomes vulnerable, he can "be let down." For Hosea there is only one reason for Israel not to have corresponded to God's unconditional love: lack of knowledge of God.[91] It is because the people of Israel failed to know God as he is, as contrasted with their images of him, that they broke the covenant with him.

Outcome

In the New Testament, it is impossible to find a single, unambiguous answer as to the meaning of salvation. Comparison was the strategy I employed to approach a bit more what Jesus might have had in mind by employing the word salvation. After all, the comparison between John the Baptist and Jesus is drawn in the gospels themselves in search of answers.

In the light of the comparison made in this chapter, I want to highlight four features of Jesus' "soteriology," as contrasted with John's. First, one can notice a tendency to reject apocalyptic thinking, though not completely, and to value more positively the world and creation. Second, and related to the previous, if the world is more appreciated, human history, together with human

---

90 Cf. Hansjürgen Verweyen, *Ist Gott die Liebe?: Spurensuche in Bibel und Tradition* (Regensburg: Pustet, 2014), 146.
91 Ibid., 148.

action, assume a more positive role as well. Third, and consequently, a more optimistic anthropology. Fourth, the significance of God's merciful love in God's salvation plan.

In the course of this examination, the Gospel of Luke has shown distinctive features, which, in my view, deserve a more detailed study, especially because they seem to coincide with the four features presented above. This will be accomplished in the next chapter.

4

The Soteriological Potential of the Praxis of Love in the Light of Lk 10:25-37

For several exegetes, the issue of salvation is at the core of Lukan theology.[1] In his twofold work, he makes every endeavor to elucidate how God fulfilled the promises of salvation of the Old Testament in the person of Jesus Christ and how this work continues through the Church, inspired by the Holy Spirit. The question of salvation recurs several times in his work, but, keeping in mind the purpose and topic of this work, I shall concentrate on one specific passage: Lk 10:25-37. In my view, this particular text combines three major issues which are crucial for any study about interreligious dialogue.[2] First, in his "foreword" (Lk 10:25-28) to the parable of the

---

1 See especially below, pp. 97–99.
2 Availing himself of Bosch's studies on Luke's understanding of the Christian mission, Amos Yong was one of the first theologians who suggested the parable of the Good Samaritan as well as the stormy relation between Jews and Samaritans as a point of departure for a performative theology of both the interreligious dialogue and Christian mission (Amos Yong, "The Spirit of Hospitality: Pentecostal Perspectives toward a Performative Theology of Interreligious Encounter," *Missiology: An International Review* 35, no. 1 [2007]: 55–73; this article was reprinted in Amos Yong, *The Missiological Spirit: Christian Mission Theology in the Third Millennium Global Context* [Cambridge: Clarke, 2015], chap. 4; see also Amos Yong, *The Spirit Poured out on All Flesh: Pentecostalism and the Possibility of Global Theology* [Grand Rapids: Baker Academic, 2005], 241–44; David Bosch, *Transforming*

Good Samaritan, Luke approaches the topic of salvation in a very innovative manner. Second, by telling the parable immediately after the twofold commandment of love, he succeeds in spelling out very concretely what love as well as the path to salvation, in effect, consist in. By so doing, he makes clear how indissociable belief and praxis are. Third, as the main character of the story is a Samaritan, Luke raises relevant concerns of his time such as "interreligious" relations, or, more precisely, what the (normative) principle to deal with (religious) otherness ought to be. By extension, the author of the Third Gospel seems to challenge the readers as to the fact that (religious) identity is at all relevant for the debate on salvation. Needless to say, religious/religion are modern categories and cannot be applied to the New Testament mindset. Nevertheless, the text allows us to think in these categories, too.

Now, since this parable belongs to a special source which is unique to Luke, as will be seen below, it requires a very diligent analysis and many factors are to be taken into account. This is the principal reason why I am going to avail myself, in the present chapter, exclusively of the results of exegetical research on this pericope along with its context, rather than immediately engaging in philosophic-theological reflection. As a consequence, the dogmatic unfoldment of the findings of the present chapter will be carried out in Part III.

In addition to what has been said, special attention has to be paid to the close relation between salvation and the (twofold) commandment to love, which appears to be a major concern of the evangelist Luke, particularly as he is the only one who explicitly makes this connection in his gospel. By introducing a debate on salvation with the question *"what must I do...,"* Luke appears, on the one hand, to recover the "Jewish" value of religious praxis and, on the other one, to attenuate Paul's firm conviction that salvation is attained but through faith, and no longer through works (of law). But this theme will be worked out in more detail in chapter 5.

Mission: Paradigm Shifts in Theology of Mission [Maryknoll, N.Y.: Orbis Books, 1991], chap. 3). His studies, however, do not engage as much in exegetical analysis as the present work is intended to.

The Parable of the Good Samaritan (Lk 10:25-37)

The main point of this parable is not to explain or to delimit who one's neighbor is – a highly controversial subject in Jewish circles at the time of Jesus – but, instead, to illustrate, very concretely, what love of neighbor consists in.[3] This may be assumed, especially if the way in which the parable is told is observed. It is not the victim, who is described in details, but the different possibilities of action.[4] Accordingly, Petzke and other scholars have pointed out that this text, as far as its genre is concerned, is to be classified as an "example story."[5] So being, the primary focus of interest is not to present a reflection on an issue like love of neighbor, but to offer different possible attitudes by means of the characters of the story. Ben-Chorin names this approach "narrative ethics."[6]

The context in which Luke places this parable and the question about eternal life is highly significant, too. He tells it immediately after the praises and beatitudes of verses 21 to 24. Apparently, Luke seeks to avoid any misunderstandings that could arise from those words of praise of Jesus. In the view of Schürmann, through this pericope (Lk 10:25-37) Luke seems to be saying that "[t]he 'Gospel' [the good news] would be misunderstood, if it did not comprise in itself the 'law.' Profession of faith in Christ alone does not suffice, if not

---

3 Cf. Heinz Schürmann, *Das Lukasevangelium*, vol. III/2, Herders theologischer Kommentar zum Neuen Testament (Freiburg im Breisgau; Basel; Wien: Herder, 1994), 144.

4 See esp. Joachim Jeremias, *Die Gleichnisse Jesu*, 11th ed. (first published in 1947) (Göttingen: Vandenhoeck & Ruprecht, 1998), 201f.

5 Cf. Gerd Petzke, *Das Sondergut des Evangeliums nach Lukas*, Zürcher Werkkommentare zur Bibel (Zürich: Theologischer Verlag, 1990), 217f.; Kim Paffenroth, *The Story of Jesus according to L*, Journal for the Study of the New Testament 147 (Sheffield: Sheffield Academic Press, 1997), 101; Hans Klein, *Barmherzigkeit gegenüber den Elenden und Geächteten: Studien zur Botschaft des lukanischen Sondergutes*, Biblisch-theologische Studien 10 (Neukirchen-Vluyn: Neukirchener Verlag, 1987), 78.

6 Cf. Shalom Ben-Chorin, *Jüdische Ethik anhand der patristischen Perikopen*, 102.

accompanied with deeds (cf. Lk 6:46-49)."[7] The reason why Jesus blesses the Father is not their faith in him nor the fact that they "had seen" the revelation of God, but rather because of their proclamation of the Kingdom through words and deeds (cf. Lk 10:1-16). Being so, the issue of salvation is approached by Luke quite differently than by Paul, though not in contradiction to it.[8]

Even if the similarities of the parable of the Good Samaritan with 2Chr 28:15[9] are not taken as coincidental,[10] this argument nevertheless does not suffice to deny its authenticity and its origin in Jesus' sayings. On the other hand, given that in exegesis there is no consensus yet as to the origin of this pericope, and that referring it back to Jesus' *ipsissima verba* is still far from being certain,[11] the only valid criterion is to verify whether texts like this indeed correspond to Jesus' *ipsissima intentio* and to his conduct as well. In the opinion of Schürmann, that question is to be answered in the affirmative.[12]

In the parable of the Good Samaritan, the question as to the road to eternal life becomes highly contentious, as Jesus seems to imply that the Samaritan was "justified" on account of his deed. It should be noted that a questioning of the prerequisites for inheriting eternal life occurs also elsewhere in Luke. The parable of the pharisee and

---

7   Schürmann, *Das Lukasevangelium*, III/2:148.

8   Even Paul links eternal life to a certain praxis (cf. Gal 3:12; Rom 14:10; 2Cor 5:10). Cf. François Bovon, *Das Evangelium nach Lukas*, vol. III/2, Evangelisch-Katholischer Kommentar zum Neuen Testament (Zürich: Benziger, 1996), 87.

9   "Men nominated for the purpose then took charge of the captives. From the booty they clothed all those of them who were naked; they gave them clothing and sandals, provided them with food and drink, mounted on donkeys all those who were infirm and took them back to Jericho, the city of palm trees, to their brothers. Then they returned to Samaria" (2Chr 28:15).

10 See esp. Thomas Walter Manson, *The Sayings of Jesus as Recorded in the Gospels according to St. Matthew and St. Luke Arranged with Introduction and Commentary* (London: SCM Press, 1950), 262.

11 That is still an ongoing discussion in exegesis. While authors like Eduard Schweizer and Wolfgang Wiefel argue for the origin in Jesus, Gerhard Schneider, Walter Schmithals and others see it as not plausible.

12 Cf. Schürmann, *Das Lukasevangelium*, III/2:150.

the tax collector (Lk 18:9-14) who go for prayer in the temple is a further example. Those who are too certain as to their justification might be surprised on the final day. Interestingly enough, this parable belongs to Lukan special material too. A close connection to the narrative of the final judgment in Mt 25 is almost inevitable at this conjuncture. Just as many who count their salvation for granted may be surprised, there may be many who will be astonished as they see prostitutes, tax collectors, and sinners preceding Pharisees and lawyers in the Kingdom of God (Lk 7:29f.; Mt 21:31f.).[13]

In fact, one of the points of the parable seems to be the great contrast between the Priest and the Levite, on the one hand, and the Samaritan, on the other. What is expected from the first ones is not done by them, but by the latter. Moreover, Jesus breaks the customary triad of priest, Levite, and Israelite, and substitutes the last one with a public enemy, a mingled person, which must have surprised the hearers/readers greatly.[14] The only person in the story with whom the Jews could have identified themselves was the assaulted. Having to accept help from a Samaritan might surely have been, for a Jew, at that time, an enormous challenge.

It has been often maintained that from v. 29 (the neighbor is the object of actions – passive) to v. 36 (the neighbor is the subject of actions, the one who acts with mercy) there is a discrepancy. Instead of discrepancy, however, G. Sellin[15] prefers the term "shift of aspect" (*Aspektverschiebung*). In his commentary on this parable, F. Bovon regards that kind of discrepancy positively. The key to understanding the point of the parable is Jesus' question in verse 36: τίς τούτων τῶν τριῶν πλησίον δοκεῖ σοι γεγονέναι τοῦ ἐμπεσόντος εἰς τοὺς λῃστάς; (Which of these three,

---

13   Cf. Hans Conzelmann, *Die Mitte der Zeit: Studien zur Theologie des Lukas*, Beiträge zur historischen Theologie 17 (Tübingen: Mohr, 1954), 206. "Fragen wir nach dem *Lohn* für das Durchhalten, so erfahren wir nachdrücklich, daß ein Anspruch, eine Anrechnung als Verdienst ausgeschlossen ist (Lk 6,35; 17,10)."

14   Joachim Jeremias, *Neutestamentliche Theologie*, 3rd ed., vol. 1 (Gütersloh: Mohn, 1979), 206.

15   Cf. Gerhard Sellin, "Lukas als Gleichniserzähler: die Erzählung vom barmherzigen Samariter (Lk 10 25-37)," *Zeitschrift für die neutestamentliche Wissenschaft und die Kunde der älteren Kirche 65*, no. 3–4 (1974): 166–89.

do you think, *became* a neighbor to the man who fell into the bandits' [hands]?). The verb γίνομαι (to come into being, to happen, to become) brings about a sort of change of paradigm in the whole discussion, so that even the lawyer, who, in the beginning of the story, just wanted to put him to the test, was touched by Jesus' view and seems to engage in the conversation on a different level.

By describing the attitude of this Samaritan, this parable turns everything upside down and leads the readers to critical thinking. From this point of view, "[...] there is one neighbor at either end of the communication of love: in the commandment (v. 27) the neighbor is the object of compassion, whereas in the parable (v. 36) the neighbor is the subject of compassion."[16] Love can indeed change relations between people. Interestingly, in the Gospel of Luke both the Samaritan and the sinful woman (Lk 7:36-50), who were excluded from social relations and regarded as objects of pity and compassion, are actually subjects of love.

This point of the parable evinces the relational aspect of love. In this parable, not only is the connotation of the word "neighbor" interpreted in a new manner, but also that of love. For Bovon, "becoming" a neighbor to someone implies much more than just "having" neighbors. Doing charity or showing solidarity towards someone is quite different from loving someone. What follows from it is that, in order to love, one has first "to become a neighbor" to others. "By becoming neighbors to others, we fulfill the law – the will of God – and assume the cause and attitude of Jesus."[17]

As a consequence, becoming a neighbor demands not only the submissive observance of a command, but, above all, the integration between inwardness and deeds. The answer of the lawyer in verse 37 gives a clue to this further aspect. He says: ὁ ποιήσας τὸ ἔλεος μετ' αὐτοῦ (the one who did [=practiced, showed] compassion for him). It is not enough to feel compassion, mercy, pity, etc. towards others, especially the most needy. One has also to put it into practice. Now, this kind of inwardness that is here presupposed could sound anachronistic, as the notion of subjectivity in those days was for sure not

---

16 Bovon, *Das Evangelium nach Lukas*, 1996, III/2:99.
17 Ibid.

the same as today. Nevertheless, without a minimum of inwardness and subjectivity, it seems difficult to speak of love in the same fashion as Luke did in this passage.

This parable had been probably handed down in Palestinian circles, as the story contains relevant background information about the region in which it occurs. The traditional account knows, for instance, that the way from Jericho to Jerusalem was highly dangerous, that Jericho was a place of residence of priests who served in Jerusalem, that at that time the relations between Jews and Samaritans were increasingly tense, and, especially, that it was a time in which the question whether Samaritan people ought to be accepted in Christian communities was a current issue.[18] Those circles were probably "not as much interested in Jesus' eschatological proclamation as they were both in the good news of God's commitment to the needy and in his commandment to love. Moreover, this is a tendency that can be observed also in other accounts of the *Lukan special material*."[19]

The Core Message and the Main Concerns of Luke's Special Material

The parable of the Good Samaritan is part of the so-called Lukan special material.[20] As such, it deserves particular attention, especially considering its age, "theology," concerns, and, not least, the context of its origin, conservation, and transmission. After Gadamer's *Truth*

---

18 Cf. Schürmann, *Das Lukasevangelium*, III/2:149.
19 Ibid. (emphasis in original).
20 In view of the existing formal and semantic ambiguity with regard to the usage of the term "Lukan special material," it is useful to make a general remark regarding its use in this work. For the sake of clarity, the variant "special material" will be used consequently and invariably. Other varying forms, such as peculiar source, special source, special materials, material specific to Luke, etc. will be avoided here. For the sake of variation, however, the well-established abbreviation "L" (or "L material," which is the equivalent form to the German SLk) may be occasionally used. For an overview of the current usage of it, cf. Paffenroth, *The Story of Jesus according to L*, 20–22.

*and Method,*²¹ we know that those factors are not as decisive as was assumed before in hermeneutic enterprise. Nevertheless, they provide a valuable help in comprehending why Luke includes the texts of this source in his gospel and where he places each of the stories, which is essential in order to understand his theology or the manner in which he understood Jesus' message.

The Source(s) of Lukan Special Material
One of the vexed questions among scholars has been whether this material consists of one single source or of more than one. A common tendency among scholars in the last decades has been to consider this material as consisting of different sources.²² For Gerhard Schneider, just to cite one of these scholars, there appear to be three distinct sources of special material in the Gospel of Luke: (a) the infancy narratives (1:5-2:52), (b) the Passion (chapters 22-23) and Easter narrative (24:12-53) and (c) the transmission of words and miracles of Jesus.²³ Further, some exegetes have suggested that it cannot be just taken for granted that even the latter (c) would have its origin in one single source.²⁴ Therefore, it might well be that this group of parables, sayings and stories were not embedded in one single text (or oral tradition), but composed in different places and at different times.

The first studies on the Lukan special material by Weiss and Feine had suggested, however, though arguing in different manners, that Luke's additional material (a), (b) and (c) must have proceeded from a single source.²⁵ Though working with methods and tools that

---

21 Hans-Georg Gadamer, *Wahrheit und Methode: Grundzüge einer philosophischen Hermeneutik*, 4th ed. (Tübingen: Mohr, 1975).
22 Cf. Petzke, *Das Sondergut des Evangeliums nach Lukas*, 13. Petzke shares this view himself.
23 Cf. Gerhard Schneider, *Das Evangelium nach Lukas* (Würzburg: Gütersloher Verlagshaus Mohn; Echter-Verlag, 1977), 28.
24 Cf. Petzke, *Das Sondergut des Evangeliums nach Lukas*, 211.
25 Bernhard Weiss, *Die Quellen des Lukasevangeliums* (Stuttgart; Berlin: Cotta, 1907); id., *Die Quellen der synoptischen Überlieferung* (Leipzig: J.C. Hinrichs, 1908); Paul Feine, *Eine vorkanonische Überlieferung des Lukas in Evangelium und*

cannot be compared to those at the beginning of the 20th century, scholars like Hans Klein and Kim Paffenroth arrive at similar conclusions. After careful examination of the vocabulary, style, formal characteristics, and contents of the pericopae contained in this material, Paffenroth verifies great internal similarities and common concerns. This leads him to come to the conclusion that they might have proceeded from one single source.[26] It should be highlighted, however, that such unity concerns alone the source containing the words and miracles of Jesus (c), not the infancy (a), Passion and Easter narratives (b). Whereas Weiss and Feine regarded (a), (b) and (c) as handed down through the same source, Paffenroth considers this to be the case just for (c). This view is shared by Klein as well,[27] though leaving the question as to the provenience of (a) and (b) quite open.[28] Paffenroth maintains, in turn, that there is not sufficient evidence for the existence of (a) and (b) as independent sources. He ascribes the authorship of infancy narrative to Luke himself but the Passion and Resurrection stories to Luke's redactional work. What he considers as "L material" is exclusively the series of pericopae comprised in Lk 3-19 containing some of Jesus' sayings, miracles and parables.[29]

Apostelgeschichte: eine Untersuchung (Gotha: F. A. Perthes, 1891).
26 Cf. Paffenroth, *The Story of Jesus according to L*, 139 and 143.
27 Klein groups the above-mentioned texts containing words and miracles of Jesus as follows: cures on Sabbath (13:10-17; 14:1-6), miracles (7:11-17; 17:11-19; 5:1-11; 4:25-27), justification for accepting sinners (15:4-10; 15:11-32; 7:36-50; 18:9-14; 19:1-10), the Samaritan (17:11-19; 9:51-56; 10:30-37), repentance (13:1-5; 13:6-9); approach to goods (12:13-15; 12:16-21; 14:12-14; 14:28-32; 16:1-12; 16:19-31; 19:1-10), prayer (11:5-8; 17:11-19; 18:1-8; 18:9-14), invitations (7:36-50; 10:38-42; 14:1-14; 19:1-10) and humility (17:7-10).
28 Cf. Klein, *Barmherzigkeit*, 12.
29 Cf. Paffenroth, *The Story of Jesus according to L*, 27–30. Accordingly, Paffenroth limits the pericopae as follows: Tax Collectors, Widows and Lepers (Lk 3:12-13; 4:25-27; 7:11b-15; 17:12-18; 18:2-8a; 18:10-14a; 19:2-10); Love or Compassion (Lk 7:11b-15:36-47; 10:30-37a; 15:11-32) Hospitality (Lk 7:36-47; 10:39-42; 11:5b-8; 14:8-10, 12-14; 19:2-10) Setting at Night (Lk 11:5b-8; 12:16b-20; 12:35-38); Prayer (Lk 11:5b-8; 18:2-8a,10-14a); Watchfulness (Lk 12:16b-20; 12:35-38; 13:1b-5, 6b-9); Children of Abraham (Lk 12:10-17b; 16:19-31; 19:2-10); Honor

Now, apart from the enormous relevance of the debate over the origin of L in exegetical studies, why should this be in any way pertinent to the present work and to the topic in question? It could be said, by way of answer, that for the interpretation of the texts of this corpus, it is not indifferent whether this material came from a single source or whether it was the result of Luke's gathering of stories and sayings of Jesus that were being told in his time at different places and happened to arrive, in some way, at his hands. It does make a difference, if it can be assumed, as Paffenroth and Klein suggest, that this material was embedded in a single source that was preserved and handed down by (a) determined group(s) of Christians who for certain had special concerns and, conceivably, different theological accents from those of later stages of early Christianity that, at a certain point, were established as "orthodoxy." Hence the need for further clarification as to the origin of this material.

The Composition of Lukan Special Material:
A Jewish Christian Writing?
Having set out, though summarily, some of the reasons why the Lukan special material (c) ought to be regarded as originating from one single source, some attention will be devoted to the authorship of these texts. As far as the date and place of composition of L are concerned, Paffenroth and Klein share similar opinions. Whereas Klein maintains that the community (or the communities) who conserved this tradition was settled either in Jerusalem or, if not, at least somewhere in Judea, especially considering the geographical scenery

---

and Shame (Lk 13:10-17b; 14:8-10, 12-14, 28-32; 15:11-32; 16:1b-8a; 17:7-10); Joy at Finding the Lost (Lk 15:4-6, 8-9, 11-32; 19:2-10).

of these texts,[30] Paffenroth prefers to speak only of Palestine.[31] This source's original language was with certainty Aramaic. Whether Mark and Matthew did not incorporate it in their gospels on account of its peculiar message,[32] or whether they did not because of its language or, perhaps, whether that source was unknown to them, these remain all open questions.[33] A possible dating would be between 40 and 60 CE.[34] As for the authorship, both are convinced that these texts might have been composed by Jewish-Christians living in Palestine or, more specifically, in Jerusalem (Klein).[35]

The difficult question, however, is to determine more precisely

---

30   Cf. Klein, *Barmherzigkeit*, 133. The texts tell, for example, about a Pharisee and a tax collector who go to the Temple (Lk 18:10ff.), a man who goes from Jerusalem to Jericho (Lk 10:30ff.), the blood of Galileans, which Pilate mingled with that of their sacrifices and the tower of Siloam (Lk 13:1-5) and about the need of inviting poor, the crippled, the lame and the blind when giving a lunch or a dinner (Lk 14:12-14) and the place where those people could be found for a certainty was in Jerusalem, especially near the temple.

31   Cf. Paffenroth, *The Story of Jesus according to L*, 155.

32   For Klein, Matthew and Mark wrote to Greek-speaking communities and had as a special concern the mission among pagans. Such a missionary concern can nowhere be found in this source (cf. Klein, *Barmherzigkeit*, 135). To Klein, it should be reckoned with the possibility that the peculiar content of this source might not have suited the concerns of those communities.

33   Cf. ibid., 35.

34   The reasons provided by Paffenroth (p. 155) are the following: on account of the lack of any mention of the destruction of Jerusalem in L, its dating has to be pushed back to before 70 CE; the next reasons suggest, however, to push its date of composition to an even earlier time: lack of Christological claims or titles for Jesus; extreme disinterest in any of the disciples, whom a much more important place is given in the other gospels; high level of residual orality; preservation of a great number of sayings and parables of Jesus, which are often deemed as proceeding from Jesus, especially because of their lack of allegorization. "L seems to lack the sort of christological, ecclesiastical, or allegorical developments that are found in later traditions [...]."

35   Cf. Klein, *Barmherzigkeit*, 135f; Paffenroth, *The Story of Jesus according to L*, 156.

what the constructs "Jewish Christians" or "Jewish Christianity" might stand for. In that respect, there seems to prevail, in current scholarship, a great deal of vagueness. Much research has been done in the last centuries on those two keywords.[36] Nonetheless, a methodological approach to that phenomenon has been shown to be highly complex, not least owing to the lack of data and the variegated nuances between different groupings[37] spread out over a vast geographic territory which would likely fall under such a label. Obviously, entering into further details in this respect would certainly go beyond the scope of this investigation.

Irrespective of those fine differing shades between different groupings, though, what can be safely assumed, according to Broadhead, who dares a definition, is the existence of "[...] persons and groups in antiquity whose historical profile suggests they both follow Jesus and maintain Jewishness and that they do so as continuation of God's covenant with Israel."[38] As many researchers of Jewish Christianity nowadays do, Broadhead acknowledges that this definition is quite a recent "label." As such, it cannot be construed as a description of

---

36 For a brief overview of the scholarly development, state of art, and main issues related to the label "Jewish Christianity," cf. Matt Jackson-McCabe, "What's in a Name? The Problem of 'Jewish Christianity,'" in *Jewish Christianity Reconsidered: Rethinking Ancients Groups and Texts*, ed. Matt Jackson-McCabe (Minneapolis: Fortress Press, 2007), 7–38; Daniélou's comprehensive study on this matter remains a classic of its kind: Jean Daniélou, *A History of Early Christian Doctrine before the Council of Nicaea*, trans. John Austin Baker, vol. 1, 3 vols. (London: Darton, Longman & Todd, 1964); see also James Carleton Paget, *Jews, Christians and Jewish Christians in Antiquity* (Tübingen: Mohr Siebeck, 2010); Edwin K. Broadhead, *Jewish Ways of Following Jesus: Redrawing the Religious Map of Antiquity* (Tübingen: Mohr Siebeck, 2010); Giorgio Jossa, *Jews or Christians? The Followers of Jesus in Search of Their Own Identity* (Tübingen: Mohr Siebeck, 2006); Petri Luomanen, *Recovering Jewish-Christian Sects and Gospels* (Leiden; Boston: Brill, 2012).

37 For Paget, this plurality has led some scholars to solve this difficulty by employing the plural "Jewish Christianities," though unsuccessfully, as he himself acknowledges (Paget, *Jews, Christians and Jewish Christians*, 317).

38 Broadhead, *Jewish Ways of Following Jesus*, 56.

reality, but rather as a "synthesizing construct of modern scholarship"[39] in order to approach this phenomenon and identify some of its main features. Yet, through this *minimal* definition, Broadhead believes to be able to overcome the historical difficulties in defining Jewishness either in terms of ethnic origin, or doctrinal beliefs, or forms of practice, or opposing orientation towards Pauline theology,[40] and to account adequately for what this phenomenon might have consisted in. If this definition is correct, it could be assumed that, in first-century Christianity, no substantial differences between Jewish Christians and other contemporary Jews could be verified, except for the fact that the former professed Jesus as the messiah of Israel.

However, apart from the question of what might have precisely constituted the identity of the so-called Jewish-Christians, what is important to observe is that in all likelihood these texts were handed down in Jewish-Christian circles and that they certainly reflected some of the main concerns of those communities.

A Possible Theology and a Few Apparent Concerns of the Texts
If what has been said above on Jewish Christianity is correct, a few similarities to Klein's theory about Lukan special material may be noted, inasmuch as he argues that those texts must have been both conserved by and addressed to a group of Jews who found in the message of Jesus a real possibility of renewal for their Jewishness and, on that account, became his followers. Following Jesus must have been understood in terms of determined practices. Moreover, what can be inferred from the texts of this source, according to Klein, is a "reticent attitude" towards the Pharisees and particularly towards the sacrifice cult in Jerusalem, including its performers (cf. Lk 10:30-37).[41] This would in fact support the conjecture that Luke might have replaced the cult criticism[42] at the end of Mark's dispute over the

---
39 Ibid., 28.
40 Ibid., 51f.
41 Klein, *Barmherzigkeit*, 134.
42 The scribe replies to Jesus in Mk 12:33: "To love him with all your heart, with all your understanding and strength, and to love your neighbour as yourself, this is

"greatest commandment" (Mk 12:28-34, par.) with the parable of the Good Samaritan (Lk 10:25-28), the message of which urges an attitude that surpasses any sacrifice. But this would in any case allow the assumption that, firstly, there was a group behind this source and, secondly, the self-understanding of this group might have been as differentiated from other Jewish groupings of that time as from the prevailing understanding of Judaism.

The second aspect considered by Klein as well as by Paffenroth in this material is a differentiated view on money and properties from Luke's own. Whereas Luke tends to have a more radical, very often even negative take on private possessions,[43] L texts seem to have a more moderate one. This observation might suggest that, other than having been wandering missionaries, such people might have had goods and properties at their disposal and were greatly encouraged to share them to meet the concrete deeds of the most needy: the poor, lepers, outcasts, widows, sinners, tax collectors, the sick, the Samaritan etc.[44] As this community might have been made up by people who were settled, instead of wandering preachers, and an apocalyptic view was not so welcome among them, renouncement of property and goods was not so strongly encouraged as sharing, giving and helping might have been. Again, there seems to be an emphasis on the right practice, be it based on Torah observance, or whatever, rather than alone on the "right belief." Klein holds that there is an awareness in this group(s) that the path to salvation is known. And the path consists in the acceptance of, the care for and the assistance to "the poor, the miserable, and the outcasts."[45]

It should be noted that, as far as this ethical approach towards the neediest is concerned, there is no inconsistency or rupture with the Jewish ethics of the Old Testament. As will be seen below,[46] by

---

far more important than any burnt offering or sacrifice."

43   In his redactional work of Markan as well as Q material, Luke urges the followers of Jesus to give up everything (πᾶς). Cf. Paffenroth, *The Story of Jesus according to L*, 122f.
44   Cf. Klein, *Barmherzigkeit*, 134.
45   Ibid., 125.
46   See below p. 153f.

grounding ethical life theologically rather than genealogically in texts such as Ex 22:20-26, the exegete Eckart Otto sees the precondition met for both rendering ethics universal and making love of neighbor (*"Nächstenliebe"*) into universal love (*"Fernstenliebe"*).[47] Just as the Lord is righteous and merciful, every Israelite is expected to fulfill the duty of being righteous and merciful himself.[48] Conversely, as long as the entire people of Israel is not merciful just as the Lord is, particularly towards the slave, the poor, the orphan, the widow etc., its salvation is in jeopardy.

The parable of Lazarus and the rich man (Lk 16:19-31), which is equally part of this special material, serves as an impressive example to illustrate the orientation of this community (these communities) as well as the consequences of a neglectful attitude toward the needy. The parable of Lazarus and the rich man refers to the next central issue of that source, which is the deliberate rejection of any sort of apocalyptic beliefs.[49] Beyond doubt, this approach differs to a great extent from that of the gospels of Matthew, Mark, in some respects from that of Luke, and all more from John's and Paul's theology. Strong as the images of this parable are, its crucial point appears to be less in the parable itself than in its appendix (Lk 16:27-31).[50] "If they will not listen either to Moses or to the prophets, they will not be convinced even if someone should rise from the dead" (v. 31b). A kind of tension can be perceived here even with regard to the belief in Jesus' resurrection. By means of this verse, any appeal to the extraordinary, to the marvelous and to the prodigious in the line of argumentation is decidedly put in question, if not refused.

---

47 Cf. Eckart Otto, *Theologische Ethik des Alten Testaments* (Stuttgart: Kohlhammer, 1994), 84f.

48 See also Dirk Ansorge, *Gerechtigkeit und Barmherzigkeit Gottes: die Dramatik von Vergebung und Versöhnung in bibeltheologischer, theologiegeschichtlicher und philosophiegeschichtlicher Perspektive* (Freiburg im Breisgau; Basel; Wien: Herder, 2009), 81.

49 For a contrary opinion, see Daniélou, *History of Early Christian Doctrine*, vol. 1, chap. 6 (Jewish Christian Apocalyptic).

50 As for the reasons for being an appendix, see Schneider, *Das Evangelium nach Lukas*, 341; Klein, *Barmherzigkeit*, 98.

Accordingly, Jesus' resurrection, might have been likewise understood in the sense of the resurrection of the upright (Lk 14:14), and not as something absolutely extraordinary and unique. This would again speak in favor of an older dating of this source. Klein does not hesitate to claim that, in the eyes of that community, Jesus actually did not bring anything completely new to them "except for a new practice and his call for repentance."[51] Instead of being the revealer, as John presents him, or the Son of God, as Mark does, Jesus is portrayed here as a true prophet of God, who calls both for repentance and for the service to the needy.[52]

This observation with regard to the absence of apocalyptic views in L may be supported by the pericopae on watchfulness (Lk 12:16b-20; 12:35-38; 13:1b-5,6b-9). What can be inferred from these four pieces is a warning "in the face of imminent judgment" and an awareness of accountability. Furthermore, there is a belief that God in fact intervenes in history and, occasionally, punishes according to people's deeds. Nevertheless, none of these texts make any explicit mention to the coming of the Kingdom or to the parousia.[53] Rather than being apocalyptic threatenings – which are usual in other warning texts – they point to the seriousness of one's life and to the responsibility for one's deeds or way of living. Klein notes in L a tendency towards making any demand to appear understandable to the followers of Jesus. "No one is asked to do what seems to her/him implausible or unjustifiable."[54]

In view of what has been said above, Klein points out, further, that the line of argument of these texts to convey their message on Jesus is neither moral, nor paraenetic, nor Christological,[55] nor missionary,

---

51 Klein, *Barmherzigkeit*, 129.
52 Cf. ibid.,130.
53 Cf. Paffenroth, *The Story of Jesus according to L*, 133.
54 As examples for this approach, Klein cites Lk 14:8-14; 16:9-12; 17:7-10 (*Barmherzigkeit*, 123).
55 Ibid., 124f.; the absence, or maybe renouncement of sovereign titles for Jesus is, for instance, one of the characteristics of this source. A different view is held by Petzke, who ascribes to L a much greater Christological character (Petzke, *Das Sondergut des Evangeliums nach Lukas*, 242f.). This, however, may be influenced by the fact that

nor apocalyptic,[56] but sapiential.[57] The sapiential character of this source becomes particularly visible in the parables that are handed down. As a matter of fact, Paffenroth observes that parables make up the most part of the corpus of this source. Out of the 26 L pericopae, 14 are parables. These are all taken from daily-life situations and sound reasonable enough to the hearers. As contrasted with the parables taken by Luke from Mark, which often draw their images and analogies from the agricultural world or inanimate objects, nearly all L parables are based on interpersonal relationships. This an important feature of theirs, particularly as it applies to Q parables as well, which would push their dating back to an earlier stage of Christian tradition. A further indicator for its oldness is the absence of allegorization, which is frequently considered by exegetes also as a criterion for their authenticity as told by Jesus.[58]

Open Questions concerning Jewish Christianity
Klein's theory about Jewish Christians could be subsumed under two basic ideas: a) the adjective "Jewish" in the construct "Jewish Christians" would stand for an emphasis on a determined practice (perhaps as a consequence of Torah observance); b) this was a closed group, differing from other "Christian forms." Although scholars such as Paget and Jackson-McCabe observe in many recent studies a trend toward defining Jewish Christianity in terms of Jewish practice, they warn about the predicaments entailed in attempts of this kind. According to them, neither should scholars yield to the temptation to conceive it in the traditional sectarian sense of the term, nor can they be as sure about the borderline between Christianity and Judaism in "early Christianity" as they would wish.[59]

---

he considers the infancy narratives and the Passion stories as belonging to L as well.
56 Cf. Klein, *Barmherzigkeit*, 122–24.
57 Paffenroth disagrees with Klein on this point. In his opinion, L community does not seem to value sapiential traditions, just as Luke himself does not (see Lk 12:19; 13:1b-5,6b-9). Cf. Paffenroth, *The Story of Jesus according to L*, 156.
58 Cf. ibid., 97.
59 Cf. Paget, *Jews, Christians and Jewish Christians*, 317f.; Jackson-McCabe, "What's in a Name?," 36.

Both authors consider Daniélou's work a significant contribution to the discussion towards overcoming such a sectarian view prevailing in his days, which for certain broadened the horizon of traditional research. Daniélou's major achievement, one might say, was the fundamental shift from thinking of Jewish Christianity as a group to approaching it in discursive terms, i.e. as "[...] *the expression of Christianity in the thought-forms of Later Judaism.*"[60] Though acknowledging the great influence of Daniélou's thought in contemporary research, Paget holds his view responsible for the vagueness that prevailed after him in the discourse on Jewish Christianity, insofar as any text could fall under the category "Jewish Christian" since then.[61]

Due to such elasticity of the term, which, in the end, renders it of no help to scholars, Jackson-McCabe regards the above-mentioned practice-based trend on the part of many scholars in recent times as "understandable," insomuch as it is a reaction to the vagueness prevailing in the current discourse, yet misleading. His criticism of approaches like Daniélou's is, rather, to which extent one can apply the category "Christianity" to a movement within Judaism that was not the only one of its kind. This has actually been the critique of post-Holocaust scholarship of the theories of early Christianity, and ought to be given much more awareness. Thus, defining Christianity merely as belief in Christ appears to be as problematic as a definition of Jewishness just as Torah observance. To be more precise, is belief in Christ a sufficient "rationale for including any given ancient group or text within the class 'Christianity' rather than 'Judaism'"?[62] After all, there were, in ancient Judaism, innumerable movement leaders who were held by their followers to be the messiah, and they are nevertheless regarded as Jewish. Can one at all speak of the *essence* of a movement, or religion? Can one pick an "essential trait" and turn it into a criterion to approach phenomena without coming into methodological shortcomings? These are the questions that remain open, and yet provide scholars with a new awareness.

---

60   Daniélou, *History of Early Christian Doctrine*, 1:10, italics in original.
61   Cf. Paget, *Jews, Christians and Jewish Christians*, 318.
62   Jackson-McCabe, "What's in a Name?," 35.

Consequences of the Study on Lukan Special Material
Now, bearing in mind the recent critique of Jewish Christianity theories, Paffenroth's as well as Klein's claims that L must have been both conserved and practiced in the context of one community – or more than one – must remain open, owing to the methodological questions mentioned above. On the other hand, turning back to the question of origin and transmission of the parable of the Good Samaritan, which actually was the prime purpose of this section on L, there are a few questions that, on account of their relevance to the topic being treated, are to be given particular attention, regardless of whether L was handed down within a community or not. Answers need to be ventured despite all the intricacies involved in it.

Accordingly, there appear to be three questions of particular interest for the purposes of this investigation. The first one concerns the "interreligious" problematic and the conflicts related to religious affiliation at that time; to be more precise, whether the Samaritan played any special role for that context (or for that assumed community); secondly, whether the point of this parable is indeed the commandment of love; finally, what understanding of salvation could be implied in the texts of this source, or, following Klein, what view of salvation that community could have possibly tried to convey through that parable.

Conflicts between Jews and Samaritans. As far as the first question is concerned, the conflict between Samaritans and Jews, particularly at the time of Jesus, is well known and an extensive description of its causes as well as development and escalation would lie beyond the scope of this research.[63] What can be assumed for certain is that the

---

63 Suffice it to mention three of the main differences and points of conflicts between the Samaritan and Jews: firstly, Samaritans recognize down to the present day alone the Pentateuch as holy Scripture (actually an ancient version which differs to a great extent from that of the Masoretic text), thereby not recognizing the prophets and other texts; secondly, for them, the chosen place in which "our fathers adored God" (cf. Jn 4:20) remains to the present day Mount Garazin instead of Mount Sion; thirdly, since they recognize only the Pentateuch, their Messiah has no relation whatsoever with the House of David, and their belief in this regard corresponds to

hatred between Jews and Samaritans can be clearly sensed between the lines of the gospels and that the word Samaritan was used as a "sharp curse word."[64] Accordingly, the lawyer, in the parable of the Good Samaritan, when asked who of the three was a neighbor to the half dead man, does not have the courage to even utter this word. He simply answers: "the one who showed pity towards him" (Lk 10:37).

"While Mark never mentions the Samaritan, and Matthew just once, though in a negative sense (Mt 10:5), the Lukan double work and the gospel of John devote them special attention."[65] In the case of Luke, all three texts related to the Samaritan belong to the Lukan special material.[66] On account of that, it is plausible to assume that Luke and the community who conserved those texts had an important common concern: a special care for the despised and outcasts.[67] In the places where this community was living – in Jerusalem or somewhere else in Judea – there certainly were Samaritans who experienced humiliation, exclusion and all sorts of hostility on the part of Jews. To be sure, the Samaritan behaved in the same way towards Jews. According to Luke, Jesus was treated with hostility by the Samaritan because he was on his way to the Temple in Jerusalem (Lk 9:51-56). Nevertheless, the sufferings that many Samaritans had to go through while living among Jews were real needs in the eyes of those communities, which demanded from them concrete answers. As a result, it is possible to assume that the very fact that these texts were conserved by this group of people and later on incorporated by Luke into his gospel is by no means accidental. Neither is it by chance

---

the description of Dt 18:15-19. Cf. Joachim Jeremias, "Σαμάρεια," *Theologisches Wörterbuch zum Neuen Testament* (Stuttgart: Kohlhammer, 1964), 89–90.

64 Ibid., 91.

65 Ibid.; Gijs Bouwman, "Σαμάρεια," *Exegetisches Wörterbuch zum Neuen Testament* (Stuttgart; Berlin; Köln: Kohlhammer, 1992), 540. Cf. Lk 9:51-56; 10:30-37; 17:11-19; Acts 1:8; 8:1-25; 9:31; 15:3 and Jn 4:4-42.

66 In the case of the Gospel of John, the account of Jesus' encounter with the Samaritan woman ought to be understood as an authoritative text, in order to trace back the mission among the Samaritan to Jesus himself (cf. Bouwman, "Σαμάρεια," 541).

67 Ibid.

that two Samaritans[68] are portrayed as good examples in their deeds, whereas the Jewish chosen people are presented, more often than not, as unfaithful, stubborn and lost.

The most difficult question is, of course, which approach Jesus might have possibly had towards the Samaritan. Jeremias maintains that, even for Jesus, the Samaritans were a "mingled people," which, for that reason, does not count as part of the people of Israel.[69] The clear instructions given in Mt 10:5f. attest to that assumption. That stresses the conviction that Jesus might have understood his own personal mission as being, primarily, the gathering of the lost sheep of Israel.[70] In the view of Jeremias, it is quite complicated to understand Mt 10:5f., if one claims that Jesus was much ahead of his time and did not share any of the views of his contemporaries. Therefore, he considers such a claim as problematic. Jesus might indeed have thought that, according to the promises of the fathers, the gathering of Israel was to take place before the other peoples were incorporated.[71] However, Jesus must have been aware that through his activity and the mission of the apostles, the Kingdom of God and the time of salvation had already begun and no one could be excluded from it. Furthermore, Jesus' conduct towards these people might have had a strong impact on the disciples as well as on various people who met him, which might have been seen as a visible manifestation of the fulfillment of the prophecies.[72]

The Point of the Parable of the Good Samaritan. In the light of this special source, one could further ask whether the point of this

---

68 The one is the Good Samaritan (Lk 10:30-37) and the other is one of the ten lepers who were cured by Jesus who came back alone to give thanks for his cure (Lk 17:11-18). As to the origin of these two parables, Klein regards the first one as having its origin in the mouth of Jesus, while the latter not (Klein, *Barmherzigkeit*, 78–79).

69 Jeremias, "Σαμάρεια," 92.

70 Cf. Raymund Schwager, *Jesus im Heilsdrama: Entwurf einer biblischen Erlösungslehre*, Innsbrucker theologische Studien 29 (Innsbruck; Wien: Tyrolia, 1990), 59–61. For that matter, see Mt 9:36; 11:28; 12:30; 23:37 par; Mk 6:34.

71 Jeremias, "Σαμάρεια," 93.

72 Ibid.

parable is indeed the commandment of love. The context in which the parable of the Good Samaritan was embedded is most likely a result of Luke's redactional work.[73] According to Klein, it is unlikely that the community that conserved this parable might have told it in association with the commandment of love. He goes on to say that what this community most cherished was neither faith contents, nor the reformulation of commandments, nor even a special appeal in the form of the commandment of love.[74] This community "lives with the certainty of its chosenness (Lk 18:7) and is convinced that it knows what the right deed is."[75] That being so, the question that follows is why Luke inserts it in the context of the commandment of love.

First of all, it is important to emphasize that Luke embedded it deliberately within the context of the commandment of love and that the whole environment might have been created by Luke to accommodate it better.[76] Even though the original wording was modified, he made an effort to preserve its meaning. Two main evidences can support it. First the expression "Kingdom of God" does not occur in the Lukan special material.[77] Formulations such as resurrection of the upright (Lk 14:14), eternal dwellings (16:9) and Abraham's embrace (16:22) are used instead. That is a plausible reason why Luke opens this pericope with a question about the right deed in order to "inherit eternal life." The second evidence is that an orthopraxis (right conduct, right deeds) would be in perfect accordance with the orientation of the Lukan special material whose fundamental conviction was that "something must be *done*" in order to enter the eternal dwellings.[78] These two ideas are taken up again by Luke at the conclusion of the parable in verses 28 and 37.

Bovon highlights that the Samaritan acts out of profound

---

73 Cf. Klein, *Barmherzigkeit*, 74. Already A. Jülicher had noticed it (*Die Gleichnisreden Jesu*, vol. 2, Tübingen: 1899, pp. 595–597). See also Hermann Binder, "Das Gleichnis vom Barmherzigen Samariter," *Theologische Zeitschrift* 15 (1959): 178.

74 Cf. Klein, *Barmherzigkeit*, 128.

75 Ibid.

76 Ibid., 74.

77 Ibid., 76.

78 Ibid., 77. Other texts which confirm it are Lk 16:9 and 14:12-14.

compassion. The motive to act with compassion towards one's neighbor, as handed down in L, is not Christological, as in Mt 25:31-46, but plainly anthropological, human. This can be assumed based on the use of the verb σπλαγχνίζομαι[79] in Lk 10:33. The verb σπλαγχνίζομαι means "to be moved in one's innermost" and is used by Luke elsewhere also to describe Jesus' and God' love.[80] There is a very clear connection between inner life and deed. What is more, it is by "doing something" in tune with his innermost compassion to solve a concrete problem demanded from him by reality that he inherits eternal life. No one of the hearers would expect that deed from the Samaritan; nevertheless this consonance between concrete situations, deeds, and one's conscience can help one overcome all possible barriers between human beings (cultural, racial, ethnic, religious etc.). Bovon remarks, though, that compassion, as emphatically described here, is not just a "feeling," but is associated with the inwardness demanded by the first commandment (cf. v. 27). For sure, this is a very important evangelical attitude and is intended by Luke to be followed by the disciples of Jesus as well.[81]

If that is so, the assumption that Luke regarded this parable as the best possible illustration of the commandment of love may be correct, too. Luke might have also been aware of the strong message of this parable, especially as regards the figure of the Samaritan. To be sure, the very fact that a Samaritan was proposed as an example of deeds and behavior was, to the ears of Jew-Christians, something very difficult to be faced with. And all the more scandalous was the

---

79 The verb σπλαγχνίζομαι occurs three times in L (Lk 7:13; 10:33; 15:20). Considering the fact that Luke omits this verb three times while editing the texts of Mark (Mk 1:41 par. Lk 5:13; Mk 6:34 par. Lk 9:11; Mk 9:22 par. Lk 9:42; plus the absence of any parallel for Mk 8:2) and that Luke appears to have a sort of "aversion to depicting Jesus' emotions" it is very unlikely that this word was added by Luke, which, in turn, would attest to its authenticity. Since love (ἀγαπάω, in Lk 7:36-47) and compassion are the issue of four of the fourteen parables of L, Paffenroth regards them as one of its major concerns. Cf. Paffenroth, *The Story of Jesus according to L*, 77f.; Klein, *Barmherzigkeit*, 127.
80 Cf. Bovon, *Das Evangelium nach Lukas*, 1996, III/2:90.
81 Cf. ibid.

statement that a Samaritan could have precedence over a priest or a Levite in the Kingdom of God.[82]

A Different Understanding of Salvation? As far as a concept of salvation is concerned, that community could have possibly tried to convey, particularly through the underlying message of this parable, one of their deepest convictions, which could be summed up as follows: in order to be received in the "eternal tents," or to take part in the resurrection of the upright, one has to have *done* something.[83] As has been seen above, this community was very much touched by the message of Jesus and tried to live it out in daily life. Its critique of cult and apocalyptic faith might have been strong, but they never engaged in missionary activities nor in faith formulations. For them, Jesus' message and praxis had touched a central point of Israel's faith, which had been increasingly neglected over the centuries, that is, a special love, care and assistance towards the foreigner, the orphan, the widow, the most needy. According to their conviction, that kind of practice probably was the only thing that could justify their existences before God and give hope to the people of Israel, God's chosen people, particularly in the face of its unfaithfulness. As opposed to John the Baptist's theology,[84] this community might have held firmly on to the belief of the sonship of Abraham as well as God's election. Accordingly, their assistance towards the needy should be understood in consequence of God's covenant with them, rather than as a merit to attain salvation.

Furthermore, as opposed to Paul's idea of the "time of salvation" (2Cor 6:2), this community might have understood itself "in

---

82 See also Mt 21:31 to understand this inference. Whereas Jülicher (*Die Gleichnisreden Jesu*, pp. 595–597) claims that this conclusion can be drawn from the parable, Klein doubts it, since, for him, there are no hints whatsoever of the Kingdom of God in this source (Klein, *Barmherzigkeit*, p. 76).

83 Klein, *Barmherzigkeit*, 77, italics in original. "Eternal tents" (αἰωνίους σκηνάς, cf. Lk 16:9) and "the resurrection of the upright" (ἐν τῇ ἀναστάσει τῶν δικαίων, cf. Lk 14:14) might have been the designations of L for other equivalents such as "Kingdom of God" (synoptics), "eternal life" (esp. Johannine literature) and salvation.

84 Cf. above, pp. 44–45.

continuity with the Old Testament piety"[85] and, in a way, much more committed to a daily "orthopraxis." No wonder that this community preferred to live out and radicalize its commitment with the "God of Israel" and did not engage as much in missionary activities among pagans as Hellenistic Christians did.

Luke's Primary Concerns in His Twofold Work

The very fact that Luke incorporates a great number of passages from L in his gospel does not mean that he shares the same interests and views of that source. Nevertheless, there is a great deal of agreement between them. Therefore, to gain a comprehensive picture of the parable in question, I find it important to devote the present section to Luke's main concerns and theology.

The Poor and the Rich

Neumann maintains, in his recent study, that Luke might have had in mind people who either possessed Hellenistic education or were at least acquainted with Hellenistic thought and, just as he, were concerned in a very particular way with the problem of poverty and richness in their societies.[86] The frequency of the word groups[87] "poor" (πτωχός) and "rich" (πλούσιος) furnish a picture of the relevance of this issue to the evangelist. The word group "poor" represents 0.5% and the word group "rich" 0.7% of the whole corpus of Luke's gospel, whereas it makes up an average of approximately 0.3% in the

---

85   Klein, *Barmherzigkeit*, 130.
86   Cf. Nils Neumann, *Armut und Reichtum im Lukasevangelium und in der kynischen Philosophie*, Stuttgarter Bibelstudien 220 (Stuttgart: Katholisches Bibelwerk, 2010), 19–20; for that issue, see also the detailed study by Hans-Georg Gradl, *Zwischen Arm und Reich: das lukanische Doppelwerk in leserorientierter und textpragmatischer Perspektive* (Würzburg: Echter, 2005).
87   To the word group poor (πτωχός) belong also the words πτωχεία, πτωχεύω and πτωχίζω and to the word group rich (πλούσιος), also πλοῦτος and πλουτέω (Neumann, *Armut und Reichtum im Lukasevangelium und in der kynischen Philosophie*, 18–19).

other two synoptics. The word "rich" does not even appear in the Gospel of John, for instance.

Gradl entitles his dissertation "between the poor and rich" because, for him, the place between those two opposite poles is where unity is to be sought and the Kingdom of God becomes visible.[88] It is not about an artificial unity in which problems are just ignored, but a committed attitude on the part of both the rich, who are ready to give and help generously, and the poor, who experience the love of God towards them in the form of this new community. It is the beginning of a new world, the Kingdom of God.

For Grilli, to emphasize that God carries on his work of salvation in favor of the poor through the person of Jesus is a core affirmation in the Gospel of Luke. And this is, in turn, one of the central statements of Jesus' message. The first two chapters of the gospel attest to it and make it very clear. The motif of the עֲנָוִים (*'anawīm*: the poor) is taken up by Luke and is present in different persons (Zacharias, Elisabeth, the shepherds, Simeon, Hanna, Mary and so on).[89]

However, for Luke, richness is neither an evil in itself, nor is it merely an ethical question. Rather, it ought to be understood in the light of both faith and the Kingdom of God. Indeed, Christian faith is radically challenged by the richness-poverty predicament. If Christians profess their faith in God, the father of all, and in a universal brotherhood in Christ, a "communion of goods" would be the most visible and convincing sign of faith in any society (cf. Acts 2:43-47). Such visibility in the form of communion was highly valued in the Old Testament, too, and acquires, for Luke, enormous significance.[90] Now, it is important to notice, that Luke provides neither a kind of "social program" for the civil society, nor a law system for the early church. On the other hand, he does offer concrete criteria for the way to handle money, property and richness. In the view of Grilli, "[t]he hermeneutic criterion for the

---

88 Gradl, *Zwischen Arm und Reich*, 440.
89 Massimo Grilli, "Schlussbeobachtungen," in *Handle danach und du wirst leben: Reichtum und Solidarität im Werk des Lukas*, ed. Cordula Langner (Stuttgart: Katholisches Bibelwerk, 2010), 253.
90 Ibid., 256.

discussion on richness is the primacy of the Kingdom of God."⁹¹ This is summed up well in Lk 12:31: "No; set your hearts on his kingdom, and these other things will be given you as well."

The close relation between Luke's theology and Cynic philosophy was briefly pointed out above and does not need to be developed further.⁹² What appears to be important to keep in mind at the end of this section is the inextricable connection between the awareness of social issues such as poverty and exclusion, the insistence on repentance (μετάνοια), the description of the Kingdom of God as the highest ideal to be pursued, and the suggestion of the model of solidarity as a privileged way of following Jesus and promoting his cause. Luke's concern with the poor is of great relevance for the present investigation on the parable of the Good Samaritan, insofar as it overlaps with the concerns of Luke's special material and furnishes a valuable clue as to the subject of salvation and the essential mission of the disciples of Christ.

Particular Concern with the Question of Salvation
A second concern could be summarized under the heading "salvation." In his review of the most important exegetical contributions on the Gospel of Luke, Bovon cites J. Gewiess' work "*Die urapostolische Heilsverkündigung nach der Apostelgeschichte*" (1939), which indeed places the notion of salvation in the center of Luke's theology and all other "theological *loci*" around it. In the same way, Marshall's study (1970)⁹³ equally "chooses salvation as the core of Lukan thought."⁹⁴ Although Luke's emphasis on the concept of salvation has been worked out in other sections, above and below, I will focus here on two specific aspects.

The first one is the presentation of the irreplaceable role of Jesus

---

91   Ibid., 255.
92   See Cf. p. 58f. For a detailed study on that, see Neumann, *Armut und Reichtum im Lukasevangelium und in der kynischen Philosophie*.
93   I. Howard Marshall, *Luke: Historian and Theologian* (Grand Rapids: Zondervan, 1970).
94   François Bovon, *Luke the Theologian*, 2nd ed. (Waco: Baylor University Press, 2006), 280.

for the visibility of God's salvation. The great good news of salvation proclaimed in Lk 4:16-20 is taken up again in Lk 7:18-23 and attested to. When asked by the disciples of John whether Jesus is "the messiah" or not, he does not give any direct answer, but just says: "Go back and tell John what you have seen and heard: the blind see again, the lame walk, those suffering from virulent skin-diseases are cleansed, and the deaf hear, the dead are raised to life, the good news is proclaimed to the poor; and blessed is anyone who does not find me a cause of falling" (Lk 7:22-23). According to Jeremias, this ought in no way to be understood as an enumeration of miracles, but as a reference to ancient images of the awaited "time of redemption." Jesus' words may be taken without major problems as a free quotation of Isa 35:5f.: "Then the eyes of the blind will be opened, and the ears of the deaf unstopped, then the lame will leap as a deer, and the tongue of the dumb sing for joy; for waters will gush in the desert, and streams in the wastelands." Furthermore, this answer of Jesus can be read as a sort of report attesting that this proclaimed "time of salvation" has indeed come and is there.[95] "God's gifts of salvation are signs of the presence of the Redeemer."[96] It is also in this context that the overcoming of the power of Satan, as described in Lk 10:18 when the 72 disciples return from their first mission, ought to be understood.[97] All these are signs which confirm that Jesus is indeed "the middle of time," a mark between the past history of Israel and the new time begun by the church.[98]

The second aspect, closely connected to the first one, is the stress on Jesus' search for the lost. Jesus is portrayed as a shepherd who was sent to the lost sheep of the house of Israel, to look for the lost sheep and bring them home (Lk 19:10), to gather the small flock

---

95 Jeremias, *Die Gleichnisse Jesu*, 116. Besides Isa 35:5-6, see also Isa 26:19; 29:18-19; 35:5-6; 42:18; Isa 61 (a good news to the poor). Those promises are construed as fulfilled through the coming of Jesus.
96 Ibid., 122.
97 "The seventy-two came back rejoicing. 'Lord,' they said, 'even the devils submit to us when we use your name.' He said to them, 'I watched Satan fall like lightning from heaven'" (Lk 10:17f).
98 See especially Conzelmann, *Die Mitte der Zeit*.

(Lk 12:32) etc. The three parables gathered by Luke in chapter 15 convey a very precise idea about what it means. Luke's soteriological model constitutes an interesting inversion. Even if the human being fails to find God or goes astray along the way, God is going to do everything to find him/her. It goes without saying that this soteriological inversion has also implications for the disciples of Jesus. For, just as he came to seek the poor, the sinners, the tax collectors, the outcasts, the lost ones, every follower of him is invited to look after those people as well.

The Model of Solidarity
The model of solidarity is, in reality, a consequence of the previous two sections. The explanations about the parable of the Good Samaritan should have made it clear what significance is attached to the virtue of solidarity both in the Gospel of Luke and in Lukan special material. Yet the ideal of solidarity intended by Luke is not only limited to material needs. Jesus' search for the lost is, in a sense, a form of solidarity, too. Not by chance was the Good Samaritan of Lk 10:30-37 for a long time in the early church and subsequently allegorically construed as the Christ himself. Bovon provides various examples from the allegories of Irenaeus, Origen, Clement of Alexandria etc. in which this parable is interpreted christologically.[99] All the actions of the Samaritan are accurately described and applied to Christ in a metaphorical sense. Some of these Church Fathers draw also ethical consequences from this example set by Christ.

Through the theological strategy of the *imitatio christi*, Christians were encouraged to follow Christ's example and do the same towards their fellow brothers and sisters whom they constantly find lying on the roadside. The model of solidarity allows Christians to reconceive traditional soteriological models in which salvation was understood in too passive a fashion and to make room for active and cooperative ones.

---

99 Cf. Bovon, *Das Evangelium nach Lukas*, 1996, III/2:93–95.

Other Similar Approaches in the Synoptic Tradition

What has been said so far about the parable of the Good Samaritan and the Gospel of Luke could convey the impression that this way of considering issues such as salvation and religious difference ought to be regarded as a particular interpretation of Luke and cannot apply to Jesus' "original" message. Lest such an impression be created, it appears to be meaningful to analyze other pieces of writing contained in the other two synoptics in order to verify whether this parable alongside its context is an isolated case or even an "erratic block" within the Gospel of Luke or not. To this end, two texts shall be considered in the following: Mt 25:31-46 and Mk 7:24-30.

Mt 25:31-46: The Unity between Love of God
and Love of Neighbor Made Concrete
In some parts of the elucidation of the parable of the Good Samaritan and its background, some readers might have surely been reminded of certain similarities to Matthew's text about the Final Judgment (Mt 25:31-46).[100] Both texts possess eschatological value as they address the issue of afterlife; both of them appear to be concerned with the right deed, the right conduct or, in a word, with the lifestyle that may justify one's existence before God at the end of one's days. Moreover, both texts contain universal claims and appear to have been thought of from a universal perspective, rather than ecclesial. Furthermore, both of them emphasize the right attitude towards people who are in extreme need. For those reasons, it appears to be adequate to have a closer glance at this text, too, so as to explore new possibilities for this investigation.

Eschatological Genre. As far as the context of this text is concerned, it is embedded in the last two chapters of Matthew's gospel, immediately before the account of Jesus' passion. This is the last set of discourses before Jesus' death, and they are all related to the last

---

100 The close relation between Lk 10:25-37 and Mt 25:31-46 has been noticed and highlighted by many theologians. A reference to J. Jeremias should suffice (*Die Gleichnisse Jesu*, 206).

days, to the *eschaton*. Considering the nature of the text in question, it is crucial to understand what the concept of eschatology means. According to Schürmann, for instance, one of the essential elements of Jesus' eschatology is that it can in no way be defined and qualified through the category of time (imminent eschatological expectation). Although this category may be an important element of apocalyptic thinking, he argues for an eschatology for the present time (*Gegenwartseschatologie*).[101]

Despite some similarities between this and other texts of the Jewish apocalyptic, Jesus' message introduces something different. Whereas in the Jewish understanding, the present and the future aeon seem to be in "antithetic" opposition to each other, considering that the present age can never be even compared to God's justice, Jesus proclaims, through his words and deeds, that God's justice has already begun in the present aeon and is on its way toward consummation through "the practice and works of love."[102] Thus, the texts of the gospels bear witness to both the experience and the conviction of the dawning of the new era. The eschatological time has already begun and there is no reason to wait further. The present time is no longer just a time of promises, but a time of fulfillment as well (cf. Mk 1:15; Mt 11:12f.; Lk 7:18-23; 10:23f.; 11:20; 17:20f.).[103]

Consequently, the eschatological message of Jesus is by no means detached from the world, but, conversely, very much related and committed to it. If the dawning of the Kingdom of God was already "heard, seen and touched" by human beings, one has no longer to wait for its coming. One can, instead, engage in God's plan of salvation for the world through the practice of the love of God and the love of neighbor.[104] As the eschatological message of Jesus is not

---

101 Cf. Heinz Schürmann, "Eschatologie und Liebesdienst in der Verkündigung Jesu," in *Kaufet die Zeit aus: Beiträge zu einer christlichen Eschatologie*, ed. Hermann Kirchhoff (Paderborn: Schöningh, 1959), 58.

102 Johannes Friedrich, *Gott im Bruder? Eine methodenkritische Untersuchung von Redaktion, Überlieferung und Traditionen in Mt 25,31-46* (Stuttgart: Calwer, 1977), 302.

103 Schürmann, "Eschatologie und Liebesdienst in der Verkündigung Jesu," 55.

104 Ibid., 70.

about future expectations, but primarily proclaims the beginning of a time of salvation, the disciples of Jesus ought to bear great responsibility for the world and for history.[105]

The Unity of Love. For the exegete Johannes Friedrich this text contains the strongest image of the unity between the love of God and the love of neighbor in the New Testament. This unity is such that both become just one, even if that may not be so explicit at first glance.[106] It is true that such an interplay between both commandments can be abundantly found in the first letter of John as well. However, in the case of John, love is limited to the community members or, in a best-case scenario, to Christian brothers.[107] Paul, on the other hand, emphasizes at times the love of God (Rom 8:28; 1Cor 8:3; Eph 6:24) and at times the love of neighbor (Rom 13:8; see also 1Pet 1:22; 2:17), but never both together such as here. In this parable of Jesus, by contrast, anyone can be one's neighbor and, therefore, subject/object of love and compassion.

Obviously, this inextricable unity between both commandments has serious implications for the life of Christians. "To love Jesus means to love one's neighbors who are in need. 'Worship to God' occurs through one's love towards other fellow human beings."[108] The possibility of such an inference from the text is based on the belief that Jesus regarded himself as somebody "who has an extremely close relationship to God" (cf. v. 34: God is his Father) and "the most authoritative interpreter of the true will of God." In addition to that, Jesus is presented in the Gospel of Matthew not only as the interpreter of God's will but also as the doer of his will and, therefore, as the revealer of it. To the community of Christians, which listens to this parable, there is no contradiction, because they can

---

105   Ibid., 71.
106   Friedrich, *Gott im Bruder?*, 231f.; see also Paul Christian, *Jesus und seine geringsten Brüder: Mt 25,31-46 redaktionsgeschichtlich untersucht* (Leipzig: St. Benno, 1975), 59. According to Christian, the "synthesis between love of neighbor and love of Christ" determines, in this text, the relation between ethics and Christology.
107   Cf. Friedrich, *Gott im Bruder?*, 231f. See esp. 1Jn 2:9f.; 3:10,14ff.; 4:20f.
108   Ibid., 286.

recognize that the criteria for the final judgment are, in truth, nothing beyond that which Jesus revealed through his life, his approach to other human beings and his message, which was then confirmed by God himself through the resurrection of Jesus.[109]

The demands implied in the double commandment of love can be verified in various ways in Jesus' deeds as well. Firstly, he seeks the encounter with the outcasts, the hungry, the sick, the crippled, the sinner, the tax collectors and so on. Besides this, Jesus himself holds table fellowship with those people, which has enormous significance and implications. What is more, Jesus himself feeds the hungry (Mk 6:30-44; 8:1-10 par), he heals the sick (Mt 8-9 par), he cares for the foreigners (Jn 4; Mk 7:24-30). None of these deeds or attitudes can in any way be doubted about the person of Jesus. Thus, the text of the final judgment should be understood as a set of instructions for a life in discipleship.[110]

Also Schnackenburg is of the opinion that it is possible to affirm, exegetically, that the efforts of people who do not know God, or belong to other religious traditions, or are atheists to promote and love other human beings are going to be recognized by God in his judgment, in spite of their not belonging to the Church.[111] For the Kingdom of God does not know any boundaries. According to Luke's narrative, "[...] people from east and west, from north and south, will come and sit down at the feast in the kingdom of God" (Lk 13:29). The strict condition to enter it is the commandment of love. The commandment of love is, in turn, to be understood on the basis of a double background: the proclamation of the Kingdom of God (i.e., that God is the Lord of history) and the revelation of God (i.e., that God is our father, that God is good, benevolent and merciful).[112] Indeed, Jeremias goes so far as to consider love to be "the law of life" in the Kingdom of God, insofar as the example for

---

109   Ibid., 286.
110   Ibid., 300.
111   Cf. Rudolf Schnackenburg, "Die Forderung der Liebe in der Verkündigung und im Verhalten Jesu," in *Prinzip Liebe: Perspektiven der Theologie*, ed. Eugen Biser (Freiburg im Breisgau; Basel; Wien: Herder, 1975), 101.
112   Schürmann, "Eschatologie und Liebesdienst in der Verkündigung Jesu," 67f.

love is set by God himself and applies to every human being: γίνεσθε οἰκτίρμονες καθὼς καὶ ὁ πατὴρ ὑμῶν οἰκτίρμων ἐστίν (Be compassionate just as your Father is compassionate, Lk 6:36).[113]

Mk 7:24-30: Jesus Learns from a Pagan Woman
The parable of the Good Samaritan is neither an isolated case to approach the issue of interreligious and/or intercultural encounters nor is the victim therein coincidentally a Samaritan. The New Testament attests to several other texts which deal with this issue in different ways. An appropriate attitude towards the Gentiles, the Hellenist, the Samaritan, the Jews etc. was a common concern for Paul, John and the other synoptic evangelists, too. It constituted a real challenge for early Christians and early communities. As is the case with the other gospels, Mark reports as well a couple of encounters and interactions of Jesus with people belonging to different religious and cultural milieus. However, considering the question of interreligious dialogue while keeping an eye especially on the question of access of non-believers to salvation, one of Mark's accounts deserves careful attention: the encounter between Jesus and the Syrophoenician woman.

The account of Mk 7:24-30 tells of an encounter of Jesus with a Hellenist woman in the territory of Tyre. The first order of concern which the story addresses is the multitude of real conflicts that existed in border regions between Tyre and Galilee as well as usual relations between Jews and Gentiles in such a place. Moreover, Jesus' Jewish "theology" and world view are confronted with a real need expressed by the woman.[114] Secondly, the text astonishingly implies an inner transformation and a clear change of mind on the part of Jesus in the face of this encounter, which has, of course, consequences for the Markan Christology. Thirdly, in the opinion of scholars like Alonso, this text is probably not used to justify Christian mission among Pagans by presenting Jesus as the first who did it. The mission among Pagans was already widespread when the gospel was written.

---

113 Cf. Jeremias, *Neutestamentliche Theologie*, 1:204–6.
114 Pablo Alonso, *The Woman Who Changed Jesus: Crossing Boundaries in Mk 7:24-30* (Leuven; Paris; Walpole: Peeters, 2011), 339f.

Through this account Mark might have rather intended to approach the issue of inclusion in his community and to depict Jesus as an example for coping with such conflicts.¹¹⁵ Of equal importance is how access to salvation and endowment with God's favor is here theologically understood and defined.

Nonetheless, for Alonso, "[...] the key element for the interpretation of the passage is the woman's word, her λόγος [...]. The importance of this word is emphasized by the absence of any other word casting out the demon."¹¹⁶ In contrast to other miracles in the Gospel of Mark, no mention is made here of faith. Her desperate need seems to suffice.¹¹⁷ Or perhaps her great love for her daughter that empowers her to overcome all those barriers, approach Jesus with her concern, and even argue with him in her favor, in spite of Jesus' authority – which becomes manifest through her address to Jesus as Lord, κύριος. Alonso observes that, even though "faith and miracles" are usually linked in the Second Gospel, the very fact that Mark avoids it explicitly offers clear evidence for respecting it, rather than doing violence to the text and regarding the woman as a "new believer." Furthermore, the absence of any reference to faith is a feature of other healings and exorcisms, too.¹¹⁸

Renate Fink points to another unusual aspect. Jesus, as a Jew, is

---

115 Ibid., 341.

116 Ibid., 341f.

117 Although in the parallel version of Matthew, Jesus praises the woman with the words "Woman, your faith is great" (ὦ γύναι, μεγάλη σου ἡ πίστις), that alteration is certainly due to the differing theological understanding of Matthew regarding the existence of faith among pagans as well as his conviction that salvation is granted exclusively through faith. Accordingly, this redactional edition of Matthew "[...] is probably inspired by the praise given to the centurion in Q (cf. Mt 8,10 par. Lk 7,9). Both are Gentiles" (ibid., 274f.).

118 Cf. Mk 1:21-28; 1:29-31; 1:32-34; 1:40-45; 3:1-6; 5:1-20; 7:31-37; 8:22-26. As against this opinion, Gnilka maintains that her faith is implicit in her words. As evidence, he points out that she is the only person in the Gospel of Mark who addresses Jesus with the title Lord (κύριε), despite being Gentile (Joachim Gnilka, *Das Evangelium nach Markus*, vol. II/2, Evangelisch-Katholischer Kommentar zum Neuen Testament [Zürich; Einsiedeln; Köln: Benziger, 1979], 293).

in an unclean territory. All of a sudden, he finds himself involved in an unwilled (vv. 24b and 25a) conversation with an unclean woman. She was reckoned both as impure, on account of her provenience (Gentile), and as untouchable, on account of the unclean Spirit that her daughter was possessed by. From the perspective of a Jew, that woman along with her daughter were stigmatized for three reasons: "they were foreigners, women, and possessed."[119] Yet, Jesus appears to keep his (Jewish) views aside and engages in a conversation with the woman, at the end of which her wish is granted. Therefore, for Alonso, Jesus' attitude of openness, especially in the face of people who are in need, is a key feature of Mark's Christology that cannot be lost sight of. Equally important is the awareness that Mark recognizes and respects the action of God everywhere and in everyone, no matter whether explicit faith in Christ is present or absent.[120]

A further study of this pericope would unavoidably lead us to knotty theological issues such as the consciousness of Jesus and his understanding of his mission, issues which, of course, lie beyond the scope and purpose of our study. Yet, this text reveals a very peculiar side of Jesus, not least because of his harsh reply to the woman. In effect, many Christians struggle with Bible passages like this, as it may shake their image of Jesus. For one can affirm, without doing violence to the text, that this encounter certainly does something with Jesus. He may not learn *something* new from or about the woman, but the text allows to infer that he does learn something new about himself or his mission. He gives up the control of the situation and allows to be "changed" by those particular circumstances, as Alonso put it. This is precisely what encounters can effect. Rather than new contents, the real learning process they trigger is the confrontation with one's self-understanding, world view, beliefs etc. Christians are invited to follow Jesus' example.

---

119 Renate Fink, *Die Botschaft des heilenden Handelns Jesu: Untersuchung der dreizehn exemplarischen Berichte von Jesu heilendem Handeln im Markusevangelium* (Innsbruck; Wien: Tyrolia, 2000), 148.
120 Alonso, *The Woman Who Changed Jesus*, 342.

Outcome

The parable of the Good Samaritan makes it clear that more important than the question "Who is my neighbor?" is the one, "How can I *become* a neighbor?" The parable addresses very delicate issues such as religious minorities, enemies, stigmatized people etc., and demands a particular attitude towards such people which can only arise out of love. Instead of providing a ready-made recipe, the parable encourages us to become watchful and merciful. Indeed, the parable poses a very relevant question: what is the basis of human agency? Moral codes, laws, customs, traditions? The story tells that the Samaritan acted solely out of compassion (ἐσπλαγχνίσθη), i.e., as a human being. His deed was not coded by religious precepts or civil laws. So being, the text is perfectly compatible with modern theories of human subjectivity and agency. Human agency is indeed one of the issues at stake in this parable. By contrasting the Samaritan's attitude with that of the priest and the Levite, who were expected to act otherwise, the paradoxes of human agency become even more patent. But this challenge will be faced in Part III, below.

It is important to note that, in this parable, Jesus does not demand of this Jewish lawyer to follow him, even though the issue of following is a central one in the Third Gospel.[121] Jesus respects the choice of the lawyer and gives him even the possibility of interpreting the Torah in his own way, considering that his way of reading it was by no means consensus among Jews. It seemed important to Jesus that this man found his own answers and his own path to "eternal life."

Although divergent from each other in some respects, Luke's theology and that of his special material coincide in the parable of the Good Samaritan, soteriology and its concern with the less privileged being its principal elements. Thus, Luke distances himself from a model of discipleship grounded predominantly in profession of faith and decidedly opts for a form of discipleship in which one's commitment to Jesus' cause, namely, his option for the poor, the outcast and the less privileged, acquires much more significance.[122] Needless to

---

121 Compare it with Lk 18:18-23 par.
122 Cf. Lk 6:46-49; 13:25-27; Mt 7:21-23. This does not mean to say, though,

say, the consequences for Christian soteriology are very profound.

In a few circles of Judaism, the Samaritans were not regarded as worthy of the love of a Jew, insofar as they were not considered their neighbors (cf. p. 123ff). Being so, by acting as they did, the priest and the Levite behaved properly. Besides questioning the notion of neighbor, the parable invites Christians to become aware of the dignity of the fallen man, which transcends any cultural or religious barrier, and to make themselves available for such an encounter.

Finally, the analysis of Mt 25:31-46 and Mk 7:24-30 has shown that the idea of salvation, the principle of unconditional recognition of otherness and the model of solidarity, which underlie Lk 10:25-37, are neither an isolated case in the synoptic tradition nor incompatible with Jesus' message. Albeit not being always in the foreground, they are perfectly in line with Christian tradition.

Turning the attention from the afterlife to one's present life is a feature of the texts of Luke's special material which characterizes both their soteriology and eschatology. This feature can be identified in Mt 25:31-46 without major difficulties. As was seen in the previous chapter, shifting the focus onto the present needs of the most suffering does make a difference in one's theological understanding of the Christian idea of salvation, and even incarnation.

As for the aspect of unconditional recognition, the tenor of Mt 25:31-46 transcends any theory of recognition inasmuch as the dignity of human beings is equated with that of Christ himself. Human dignity is thus elevated to the heights. However, in order to acknowledge the truth of such an affirmation, it does not suffice simply to state or repeat it. One must realize it existentially. The account of Mk 7:24-30 suggests that Jesus' unconditional recognition of and unlimited solidarity with the Syrophoenician woman, far from being

---

that Luke undervalues profession of faith. What he seeks is rather the right balance between faith and practice. Following that line of thought, Bovon maintains, for instance, that Lk 10:25-42 forms a whole whereby the story of Martha and Mary (Lk 10:38-42) elucidates the confessional dimension of faith, whereas the parable of the Good Samaritan (Lk 10:30-37) spells out its practical one, both remaining under the double commandment to love (Lk 10:25-29), which, in turn, comprises all dimensions of human life (cf. Bovon, *Das Evangelium nach Lukas*, 1996, III/2:82).

something natural or taken for granted, was a process triggered by that very encounter with her. This is the power of encounters, particularly those with people whose dignity may be threatened by one's prejudices.

5

The Close Relation between Salvation and the Twofold Commandment of Love

The double commandment to love is the "foreword" to Lk 10:25-37. By opening this conversation with a question on eternal life, Luke certainly assigns the twofold commandment of love, as compared with Mark and Matthew, entirely new significance. A synoptic overview could be helpful to notice the differences between them. Consequently, what Jesus teaches in Lk 10:25-37 is not solely "who one's neighbor is," but, most importantly, "how one attains salvation," that is, what the meaning of one's existence is, what to do lest one's whole life is put at stake and ends up meaningless.[1] Thus, this twofold commandment is to be understood, in the view of Luke, as a condition to inherit eternal life.[2]

To the ears of his contemporaries Luke's adaptation might not have sounded as self-evident as one would perhaps expect it to be today. However, for him, the question "what must I do" cannot be

---

1   Walter Dirks, *Die Samariter und der Mann aus Samaria: vom Umgang mit der Barmherzigkeit* (Freiburg im Breisgau: Labertus, 1985), 15f.
2   Cf. Heinz Schürmann, *Das Lukasevangelium*, vol. III/2, Herders theologischer Kommentar zum Neuen Testament (Freiburg im Breisgau; Basel; Wien: Herder, 1994), 130; similarly, François Bovon, *Das Evangelium nach Lukas*, vol. III/2, Evangelisch-Katholischer Kommentar zum Neuen Testament (Zürich: Benziger, 1996), 82. This explicit question about the path to salvation had already begun in Lk 10:17 and is drawn until v. 37. Verse 20 makes this affirmation clear.

left aside, when dealing with the question of salvation. In fact, in this pericope everything revolves around the right praxis, the right deeds, the verb to do (be it on the part of the lawyer, of Jesus, of the Samaritan, of the Levite, of the priest etc.).[3] Not coincidentally is it a Jewish *lawyer* who puts this question to Jesus with intent to put him to the test (cf. Lk 10:25).[4] If that is correct, there is no longer an exegetical basis to view the preliminary verses (Lk 10:25-28) as an alternative parallel text to Mark and Matthew regarding the "greatest commandment" (as Matthew and Mark do).[5] Luke might have altered this text and intentionally placed it before the parable of the Good Samaritan as a "foreword" to it, so that both texts be regarded as a whole. This unity will be elucidated in this chapter.[6]

In the synoptic tradition, the commandment to love one's neighbor appears in total six times (Mt 5:43; 19:19; 22:39; Mk 12:31,33; Lk 10:27). Four of them appear in the account of the double commandment of love (Mk 12:28-34; Mt 22:34-40; Lk 10:25-28), while the other two are editorial additions by Matthew. Most scholars are of the opinion that the first version of this text must have been written by Mark and that Matthew and Luke probably had this text in front of them as they wrote their gospels. It is very unlikely that each one had a different version. It is more probable that the changes in Matthew's and Luke's texts have redactional reasons on account of their respective contexts.[7] Even though the focus of interest in this section is not to offer a thorough analysis of the major differences

---

3   Bovon, *Das Evangelium nach Lukas*, 1996, III/2:85.

4   Cf. Schürmann, *Das Lukasevangelium*, III/2:131.

5   Cf. Joachim Jeremias, *Die Gleichnisse Jesu*, 11th ed. (first published in 1947) (Göttingen: Vandenhoeck & Ruprecht, 1998), 200.

6   For François Bovon this "foreword" applies to both the parable of the Good Samaritan and the following text of Martha and Mary, so that these three passages would form a unity. According to him, since the commandment of love is twofold, there are two texts explaining them in a very concrete way. See Bovon, *Das Evangelium nach Lukas*, 1996, III/2:82. For the whole exegetical argumentation, see pp. 79–117.

7   Cf. Michael Ebersohn, *Das Nächstenliebegebot in der synoptischen Tradition* (Marburg: Elwert, 1993), 155.

between the three synoptic texts, a brief overview on the distinct focuses of concern of Mark and Matthew may be helpful, in order to understand this core element of the message of Jesus in the light of Lk 10:25-37.

The Twofold Commandment of Love in the Gospel of Mark

Even a merely literary comparison between these three parallel texts in question (Mk 12:28-34; Mt 22:34-40; Lk 10:25-28) would indicate that the βασιλεία τοῦ θεοῦ (Kingdom of God) plays, for Mark, an important role. As regards Mark's version of the commandment to love, Ebersohn observes a close relation between Mk 1:15 and Mk 12:34, that is, between the programmatic beginning of Jesus' proclamation and the end of confrontations with his opponents. In his view, both verses are chiastically related to each other. "In 1:15, repentance and belief in the gospel [the good news] are demanded because of the *nearness* of the Kingdom of God and in 12:28-34 this nearness is the *consequence of* [keeping] the love of God and the love of neighbor."[8] Mk 1:15 presents the new demand of Jesus and Mk 12:28-34 the "old" [Jewish] one. Both are conditions for experiencing the Kingdom of God. "The scribe is assured of his nearness to the Kingdom of God" because of his awareness of "the correlation between love of God and love of neighbor" and of the "precedence of human action over the mechanical fulfillment of ritual duties."[9] However, unlike the children in 10:14, the Kingdom of God is not fully granted to him, but only its nearness. Something lacks, there remains a distance. This is the reason for the negative formulation: "you are not far from the Kingdom of God" (Mk 12:34).

However, the most striking thing is "the combination of both commandments in a single double commandment by a representative of Judaism."[10] What takes place here is actually something absolutely atypical of Judaism: "the *fundamental* openness of such

---

8   Ibid., 178.
9   Ibid., 176.
10 Ibid., 177.

a formulation which, on the one hand, allows subsuming different ways of acting under those commandments and, on the other hand, purposely leaves the *concrete* fulfillment up to every human being."[11] It is also due to this kind of fundamental openness that Jesus' approach towards other peoples, which goes beyond the limits of Israel (cf. Mk 7:27-30; 11:17; 13:10; 15:39), is not contradictory.[12] Actually, it is just because these two commandments are so general that they can encompass the human being entirely. The basis, however, remains Judaism and its Law. Mark's endeavor to return to the roots of Judaism in a tough time of crisis and estrangements between Christians and Jews is, in this pericope, sufficiently manifest. However, viewed from the perspective of Mark, it seems as though Judaism had lost the connection to its very basis or as though it were no longer aware of the meaning of that basis. Mark's intention is by no means to claim that Jews ought to interpret the Law as Jesus did, even though that would have been possible.[13] Instead, the evangelist wants to make it clear, on the one hand, that Christians – and Jesus as well – recognize their origin in the Jewish tradition and in the Torah as normative, and, on the other hand, that the discrepancies in current Judaism were indeed substantial, as compared to what it actually "should look like" in the view of Mark.[14]

As distinguished from the text of Matthew and Luke, Jesus literally quotes Deut 6:4f. and then Lev 19:18. There is no doubt that, by quoting Deut 6:4, the aim is to reach the core of Jewish faith. At the same time, this solemn proclamation of the oneness of the Lord is to be construed as an indication of Hellenistic context.[15] Moreover, the

---

11 Ibid.
12 Cf. ibid., 178.
13 For instance, the Jewish apocryphal writing "Testaments of the Twelve Patriarchs" attests to similar attempts to lay the double commandment of love as a foundation for ethical life. Considering such pieces of writing, the evangelist was aware that such a move would have been possible in Judaism, too. Nevertheless, he respects the differences and shows that Jews should not be actually surprised by Jesus' understanding of the Law, as it is very much rooted in Jewish thought.
14 Cf. Ebersohn, *Das Nächstenliebegebot in der synoptischen Tradition*, 179.
15 Cf. Joachim Gnilka, *Das Evangelium nach Markus*, vol. II/2,

slight variation from the original text in Mark's version of Dtn 6,5 provides further evidences for such influences. Whereas the words of the original Hebrew text are לְבָב (heart), נֶפֶשׁ (soul/life) and מְאֹד (force), which, in turn, had been translated, in the LXX, respectively, as καρδία, ψυχή and δύναμις, Mark substitutes δύναμις with two words: διάνοια (reason, intellect) and ἰσχύς (strength). Thus, the rational dimension of human life is given a bit more emphasis. Interestingly, in the reply of the scribe there is one more variation of the original text, which equally stresses that intellectual side: instead of ψυχή (soul/life) the scribe says συνέσεως (the faculty of understanding, comprehension, sagacity). Such an emphasis on comprehension is to be understood in the context of the cult criticism, which again attests to Hellenistic influence.[16] The similarity to the prophetical cult criticism is here undeniable: "[…] for faithful love is what pleases me, not sacrifice; knowledge of God, not burnt offerings" (Hos 6:6; see also Isa 1:11; Mt 9:13; 12:7).[17] This cult criticism could not have been portrayed in a stronger way than it was by Mark: it is a Jewish theologian who utters such words "in the middle of the temple square, the place of the offerings."[18] Moreover, that takes place after Jesus' purification of the Temple (Mk 11:15-17).

At the end of this pericope, one would expect, on the part of Jesus, an invitation to follow him. In the view of Gnilka, the absence of such a request is by no means casual, as the core concern of this theological dispute is to call attention to "the conformity between Jesus' understanding and some of the fundamental beliefs of Jewish faith."[19] As a

---

Evangelisch-Katholischer Kommentar zum Neuen Testament (Zürich; Einsiedeln; Köln: Benziger, 1979), 165.

16 Therefore, considering the compelling evidence of those influences in this pericope, Gnilka deems the factuality of this account in the life of Jesus as highly unlikely (ibid., II/2:167).

17 This prophetical cult criticism had been prepared in some currents of the Old Testament literature (see 1Sam 15:22; Ps 51:20f.; 40:7; Prov 21:3; 16:7). In Jesus' time, this kind of criticism was present, in a particular fashion, in the community of Qumran, and, to some extent, in Hellenistic Judaism (cf. ibid., II/2:166).

18 Ibid.

19 Ibid.

consequence, there would have been, for the scribe, no formal impediments of any kind to join Jesus and embrace Christian faith.

The Twofold Commandment of Love in the Gospel of Matthew

In Matthew, the commandment to love one's neighbor is not just quoted, but, like in the other gospels, intentionally placed within a sequence that comprises three other edited texts around it, thereby keeping, in his report of Jesus' last activities in Jerusalem, the same structure as Mark.[20] This commandment is placed, in 22:34-40, as a summary of ethics, which is something fairly new for that time, peculiarly for Christians coming from Judaism. More precisely, what was new to them were not the ethical demands of the Law, but those of Jesus. That might be the reason, according to Ebersohn, why Jesus does not conclude the sermon of the mountain with a quotation of the Torah, but with the golden rule (cf. Mt 7:12).[21] This element is new as well and is presented as contrasting to the Law. Matthew makes every effort to highlight the newness of Jesus' message and, especially, the radical differences vis-a-vis Judaism. In other words, what goes on at different levels in Matthew's gospel is a struggle for interpretation.

A quick look into the historical background of Matthew's time would be particularly helpful to understand such a need. The phase of apologetics in the face of Judaism, which is manifest in the Gospel of Mark, seems to be over. The rupture with Judaism seems to be consummated and irreparable. Whereas in Mark there seemed to be an attempt to reach a sort of compromise with Judaism, Matthew seems to deliberately seek rupture. Moreover, Matthew's community was faced with a fundamental dilemma. Outwards (in the face of Judaism and the Romans), they had to take their own position in

---

20 Both in Mark and Matthew, the sequence consists of four texts which concern important aspects of (Christian) life: world matters = Mt 22:15-22; eschatology = Mt 22:23-33; ethics = the double commandment to love; Christology = Mt 22:41-46.

21 Cf. Ebersohn, *Das Nächstenliebegebot in der synoptischen Tradition*, 210.

society, whereas inwardly, they needed to build a functioning way of living together (ethics). On that account, the *interpretation of law* through the authority[22] of Jesus, the son of God, who now lays the foundations for a new ethics, is, for Matthew, very much an issue.[23]

As to the meaning of the double commandment to love in Matthew, Luz points out that to assign the Hebrew verb אהב (*'ahab*: to love) a precise meaning is rather a complex task, given its broad and open range of meanings.[24] It can vary between sexual love, love to family members, friends, loyalty in political relations and the relationship to God.[25] However, what can for certain be maintained is that "[i]n the Jewish interpretation of Deut 6:5, love of God is first and foremost expressed through deeds of obedience, piety and faithfulness to the Torah. To love God means to devote one's life to his commandments."[26] As a consequence, the adverbs involve three fundamental dimensions of human beings: ἐν ὅλῃ τῇ καρδίᾳ σου: the wholeheartedness of one's obedience to God; ἐν ὅλῃ τῇ ψυχῇ σου: the

---

22   Jesus' authority can be best perceived in the formulation ἐγὼ δὲ λέγω ὑμῖν (but I say to you...) used in the sermon of the mountain to spell out the implications of the "greater justice" (cf. Mt 5:20-48). Jesus, the son of God and the new Moses, has now brought a new interpretation of the Law in complete conformity with the will of God. Law is now brought to completion alone through the observance of this new interpretation (cf. Mt 5:17).

23   Cf. Ebersohn, *Das Nächstenliebegebot in der synoptischen Tradition*, 210.

24   For further details on the different connotations of love in the Old Testament, see below on p. 124.

25   Cf. Ebersohn, *Das Nächstenliebegebot in der synoptischen Tradition*, 43–46; Hans-Peter Mathys, *Liebe deinen Nächsten wie dich selbst: Untersuchungen zum alttestamentlichen Gebot der Nächstenliebe (Lev 19,18)*, Orbis biblicus et orientalis 71 (Freiburg, Switzerland; Göttingen: Universitätsverlag; Vandenhoeck & Ruprecht, 1986), 12–28; Ulrich Luz, "Das Evangelium nach Matthäus," *Evangelisch-Katholischer Kommentar zum Neuen Testament* (Zürich; Neukirchen-Vluyn: Benziger; Neukirchener, 1997), 279.

26   Luz, "Das Evangelium nach Matthäus," 279; for evidences in that regard see Andreas Nissen, *Gott und der Nächste im antiken Judentum: Untersuchungen zum Doppelgebot der Liebe*, Wissenschaftliche Untersuchungen zum Neuen Testament 15 (Tübingen: Mohr, 1974), 203–11.

witness to one's faith in God, which one bears in concrete life; ἐν ὅλῃ τῇ διανοίᾳ σου: the intellect, the faculty of thinking, understanding, hence the knowledge of God. Therefore, what love of God implies here is neither a feeling, nor prayer duties (after all, Deut 6:5 is a Jewish daily prayer), nor a sort of mysticism alienated from the world, "but the knowledge of the one God and the obedience towards him in the world."[27] If that is so, an inner connection between love of God and love of neighbor seems undeniable, given that both depend on each other and are given the same importance (cf. δευτέρα δὲ ὁμοία αὐτῇ = but the second is similar to it). Christian tradition has always insisted on the unity of both, especially through the quotation of 1Jn 4:7f.,20. Yet Luz insists that, according to the text and to the message of Jesus, the commandment of love of God is the first and foremost one, while the love of neighbor is to be practiced on the basis and/ or as a consequence of the love of God.[28] On that account, he shows his concern for certain liberal approaches which take no account of love towards God and reduce religion to ethics alone.[29] For him, it is love of God that justifies and ensures the consistency of the love of neighbor, not the other way round.

In addition, Ebersohn points out that the commandment of love of neighbor ought to be read in the context of Mt 5:43ff. (love of enemies) and Mt 19:21 (love towards the poor). As a result, the meaning of loving acquires a new (ethical) connotation (no longer like in Lev 19:18). It now takes on the meaning of non-violence and renunciation of vengeance, as far as the *enemies* are concerned (Mt 5:38-42) and mercy, charity, alms and benevolence, as far as *the poor* are (Mt 19:21).[30]

Luz draws attention to a further aspect of this text, which has been very often neglected, particularly due to its historical background: one's self-love (You shall love your neighbor *as yourself*). Self-love was in no way a problematic issue either in Jewish thought or in

---

27 Luz, "Das Evangelium nach Matthäus," 279.
28 Ibid.
29 Cf. ibid., 275. He thinks back, for instance, on the liberal theology, in the 19th century, and on authors like Adolf von Harnack (Das Wesen des Christentums).
30 Cf. Ebersohn, *Das Nächstenliebegebot in der synoptischen Tradition*, 207f.

the early church, but regarded positively and as a sound standard to "measure" one's love of neighbor. Problems with it came later on, especially during the Reformation, when sin began to be understood as self-righteousness, thereby taking on quite a negative meaning.[31] Hence the need to find, in today's world, a new understanding of self-love,[32] a new balance between absolutization of the individual and lack of self-esteem. According to Luz, such a new understanding of self-love can only be acquired through one's love of God and is the key element towards a more genuine love of neighbor.[33]

The Twofold Commandment of Love in the Gospel of Luke

Luke's account of this pericope (Mk 12:30f.; Mt 22:37-39) is marked by two significant changes. First, instead of putting in the lawyer's (νομικός) mouth a question about the first (Mk) or the greatest (Mt) commandment, Luke begins this text with the following question: "Master, what must I do to inherit eternal life?" (Lk 10:25). Second, out of the two commandments,[34] Luke makes just one: "You shall love the Lord your God [...] and your neighbor as yourself."[35] And the fulfillment of this "comprehensive commandment" is presented as the road to eternal life.[36] This section will be devoted to these two issues, starting with the latter.

---

31 Cf. Luz, "Das Evangelium nach Matthäus," 283.
32 Cf. ibid., 284f.
33 Ibid.
34 These two commandments are taken by Mark from Deut 6:5 and Lev 19:18. The distinction between πρώτη and δευτέρα ἐντολή (first and second commandment) is not found in Luke's text.
35 Cf. Michael Wolter, *Das Lukasevangelium*, Handbuch zum Neuen Testament 5 (Tübingen: Mohr Siebeck, 2008), 392. A quick synoptic overview of these texts can make the development from Mark to Luke clear: from a literal quotation (Mark) to an own formulation, i.e., detached from Judaism.
36 Cf. Gerd Petzke, *Das Sondergut des Evangeliums nach Lukas* (Zürich: Theologischer Verlag, 1990), 109.

Summarizing the Whole Torah in One Single Commandment
As a matter of fact, there was, in Hellenistic Judaism, "an endeavor to sum up the whole Torah in 'two main points'[37] [...] which include both the relation to God and the relation to other human beings." The background of that is the Hellenistic "Canon of Two Virtues." This tendency can be observed, for example, in the "Testament of the Twelve Patriarchs."[38] But even Paul sums up the whole Torah in the commandment of love in Rom 13:8-10 and Gal 5:14.

Nonetheless, such an endeavor was, for the German philologist Albrecht Dihle, "completely foreign to Jewish original thinking"[39] and ought to be rather situated in the context of the interplay between Hellenistic and Jewish philosophy.[40] A general and summarizing formulation of the entire Law can be found neither in the whole Old Testament literature nor in the literature between both Testaments. In the view of Ebersohn, that would violate the very inner logic of the Torah and Jewish theology as well, since, *in principle*, given their

---

37 Cf. Philo, *Spec. Leg.* 2,63: δύο τὰ ἀνωτάτω κεφάλαια apud Wolter, *Das Lukasevangelium*, 393.

38 Cf. Bovon, *Das Evangelium nach Lukas*, 1996, III/2:86. For Bovon, even if such a tendency might have been strongly influenced by Hellenism, such a move certainly had also advantages: the balance between faith and ethics is kept and more emphasis is laid on moral life than on the prescriptive (submissive) observance of ritual practices. This might have been even more so after the destruction of the Temple in 70 CE.

39 Albrecht Dihle, *Die goldene Regel: Eine Einführung in die Geschichte der antiken und frühchristlichen Vulgärethik* (Göttingen: Vandenhoeck & Ruprecht, 1962), 83.

40 The most known example is found in the teachings of the Pharisee Rabbi Hillel the Elder (approx. 32 BC-7 CE). According to the story, a heathen went to him asking, "Make me a proselyte, on condition that you teach me the whole Torah while I stand on one foot." "... [H]e said to him, 'What is hateful to you, do not to your neighbour: that is the whole Torah, while the rest is the commentary thereof; go and learn it'" (Babylonian Talmud: Tractate Shabbath, 31a). Further evidences for that kind of interaction are Letter of Aristeas, 207 (130 BC), Sir 31(34):15 and Tobi 4,15. Cf. Hans-Peter Mathys, "Goldene Regel (I. Judentum)," *Theologische Realenzyklopädie* (Berlin: de Gruyter, 1992), 570.

common origin from God, all 613 commandments are of equal value.[41] On the other hand, even if that is the case, the way Jesus conceives both the unity of these two commandments and their necessity for inheriting eternal life is quite unique and cannot, therefore, be equated to those attempts in Hellenistic Judaism.[42]

Indeed, Mussner affirms that, as far as the double love command is concerned, Jesus has not brought anything "new" into the world. However, he also considers the close correlation between Deut 6:5 and Lev 19:18 to be new.[43] This is endorsed by Gnilka, who likewise sees a clear difference between Jesus' combination and the relation between worship of God and love of neighbor, just as it was conceived of by Philo of Alexandria.[44] However, the differences in the synoptic account of this pericope do constitute a difficulty in reconstructing Jesus' original speech.

Yet the exegetical difficulty of tracing back the double love command to Jesus as his *ipsissimum verbum* does not lessen, in any way, the authority of this pericope. According to Schürmann, who, in that regard, relies on Bultmann's approach, since there is still insufficient evidence to attest either that this formulation originates from Jesus or that it was formed by the post-Easter community, one valid criterion would be whether this word finds echo in Jesus' life and attitude.[45] As Bultmann puts it in his history of the synoptic tradition, even though it is likely that Jesus was put questions such as this, the form in which the post-Easter community tells it may correspond to the "spirit" of

---

41 Cf. Ebersohn, *Das Nächstenliebegebot in der synoptischen Tradition*, 170, 250; Nissen, *Gott und der Nächste*, 337–42, 415f.; Gnilka, *Das Evangelium nach Markus*, II/2:164; Luz, "Das Evangelium nach Matthäus," 278, although Luz relativizes it a bit.

42 Cf. Schürmann, *Das Lukasevangelium*, III/2:135.

43 Cf. Franz Mussner, *Was hat Jesus Neues in die Welt gebracht?* (Stuttgart: Katholisches Bibelwerk, 2001), 49; Gnilka raises the same question in *Das Evangelium nach Markus*, II/2:167.

44 Gnilka, *Das Evangelium nach Markus*, II/2:167.

45 Cf. Schürmann, *Das Lukasevangelium*, III/2:140.

Jesus, rather than to the historic fact.[46] Similarly, the theologian Werner Jeanrond affirms that, more important than knowing whether or not Jesus was the first one to introduce this combination of both commandments is "to appreciate the significance of this double commandment for the proclamation of God's reign in the Synoptic Gospels."[47] Jeanrond sees in the idea of love the central element for one's relationship both to God and to other human beings.

The Linkage between Love and Salvation
Let us turn our attention now to the linkage between salvation and the commandment of love, as suggested by Luke. According to the exegete Wolter, this attempt of Luke has to be contextualized within the process of separation between Christians and Jews. Unlike the view of most Hellenistic Christians, the very fact that an expert in law confirms that one, in fact, fulfills the law – i.e., the whole Torah – through the practice of love might have sounded as a piece of good news for (Jewish) Christians and perhaps even as a comfort. On that account, Wolter holds that this pericope has, for Luke, less to do with parenesis than it has with apologetics.[48] That would imply that Luke's greatest concern here would have been to make it clear that the observance of the Torah in fact applies to Christians as well, on a normative level. The reason for such a strong apologetics on the part of Luke could be construed as an attempt to correct certain currents, especially in Hellenistic Christianity, which were intent on abolishing any commitment or obligations with regard to the Torah and Jewish traditions.

It can be assumed that from the second century B.C. onwards there was the belief that after death one would not simply be put in

---

46 Rudolf Bultmann, *Die Geschichte der synoptischen Tradition*, 10th ed., 1st ed. 1921 (Göttingen: Vandenhoeck & Ruprecht, 1995), 57.
47 Werner G. Jeanrond, *A Theology of Love* (London: T & T Clark, 2010), 33.
48 Wolter, *Das Lukasevangelium*, 394. Wolter refers here especially to the theory of Günther Bornkamm, "Das Doppelgebot der Liebe," in *Geschichte und Glaube*, Beiträge zur evangelischen Theologie 48 (München: Kaiser, 1968), 45. Differently, Bovon tends to emphasize more the ethical aspect (Bovon, *Das Evangelium nach Lukas*, 1996, III/2:82ff.).

the netherworld, but enjoy a sort of "true 'life,' an 'eternal life' in and together with God."[49] Apparently, they knew well that this eternal life is a gift and can, therefore, only be inherited (cf. Lk 10:25), albeit not completely dissociated from a certain praxis, from a certain "doing." Luke suggests, in this text, that there is a close connection between "eternal life" and agape. He reflects on the love of God from the perspective of the concrete love of neighbor, which, in turn, is ultimately decisive for his understanding of the love of God.[50]

For the exegete Ulrich Luz, such an understanding of salvation is by no means an isolated approach unique to Luke, but can be found, even if a bit more implicit, in the Gospel of Matthew as well. In his gospel, this "Jewish Christian" tries to oppose a group of people that can be referred to as "radical antinomians." These were convinced that, with the advent of Christianity, the Law in the Torah was to be abolished. "For Matthew, Jesus' authoritative[51] interpretation of the Law is decisive, making the commandment to love the greatest commandment under all circumstances and the one on which all the rest depends (cf. Mt 22:40)."[52] Matthew's formulation ἐὰν μὴ περισσεύσῃ ὑμῶν ἡ δικαιοσύνη πλεῖον τῶν γραμματέων καὶ Φαρισαίων...[53] is the heading verse to the so-called greater righteousness theses. The δικαιοσύνη (righteousness) demanded of Christians is the commandment to love, practiced in its radicalness, which, in turn, is God's will. Fulfilling this command is equated with

---

49 Schürmann, *Das Lukasevangelium*, III/2:132.

50 Ibid., III/2:133. Interestingly, Paul also talks more often about the love of neighbor than he does about the love of God (cf. Gal 5:14; Rom 13:9). For this matter, see Rudolf Schnackenburg, "'Das Gesetz des Christus' (Gal 6:2): Jesu Verhalten und Wort als letztgültige sittliche Norm nach Paulus," in *Neues Testament und Kirche: für Rudolf Schnackenburg zum 60. Geburtstag*, ed. Joachim Gnilka (Freiburg im Breisgau; Basel; Wien: Herder, 1974), 282–300.

51 The verb ἦλθον (I have come...) gives the sentence the status of a Christological statement and emphasizes the mission of Jesus as revealer of the will of God (cf. Ulrich Luz, *Studies in Matthew* [Grand Rapids, Cambridge: Eerdmans, 2005], 201).

52 Cf. ibid., 205f.

53 "[...] if your uprightness does not surpass that of the scribes and Pharisees, you will never get into the kingdom of Heaven" (Mt 5:20).

the "perfection" (cf. Mt 5:48).[54] "Matthew must seek above all to establish the commandment to love, whose practice is central to the community, as the *biblical* will of God."[55] Matthew puts it even as the *condition* for entering the kingdom of heaven.[56] Indeed, verse 20 "contains the most definitive connection between deeds and promise of salvation" (as condition).[57]

However, Matthew's theology may not be classified under the label of "justification by work" in opposition to Paul's. "[...] [F]or Matthew, the will of God revealed in Jesus Christ as 'will of the Father' is already grace in itself [...]."[58] The main factor that has to be taken into account is that Paul and Matthew write in completely different times, and have in mind very different addressees.[59] For Matthew, "[...] grace is given in the form of commandment, and the commandments in turn are the epitome of grace. This enables him, in exemplary manner, to see practice as the essence of the Christian faith, with the effect of grace evidenced in Christians being sustained in action and called on to act."[60]

The Controversies around the Idea of Neighbor
Traditionally, exegesis has read the lawyer's question (Lk 10:25) in the context of interpretation of Lev 19:18b. That being the case, it was apparently important not only to affirm *that* one has to love, but also to define *whom* one has to love. Indeed, there was in Judaism at

---

54 Cf. Luz, *Studies in Matthew*, 207.
55 Ibid., 210 (emphasis in original).
56 Cf. ibid., 214.
57 Cf. ibid.
58 Ibid., 216.
59 Cf. ibid., 217. According to Luz, whereas Paul writes in a context in which there still was a hope that Jews would embrace Jesus Christ, and Paul's main concern was to explain how one (especially a Jew) *becomes* a Christian, Matthew's concern is, one generation later, how one *remains* a Christian. As the setting in which Matthew writes his gospel is marked by a strict separation between Christian and Jewish communities and many conflicts and issues have to be settled, he cannot ignore the issue of the right praxis (orthopraxis) of Christians vis-a-vis Jews.
60 Ibid., 218.

that time an intensive ongoing debate on that issue, particularly as far as the meaning of the word רֵעַ (*rēᵃᶜ:* friend, fellow, companion, neighbor etc.) was concerned.[61] There is enough evidence to affirm that the Hebrew word רֵעַ might have in fact connoted, in Lev 19:18, exclusively one's own countryman. For Schürmann, however, Lev 19:34 and Deut 10:19 appear to prescribe the inclusion of foreigners living in Israel, too, in the group of those whom an Israelite was supposed to love.[62] Moreover, these three verses are the only ones, in the Old Testament, that demand from the Israelites such a love "towards a determined group of people,"[63] which could suggest a close relation between them.

Nevertheless, Ebersohn holds that those two latter verses are probably linked to each other, but may have little to do with Lev 19:18. Both verses have the same structure and give the same explanation why one ought to proceed in that way,[64] while Lev 19:18 is to be understood in the context of the "Holiness Code" (Lev 17-26). According to him, the context in which the word גֵּר (*gēr:* foreigner, guest worker) is used in Lev 19:34 and Deut 10:19 is different from that of Lev 19:18. The only common denominator is the verb אהב (*ahab:* to love),[65] though the connotation of this verb is, in

---

61 Cf. Schürmann, *Das Lukasevangelium*, III/2:142; see also Mathys, *Liebe deinen Nächsten wie dich selbst*, 12. The debate was about both the definition and domain of the Hebrew term רֵעַ (*rēᵃᶜ*) and its equivalent Greek translation τὸ πλησίον (fellow man, neighbor).

62 Cf. Schürmann, *Das Lukasevangelium*, III/2:142.

63 Cf. Mathys, *Liebe deinen Nächsten wie dich selbst*, 12.

64 Compare: "You will treat resident aliens as though they were native-born and love them as yourself – for you yourselves were once aliens in Egypt" (Lev 19:34). "You will love the stranger, for you were once strangers in Egypt" (Deut 10:19).

65 This Hebrew verb has five different meanings: a) love between man and woman (sexual love); b) in familiar bonds (Gn 22:2; 25:28); c) ties between friends (Saul and David or Jonathan and David, cf. 1Sam 18:1,3; 20:17; 2Sam 1:26), which involve also feelings, despite being, normally, a relationship of protection; d) in political sense, a loyal relationship between king and subject such as in a vassal contract; the subject was supposed to love his king as much as himself; in the Old Testament, it also applies to the relationship between David and Hiram of Tyrus (1Kgs 5:15; cf. 2Sam 5:11; 2Chr 19:2), which again implies protection, support and help (1Sam

Deut 10:18, quite specified, thereby taking on a different meaning. Whereas in Deut 10:18, to love means to give him [the foreigner] "food and clothing," that is, to assure his most basic needs,[66] in Lev 19:18 the verb to love is used to positively affirm all the prohibitions which were negatively stated in the previous verses (Lev 19:11-18). All commandments and prohibitions are now, in v. 19, generalized positively. Although the people who had a lower status (cf. Deut 10:18f) may also be included in this commandment in the sense of protection, the commandment to love is intended, in Lev 19:18, for the "full Israelite citizens." "Love is to be understood as mutual solidarity within a community that, by holding on to Yahweh's traditional faith, strives to join forces together and to hold together."[67]

This appeal to mutual support and protection among the sons of Israel in the form of a commandment appears to have been nearly a question of survival during the horrible context of exile in which this text was composed. It was added to the Priestly Source in the time of exile to call on the people who were living there to remain united and to support one another. It is addressed to the members of the People of Israel, more precisely, to the adult male full citizens. They are requested not to oppress their neighbors and, whenever necessary, to provide the neighbor with the same position that one has and which the neighbor has a right to. Therefore, what is meant here, according to Ebersohn, is not primarily solidarity with the weaker, the poor, the foreigners, but solidarity among Israelites who possess the same status. Such a general commandment is nowhere else to be found in the Old Testament. That can be explained with reference to the exceptional circumstances in which the text was written, namely, the Exile. What is therein intended is to provide a programmatic ideal picture for living together. Interestingly, the exegete Mathys uses

---

16:21); finally, it is used in the relationship between David and the people (cf. 1Sam 18:16; 18:5; 18:22); e) in a theological sense: the relationship between Yahweh and Israel and the obedience of Israel towards Yahweh (demanded by Him in Deut 6:5; 10:12f.). For a more comprehensive view of the range of meanings of this word, see Ebersohn, *Das Nächstenliebegebot in der synoptischen Tradition*, 43f.

66 Cf. also Mathys, *Liebe deinen Nächsten wie dich selbst*, 13.
67 Ebersohn, *Das Nächstenliebegebot in der synoptischen Tradition*, 46.

the same argumentation line as Ebersohn to demonstrate how Deut 10:19 demands the same as in Lev 19:18, 34.[68]

This short look into the controversial interpretation of Lev 19:18 within Judaism could hopefully deliver a picture of the hermeneutic predicaments that were then at work. Around the time of Jesus, the meaning of Lev 19:34 and Deut 10:19 had been narrowed to proselyte foreigners, that is, to foreigners who had been circumcised and then baptized.[69] Even so, there was substantial disagreement as to the exceptions that could be made among those people. In rigorous groups like the Pharisees or the Essenes, there was a tendency to exclude even other Jews from the עַם הָאָרֶץ (*the people of the land*),[70] so that among Pharisees, for example, every non-Pharisee could, in principle, be reckoned as such. Not only were people who did not know the Law well or people who were not as rigorous as the Pharisees in observing it regarded with contempt, but also sinners, heretics, the Samaritan etc.[71]

Bearing that context in mind, one thing can be stated with certainty: The idea of neighbor, which had become quite narrow in Judaism, "was reinterpreted by Jesus," particularly in the parable of the Good Samaritan.[72] And this is exactly the issue addressed by the lawyer in verse 29, which concerns the ambit and applicability of Lev 19:18b as well as all Torah prescriptions involving the neighbor. The key to understanding the intention behind the lawyer's question could be the following sentence: "But the man was anxious to justify himself [...]" (Lk 10:29). In other words, he wanted to justify his question and be in the right. He wanted to know whom precisely he was supposed to love. Jesus understands what was at stake and gives him a very concrete answer.

---

68 Cf. Mathys, *Liebe deinen Nächsten wie dich selbst*, 13.

69 Cf. Schürmann, *Das Lukasevangelium*, III/2:142; also Luz, "Das Evangelium nach Matthäus," 280.

70 עַם הָאָרֶץ (*'am ha-'areç*) was the current designation for the "people of the land," the inhabitants of a determined country, as contrasted to the foreigner (גֵּר).

71 Cf. Jeremias, *Die Gleichnisse Jesu*, 201; Schürmann, *Das Lukasevangelium*, III/2:142. According to Jeremias, this kind of contemptuous attitude on the part of the Pharisees towards these people can be sensed, for example, in Jn 7:49.

72 Gnilka, *Das Evangelium nach Markus*, II/2:167.

Luke's Emphasis on the Practice of Love

It is not easy to find in Luke a definition of love or neighbor. But if Lk 10:25-37 is taken into consideration, neighbor cannot have the same meaning as it has in Lev 19:18. For Luke, neighbor cannot be defined either sociologically or ethnically, but rather in terms of his/her needs: one's neighbor is anyone who may need concrete assistance. In that way, neighbor cannot be defined at all. Since anyone can be in need, neighbor can in principle be understood as universal.[73] To love would mean, in Luke, the praxis of mercy, charity and compassion (cf. the word ἔλεος in Lk 10:37), that is, a praxis concerned with the need rather than with the person.

At first glance, the identity of the assaulted does not seem to play any special role in Luke's story. Also Luke understands the commandment of love of neighbor as a general and summarizing demand, although quite differently from the author of Lev 19. Whereas Lev 19:18 is a generalizing formulation (inductive) that unifies different peculiarities of the law which is demanded in the previous chapters, Luke 10:27b is a "meta-ethic" sentence that has to be made concrete in every situation (deductive), a sentence from which any instruction for the practice can be derived. In any case, what becomes clear is that in the time of Luke, this sentence was an inherited tradition, but its meaning was no longer self-evident.[74]

By analyzing the structure of Luke's text, it is not difficult to notice that his main concern is not to offer a treatise on law, a solution to this hermeneutic predicament or any theoretical discussion. This is deliberately avoided. His point is exactly the opposite. The lawyer misses the point because his main concern is to justify himself or to look for theories that could justify him or his behavior (v. 29a). That is the reason why the lawyer (the learned and the clever in Lk 10:21) is put in contrast to the little children, to whom it is granted to know the truth and the Father. Luke emphasizes, by contrast, from the very beginning of the conversation, the verb to do (ποιέω, or imperative: τοῦτο ποίει). In short, salvation, for Luke, "does not

---

73 Cf. Ebersohn, *Das Nächstenliebegebot in der synoptischen Tradition*, 238.
74 Cf. ibid.

consist in practicing the *Law,* but in *practicing* the Law."[75]

The summary of the Law is also in Luke a quite general principle and everyone is free to implement it in the concrete cases of concrete life. The only condition is that one really *does* it. For the Protestant theologian Joachim Jeremias, the question as to why Jesus suggests one's *doing* (τοῦτο ποίει καὶ ζήσῃ) as the road to eternal life should be understood in this way: "all theological knowledge is of no use, if love of God and love of fellow man[76] do not determine one's conduct of life."[77] In fact, Luke places this text in a section in which the issue of salvation is dealt with. It begins in Lk 10:17 and ends in 10:37. The answer to the lawyer in 10:25 is given through the parable of the Good Samaritan and the main concern is not so much a summarizing commandment as it is a practical indication for the praxis. The lawyer's answer was correct, but Luke felt the need to clarify what it actually implies concretely. In all likelihood, there were misunderstandings in the interpretation of that command. Luke is less concerned about a definition and/or delimitation of neighbor than about the concrete meaning of loving, whereby *doing* plays a decisive role.

Agape as a Key Theological Concept of the Johannine Literature

The ethical demand of the twofold commandment to love is in no way exclusive to the synoptic gospels. Both the Johannine and the Pauline tradition know of and hand it down, too, though with different accents. To be sure, they could serve the purpose of providing as well as supporting the evidence for the originality of such a commandment in the message of Jesus. More importantly, considering

---

75 Ibid., 232 (emphasis in original). "Pointiert formuliert: Das Heil besteht nicht im Tun des *Gesetzes,* sondern im *Tun* des Gesetzes."

76 Jeremias is very careful when translating τὸν πλησίον (= $rē^{ac}$). According to him, the real historical meaning of this term would remain veiled, if τὸν πλησίον would be automatically translated with and understood in terms of *neighbor*. The Christian notion of neighbor is, for him, "a result of history, and not a departure point" (Jeremias, *Die Gleichnisse Jesu,* 201).

77 Ibid.

my efforts in making a case for a reinterpretation of the notion of salvation by means of the notion of love, it would be perfectly legitimate to expect me to take the Johannine literature as a basis for argumentation. Not only is this expectation endorsed by the abundant number of occurrences of the word "love" therein,[78] but this tendency can be observed across the history of Christian theology, too. Joachim of Fiore and the Franciscan Spirituals are just an example of this sort.[79]

There are certainly good reasons to proceed that way. First of all, the so-called Johannine communities did not know yet a hierarchical understanding of ministry as, for instance, the recipients of the pastoral letters did.[80] Consequently, the principle of equality among the members of the community is much more underscored. The reason for such equality is a gift of the Holy Spirit (Paraclete) given to all who are baptized and receive the anointing (Chrism). The First Letter of John bears witness to a very strong statement in that regard: "But as for you, the anointing (χρῖσμα) you received from him remains in you, and you do not need anyone to teach you (καὶ οὐ χρείαν ἔχετε ἵνα τις διδάσκῃ ὑμᾶς); since the anointing he gave you teaches you everything [...]" (cf. 1Jn 1:27). A statement of this tenor provides, for sure, sufficient elements to rethink not only the very foundations of ecclesiology, particularly regarding the aspects of ministry, laity, authority, doctrine and hierarchy, but also a theory of interreligious dialogue.

However, as compared to the synoptic gospels, the semantic connotation of love appears to undergo a discernible shift, whereby other aspects beyond the double commandment to love come under consideration. According to Jeanrond, two further dimensions could

---

78   Out of the 320 occurrences for the verb ἀγαπᾶν (to love) and its derivatives in the entire New Testament, 106 are found in the *Corpus Johanneum*; of a total of 55 occurrences for φιλεῖν (to love) and its derivatives, 21 are in the Johannine writings (Enno Edzard Popkes, *Die Theologie der Liebe Gottes in den johanneischen Schriften: Zur Semantik der Liebe und zum Motivkreis des Dualismus* [Tübingen: Mohr Siebeck, 2005], 18; see also Udo Schnelle, *Die Johannesbriefe* [Leipzig: Evangelische Verlagsanstalt, 2010], 163).
79   Cf. Hans-Josef Klauck, *Gemeinde – Amt – Sakrament: neutestamentliche Perspektiven* (Würzburg: Echter, 1989), 196.
80   Cf. ibid., 220.

be included: "the love of God is related, first, to oneness or harmony within the Christian community, and second, to Jesus' own example of self-sacrifice for his friends."[81] This is endorsed by the studies of the exegete Hans-Josef Klauck on John, who affirms that within the Johannine literature love is always to be interpreted Christologically.[82] This amounts to saying that claims such as "God is love" (1Jn 4:8,16) can only be inferred from the very fact that he sent his only Son to the world. There is no other basis to suppose, to assume, or to infer it from.

However, the Johannine approach seems to bring on, as a consequence, a narrowing of the meaning of love, particularly, as far as its scope is concerned. Thus, in comparison to the synoptics, the first, and, perhaps, the most significant difference that can be observed in that regard, is that love of "the others" refers not to every other, but, as it seems, almost exclusively to the fellow members of the Johannine community. Klauck remarks that the title "brother" (ἀδελφός, masculine) was used only for the members of Christian communities,[83] which conveys the impression that all other non-Christians would be automatically excluded from the love of Christians. The cohesion of the Christian communities seems to be saved at the expense of the love of "other" neighbors. This has prompted many theologians, within the exegetical tradition of these writings, to construe them as sectarian texts belonging to a sectarian group.[84] This impression leads Jeanrond to point out provocatively that, in those writings, "[...] love and oneness are linked in such a manner as to suggest that love is not so much the way to handle difference, conflict and

---

81 Jeanrond, *Theology of Love*, 35.

82 Cf. Hans-Josef Klauck, *Der erste Johannesbrief*, Evangelisch-Katholischer Kommentar zum Neuen Testament, 23/1 (Zürich; Neukirchen-Vluyn: Benziger; Neukirchener, 1991), 261.

83 Cf. ibid., 277.

84 Cf. Popkes, *Theologie der Liebe Gottes*, 3–5. In this extensive research, Popkes makes a remarkable endeavor to prove whether the supposed contradiction between God's universal love and the limitation of the love commandment to the boundaries of the Christian community is, in reality, just ostensible or whether this tension between both remains unresolved.

otherness as a way of avoiding – if not perpetuating – all three."[85]

Klauck, on the other hand, suggests a more differentiated view, though recognizing himself that these writings do allow a margin for such interpretations. Such readings of the Johannine theology of love as though it was written to an esoteric group can certainly be associated with its ambivalent stance on the world (κόσμος), which is most frequently construed exclusively as a negative environment. Nevertheless, at a closer glance, generalizations of this kind may become relative, if the context of these communities is taken into account.

The rationales Klauck presents for his opinion are basically two. First, he draws the attention to the hostile environment surrounding these communities, especially with regard to the local authorities. This is a fact perceptible all throughout the Johannine writings. In addition, the community was going through a serious internal crisis, which was perceived as something putting in jeopardy the cohesion and even the future of the community.[86] What is more, it must be borne in mind that the price paid by those who opted for Christianity and joined these communities was quite high, insofar as they had to give up all their social securities and every kind of support. Therefore, they were entirely dependent upon the support of other community members, should any need arise.[87]

Second, he suggests a differentiated look at the commandment of love of neighbor, as presented by the synoptics. Contrary to the general view of it as applying to the whole humanity in the sense of a universal love, he argues that this command concerns, primarily, one's very concrete neighbor, that is to say, someone whom one has contact with, someone visible, rather than abstract. For, he goes on to say, even the love of enemy, a highly abstract ideal, implies proximity, concreteness: "If someone slaps you on your right cheek […]"

---

85 Jeanrond, *Theology of Love*, 37.
86 In addition to this internal crisis, Popkes argues that the intimate atmosphere in which Jesus gives the commandment to love to his disciples (Jn 13:34f.), as contrasted with the synoptics which place the commandment to love within a public controversy, may not be construed as a sectarian act, but rather as a consequence of the Johannine Christology. Cf. Popkes, *Theologie der Liebe Gottes*, 260.
87 Cf. Klauck, *Der erste Johannesbrief*, 279.

(Mt 5:39). Such a concreteness is intended in the writings of John, too, and, if that is correct, such supposed discrepancy between the synoptics and the Johannine literature could be bridged. For in the view of the composer(s) of these writings, only by means of such concrete love of one another among fellow Christians can the disciples of Christ become light and witness to the world and fulfill Jesus' command.[88]

Notwithstanding, looking for similarities to or even for a continuity between the synoptics and the Johannine writings regarding the command to love seems to yield no fruitful results. One may be even confused about John's usages such as *old* command (1Jn 2:7), *new* command (Jn 13:34), and *my* command (Jn 15:12). In view of this state of affairs, the exegete Oda Wischmeyer believes to have good grounds to claim that *new* (καινός) is to be construed, in this context, as given by Jesus, thereby referring to the newness of it.[89] No connection whatsoever is made to the Torah nor to any other authoritative source of that time. Jesus alone is presented as the authoritative source of this command,[90] the one who entrusts this command (ἐντολή) exclusively to his disciples (οἱ μαθηταί αὐτοῦ).[91] The main issue for the composer(s) of the Johannine writings is to create such a new linkage between love, new and command that this becomes as much the *unique* as the *only one* command given by Jesus: "ἐντολὴν

---

88 Cf. ibid., 278f.

89 Cf. Oda Wischmeyer, "Das alte und das neue Gebot: Ein Beitrag zur Intertextualität der johanneischen Schriften," in *Studien zu Matthäus und Johannes / Festschrift für Jean Zumstein*, ed. Andreas Dettwiler and Uta Poplutz, Abhandlungen zur Theologie des Alten und Neuen Testaments 97 (Zürich: Theologischer Verlag Zürich, 2009), 210.

90 Besides the aspect of Jesus' authority, Popkes points to Jesus' sovereignty, as is typical of John, while giving this commandment. Unlike the synoptic account, in which Jesus' authority is questioned by a scribe (cf. Mk 12:28-31; Mt 22:34-40; Lk 10:25-28), so that Jesus reacts to him, in the account of John it is Jesus himself who takes the initiative and deliberately acts (Popkes, *Theologie der Liebe Gottes*, 260).

91 John adopts the term μαθηταί to refer to the disciples of Jesus, just as in the synoptics. Yet there are other terms which are peculiar to John, such as οἱ ἴδοι (those who are his own) φίλοι (friends).

καινὴν δίδωμι ὑμῖν..." (I give you a new commandment, Jn 13:34).[92]

There is no doubt that the Jewish notion of commandment, as handed down through the Septuagint and as received by the synoptics, was known and presupposed. But in that case, speaking of a new command would make no sense to the addressees of the writings, unless this kind of "rupture," as described above, is assumed as being the case.[93] In Jn 13 and 15, Jesus speaks as the Son of God. Thus, his authority supersedes definitively the authority as well as the commands of Moses.[94]

Similarly, this connection between the law and the commandment(s) in the Johannine literature is seen by Johannes Beutler in the context of the controversies between the Johannine community and the Jewish Synagogue.[95] He maintains that both the noun ἐντολή (commandment) and the verb ἐντέλλομαι (to command) are related, to a great extent, to the notion of νόμος (law).[96] In the course of those controversies, ἐντολή opens up a new semantic field, insofar as it comprises two essential elements of Johannine theology: to reveal (the will of) the Father himself (cf. Jn 12:49f.) and to lay down one's own life (cf. Jn 10:18; 14:31).[97] This (new) command is in perfect accordance with the will of the Father himself and the greatest example has been set by Jesus, the revealer.

Therefore, even on the ethical plane the "old commands" have no chance at all to compete with Jesus' "new one," precisely because the (new) measure for the love of Christians is not self-love, as in Lev 19:18, in the synoptics and in the Pauline letters, but the very love of Jesus showed to his disciples, which comes to its most significant expression on the cross.[98] Therefore, Wischmeyer argues that

---

92 Cf. Wischmeyer, "Das alte und das neue Gebot," 211.
93 Cf. ibid., 212.
94 Cf. ibid.
95 Cf. Johannes Beutler, "Gesetz und Gebot in Evanglium und Briefen des Johannes," in *Neue Studien zu den johanneischen Schriften*, Bonner Biblische Beiträge 167 (Göttingen: Bonn University Press, 2012), 14.
96 Cf. ibid., 16.
97 Cf. ibid.
98 Cf. Popkes, *Theologie der Liebe Gottes*, 262f.

the expression "new commandment" attests to an inner development taking place in the Johannine communities, be it in relation to the synoptics or other early Christian writings, be it in relation to the Johannine theology itself.[99]

A contrary opinion is offered by Augenstein. He argues that the Johannine commandment to love is a reinterpretation of Lev 19:18 and that "old command" is an expression of the continuity of the will of God between the Old and the New Testaments.[100] The consequence he draws from his assessment is that categories like conventicle ethics, φιλανθρωπία (love of mankind, benevolence), or φιλαδελφία (love of one's brothers, in a wide sense) are in no way appropriate to characterize the Johannine understanding of the commandment to love. John's theology is to be viewed, primarily, as a new reading of Lev 19:18 and the synoptics alike.[101]

On the other hand, exegetes such as Schnackenburg draw attention to the fact that assertions such as Jn 15:13 could not have been taken up from Judaism.[102] They are rather to be accounted for by general views of the antique ethics of friendship prevailing in the Greek-Roman world of that time. That the greatest expression of one's love is to lay down one's own life for one's friends is an idea that cannot be understood but in the context of Hellenistic influence.[103] Now, if that is correct, there would be sufficient room for criticisms which regard the command to love as conceived of by the Johannine theology as partisan and sectarian, or even at variance with Jesus' original teachings. Yet, in the opinion of Scholtissek, this must not necessarily be seen as negative. For him, the undeniable traits of the Hellenistic-Jewish ethics of friendship and family metaphors are to

---

99 Cf. Wischmeyer, "Das alte und das neue Gebot," 220.

100 Cf. Jörg Augenstein, *Das Liebesgebot im Johannesevangelium und in den Johannesbriefen* (Stuttgart: Kohlhammer, 1993), 183.

101 Cf. ibid., 177.

102 "No one can have greater love than to lay down his life for his friends" (Jn 15:13).

103 Cf. Rudolf Schnackenburg, *Das Johannesevangelium*, vol. 3, Herders theologischer Kommentar zum Neuen Testament 4 (Freiburg im Breisgau; Basel; Wien: Herder, 1975), 125.

be regarded as a remarkable effort of inculturation on the part of the Johannine theology, which does not simply take up those imaginaries, but reinterprets them and fills them anew with soteriological as well as ethic motifs.[104]

Paul's Understanding of the Commandment to Love

To consider Paul's peculiar understanding of agape constitutes an unavoidable task to the present study, not only because of the importance of Paul's new insights for both theological reflection and Christian praxis, but particularly owing to the historical impact and reception of his thoughts. As Thomas Söding sees it, Paul's conception of agape has exerted a profound influence upon three fundamental areas of Christian theology. *Firstly,* Paul's *paraklesis* (exhortation) of love has determined the relation between exegesis and systematic theology. The main aspects that could be highlighted here are the search for both a definition of Christian love (dogmatic theology) and the place of love in Christian ethics or moral conduct. *Secondly,* most of the confessional controversies on the doctrine of justification depend on how one construes the relation between faith and love or the one between soteriology and ethics in Paul's writings. More precisely, the Lutheran *sola fide* and the Catholic *fides caritate formata* owe their legitimacy, to a great extent, to the way one interprets verses like Gal 5:6 (ἀλλὰ πίστις δι' ἀγάπης ἐνεργουμένη: "[...] but faith working through love").[105]

---

104 Cf. Klaus Scholtissek, "'Eine größere Liebe als diese hat niemand, als wenn einer sein Leben hingibt für seine Freunde' (Jn 15,13): Die hellenistische Freundschaftsethik und das Johannesevangelium," in *Kontexte des Johannesevangeliums: das vierte Evangelium in religions- und traditionsgeschichtlicher Perspektive,* ed. Jörg Frey and Udo Schnelle, Wissenschaftliche Untersuchungen zum Neuen Testament 175 (Tübingen: Mohr Siebeck, 2004), 438f.
105 For that matter, see esp. Miriam Rose, *Fides caritate formata: das Verhältnis von Glaube und Liebe in der Summa Theologiae des Thomas von Aquin,* Forschungen zur systematischen und ökumenischen Theologie 112 (Göttingen: Vandenhoeck & Ruprecht, 2007).

Thirdly, since Paul quotes, in Gal 5:14 and Rom 13:8-10, the Jewish commandment to love as it is found in Lev 19:18, this offers a great chance for a fruitful dialogue between Jews and Christians about the very foundations of ethics.[106]

Similarly to the synoptics,[107] Paul makes an effort to read and sum up the entire Torah in the sense of Lev 19:18 ("You shall love your neighbor as yourself"). This occurs, explicitly, in Gal 5:14 and Rom 13:8-10 and, implicitly, in several other passages about agape. In so arguing, his intention is to subsume both the Jewish and the Greek-Roman way of conceiving the law in such a way that this command may sound plausible to all Christian communities, notwithstanding his harsh criticism of law.[108]

The question then arises, why Paul "needs" at all such a commandment, if Christians have been set free through Christ so as to remain free and exempted from the yoke of slavery to which one is subjected through the law (cf. Gal 5:1). This question becomes particularly vexed, if one takes into consideration that Paul's commandment to love is the outcome of a development in his thought which takes its clearest shape in the letters to the Galatians and to the Romans in which he spells out more elaborately his doctrine of justification and his criticism of law.[109] How to conciliate these two latter with the *commandment* to love, then?

To start with, a subtle distinction has to be made. Fundamental as it is for Paul's entire ethics, the love commandment should not be confused with a general instruction for each and every situation in daily life. Rather, Paul confers on this command a "unique theological quality." The reason for this is that, in his view, "[...] solely the idea of agape can ensure that both the will and the actions of

---

106 Cf. Thomas Söding, *Das Liebesgebot bei Paulus: die Mahnung zur Agape im Rahmen der paulinischen Ethik* (Münster: Aschendorff, 1995), 1–10.
107 In so arguing, Paul stands in the tradition of the so-called Jewish-Christian Scriptural interpretation (cf. Mt 5:43; 7:12; 19:19; 22:39; Mk 12:28-34; Lk 10:27).
108 Cf. Schnelle, *Die Johannesbriefe*, 163; Oda Wischmeyer, "Das Gebot der Nächstenliebe bei Paulus: Eine traditionsgeschichtliche Untersuchung," *Biblische Zeitschrift* 30, no. 2 (1986): 181.
109 Cf. Söding, *Das Liebesgebot bei Paulus*, 272.

human beings be determined by the dynamics of God's salvific activity."[110] Accordingly, the love of God, which has become manifest in a unique manner in Christ's death and resurrection, can find a correspondence in the command to love. Agape is, therefore, not so much of an instruction to be followed in daily life as it is a criterion through which the "authenticity of Christian conduct" is assured.[111] What follows is a dynamic interplay between both that could be put in these terms: on the one hand, the command to love cannot be reduced to moral instructions, as its theological quality stands on a higher level than morality; on the other hand, nevertheless, no instruction for Christian life can stand in disagreement with agape.[112]

A second question that has to be posed, considering the topic in question, concerns the status of agape in salvation or, as Paul prefers it, in justification before God: whether it just contributes towards a peaceful, friendly coexistence among the members of the community or whether agape, besides that, plays any role in God's salvific plan as well.

The key verse to this issue is, according to Söding, Gal 5:6.[113] The immediate context of this verse is Gal 5:1-11. Therein, Paul recapitulates his doctrine of justification, previously elucidated in Gal 2:16-4:31, and addresses the concrete issue of circumcision.[114] To be sure, faith (πίστις) is the core of this section, just as it was in 2:16, and is reiterated as the only means of justification (δικαιοσύνη) for believers. However, this justifying faith is defined a shade more precisely by Paul in Gal 5:6 and prepares for the insertion of the commandment to love in Gal 5:14b. The justifying faith is now defined as one "working through love," which amounts to saying that faith is *made effective* through the dynamic power of agape. Ἐνεργουμένη, being a participle in the present tense, indicates an ongoing action of the

---

110   Ibid.
111   Ibid.
112   Ibid., 273.
113   Cf. ibid., 197; already maintained by Oda Wischmeyer, *Der höchste Weg: das 13. Kapitel des 1. Korintherbriefes*, Studien zum Neuen Testament 13 (Gütersloh: Gütersloher Verlagshaus Mohn, 1981), 225.
114   Cf. Söding, *Das Liebesgebot bei Paulus*, 197.

verb ἐνεργέω, which means to be at work or operative, to bring about something, to accomplish, to be or become effective.

Yet this does not mean that agape owes its origin to the subject. In Pauline theology, agape is a "fruit of the Spirit" (Gal 5:22), as much as faith is a gift of God. Thus, love is presented here, also in accordance with Phil 1f. and 1Cor 13, "[...] as a manifestation of God's powerful grace aiming at the practice of the love of neighbor."[115] As a consequence, the absolute affirmation of God, through faith, entails assenting to his salvific will just as much. This consists in creating, already in the present time, an anticipation of God's final salvation, as it were, i.e., a correspondence between his justifying grace and the communicative, ecclesial and social dimensions implied by it.[116] Through agape, Christians can, therefore, already experience in this world, though in anticipation and imperfectly, what God's salvation is all about: a communion of the whole creation with him, in his glory, through Jesus Christ (cf. 1Cor 13:12; Rom 5:2).

Therefore, in the opinion of Oda Wischmeyer, agape can be defined as the mode of Christian existence. She asks herself, in her study on 1Cor 13, why Paul contrasts the spiritual charismata of the community of Corinth with an ethical value such as agape, instead of a spiritual one such as faith, for example. Similarly to Söding, she does not think that Paul's intention is to downplay the importance of faith through love. On the one hand, Paul has no doubts about the fact that faith is the only form of relationship with God that can attain salvation. On the other hand, he knows that one's relation to God does not cover the entirety of human existence. As pointed out above, just as in Gal 5:6 faith was said to be determined through agape, so too agape is presented, in 1Cor 13, as the determining value of the entirety of Christian existence. She goes so far as to say that πίστις (faith) is but "an expression of ἀγάπη" in one's relationship to God, and not the other way around.[117]

Interestingly enough, in his hymn to agape, in 1Cor 13, neither does Paul elevate ἀγάπη to the dignity of a divinity, as the Greeks

---

115   Ibid., 199.
116   Cf. ibid.
117   Wischmeyer, *Der höchste Weg*, 225.

did with ἔρως (eros), nor does he turn it into an instrument of God, as Jewish circles influenced by Hellenism did with the ideas of σοφία (wisdom) and ἀλήθεια (truth), by making them into hypostases. As deliberately opposed to those current forms of praise, Paul chooses to tie agape exclusively to human activity. In verses 4-7, love acquires such a significance that no other gift of the Spirit can be compared to it. For in these verses agape excels both all other known ethical virtues and all other spiritual gifts. Yet love does not assume any independent (hypostatic) existence.[118]

For believers who were acquainted with the early Jewish theological tradition,[119] it should not have been difficult to recognize in the qualities of agape, as described in verses 4-7, the attributes of God himself: for longanimity, goodness, not to rejoice at injustice etc. were traditional attributes of God.[120] Therefore, when faced with the attributes and implications of love, Christians are simultaneously confronted with God's very essence, attitude and way of acting. Given that agape is rooted in God himself, Christians are exhorted (*paraklesis*) to shape their own lives and to determine their own praxis as the body of Christ, which they were, from the logic and from the very dynamics of God.

Wischmeyer's second remark concerning agape's eschatological endurance provides an even deeper insight into the matter. She observes that Paul avoids, in this text, any reference to eschatological beliefs peculiar to early Christianity, as it is the case, for instance, in 1Cor 15 and 1Thess 4-5. Also apocalyptic motifs suddenly vanish without trace in this text. Neither is God mentioned, nor Jesus Christ. Paul appears to have opted for terms and images that were generally understood by everyone. In 1Cor 13, Paul's eschatology is, in the view of Wischmeyer, wittingly "reduced to the modest framework

---

118 Cf. ibid., 226.

119 Given that Paul's assertions about agape are the first written utterances on this topic in early Christianity, Paul did not have any other sources to draw on other than the LXX literature and other extrabiblical writings of Hellenistic-Roman Judaism (Wischmeyer, "Das Gebot der Nächstenliebe bei Paulus," 161).

120 Cf. Söding, *Das Liebesgebot bei Paulus*, 131.

of 'now – then, imperfectly, towards – perfection.'"[121] The focus is, thus, laid on the present time, on "here and now."

Moreover, while juxtaposing both times, the present and the future, and depicting love as the sole spiritual gift capable of enduring both, Paul also wants to challenge the knowledge (γνῶσις) of the Corinthians. He contrasts γνῶσις with ἐπίγνωσις (1Cor 13:12). While the former is the general word for knowledge and refers to cognition processes occurring in the present time (ἄρτι), the latter is said to be the perfect knowledge, i.e., the one which will be acquired "face to face" in the future time (τότε).[122] The actual and definitive knowledge of God has, therefore, less to do with the Corinthians' γνῶσις θεοῦ and more with the very structure of agape, inasmuch as it is the only spiritual gift that is consonant with the structure of the eschatological knowledge of God (ἐπίγνωσις). Even theologically, Paul does not regard love as greater than faith and hope because love is essentially different, but because love is the only spiritual gift that is able to *endure* the new conditions of the future time. After all, in the eschatological time, faith and hope won't be required any longer, since that which we now believe in and hope for will then be revealed face-to-face. But agape remains even in the eschatological time as the mode of (Christian) existence. What has begun here on earth tentatively and imperfectly is carried on and attains perfection in eternity. Hence, if Christians want to lead their lives in anticipation of the eschatological time, they must necessarily live, in the present time, in accordance with the dynamics of agape.

Nevertheless, though conceding that 1Cor 13 is "equivalent" to the synoptic love of neighbor and love of enemies commandments, one has to bear in mind that, in Paul's theology, agape "[…] is neither

---

121 Wischmeyer, *Der höchste Weg*, 226.

122 Ἐπίγνωσις may be translated as knowledge as well, but it implies more of a first-hand knowledge, one through direct contact with the person or thing, rather than obtained from others. Possible meanings of the verb ἐπιγινώσκω: to become thoroughly acquainted with, to know thoroughly; to know accurately, know well, to recognize, i.e., to know through external signs who or what someone or something is; to recognize a thing to be what it really is (cf. Thayer's *Greek-English Lexicon of the New Testament*).

a virtue, nor an inner attitude, nor a helping activity, nor an obligatory command, but, basically, an eschatological power. Fundamentally, it is the love of God manifested in Jesus Christ which, as such, determines the life of believers from its very roots."[123] Therefore, even though not explicitly put, agape is a theological and Christological dimension of Christian existence.[124] As such, it cannot be reduced to ethics alone. To define love as an eschatological power implies, rather, that "the love of God, manifested in Jesus Christ, determines the entire life of believers."[125]

At the same time, however, to subsume under the Christian idea of agape Jewish attitudes such as patience, hope, belief and a gentle relationship towards one's neighbor, which were traditionally regarded as belonging to the category of agape as well, does not seem inconsistent to Paul, precisely on account of such an existential component of love.[126] Again, in Paul's theology, agape is the only category capable of bridging the interplay between present and future time. To that extent, there is no contradiction. Likewise, even though Paul does not combine love of God and love of neighbor in just one command, as the synoptics do, there is no discrepancy between both approaches, given that the love of God is just presupposed by Paul. What he is not agreed upon, though, is to consider agape normatively from the perspective of this life, as a human-made command, so to speak. Instead, the ground on which he bases his whole argumentation is eschatology, a reality to which one has been given access through God's revelation in Jesus Christ and the gift of the Holy Spirit.

Now, being an eschatological reality, agape questions the very meaning of human existence, thereby possessing a critical potential. In fact, in the last analysis, 1Cor 13 is an attempt to answer fairly complex questions such as: What is worthwhile in this life? What really counts at the end of the day? What is really of use in this life? When Paul critically says that, having no love, one is nothing (1Cor 13:2), that being without love is of no use whatever (ὠφελοῦμαι, 1Cor

---

123 Söding, *Das Liebesgebot bei Paulus*, 130.
124 Cf. Wischmeyer, *Der höchste Weg*, 115.
125 Cf. Schnelle, *Die Johannesbriefe*, 162.
126 Cf. Söding, *Das Liebesgebot bei Paulus*, 131.

13:2), he thinks of one's existence as a whole standing before God's love at the end of one's earthly journey.

Finally, a brief consideration about Paul's combination of the Decalogue and the love of neighbor command in Rom 13:8-10 is required on account of its importance and originality in Pauline theology. Actually, the formulation of this pericope does not differ much from that of Gal 5:14 and serves as evidence for the coherence of Paul's theology, be it with regard to his ethics or to his soteriology.[127] Yet the combination of the Decalogue and the love of neighbor, as presented in Rom 13:8-10, represents something very peculiar and is worthy of consideration. Firstly, it should be noted that there is no discrepancy between this attempt of Paul and those of the synoptics as regards the (double) commandment to love. These may be compared to other similar attempts in Hellenistic Judaism, such as the "Testaments of the Twelve Patriarchs," Philo of Alexandria, Pseudo-Philo, to set a few fundamental attitudes of Hellenistic ethics beside (not in place of) the Torah's myriad of commands.[128]

On the other hand, Paul brings this latent tendency to a climax by summing up the whole Torah in just one commandment (Lev 19:18) that serves, in his theology, as the foundation for his ethics. This step itself would go, even for Philo, too far.[129] But Paul goes even further. The foundation of his new ethics is no longer something ordered by law, but "a reality, a gift of the πνεῦμα [spirit]," in a word: agape.[130] "Therefore, the love of neighbor is, basically, for Paul, the affirmation of the creative, justifying, and saving love that God bestows on him/her through Jesus Christ."[131]

Strictly speaking, human beings cannot love their neighbor themselves. It is always the love of the Spirit that operates through Jesus Christ in one's heart and one's actions alike. However peculiar it might sound, Paul *"abolishes the law through law itself."*[132] For

---

127 Cf. ibid., 255f.
128 Cf. Wischmeyer, "Das Gebot der Nächstenliebe bei Paulus," 181.
129 Cf. ibid., 183.
130 Ibid., 185.
131 Söding, *Das Liebesgebot bei Paulus*, 271.
132 Wischmeyer, "Das Gebot der Nächstenliebe bei Paulus," 182 (emphasis in original).

agape does not proceed from the law, neither can it be inferred from it, yet it fulfills the whole law. Its provenience from God guarantees that the "principle" of the law is fulfilled. At the same time, agape supersedes the law, as the law cannot demand of individuals what agape is capable of. Through the statement of Rom 13:8-10, Paul wants to dismiss, once and for all, the accusation that the exemption from law would give rise to "ethical indifference"[133] and to make it clear that shaping one's life through agape is a good deal more demanding than through law.

As a result, one could say that Paul's agape theology offers a profound reflection on Christian ethics, informed by his theological belief. In his theology there is an essential connection between agape and faith, and, by extension, between love and salvation, insofar as faith is always (working) through love. Love is the most visible sign of the accordance of one's life with God's, which was made visible in Christ.

In the letter to the Galatians, the "purpose" of the command to love, as understood by Paul, is to ensure that very freedom which Christians have gained through Jesus Christ (cf. Gal 5:1,13). And agape consists, for Paul, in serving one another. The consequences of this thought are, basically, two. First, freedom can only be granted, never achieved. If achieved alone through one's own initiative, it goes more often than not allied with force and violence. Second, once one is granted freedom, once one is set free, the only way to preserve it is by serving, rather than fulfilling one's own desires, wishes and, ultimately, one's own will. Strange as it may sound, one can only preserve one's own freedom as long as one serves others.

On a socio-analytical plane the alternative which Paul seems to have found was that freedom, be it personal, social or political, can in effect become a reality only insofar as one becomes "independent" of the established socio-political structures and, inspired by the power and dynamics of the Spirit acting within oneself, begins a new reality – not through fighting, but through something essentially new.[134] This is, in other words, the essence of the ἐκκλησία (church).

---

133 Cf. Söding, *Das Liebesgebot bei Paulus*, 258.
134 As for this aspect, it is striking to notice how much Paul has been received

The principle that underlies the idea of the Pauline ἐκκλησία is that those who have been called (or chosen) by God through faith in Christ are now encouraged to begin a new life grounded in the Spirit. It is no longer they who live, but the love which has been poured out by the Spirit in their hearts. If faith and love really go hand in hand, as Gal 5:6 attests to, "[...] it becomes clear that God's election not only reveals a new understanding to one's existence, but it grounds, at the same time, a human *koinonia*, whose historical form is to be found in the Ekklesia."[135] The beginning of the church is the beginning of a new reality on earth, a reality which is originated and sustained by agape.

Outcome

This chapter set out to examine in more detail the close relation between the commandment to love and salvation. Even though special attention has been devoted to Lk 10:25-37, "Luke's own version" of the twofold commandment to love, which is understood by him as a condition to "inherit eternal life," has proved not to be an isolated case. Further references to the other synoptic gospels as well as to John and Paul have shown that such a view is congruous with Jesus' message and sustainable within Christian tradition.

The first important result of this chapter was that the claim implied in the typology, exclusivism, inclusivism and pluralism that all salvation is mediated exclusively through Jesus Christ ought to be assessed at best as problematic. In fact, the problem of mediation of salvation accompanies Christianity from its very beginning. According to Luke, salvation is neither something to be awaited nor something that can be ensured, which one can be sure of. Salvation is to be equated with events, happenings. They have concrete faces,

---

and rediscovered, nowadays, among prominent intellectuals such as G. Agamben, S. Žižek, A. Badiou, etc. For an overview, see Dominik Finkelde, *Politische Eschatologie nach Paulus: Badiou – Agamben – Žižek – Santner* (Wien: Turia + Kant, 2007).
135 Söding, *Das Liebesgebot bei Paulus*, 271.

backgrounds, agents, own histories. Faith in Jesus Christ is to be followed by concrete deeds, too, and in a spirit of humility (cf. Lk 6:46-49; 13:22-30; 18:9-14; Mt 7:21-23).

Second, the inextricable connection between salvation and concrete deeds is another central feature, controversial as this issue is. A closer study of Lukan special material has demonstrated how important that was in early (Jewish) Christianity. In God's salvation plan his gratuitous salvation can also be mediated by human beings who allow themselves to be led by the Holy Spirit and follow in the footsteps of Jesus. Luke does not see any boundaries for the action of the Spirit.

As seen above, there is a clear consensus in the synoptic tradition in presenting the double love commandment as being normative for Christians. However, no further theological elucidation is found in those gospels, except for Luke, to some extent. In his later writings, however, Paul sets out to go deeper into the question of agape, which he describes as the "eschatological mode of Christian existence." Besides liberating agape from the captivity of the realm of ethics, Paul succeeds, thereby, in spelling out how normativity and heteronomy are not as foreign to each other and to human subjectivity as it is often assumed. Since the disciples of Christ make room in themselves for the activity of the Holy Spirit and allow themselves to be transformed by his power, the normative attitude of agape springs from within, rather than from rules of the outside, and transforms the person herself and the context in which she lives and acts. Thus, love determines one's existence in this aeon and withstands the changes of the future one, in eternity, in the face of God. Furthermore, because, for Paul, love is inextricably linked to faith, the relation between love and salvation can be inferred from Paul's writings, too, which endorses the thesis of this chapter.

What still remains unclear is to which extent the formulation of the double love commandment was influenced by the Hellenistic background and by some attempts, in Greek philosophy, to grasp human agency in terms of virtues such as reverence and piety (εὐσέβεια and ὁσιότης), in one's relation to God, or benevolence and justice (φιλανθρωπία and δικαιοσύνη), in one's relation to other human beings. However, there can be no doubt that Jesus' message offers decisive elements to rethink not only modern issues such as human agency in a plural world, secularity, interreligious dialogue etc., but even the Christian concept of salvation. It may help Christians to shift from a paradigm of personal salvation to one of universal salvation whereby one is not concerned with one's own salvation, but fully committed to that of others, to that of the whole world, however overwhelming such a concern may feel.

6

The Notion of Love as a Corrective Ideal to the Concept of Salvation?

The previous chapters have shown the pivotal significance of agape both in the New Testament literature and in the life of (early) Christians. Moreover, the detailed examination of Lk 10:25-37 conducted above, including parallel texts and similar approaches in the New Testament, has suggested a close relation between the Christian concepts of agape and salvation. One does not have to be an expert in soteriology to assess the exegetical inconsistencies, historical controversies and theological difficulties of such an approach. For how is it possible to reconcile God's threatening judgment, which is described in various ways in the gospels, with God's unconditional love, as it is described, for instance, in the book of the prophet Hosea or in the parable of the merciful father (Lk 15:11-32)? However beautiful and moving the aspects of love and mercy may be in the context of God's salvation, one is left with the impression that, at least on a rational level, something is not quite right or that such an approach is somehow "unjust."

Therefore, let us dwell for a while more on this intricate relation, for the relation between love, salvation and justice must be explained in more detail and the apparent contradictions tackled. But before engaging in systematic reflection, my proposal is to remain awhile on the biblical level. I suggest taking a look at the Scripture as a whole once more, bearing in mind this specific predicament. Our task, in this chapter, is to verify the validity of the results of the previous chapters in the face of the Scripture in its entirety.

Salvation in the Context of God's Threatening Judgment

In the opinion of the Catholic theologian Raymond Schwager, one of the most challenging tasks of any soteriological theology is to demonstrate a plausible congruence between different affirmations about God, as handed down in the Scripture, with a particular focus on the apparent discontinuity between God's wrath and mercy.[1] So, the solution which many have found to that was to depict the God of the Old Testament as a just, merciless and revengeful judge, and the God of the New Testament as a good, compassionate and merciful father. Marcion of Sinope (circa 85 to circa 160 CE) was the first theologian to create such an antagonism that perpetuates to the present day in different fashions.[2] Notwithstanding the early church's condemnation of such a view from its outset, this appears to continue being a tempting approach.

The fundamental issue at stake here is, first and foremost, how to come to terms with both the possibility of God forgiving his chosen people despite their transgressions and their unfaithfulness to the covenant and with the meaning of the prophetic threatenings of a final judgment addressed to the entire people of Israel. Secondly, it concerns the question of the historical victims of injustice.[3] Finally, it touches upon the question whether one can be really sure that it is worth doing good and that the wicked won't go unpunished.[4]

---

1 Cf. Raymund Schwager, *Jesus im Heilsdrama: Entwurf einer biblischen Erlösungslehre*, Innsbrucker theologische Studien 29 (Innsbruck; Wien: Tyrolia, 1990), 12–22.
2 Cf. Bernd Janowski, "Der barmherzige Richter: Zur Einheit von Gerechtigkeit und Barmherzigkeit im Gottesbild des Alten Orients und des Alten Testaments," in *Der Gott des Lebens*, ed. Bernd Janowski (Neukirchen-Vluyn: Neukirchener, 2003), 76; Dirk Ansorge, *Gerechtigkeit und Barmherzigkeit Gottes: die Dramatik von Vergebung und Versöhnung in bibeltheologischer, theologiegeschichtlicher und philosophiegeschichtlicher Perspektive* (Freiburg im Breisgau; Basel; Wien: Herder, 2009), 124; for a more recent typology, see also Knut Wenzel, "Liebe als Gerechtigkeit: Zu einem Kernaspekt des christlichen Gottesverständnisses," in *Prekär: Gottes Gerechtigkeit und die Moral der Menschen*, ed. Klaus Bieberstein and Hanspeter Schmitt (Luzern: Exodus, 2008), 150.
3 See especially Ansorge, *Gerechtigkeit und Barmherzigkeit Gottes*.
4 Cf. Jan Assmann, Bernd Janowski, and Michael Welker, "Richten und Retten:

The complexity of those questions, allied with the immensity of approaches to them throughout history, are sufficient grounds for not going into minor details on it, lest the principal question may be lost sight of. Let it suffice to present one of those theories that appears to offer a convincing answer to this predicament. Basically, this theory proposed by Assmann, Janowski and Welker avails itself of the ancient Near Eastern notion of a "saving justice." To put it in a nutshell, it implies that "the deity or the King, insofar as he is a representative of hers [the deity], saves *by* judging."[5] According to that view, to judge – conceived of as punishing wrongdoings and penalizing the wicked – and to save are not seen as two actions conflicting with each other but correlative.

To start with, one has to bear in mind that the semantic field of the Hebrew words צֶדֶק and צְדָקָה (*ṣedeq-ṣĕdāqâ* = justice, righteousness, righteous etc.), when applied to God, is intimately related to the שָׁלוֹם (*šālôm* = well-being, prosperity) of the people, especially in the Psalms and Isaiah 40-66.[6] As Janowski puts it, community and justice are "two sides of the same coin," insofar as the Jewish notion of justice entails the religious, socio-political and anthropological dimensions of the community.[7] Furthermore, just as important as the collective dimension of salvation is God's "[...] saving action toward the people of Israel and the helpless individual – the poor, the oppressed, the widow, the orphan."[8] Both aspects may sound strange to the ears of individuals acquainted with the modern juridical system. Nevertheless, albeit forgotten or unknown, these are essential features of the Old Testamental idea of justice and provide, thus, a helpful clue to tackle the three main questions put at the beginning of this section.

Zur Aktualität der altorientalischen und biblischen Gerechtigkeitskonzeption," in *Die rettende Gerechtigkeit*, ed. Bernd Janowski (Neukirchen-Vluyn: Neukirchener, 1999), 221.

5   Ibid. (emphasis in original).
6   Cf. John J. Scullion, "Righteousness (OT)," *The Anchor Bible Dictionary* (New York: Doubleday, 1992), 735.
7   Assmann, Janowski, and Welker, "Richten und Retten," 232.
8   Scullion, "Righteousness (OT)," 726.

It follows that the Jewish notion of justice strongly implies any action in the cause of the community or as a sign of one's loyalty towards it, be it on the part of the Lord, as the original source of justice; be it on the part of the king, as a mediator of God's justice; be it on the part of the individual, as the receiver of and the collaborator with God's justice, especially in the case of the poor and the oppressed.[9] Viewed from this perspective, God's actions to restore justice are to be understood within a framework in which justice should be done to the oppressed and to the righteous in view of all the questions and challenges posed to them by the wicked. Precisely when this is prayed for in the psalms, it should not be confused with self-righteousness. Instead, it has more to do with a sort of legal aid that is asked for, especially in distress situations.[10] Being so, not only is the issue of the victims given attention, but also the importance of every individual practicing justice in his/her own life, not for one's own sake, but for that of the community.

Interestingly enough, the cry of the oppressed and the individual ethics of solidarity are very close related. Ansorge observes that, whereas sinners hope for God's mercy, the victims of history hope, in their helplessness, for God's solidarity towards them. Their hope is that God will prove himself mightier than the oppressors in order to overcome injustice and violence. Towards that end, prophetic voices often criticize the established order and even official rules. It is precisely at this juncture that a sort of subtle gap between right or righteousness (*Recht*) and justice or uprightness (*Gerechtigkeit*) should be given attention in order to understand what is at stake here. Whereas the former has to do with one's (the king's) fairness in upholding the law or the rules in vigor, the latter concerns the integrity of heart or the good sense with which one (the king) enforces it. But it is precisely from this gap between righteousness and God's justice that a new ethos of solidarity could emerge.[11] As was seen above, in the

---

9 Assmann, Janowski, and Welker, "Richten und Retten," 232, with the idea of the individual as a "collaborator" with God being an addition of mine to the original thought.

10 See especially Ps 7; 72; 82; cf. ibid., 237.

11 Cf. Ansorge, *Gerechtigkeit und Barmherzigkeit Gottes*, 76.

book of the prophet Hosea, the struggle between love and wrath begins in the very heart of God himself, whose attitude and behavior furnishes the key to understanding the whole issue. In the words of Hosea, it is God who finds himself caught in a dilemma in the face of Israel's unfaithfulness.[12] Yet, in consequence of his love, God cannot simply give up his people or blindly act as he might be expected to in face of Israel's faults and transgressions (cf. Hos 11:8f.). God cannot just enforce what appears to be "rightful and logical."

This new ethics is, in the Old Testament, theologically grounded and serves as basis for both moral responsibility and moral individuality. This is the foundation on which prophetic figures such as Elijah, Nathan etc. justify their criticism against the kings' rule. As a result of the dissociation of the practice of justice exclusively from the figure of the king, an individual and universal ethos comes into being. "Since God is just and merciful, no one can escape the task of practicing oneself mercy and justice."[13] This ethos is individual and universal alike.

Bearing this in mind, the result which Ansorge reaches in his survey of the Old Testamental texts is that the supposed contradiction between God's mercifulness and righteousness does not apply. The affirmations of God's (revengeful) righteousness are always the natural consequence of the hope for God's solidarity with the victims. With good reasons, therefore, he affirms that "God's justice is but a moment of his mercifulness."[14] Being so, the supposed discrepancies within the Old Testament, as mentioned above, as well as false comparisons with the New Testament along with tendentious conclusions drawn from it can be dismissed, at least for the most part.

This applies equally to the purported discontinuity between Old and New Testament. To be sure, both contain a large number of passages that are problematic and conflicting with each other, whose divergences may never be resolved. However, giving up the Old Testament for the sake of the "Christian" faith in Jesus Christ seems to betray Jesus' own faith in the God of Israel and his message as

---

12   Cf. Janowski, "Der barmherzige Richter," 119f.
13   Ansorge, *Gerechtigkeit und Barmherzigkeit Gottes*, 81.
14   Ibid., 138.

well.[15] Misusing Jesus on the pretext of denying God's revelation in the Tanakh or setting his love above or against the love of the God of Israel would not do justice to the person and message of Jesus.[16]

Moreover, the Jesus-event, as believed in and interpreted in the New Testament, would be incomprehensible without the background of the Old Testament. When, for instance, Jesus is referred to as a king or ascribed the role of mediator of God's justice, one has to firstly keep in mind what God's justice consists in; secondly, what the figure of the king meant and symbolized to the people of Israel; and, thirdly, what the role of a mediator is about. If Jesus' life, message, death and resurrection are to be believed in as God's revelation, it is rather because Jesus in fact lived out the faith of Israel, because he set himself the task of (re)gathering the entire people of Israel, because he himself took up the cause of the poor and the outcasts, because he himself prayed as a Jew with the words of Psalm 22 in the midst of his most acute distress on the cross: "My God, my God, why have you forsaken me?" (Mk 15:34; Mt 27:46). Such a prayer can be seen in the same way as the request of Psalm 7 in which the psalmist asks God to do justice to him. To do justice means, in this case, to endorse all one has believed in, practiced and lived out in one's lifetime. Moreover, given the fact that Jesus was a victim of violence himself and died as Jew, praying as a Jew, believing in the God of his religious tradition, hoping for his justice in the face of the violence inflicted upon him, and given the fact that the holy authors interpreted Jesus' fate in the light of the Jewish Old Testamental tradition, there are no compelling reasons to cast doubt on the congruence between these both Testaments.

---

15 In recent years, the controversial essay by the Protestant theologian Slenczka sparked off, in Germany, a heated debate on this issue (cf. Notger Slenczka, "Die Kirche und das Alte Testament," in *Das Alte Testament in der Theologie*, ed. Elisabeth Gräb-Schmidt, Marburger Jahrbuch Theologie 25 [Leipzig: Evangelische Verlagsanstalt, 2013], 83–119).

16 Cf. Bernd Janowski, "Der eine Gott der beiden Testamente: Grundfragen einer biblischen Theologie," in *Die rettende Gerechtigkeit*, ed. Bernd Janowski (Neukirchen-Vluyn: Neukirchener, 1999), 282.

Love Alone Can Break the Cycle of Violence

Bearing in mind what has been said so far with respect to the relation between mercy and justice, one can note that a conception of God as love is by no means something completely new in the history of Israel or even peculiar to the New Testament. The "gap" between law (right/legislation) and justice is not simply known in the Ancient Near East, but rests on the very foundation of the Jewish ancient covenantal theology.[17] Accordingly, the person or institution of the ruler was invested with due sovereign power in order to "*guarantee peace and order*" within his jurisdictional territory.[18] By taking the examples of Ancient Egypt and Mesopotamia, it becomes evident that the particular prescriptions contained in their respective conduct codes were not sufficient to ensure the overall welfare of those societies.[19] The existence of derogations from the ordinary rule, which used to take place in their annual feasts, and the granting of amnesties for the transgression of the established rules, in determined cases, serve as evidence to that. Bearing that in mind, it could be said that a just king was not the one who mercilessly enforced each and every prescription of law, but the one who could weigh and discern in the face of the overall well-being of his subjects the one who was able, under certain circumstances, to grant amnesties, economical abatements and acts of grace.[20]

One of the peculiarities of the Old Testament is that such sovereignty above justice is attributed to God alone, rather than to the kings of Israel. It is precisely this theological turn in the conception of justice that gives authority to the prophets to criticize and even oppose the kings "in the name of God," in order to implement God's own justice. The kings of Israel did not possess the freedom to decide whether or not they should promote solidarity, benevolence and social justice. On the contrary, since the only one valid measure for

---

17 Cf. Ansorge, *Gerechtigkeit und Barmherzigkeit Gottes*, 77.
18 Ibid., 78 (emphasis added).
19 For further details on it, see Jan Assmann, *Herrschaft und Heil: politische Theologie in Altägypten, Israel und Europa* (München: C. Hanser, 2000).
20 Cf. Ansorge, *Gerechtigkeit und Barmherzigkeit Gottes*, 78.

justice is that of God the Lord, the kings were obliged to follow it. In the view of the exegete Eckart Otto, the fulfillment of that duty can be particularly seen in the king's commitment towards the most needy and weak of his society. As a consequence, God's solidarity and mercifulness become the solid foundation on which the Jewish ethics of solidarity and mercifulness rest.[21]

As a result, one can say with Ricoeur that, if assumed that the aim of any organized society or ruling system is to attain "states of peace" and harmony among its members, justice "fails the test," as it "[...] does not exhaust the question of putting an end to the dispute begun by violence and reopened by vengeance."[22] By contrast, the idea of equivalence, inherent in the principle of justice, appears to be "the seed of new conflicts." The vicious cycle of hatred and vengeance cannot be broken by means of the justice of the law. Feasts such as Yom Kippur are evidence for that. Forgiveness, which is a consequence of love, is just as hypermoral as love. As a consequence, they cannot be commanded nor can they pertain to the ordinary legal procedures of any given society.[23] The concept of love can only function as a corrective to the principle of justice.[24]

---

21 See especially Ex 22:20-26 (Eckart Otto, *Theologische Ethik des Alten Testaments*, Theologische Wissenschaft, 3,2 [Stuttgart: Kohlhammer, 1994], 84f.; see also Ansorge, *Gerechtigkeit und Barmherzigkeit Gottes*, 81).

22 Paul Ricoeur, *The Course of Recognition*, trans. David Pellauer (Cambridge, Massachusetts: Harvard University Press, 2005), 220.

23 See especially Paul Ricoeur, *Memory, History, Forgetting* (Chicago: University of Chicago Press, 2004), 452–56; Knut Wenzel, *Glaube in Vermittlung: theologische Hermeneutik nach Paul Ricoeur* (Freiburg im Breisgau; Basel; Wien: Herder, 2008), 253–55.

24 See especially Paul Ricoeur, "Love and Justice," in *Paul Ricoeur: The Hermeneutics of Action*, ed. Richard Kearney, trans. David Pellauer (London; Thousand Oaks; New Delhi: Sage Publications, 1996), 23–39.

The New Testament Notion of Agape

In his theory of early Christianity, Gerd Theißen puts out that the commandment of love was the principal element of Christian ethics. It enabled the mission among pagans, the spreading of Christianity, and the possibility of living together in communities amidst a plurality of religions and cultures. "Early Christian love wanted to overcome those barriers [existing among different groups]."[25] Besides that, there was very high aspiration to overcome the oriental ethics of mercy, which is at the basis of Lev 19:18,34 and amounts to helping the poor, the widow and the orphan. In the message of Jesus, there is a clear awareness that the borders of love of neighbor are firstly to be expanded towards three major marginalized groups: a) the enemies (not only personal, but also enemy groups like the dominant class, the Romans, etc. – cf. Lk 6:27; Mt 5:43); b) towards the foreign (cf. Lk 10:25-37); c) towards the sinner (cf. Lk 7:36-50). Finally, since the second core value of early Christian ethics was the renunciation of status whatsoever, the standard of agape was so high as to demand of Christians to overcome any kind of hierarchical barrier within their communities (see esp. Jn 13:1-15).[26]

---

25   Gerd Theißen, *Die Religion der ersten Christen: Eine Theorie des Urchristentums*, 3rd ed. (Gütersloh: Kaiser, 2003), 102; see also Philip F. Esler, "Jesus and the Reduction of Intergroup Conflict: The Parable of the Good Samaritan in the Light of Social Identity Theory," *Biblical Interpretation* 8, no. 4 (2000): 325–57. In this article, Esler analyzes not only the intergroup conflicts of Jesus' time but also draws consequences from Jesus' message for the solving of contemporary problems of that nature.

26   Cf. Theißen, *Die Religion der ersten Christen*, 103–6. Now, while this is the connotation of agape which can be inferred from the synoptic gospels, texts like the letters of Paul and the Pauline literature may diverge considerably from them. In the letters of Paul there is a substantial move from encouraging love towards everyone (in 1Thess 3:12) to the exhortation to love especially the brothers and sisters in faith (Gal 6:10; Rom 12:9-12). This approach is even more radical in the Johannine literature, especially on account of the strong dualism between world and faith community (cf. 1Jn 2:10; Jn 13:35; Jn 3:16). Accordingly, in those writings, the focus of the commandment to love is rather limited to the Johannine community (cf. ibid., 108).

Theißen goes even so far as to say that the very symbolic language contained in the symbols, rites, parables and expressions of early Christianity contributed largely to the overcoming of the spiral of violence as well as to the integration of aggression in the lives of individuals and society alike. In such a vision, the commandment to love definitely played a decisive role, but, alongside it, also the innumerable exhortations for the renunciation of any kind of violence, aggression, revenge etc. A closer psycho-sociological look at texts like Lk 3:9; 19:27; Mt 25:46; 8:12; 13:42, which at first glance might shock because of their cruel images, may interpret them as a means of addressing those areas of human life. The crucial point here is to note that there is an awareness that judgment and punishment are reserved for God alone. As for us, "we are useless servants: we have done no more than our duty" (cf. Lk 17:10).[27]

In the last decades, the New Testamental agape model of love has been frequently criticized for demanding of human beings too much selflessness and altruism. Moreover, since its very principle is to give without expecting anything in return, it also entails a lack of reciprocity, which constitutes an essential element of love, too.[28] This is particularly manifest in the form of love of enemy, which indeed overwhelms the subject with too high expectations. On the other hand, the agape model of love did allow a new ethical development, especially in contrast with both the Platonic eros-model, based on loss of and separation from the object of love, and the oriental ethics of mercy, based exclusively on material aid.

Since, in the synoptic gospels, the focus of the present investigation, nothing explicitly is said about God's love,[29] as it is the case in the letters of John or other writings of the New Testament, this

---

27 Cf. Gerd Theißen, *Die Jesusbewegung: Sozialgeschichte einer Revolution der Werte* (Gütersloh: Gütersloher Verlagshaus, 2004), 269–89.

28 See, for example, Angelika Krebs, "Liebe," ed. Petra Kolmer and Armin G. Wildfeuer, *Neues Handbuch philosophischer Grundbegriffe* (Freiburg im Breisgau: Karl Alber, 2011), 1473.

29 William Klassen, "Love (NT and Early Jewish)," ed. David Noel Freedman, *The Anchor Bible Dictionary* (New York: Doubleday, 1992), 385.

section shall remain limited to the human dimension of agape (love of neighbor and love of enemy).[30]

Beyond Ethics

For the exegete Schnelle, the commandment to love, considered in its threefold form, namely, as love of neighbor (cf. Mt 5:43), as love of enemies (cf. Mt 5:44) and as twofold commandment to love (cf. Mk 12:28-34), "constitutes the core of Jesus' ethics."[31] If that is the case, the first important question to devote attention to is whether such a radical demand can at all be commanded, that is, whether it falls into the realm of ethics or not.

In the view of Kierkegaard, the commandment to love must necessarily remain a command in order to remain protected against any change. For if love is left up to the individual's choice, if love remains spontaneous, it is no longer secure. "Consequently, *only when it is a duty to love, only then is love eternally secure*. This security of the eternal casts out all anxiety and makes the love perfect, perfectly secure."[32] This is for him the only way to keep faithful to God's command and to one's duty vis-a-vis one's neighbor.

Also Schillebeeckx sees a connection between ethics and religion, even though the latter cannot be limited to the former and even though he would not see love as a command as Kierkegaard did. Christian ethics, as ethics, does not "add" anything special to an "autonomous morality" oriented towards the human being and his/her dignity. For him, the crucial difference between those two is that Christian ethics is prompted by a spirituality based on the theological virtues of faith, hope

---

30 For more details about the commandment to love, see chapter 5.

31 Udo Schnelle, *Die Johannesbriefe*, Theologischer Handkommentar zum Neuen Testament 17 (Leipzig: Evangelische Verlagsanstalt, 2010), 162; see also Udo Schnelle, *Theologie des Neuen Testaments* (Stuttgart: Vandenhoeck & Ruprecht, 2007), 101–4.

32 Søren Kierkegaard, *Works of Love: Some Christian Reflections in the Form of Discourses*, trans. Howard and Edna Hong (New York: Harper and Row, 1962), 47 (emphasis in original).

and charity. If ethics is not based in those virtues, one is indeed overwhelmed with "excessive demands" and one's ethics tends to become *merci-less*. As a consequence, "[...] there is [no] ethics without the element of love which brings happiness, in which love of God and human love are one and the same indivisible basic attitude or virtue."[33] For Schillebeeckx, therefore, it is impossible to think of any Christian ethics that is not based on "theologal life" as a response of Christians to something which is prior to any moral act, a response to God's grace. The main difference from Kierkegaard's view seems to be that love is not thought of purely as an ethical category, but as a condition of possibility for truly Christian ethics. Therefore, "[...] from the Christian perspective the starting point of this ethic [*sic*] is not (unliberated) universal 'moral reason' (which often works to the detriment of the 'little ones'), but belief in God, which leads to the historical enterprise of the praxis of human liberation and provokes reflection."[34]

The question arises whether "secular ethics" or any moral approach which is not sustained by such a spirituality can serve as a means of salvation. Rahner's answer to that question is a negative one. Since ethics is not sufficient to attain salvation, even secular people, atheists or non-Christians need what he calls "anonymous faith."[35] Such "anonymous faith" is characterized by every person's search for self-transcendence, meaning and purpose in life. That search is referred to by Rahner as a "searching Christology," pursued by every human being whether one is aware of it or not. This searching Christology finds expression in the way one deals with three essential dimensions of one's life: the practice of the absolute love of neighbor, the readiness for death and the hope for the future, which, in turn, are respectively related to the explicit faith in Jesus' life, death and resurrection.[36] Those three dimensions of life or "appeals,"

---

33 Edward Schillebeeckx, *Church: The Human Story of God*, The Collected Works of Edward Schillebeeckx 10 (London: Bloomsbury, 2014), 31.

34 Ibid., 30.

35 Cf. Karl Rahner, "Anonymer und expliziter Glaube," in *Schriften zur Theologie*, vol. 12 (Zürich; Einsiedeln; Köln: Benziger, 1975), 76f.

36 For a brief overview on it, see Ekkehard Wohlleben, *Die Kirchen und die Religionen: Perspektiven einer ökumenischen Religionstheologie* (Göttingen: Vandenhoeck & Ruprecht, 2004), 95–99; Pamela Dickey Young, "Rahner's Searching

as Rahner calls them, have much in common with Schillebeeckx's suggestion of the theological virtues, which makes both theories compatible with each other. Obviously, what they both suggest has unquestionable points of contact with several ethical issues. Nevertheless, they substantially transcend ethical life.

Still, there are approaches nowadays, even in moral theology, in which moral life is grounded in the power of the notion of love. However, interestingly enough, to be able to serve that purpose, love must be divested of a merely juridical, normative character and be rather conceived of as an attitude or something to that effect. In his attempt to do so, Kirchschläger argues that, even if love constitutes the foundation of Christian ethics, this is not to be understood in terms of a command given "externally" by God. Instead, the responsibility for one's neighbor and for the world begins to be "shared" with God by human beings as early as in the act of their creation in his image and likeness, so that one can speak of a "dialogic responsibility" between God and human beings.[37] Viewed from that stance, the double commandment to love is conceived of as being embedded in a relationship between God and man and should be construed in terms of cultivating that relationship, rather than in juridical ones.

What seems to be common to the approaches mentioned here is that there is in fact a very close link between ethics, salvation and love. However, ethics cannot by itself generate either of the others. Rather, it is the other way round that must be pursued. For one can do charity out of genuine love and compassion, another to obtain tax advantages and a third one may perform it with contempt and disdain for the person in need. In all three cases an ethical deed towards someone in need of help has been performed and has its own value, although the inner attitude differs from case to case. Thus, what qualifies an act as just, good or righteous is not alone its performance or the observance of law. Furthermore, the crucial element to discern it seems to lie beyond ethical codes of conduct or even a so-called universal moral reason.

Christology," *New Blackfriars* 68, no. 809 (1987): 437–43.
37 Peter G. Kirchschläger, "Nächstenliebe – das Leitprinzip christlicher Moraltheologie," *Zeitschrift für katholische Theologie* 137, no. 2 (2015): 191.

As against the approach of Enlightenment or liberal theologies to this respect, whose aim was indeed to reduce religious life to ethics, the position defended here is that Jesus' primary concern in his preaching was not to suggest an ethical code of conduct, but to address an issue that transcends it and has more to do with one's inner attitude than with one's outer deeds, though both are intimately related. In the synoptic gospels, this aspect finds expression in the discourse of love (agape).

No Love without Justice

One of the biggest challenges of any theology of love in the present times is, undoubtedly, to do justice to it as a philosophical and theological concept in the face of its long history, but particularly considering the plurality of possibilities of interpreting it. Not rarely, misleading or very partial views on love may make such a task all the more difficult. Also the French philosopher Paul Ricoeur asks himself at the beginning of his essay "Love and Justice" whether it is at all possible to talk about love without either simply exalting it as something extremely ideal or "falling into sentimental platitudes." The way he suggests in order to accomplish that task "with justice" is to approach love by considering its dialectical relation to justice.[38] What he means by dialectics is, on the one hand, the "initial disproportionality" between both terms and, on the other hand, the "search for practical mediation between them." Ricoeur misses such kinds of dialectical approach in ethicists, theologians or philosophers who, by means of the method of conceptual analysis (analytic philosophy), claim to be able to extract from concepts, irrespective of circumstances of any sort, their "normative contents."[39]

Obviously, love and justice have different logics (the logic of superabundance and that of equivalence) and both are part, in one way or the other, of daily life. Ricoeur does not argue for the

---

38   Ricoeur, "Love and Justice," 23.
39   As an example for that kind of approach, Ricoeur takes the work by Gene Outka, *Agape: An Ethical Analysis* (New Haven; London: Yale University Press, 1972).

prevalence of either of them or for the suppression of the one at the expense of the other. Rather, the point he makes in his essay is that "justice [is] the necessary medium of love; precisely because love is hypermoral, it enters the practical and ethical sphere only under the aegis of justice."[40]

Although both love and justice are frequently employed as attributes to God, when both words are put next to each other, many aporias begin to arise. This becomes particularly patent in the question of theodicy, for instance, albeit not exclusively. A way out of that impasse has been found, at times, by means of typologizations in which both are presented over against each other, similarly to the oppositions between God's mercy and righteousness seen above. Wenzel takes as an example the theory of the German philosopher and literary critic Friedrich Schlegel which portrays Judaism as "a religion of Law" as well as a preparation for Christianity, which is "the religion of love."[41] From that perspective, love and justice could even exist independent of each other or deny each other, which does not seem to be in accordance with biblical and traditional Christian understanding.

Therefore, in an endeavor to do justice to both concepts within Christian tradition, Wenzel comes up with the idea of unconditional recognition. He considers it as the common structure to both love and justice. Accordingly, Christian love can only take place *asymmetrically*. A lover cannot demand from the other (the beloved) anything in return. If any condition is set out, love ceases being free. Secondly, love ought to be free from any sort of apparency, feeling, etc. That is the reason why the New Testament attests to a sort of resistance to the semantically similar Greek words ἔρως (eros) and φιλία (philia). In contrast with these, αγάπη (agape) would be more of a "sober" and "demanding" love,[42] since it is not based on affinities, tastes, feelings or preferences. Every other should be recognized as he/she is, irrespective of race, color, gender, nationality etc. If the Jesuanic

---

40   Ricoeur, "Love and Justice," 36f.
41   Friedrich Schlegel, *Von der wahren Liebe Gottes und dem falschen Mystizismus [1819]*, Kritische Friedrich-Schlegel-Ausgabe, VIII (Paderborn; Zürich, 1975), 529–45, apud Wenzel, "Liebe als Gerechtigkeit," 150.
42   Cf. Wenzel, "Liebe als Gerechtigkeit," 152f.

message of the love of enemies is brought to the discussion, such asymmetry becomes all the more transparent.[43] In this case, there is no reciprocity (symmetry) whatsoever. Moreover, love of enemies poses such an enormous challenge to (distributive) justice as to be considered silly, a case of nonsense.

Now, if one is willing to put love into practice, if one wants to love somebody else, one does it, in order to *do justice* to the other.[44] This is the junction where love and justice meet. The asymmetry of love implies that every human being is worthy of love and recognition. While the philosophical basis for that could be the categorical imperative, the theological one is the biblical belief in the likeness of God.[45] Accordingly, because every person has been created in the image and likeness of God, if justice is to be done to this kind of relation among human beings, one has to recognize every other person as bearer of such dignity and worthy of unconditional love. For to love someone means saying to him/her without reserves: "I want you to exist, […] I want you to be yourself, as you are."[46]

However, despite their common denominator, love and justice are not the same. They pursue different goals. Whereas such an unconditional recognition can only be realized within the sphere of love, it is because of the notion of justice that concrete and material deeds may render the concern to do justice to others visible.[47] Hence the necessity of combining both complementarily: "Justice alone cannot afford to point up the unconditional reasons for the dynamics of recognition inherent to itself and needs, for that purpose, love. Love, on the other hand, runs the risk of becoming non-committed if it is not put into practice through deeds whose purpose is to do justice to the other."[48] In the words of Pröpper, "[…] justice without love is bound to remain outward, and love without justice would be untruthful."[49]

---

43 Cf. ibid., 154.
44 Cf. ibid., 155.
45 Cf. ibid.
46 Cf. ibid., 157.
47 Cf. ibid., 155.
48 Ibid.
49 Thomas Pröpper, *Evangelium und freie Vernunft: Konturen einer theologischen*

For Paul Tillich, the close relation between love and justice occurs on the ontological level. He himself acknowledges that it is very hard for us today to grasp what the Latin *esse-ipsum* (being-itself) and the Greek ὄν ἦ ὄν (being-in-so-far-as-it-is-being) really mean. On that account, he says that all of us "are nominalists by birth."[50] However, he makes an effort to render it plausible, that unless one begins on this level, it is impossible to grasp both the range and the spectrum of concepts such as love, power (will) and justice. It is not by chance that most of the great thinkers of antiquity included these concepts in their ontologies. The reason for this fact is that they are part of the structures which are "common to everything that *is*, to everything that participates in being."[51] As a result, no theory can succeed in comprehensively describing the nature and the interrelation of those ideas, unless there is an endeavor to search for their very "root meanings."[52]

As opposed to Kierkegaard, Nygren, Barth, and Jüngel, Tillich overcomes the dichotomy between eros and agape (33).[53] He regards all dimensions of love (eros, philia, epithymia, and agape) as complementary traits of it serving the purpose of uniting. "Love is the drive towards the unity of the separated" (25). In this regard, he follows Plato's theory of love. However, for Tillich, not only does eros contain an element of desire (epithymia), but also philia, so that they both lead towards union. Love is, therefore, for Tillich, more than just an emotion, though it includes it too, and more than passion, or pleasure. Instead, it is the union "with that which fulfils the desire" (29). Agape, in its turn, is "the depth of love," inasmuch as it describes love's "relation to the ground of life," as though love, as agape, were "cutting into love." "One could say that in agapē ultimate reality manifests itself and transforms life and love" (33). In the final analysis, it is God, the ground of life, who transforms reality, but not dissociated from or opposing human love.

Hermeneutik (Freiburg im Breisgau: Herder, 2001), 54.
50 Paul Tillich, *Love, Power, and Justice: Ontological Analyses and Ethical Applications*, reprint (London: Oxford University Press, 1968), 18.
51 Ibid., 19 (emphasis added).
52 Ibid., 1.
53 See also Werner G. Jeanrond, *A Theology of Love* (London: T & T Clark, 2010), 136.

Thus, Tillich sums up his ontology of love as follows: "Life is being in actuality and love is the moving power of life. In these two sentences the ontological nature of love is expressed. They say that being is not actual without the love which drives everything that is toward everything else that is" (25).

This being so, Tillich posits love as the principle of justice.

> Love does not do more than justice demands, but love is the ultimate principle of justice. Love reunites; justice preserves what is to be united. It is the form in which and through which love performs its work. Justice in its ultimate meaning is creative justice, and creative justice is the form of reuniting love.[54]

Therefore, it is false to claim that love gives what justice cannot give. Tillich remarks that, more often than not, this is "a clever way of trying to escape the responsibility and the self-restriction demanded by justice" (82). People who "deny justice to others but say that they love them [...] combine injustice with sentimentality and call this love."[55] However, love can transcend justice, though without destroying it. Love is, as it were, "the creative element in justice" (83). As a result, the relation of justice to love in interpersonal encounters may be described in terms of three basic functions of so-called creative justice: listening, giving and forgiving (84). By following Paul's as well as Luther's theologies of justification by grace on this point, Tillich goes on to say that, even though these features might seem contradictory to the human experience of justice, in reality they are but "the creative fulfilment of justice."[56]

Apart from the way one explains it, this conviction rests upon the experience that no life – be it personal, interpersonal or social life – can be carried on without forgiveness of sin, i.e., that failed life needs to be given a new chance for a new beginning. But forgiveness can neither be imposed by law, nor can it be inferred from the principles

---

54 Tillich, *Love, Power, and Justice*, 71.
55 Paul Tillich, *My Search for Absolutes* (New York: Simon and Schuster, 1967), 108.
56 Cf. Jeanrond, *Theology of Love*, 138.

of justice. Only love can render such a new beginning in human relationships possible, which applies, of course, to the relation to God as well. Only through love is justice endowed with such creative potential which alone is capable of giving life new chances to blossom.

Towards the end of his life, Tillich reflects once more on the relation between love and justice, but especially on the most distinguishing aspect of agape in moral decision-making. Although he values the Old Testamental notion of righteousness (*tsedeq* – צֶדֶק), and even raises it to the category of "creative justice," given that it recognizes the other person and goes beyond proportionate justice, he sees in the New Testamental idea of justice an additional element, which is the notion of agape. The distinctiveness of agape relative to other features of justice and love itself is its drive towards reunion with the other and everything, despite all apparent obstacles and contradictions.

> Its greatness is that it accepts and tolerates the other person even if he is unacceptable to us and we can barely tolerate him. Its aim is a union that is more than a union on the basis of sympathy or friendship, a union even in spite of enmity. Loving one's enemies is not sentimentality; the enemy remains an enemy. In spite of this, he is not only acknowledged as a person; he is united with me in something that is above him and me, the ultimate ground of the being of each of us.[57]

On that account, love is, for Tillich, the absolute moral principle for any moral decision. If the biblical conviction of the human being as an *imago Dei* is to be consequently held on to, this greater dimension of the "ultimate ground of the being" is to be sought and pursued, in spite of all contradictions, opposition, persecution and hostility.

Outcome

A closer examination of the concept of salvation within the context of Jesus has shown the various predicaments that it involves, the most difficult of which being that between God's justice and

---

57 Tillich, *Search*, 108.

mercifulness. The category of justice, usually associated with the idea of a final judgment, has proved to be insufficient and even misleading to convey what the New Testamental notion of salvation might have meant. The human experience of justice provides ample evidence for that claim. By contrast, the New Testamental concept of agape seems to complement and serve as a corrective to that of justice in many respects. It should be noted that, although the early communities and the sacred authors, by following Jesus' message, laid great emphasis on the ideal of agape, this is not to be regarded as an exclusive invention of the New Testament. Instead, its roots are to be sought in Jewish prophetic theology as well.

On the other hand, the interrelationship between love, justice and salvation is quite an intricate one. Firstly, neither justice nor love, albeit essentially distinct from each other, can be fully grasped without the aid of the other. Moreover, since salvation cannot be generated either by human intention, or human will, or human deeds, the point of intersection between them has to lie beyond ethical life. Yet, given that salvation has to be mediated through human history, it must involve in some way human cooperation. In the face of those challenges, love has been described as an inner *attitude* which can neither be reduced to ethics, though it enables ethical life, nor be equated with salvation, though it may play a valuable part in God's salvific plan.

In spite of the apparent inconsistencies between the Old and New Testament or between God's justice and love, wrath and mercy, the present chapter has shown a way of reading that copes with those difficulties. Thus, the core thesis that the road to salvation implies, particularly, the fulfillment of the double love commandment and a deep commitment to the cause of the most needy, formulated above especially with basis on Lk 10:25-37, has proved not to be incongruent with the whole of the Scripture. The next task is now to work it out systematically, taking account of the philosophical and theological challenges implied in it, which will be accomplished in the following chapter, in Part III.

PART III

Theological Implications

7

Agape: A Valuable Concept for the World

The previous chapter has shown how inextricable the relation between (the commandment to) love and salvation was in the message of Jesus. Innovative and essential as the notion of love (αγάπη) might have been to early Christians and to the very identity of Christianity, one might often have to face the objection that, on the theoretical level, love would be nothing but a stopgap solution to complex predicaments. Accordingly, to appeal to this concept would introduce a line of argumentation in which "everything goes." In addition, the word "love" would be so worn-out that it can be considered valueless to tackle complex contemporary issues. Finally, on account of its wide range of meaning, it gives rise to innumerable ambiguities and misunderstandings which render it much more harmful than helpful.

On the other hand, bearing in mind the outstanding importance of the concept of love in the soteriological proclamation of Jesus and in the life of the (early) church, it seems impossible to simply give up such a great ideal. Moreover, the examination of Jesus' message on love has shown so far that this idea has, in the gospels, very little to do with warm feelings or sentimental attitudes. It is rather related to the Jewish notion of justice and mercy, the observation of Torah and the overcoming of social barriers and conventional patterns of behavior. Therefore, a determined effort should be made in order to recover its original meaning and significance for Christians.

Furthermore, this chapter builds on the awareness that the conceptual discourse on agape is in no way Christianity's private ownership, nor is it exclusively reserved to theological circles. As has been ever since early times, in Christianity, the notion of agape (*amor, caritas, dilectio*) awakens still today interest among theoreticians of various areas of knowledge such as philosophy, sociology, psychology and, of course, theology. Therefore, in this chapter, a few relevant and exemplary approaches to love taken from different perspectives shall be briefly examined in order to acquire a more comprehensive understanding of this sophisticated concept. Besides the purpose of exploring the semantic field of the word "love" within the Western tradition of thought, this section constitutes a modest effort to demonstrate the variety of areas of human life that love covers and exerts a profound influence upon.

Agape's Theological Relevance

Thomas Pröpper cannot imagine any word other than *love* to "translate" and to make concrete the contents of what is meant by salvation and revelation. That would be enough reason not to give up the concept of agape. To be sure, he is aware of the various objections to it, especially on account of romantic and bourgeois influences on its connotation. On the other hand,

> [...] no other word can enable so integrative an understanding of all soteriological aspects of Revelation as it [love] can: to these belong the aspects of forgiveness and reconciliation, the liberation from manifold sorts of alienation, the rescue from one's helplessness in the face of the powers that enslave life, and, not least, the promise which surpasses all human possibilities and present expectations.[1]

In a word, God's definitive act of salvation and revelation manifested in Jesus Christ owes its character of ultimacy to the fact that God approached the human being in a human manner, through love. Therefore, one can say that God's historical revelation through the

---

1 Thomas Pröpper, *Evangelium und freie Vernunft: Konturen einer theologischen Hermeneutik* (Freiburg im Breisgau: Herder, 2001), 53.

person of Jesus Christ is, actually, a self-revelation. God reveals himself as love.[2] Yet the veracity of an affirmation of that nature can only be ensured, insofar as it *occurs* in real life, or else it runs the risk of being nothing beyond beautiful, idle words. But since this unconditional, unmerited act of love factually took place in the life of Jesus, one can assert that this self-revelation is indeed truthful and definitive.

That notwithstanding, the Catholic theologian Hansjürgen Verweyen questions, in one of his most recent books, whether a Christian can nowadays still claim that God, as he is experienced and described in the Bible, is [the] love. Admittedly, the greatest objection to the common reason still remains the question of theodicy. However, he is aware that there are a few other aporias in Christian tradition that must be revisited and reinterpreted if one wants to understand what it means to claim that God is love. The crucial point of this work of his is the method he chooses. He does not set out to trace in the Bible every "instance" which may affirm *that* God is love. His interest is, instead, *what* love is all about. "Those who do not take this question seriously into consideration run the risk of searching Scripture and tradition for 'quotations' which fit their preconceived concept of love and end up confirming it."[3] For him, this "*what*" can be defined neither through speculation nor through mystic knowledge. The source to be investigated is the millenary Jewish-Christian tradition, in which God has revealed his concrete love and his very essence. In effect, this is a well-established praxis in contemporary theology.

Albeit sharing Verweyen's view, Jeanrond draws attention to the fact that even within Christian tradition no one can claim that love is a clear and unequivocal concept. Any serious hermeneutic analysis of this concept will show a great amount of ambiguities arisen from cultural (e.g. the patriarchalism inherited from the Jewish-Graeco-Roman background) and language (e.g., the word *eros* was avoided altogether already in the Septuagint translation) issues.

---

2 Ibid., 45.
3 Hansjürgen Verweyen, *Ist Gott die Liebe?: Spurensuche in Bibel und Tradition* (Regensburg: Pustet, 2014), 13.

"Love is neither a Christian invention nor a Christian possession."[4] Also, there is not something like the one Christian praxis of love. On the contrary, the Christian praxis of love has always been a pluriform phenomenon. There have always been tensions and shifts in emphasis from one Christian experience and conceptualization of love to another.

Therefore, one must say that there is not a single matrix for the praxis of love. As a consequence, Christians can neither expect non-Christians to accept their matrix, nor can they claim that there is a single matrix for Christian love. The dynamics of love slip across any religious borders and cannot be confined to the Christian experience of agape. It occurs anywhere and in pluriform ways. Being so, let us now consider a few relevant approaches to agape from other areas of knowledge and realms of life.

Love as Universal Power

Curiously enough, it is the French Marxist philosopher Alain Badiou who delivers us quite a refreshing reading of Paul concerning the unity between thinking, will, human agency and love in the process of subjectivation.[5] His thesis appears to be relevant to our focus of

---

4 Werner G. Jeanrond, *A Theology of Love* (London: T & T Clark, 2010), 29.

5 This attempt of Badiou to make some contents of Christianity fruitful for contemporary philosophical reflection, no matter whether in atheistic or Marxist circles, is in no way an isolated case. See also, for instance, the works of Slavoj Žižek, *The Fragile Absolute: Or, Why Is the Christian Legacy Worth Fighting For?* (London; New York: Verso, 2000); Giorgio Agamben, *Il tempo che resta: un commento alla Lettera ai Romani* (Bollati Boringhieri, 2000). The former explores particularly a few similarities between Jesus' "good news" and Marxism such as the inversion of hierarchical ranks (the poor, the outcasts, the prostitutes become the privileged, p. 123) and the primacy of love in social life in order to "disrupt the circular logic of revenge or punishment destined to re-establish the balance of Justice" (p. 125). The latter, in turn, explores Paul's idea of messianic time, the remaining time, the καιρός-time, the time of the now. By contrasting πίστις with νόμος, Agamben sees the possibility and necessity of indeed overcoming law in its most juridical sense, in or-

interest inasmuch as he sees in the Pauline idea of αγάπη (love) the element of unity between thinking and human agency.[6] Obviously, he reads Paul neither as an exegete, nor as a believer. Instead, his epistemological interest in Paul concerns the subjective structure that underlies his thought. The contents of Paul's theology are, therefore, left apart and the focus of analysis is laid on him as an ancient thinker.[7]

For Badiou, Paul's unprecedented accomplishment was to ground the philosophical category of universalism. He succeeded, thus, in "subtracting truth from the communitarian grasp"[8] – thereby not being kept captive any more by any people, city, empire, territory or social class – and to place it in the subject as a "procedure." Being aware, as he is, that the borderline between truth and fable may not appear to be, at first glance, sufficiently sharp, Badiou holds firm to the conviction that the sole criterion for the truthfulness of something cannot be the feasibility of tracing back to or basing on an objective aggregate, either to its possible cause or to its destination. For what matters, even if the truthfulness of a given content should be proven false, is the subjective structure in view of the conditions of universality, i.e., the "form of these conditions and, in particular, the ruin of every attempt to assign the discourse of truth to preconstituted historical aggregates."[9] Badiou cannot think of truth but as being a "truth procedure,"[10] a militant struggle.[11] Truth is, in a word, entirely "subjective."[12] As an example, he observes that, for Paul, the one solid foundation for Christian faith is the resurrection of Christ, and not, for instance, his birth or his public life. The interesting thing

---

der to establish the time of the "messianic community," which does not necessarily coincide with the church, but definitely with a new social order.
6   Alain Badiou, *Saint Paul: The Foundation of Universalism*, trans. Ray Brassier (Stanford, CA: Stanford University Press, 1997), 88.
7   Ibid., 1–3.
8   Ibid., 5.
9   Ibid., 6.
10 Ibid., 84, among others.
11 Ibid., 88: "Truth is either militant or is not."
12 Ibid., 14.

is that, in fact, resurrection cannot be bound to historical, objective proofs. The event of resurrection escapes any logical framework of human experience and is bound to nothing else but faith. Even if resurrection were just a myth,[13] this does not constitute any serious problem of consistency for the searcher of truth, as the content of this belief does not count as much as the "subjective gesture" of believers.[14]

If that is right, how can one be freed from arbitrariness in one's search for truth? For Paul, the material certainty of a true subjectivation is the *public profession* of the event[15] of resurrection. Thus, the act of πίστις (one's conviction, one's faith) does not take place in one's heart alone, but, in particular, through one's mouth (στόμα).[16] For truth is a militant act performed in the public sphere. "What grants power to a truth, and determines subjective fidelity, is the universal address of the relation to self instituted by the event, and not this relation itself."[17] Indeed, there is nothing more universal than the proclamation of the event of the resurrection of Jesus Christ. On account of its absolute gratuitousness – there are no conditions whatsoever – everyone can adhere to it.

However, it is not one's [personal] relation to the event that validates truth, but the universality of that relation, which can be safeguarded alone through love. The subjective form of universality is called by Paul ἀγάπη and "[...] consists in its tirelessly addressing itself to all the others, Greeks and Jews, men and women, free men and slaves."[18] As the subjective process of a truth claim is "one and the same thing as the love of that truth,"[19] ἀγάπη could be referred to as the consistency of the truth of the event over one's lifetime. There

---

13 Ibid., 107f.
14 Ibid., 6.
15 The category of event plays, in Badiou's philosophy, a decisive role. See especially his major work *Being and Event*, trans. Oliver Feltham (London; New York: Continuum, 2007).
16 See esp. Rom 10:8-10 (Badiou, *Saint Paul*, 88).
17 Ibid., 90.
18 Ibid., 92.
19 Ibid.

is no instantaneous redemption. The process of subjectivation, which is the validation of the truth of the event within the subject, can only occur through one's own labor. "'Love' is the name of that labor."[20] Truth means, for Paul, after all, "faith working through love" (cf. Gal 5:6).

Without love, the gap between thinking and acting cannot be filled, because the will is held captive by sin. Paul cannot understand what is "wrong" with him: οὐ γὰρ ὃ θέλω τοῦτο πράσσω, ἀλλ' ὃ μισῶ τοῦτο ποιω (Rom 7:15b, literally: I do not practice that which I will, but I do that which I hate). In the previous verses (vv. 7-14) Paul gives an account of the causes for that state of affairs. It is the activity of sin through the means of law. Sin is not defined by Badiou in a moral sense, but as an automatism, as a sort of independence of desire from the will of subject by virtue of law. So long as one lives under the rule of law, one's desire is determined and fixed by law.[21]

To love does not mean, however, to act against the law or to delegitimate it. On the contrary, the law in itself is good, holy and righteous (cf. Rom 7:12). Yet, how to understand the apparent antinomy between the following sentences? a) "Christ is the end of the law" (τέλος[22] γὰρ νόμου Χριστὸς in Rom 10:4); b) "Therefore, love is the fulfillment of the law" (πλήρωμα οὖν νόμου ἡ ἀγάπη in Rom 13:10). This contradiction can only be overcome if a peculiar aspect of Paul's anthropology is shortly explained. For Paul, the subject is in no way a harmonic whole, but the struggle between two subjective paths, which he calls σάρξ (flesh) and πνεῦμα (spirit).[23] Although the law is in itself good, it grounds a life according to the flesh, enables the automatism of sin and leads to death. If there should be a complete break with the law, and if love should be the fulfillment of the law, then love must be in some way related to the law. For Badiou, Pauline love grounds, actually, a new law, the law according to the spirit (πνεῦμα). Rather than consisting of a prescriptive list

---

20   Ibid.
21   Ibid., 79.
22   It should be clear that τέλος (end) is employed, in this verse, in the sense of termination, cessation, conclusion, and not in the sense of a purpose.
23   Badiou, *Saint Paul*, 55.

of commandments, Paul's commandment of love in Rom 13:8-10 is an affirmative maxim, which is not related to any specific object.[24] "Under the condition of faith, of a declared conviction, love names a nonliteral law, one that gives to the faithful subject his consistency, and effectuates the posteventual truth in the world."[25] Thus, the subject is given the chance to find once more the unity between thinking and acting. Such unity owes its condition of possibility to the power of love that overthrows sin from its reign and autonomy. For faith does not own such a power. Faith can only point to the possibility that thinking can be freed from its impotence, but love alone can effect it, as it gives to self-love a universal determination.[26] Through the path of love, and by being faithful to the truth of the event, life in sin comes to its end and an anticipatory glimpse at what participating in the resurrection of Christ might look like is made available to the believer. "When the subject as thought [i.e., as a thinking subject] accords with the grace of the event – this is subjectivation (faith, conviction) – he, who was dead, returns to the place of life."[27] Whether this point can be arrived at is by no means guaranteed.

Having said that as a basic prerequisite to follow Badiou's thesis, let us now return to the initial question: why does love play, for him, so decisive a role in the inner process of subjectivation of individuals, particularly as far as the interplay between thinking, acting, autonomy and will are concerned?

For Paul, law contains an element of particularity, which is incompatible with the *one* God for all peoples (πάντα τὰ ἔθνη). Such unity of God in Paul's monotheism is in no way metaphysical speculation, but rather a consequence from the structure of the universal address of this truth, namely, to everyone, without exceptions.[28] For, if the message of salvation is to be addressed to every human being, law cannot function as a condition, given that it is always particular. Whereas "[...] law 'objectifies' salvation and forbids one from relating it to the

---

24 Ibid., 89.
25 Ibid., 87.
26 Ibid., 90.
27 Ibid., 87.
28 Ibid., 76.

gratuitousness of the Christ-event (see especially Rom 3:27-30),"[29] "[g]race is the opposite of law insofar as it is what *comes without being due*."[30] As a result, God's grace enables human freedom which is, in turn, the condition of the possibility of love. "It is from this point of view that, for the Christian subject, love underwrites the return of a law that, although nonliteral, nonetheless functions as principle and consistency for the subjective energy initiated by the declaration of faith."[31] The primacy of love in human life, grounded in the exemption of any particular law, justifies, thus, not only human freedom, but especially human autonomy. The strongest expression of such an autonomy and equality among Christians is found in 1Cor 3:9: "we [all] are God's co-workers" (θεοῦ συνεργοί). There is plenty of room for creativity, free initiative and charisma, inspired by the Spirit. The logic of the master (*maître*) no longer reigns, but that of the Son in whom we are all brothers and work together towards the construction of the kingdom (συνεργοὶ εἰς τὴν βασιλείαν τοῦ Θεοῦ, Col 4:11).[32]

The Social "Function" of Love

Quite different from Badiou's subjective theory of love, Niklas Luhmann's systems theory ascribes a rather regulative role to love. What accounts for the need of including such a sociological approach in this work is its compatibility with modern and plural societies, as the focus is laid on functionality, rather than on stratified structures. For that reason, Luhmann's theory could be particularly helpful as an analytical tool in order to understand the phenomenon of pluralism and, perhaps, even cast new light on it. Furthermore, Luhmann's contribution could be of use, in order to approach love not exclusively on the basis of its semantic unfoldment, but much more comprehensively.

Incorporating the perceptions of social sciences in theological treatises is quite a well-established tradition in certain theological

---

29   Ibid., 75.
30   Ibid., 77.
31   Ibid., 89.
32   Ibid., 59f.

circles, like liberation theology. This can by no means be taken for granted, though, especially on account of methodological inconsistencies. However, considering that the following section is not as much of a sociological analysis as it is a way of approaching the concept of love from an entirely different and striking perspective, this should not constitute any incoherence for the work so that further clarification in this respect may be dispensed with.

Now, apart from the aforementioned reasons why Luhmann's theory on love would be of significant advantage to this work, one additional factor should be taken into account. Luhmann claims that in highly complex, differentiated and plural societies it is no longer possible to operate with the ancient notion of love conceived of as philia or agape, that is, with the categories of political and religious love. This thesis undoubtedly raises strong objections against the conclusions reached above, in chapter 4, and deserves, therefore, closer consideration.

Luhmann's Systems Theory: A Brief Overview

What interests Luhmann most in his research on love[33] is not so much the wide semantic range of meanings of this concept down the centuries as it is the question of what kind of problems this "word" addresses in a given social system and, above all, what solutions it offers to tackle them.[34] From that perspective, love is to be dealt with as a *communication medium,* as Luhmann terms it.[35] Besides love,

---

33 Luhmann's most comprehensive study on love is *Liebe als Passion: Zur Codierung von Intimität,* 6th ed. (Frankfurt am Main: Suhrkamp, 1992); Luhmann actually wrote his first text on love (as passion) in 1969. This text, however, served only his teaching purposes at the University of Bielefeld, remaining unpublished until 2008, when it was discovered in his office among his belongings. This text was shortly thereafter published under the title "Liebe als Passion (1969)," in *Liebe: Eine Übung,* ed. André Kieserling (Frankfurt am Main: Suhrkamp, 2008), 9–91.

34 Luhmann, "Liebe als Passion (1969)."

35 Ibid., 10; Luhmann had already outlined this theory of communication media in his article "Soziologie als Theorie sozialer Systeme" in the *Zeitschrift für Soziologie und Sozialpsychologie* (vol. 19, pp. 615–644, 1967). The article was republished in Niklas Luhmann, "Soziologie als Theorie sozialer Systeme," in *Soziologische*

Luhmann observes, in complex societies, the activity of three other media: truth, power and money. He ascribes to those media a crucial role in societal life, and they are to be understood in the context of his systems theory, a lifelong project of his.[36] Although this highly elaborate theory would deserve a much more in-depth elucidation on account of its complexity, a brief overview should suffice to fulfill the purpose of describing the function of love as a communication medium in society.

Social systems are engendered through communication. Their purpose is to reduce the complexity of the world, given that being in the world necessarily entails the experiences of enormous complexity and radical contingency. The world may be said to be highly complex, because no one can ever claim to be able to experience the "naked" world as such, without any (social) mediations. Contingency is given account for, if assumed that every act, or every communication, is just one possibility among innumerable others. Only within a social system can possibilities of action or communication be considerably and meaningfully reduced. These are called by Luhmann *selections* (*Selektivität*).

Selections are performed through the combination of *information, utterance and understanding*. Complexity is, thus, processed by systems in the form of meaning, which may be defined as "the continuous processing of the difference between actuality and possibility."[37] That means that in the world the realm of possibilities is open to the infinite. Whereas in the world everything is, and remains, fully open, systems serve the purpose of processing information and

---

Aufklärung, vol. 1 (Köln; Opladen: Westdeutscher, 1970), 113–36, esp. pp. 127–28. For a brief overview of Luhmann's communication media theory, see also Niklas Luhmann, "Einführende Bemerkungen zu einer Theorie symbolisch generalisierter Kommunikationsmedien," in *Soziologische Aufklärung*, vol. 2 (Köln; Opladen: Westdeutscher, 1970), 170–92.

36 Although this theory may be found in many of Luhmann's (early) writings as well, he describes it most comprehensively in his major work *Soziale Systeme: Grundriß einer allgemeinen Theorie* (Frankfurt am Main: Suhrkamp, 1984).

37 Harro Müller and Larson Powell, "Luhmann's Systems Theory as a Theory of Modernity," *New German Critique*, no. 61 (1994): 43.

generating meaning so as to provide individuals with a number of "pre-established" selections and to enable "functioning" communications. At this juncture, it is important to note that in the Luhmannian theory neither are systems limited to human beings nor are human beings their point of departure. All that counts in social systems is communication.[38]

Now, selections have to be transmitted. For him, it should be possible to assume the possibility of transmission of selections by means of intersubjective relations. Otherwise, everyone would have to both reduce the complexity of the world and generate meaning on one's own, which is impossible.[39] This creates, in turn, a need for so-called *communication media*. The major function of *generalized communication media* is, thus, "to render reduced complexity transferable."[40] As a consequence, everyone should be able to base one's own experiences and deeds on other people's selections. This presupposition lays the foundation for the transferability of performed selections in intersubjective relations and enables the proper functioning of any social system (successful communication).

The full form of this term is *"symbolically generalized communication media."* The sense in which this phrase is meant may be summed up as follows. They are designated as media because they are not real objects, but can only *convey* meaning; they are communication media, because they serve the purpose of reproducing social systems through communication; generalized means that they are general and broad statements, rather than particular or personal ones and, therefore, accessible to everyone in a given society; to affirm that they operate symbolically implies that they are not factual or verifiable realities, but that they represent imagined entities instead.

---

38 Statements like that gave rise to the debate whether Luhmann ought to be considered, in fact, an anti-humanist or not. As a response to that, he warns himself by saying that such formulations may be misleading. His goal was to question the premises of classical humanism by redefining his/her "place" in society: instead of standing above it, being just part of it (cf. Luhmann, *Soziale Systeme*, 288).

39 Cf. Luhmann, "Soziologie als Theorie sozialer Systeme," 126.

40 Luhmann, "Einführende Bemerkungen zu einer Theorie symbolisch generalisierter Kommunikationsmedien," 174.

Through these media, communication is conditioned in such a way that they may work as means of motivation as well, thereby "guaranteeing sufficiently the compliance with the suggestion of selection."[41] Communication media combine, therefore, both selection and motivation mechanisms. "[...] [T]hrough the way of their selection, they motivate to the assent of the selected meaning."[42]

Symbolically generalized communication media are "semantic devices" serving the purpose of "[...] ensuring the success of unlikely communication despite its unlikeliness. 'Guaranteeing success' means, in this case, to increase one's readiness to accept communications in such a way that communication may be dared, rather than refused right from the outset as something hopeless."[43] Unlikelihoods discourage individuals from acting in the way the unlikelihood points to. However, if communications succeed in proving certain unlikelihoods false there is a chance for social systems to come about or to be reproduced. This does not imply that media like love, truth, money and power are mere illusions (unlikely to come true). It implies, instead, that they are not realities as such, but means of selection and motivation. For instance, it is highly unlikely that someone is going to be happier than he is, if the amount of money he owns increases significantly. However, the medium money gives him/her the promise of satisfying all his/her needs and becomes a motivation towards that end. Whether he/she becomes happier may not even be verified, but the medium money operates in that way.

The necessity of such a device can be explained by the impossibility for individuals to constantly have to consciously assimilate experiences in a highly complex world.[44] Thus, social structures give a certain (rigid) form to processes, so that under similar circumstances certain patterns of behaviors may be expected from individuals.[45] Being so, every social system provides its members with "predefined" possibilities of selection (*Selektivität*) or choice. That implies that

---

41   Luhmann, *Soziale Systeme*, 222.
42   Luhmann, "Liebe als Passion (1969)," 13f.
43   Luhmann, *Liebe als Passion*, 21, translation slightly modified.
44   Luhmann, "Soziologie als Theorie sozialer Systeme," 116.
45   Ibid., 119f.

from a huge quantity of information available "out there," in the world, individuals living in a given system (society) can make sense out of that by means of a limited amount of information and interpretation possibilities. In less complex – that is, in functionally undifferentiated – societies, for example, such performance of selection (*Selektionsleistung*) is transferred through a common (shared) "construction of reality," as being a pre-established order regarding being and nature (natural law, for instance). In functionally differentiated societies, by contrast, this performance of selection may be increased by means of two different ways: either through reflexivity or through the aforementioned communication media.

Media are attributes of sentences, feelings, means of exchange etc., not those things in themselves, even though individuals may employ them so when communicating. Media are instructions given by communication, which have less to do with actual reality.[46]

As for the communication media, each of them transmits, in complex societies, determined selections of information which are agreed upon. They may work independently of each other, as they form subsystems. Accordingly, truth conveys meanings, power enables individual decisions, love ascribes another person (or other persons) the authority to become one's co-interpreter of the world, and money transfers possibilities of satisfaction of one's needs within a given society.[47]

Love as a Social Code
Now, the key point to understanding the relevance of such media in any given society is that they do not exist for their own sake, but that they owe their existence to the need for solving determined social problems. That would amount to saying that depending on which manner love is portrayed in a society, depending on which way it is either idealized or mythologized, depending on which social problems it serves as a solution to, new keys are made available to the

---

46 Luhmann, *Liebe als Passion*, 22f. It is no wonder that every communication medium has a peculiar relation to one elementary organic process: for the medium power – physic, violence; truth – perception; money – satisfaction of needs; Love – sexuality (ibid., 32).

47 Luhmann, "Soziologie als Theorie sozialer Systeme," 127f.

researcher in order to understand that society better. Depictions of love found in literature, arts, humanities etc. are by no means casual, but rather a sort of reaction to relevant social issues.[48] Approaching love in that manner may be considered, therefore, as one of Luhmann's most original and innovative insights for the topic of love.

If that is the case, what would be the main problem which the medium love tries to address in modern societies? According to Luhmann, it is the problem of "highly personal communication," that is to say, a kind of communication "through which the speaker seeks to distinguish himself from other individuals."[49] Such a need arises particularly when the relation of individuals to the world begins to become more and more personal and, as a consequence, it is no longer possible to reach social consensus. Most people, in one's society, do not bother at all about the way one relates to or sees the world, about one's views and way of being. In other words, what is at issue, here, is the question of identity. Transcendental philosophy knew it as "one's transcendental self," the "Self of one's Self,"[50] and it attests to the effort, in modernity, to validate one's own perception and act with autonomy, instead of being acted upon or being determined by external forces. However, in view of the decrease of perception of one's Self's presentation in everyday life, owing to modern life, one depends on someone who is "indifferent enough" to point to one's discrepancies between being and appearing.[51] No one is neutral enough to assess oneself adequately, to be one's own judge. To put it technically, systems need each other to reproduce themselves through communications and to perpetuate themselves.

However, given that, in plural societies, it has become extremely difficult both to experience oneself and to act as a unity, as a whole, particularly on account of the myriad impersonal relations that have become part of daily life, Luhmann affirms that, in fact, what one avidly seeks in love or in an intimate relationship is *"the validation of one's*

---

48   Cf. Luhmann, *Liebe als Passion*, 24.
49   Ibid.
50   Cf. ibid., 207f.
51   Cf. ibid., 209.

self-portrayal" (*Validierung der Selbstdarstellung*).⁵² All that one seeks is that one's self-perception, one's deeds and one's life as a whole may be deemed to be authentic and coherent in the eyes of someone else.

Through the notion of interpenetration, Luhmann succeeds, in his theory, in joining acting (*Handeln*) and experiencing (*Erleben*),⁵³ inasmuch as systems can only subsist by combining both of them. By choosing the term "interpenetration," he is determined to do away with any understanding of love which would entail the ideas of reciprocity, fusion or *unio mystica*,⁵⁴ especially if the radical asymmetry between systems is taken into account. After all, the aim of intimate relationships is not to reach a point in which both have common hobbies and interests or even become one (flesh), but a point in which both understand each other. Now, Luhmann's notion of interpenetration, meaning the interchange of communications of autonomous systems, cannot be properly comprehended, unless a little attention is devoted to the semantic shift of the notion of love across history. Only thus can one grasp its relevance.

Luhmann refers, for instance, to a few studies on love suggesting that in ancient Greek literature the root word to express what we, today, assign to the word love existed solely as adjective: φῖλος. It could be translated as "dear, or close to (someone)," "belonging to someone," being applied to things, animals and one's own body as well.⁵⁵ The need for the noun φιλία arises in the course of Greece's civilizational move, which finds its high point in the πόλις (city). As a result of this political connotation, however, the concept becomes much more abstract. Philia was an attempt to combine the elements of benefit and affection. As it arose in a context determined by political interests, its connotation was very much shaped by idea of κοινωνία (especially πολιτική κοινωνία, Lat.: *societas civilis*). For Luhmann, the central issue at stake in this connotation of love may be expressed in the semantic field of solidarity.⁵⁶ "True love is grounded on the same

---

52 Cf. ibid., 208.
53 Cf. ibid., 200.
54 Cf. ibid., 219.
55 Cf. Luhmann, "Liebe als Passion (1969)," 28.
56 Cf. ibid.

principle as society is [...],"⁵⁷ first as political love, and then as religious love. In those social systems, the function of the medium love was to strengthen the bonds between fellow individuals belonging to the same society (political love) and to promote a certain reserve towards foreigners. This project was then enhanced by extending political love to the whole humanity (religious love). To Luhmann, this remained a utopian enterprise, though.⁵⁸

This understanding of love endures until the beginning of modernity, passing through the whole period of the Middle Ages. Admittedly, intimate love and strong affections were there, too, in those periods, though rather unwanted and regarded as a disturbing energy which had to be kept under control.⁵⁹ For Luhmann, the great "evolutionary" achievement of modernity was to promote the other way round: the function of the medium was no longer fulfilled through its universality, but through its limitation and differentiation. The effectiveness of the medium love does not consist any more in loving everyone, but in loving someone particular and chosen.⁶⁰

In fact, the late 17th century faced, particularly in France, great struggles with the traditional understanding of love and witnessed important changes towards the formulation of a new code.⁶¹ Luhmann terms this new code *passionate love*. As early as in antiquity, there had been the belief that passionate love was to be treated as a disease, a disorder.⁶² This understanding was carried on during the Middle Ages, peculiarly in the form of courtly love, in which the beloved was idealized and love had to be proved through brave deeds. In courtly love, the major concern seems to have been to demonstrate one's nobility and to avoid, in every way, being vulgar.⁶³ Moreover, the attributes of the beloved were of crucial importance. The beloved

---

57   Ibid., 29.
58   As for the notion of love/charity in the Middle Ages, Luhmann refers specially to Thomas Aquinas' *Summa Theologica* (esp. II-II, q. 23).
59   Cf. Luhmann, "Liebe als Passion (1969)," 30.
60   Cf. ibid.
61   Cf. Luhmann, *Liebe als Passion*, 57.
62   Cf. ibid., 63.
63   Cf. ibid., 50.

had to be perfect. Beauty and nobility were decisive factors. That code of morality regulated interpersonal relations in such a way that there was hardly any possibility to overcome the solid barriers of those conventions. What took place in the 17th century were gradual efforts to attain freedom in love relationships. For the first time in history there was a setting which enabled women, for instance, to decide whether they wanted a relationship or not, regardless of proofs of love and external determinations.[64] Moreover, if the freedom of the lovers is now valued and taken seriously, the orientation towards specific characteristics of the partners could be undermined and replaced with the orientation towards their love alone.

To be sure, this was a process that lasted until the 19th century, but it surely laid the first foundations for the new code of love as *passion*. The principle of this new code implies, summarily, that what counts are no longer the specific characteristics, idealizations or proofs of love, but "to be in love," that is, to be in a process.[65] The paradox of love as passion in a society in which rationality is highly appreciated and logic is the only sound way of reasoning can be taken for granted. The main reason is that in the new code of love, there is nothing to which one can ascribe the cause or the origin of a love relationship. One just falls in love. Intimate relationships escape, thus, any kind of external determinations.

Nevertheless, the medium love cannot be identified with a feeling, but exclusively as a communication code. This code has determined rules that are to be followed by the participants of the communication. By observing those rules, certain feelings may be then generated, expressed, denied, simulated etc.,[66] but they cannot be referred to as love. Indeed, as Luhmann asks about the origins of love, he warns the reader that this can be found neither anthropologically (perhaps certain feelings, or sexuality may even be, but love definitively not), nor in epochal changes (considering that something completely *new* rarely comes about in such changes; normally something already existing is reinterpreted). According to him, it is more beneficial to

---

64 Cf. ibid., 59f.
65 Cf. ibid., 62.
66 Ibid., 23.

search for it in "central moments in which the giving of meaning is altered."[67] He observes, for instance, that the need to assign to love a new meaning is a parallel development to the need for regulating both intimate relations and sexuality differently. What he has in mind in that regard is the gross misconduct on the part of the nobility in the late Middle Ages. Luhmann points out that love, peculiarly during the shift to romanticism in the early 19th century, acquires a function, rather than remaining a noble ideal to be pursued. Its function consists, precisely, in leading autonomy to reflection. As a consequence, love turns out to be *"reflection on autonomy, on self-reference."*[68] That amounts to saying that every autonomous act of/in love can only find its meaning inasmuch as it finds resonance in the systems of both involved. The author (lover) of the communication (deed) should have reflected upon it, and the receiver (beloved) should be able to see (experience, *erleben*) in that deed an authentic and exclusive sign of the lover's love. Precisely on that account, it demands from the lovers a continual effort, in order to make what they mean, and believe, "observable" to the beloved, in such a way that the beloved can see an identification between the action and its actor. If love is not lived as a continual process of communication which demands the commitment of both sides, if both sides are not ready to surrender themselves to each other by revealing their very identities, there is less hope that this interpenetration between those two systems may subsist. "Wedding ceremonies are celebrated in heaven and dissolved in the car," says Luhmann, pointing to the fact that the driving style of one of the partners often becomes an issue that ends up in terrible quarrels.[69] That reveals how unstable a love relationship can become over time. Luhman does not hesitate to attribute the establishment of marriage as an institution to such a constant feeling of instability in such a relationship.[70]

The real "problem" of modern societies – and modern persons – is that the achievements of modernity can no longer be regarded

---

67   Cf. ibid., 50.
68   Ibid., 51.
69   Ibid., 42.
70   Cf. ibid., 29. Cf. ibid., 29, chapter 14.

as desiderata. They are realities and must be shaped.[71] Instead of looking for the perfect or for the most beautiful partner, one has to shape this relationship to the best of his/her capacities. For the first time in history the whole responsibility for the institution of marriage has been handed over to the individuals who marry, and no longer kept in the hands of parents or in social structures.[72] This was a huge achievement, although it may be, at times, quite overwhelming. Love cannot be experienced as a reaction. Rather than reactive, love ought to be "proactive acting."[73] After all, "[...] the lover is himself the source of his love,"[74] and that is by no means self-evident. It is, instead, a fruit of evolutionary processes. One does not have to fulfill social expectations, but has much more freedom for one's spontaneity and creativity. "Only by acting on his/her own initiative and in advance of the beloved, to whom one adjusts oneself completely, can the lover preserve his/her own freedom and self-determination."[75] What holds an intimate relationship is, for Luhmann, less the fulfillment of duties (as a spouse) than the creativity of surprising the beloved through actions that will be understood and experienced by him/her as authentic. Moreover, this is the only manner in which the chains of submission can be broken and the real sense of daily life becomes manifest: "to act as the Self of one's own Self, as source of one's own love."[76] Having to select from one's own possibilities is the new and toughest challenge of modernity.

Acting out of love is something much more pretentious than the willingness to please the beloved or to fulfill his/her wishes. It goes beyond submission and complacency. Acting out of love is all about "finding sense in someone else's world," inasmuch as only one's beloved can understand what a determined deed (of love) really means. Therefore, one could assume that the core element of the code

---

71 Cf. ibid., 199.
72 Cf. ibid.
73 Cf. ibid., 209.
74 Cf. ibid., 208.
75 Ibid., 210.
76 Ibid.

of intimacy is *understanding*.⁷⁷ This presupposes that the processing of information between two systems on the basis of their communication (also through deeds) is insomuch coupled that they can decode them and find meaning. Not, however, *the* [one] meaning of life, but meaning that is generated, selected and understood within those systems.

Agape as a Competence to Reach States of Peace

The idea of agape finds resonance in Ricoeur's philosophy as well. His considerations in this respect may be found particularly in two works of his: "Love and Justice"⁷⁸ and "The Course of Recognition."⁷⁹ Rather than defining it, Ricoeur prefers to elucidate it in dialectic tension with the idea of justice, in the case of the former work, and in contradistinction to the Hegelian idea of a "struggle for recognition," in the case of the latter. By so proceeding, Ricoeur does not seem to be as much interested in a mere philosophical analysis of the term as he is in the role played by agape in individual as well as societal life, particularly in social actions. He avails himself of a major study on love and justice carried out by Luc Boltanski within the framework of a sociology of action whence he also borrows the notion of "states of peace."⁸⁰ It is precisely this focus of interest that makes Ricoeur's approach especially helpful to our investigation, which is similarly concerned with the "practice" of love.

In both essays, though taking different detours, he appears to point to the same direction. What he envisions on the horizon towards which the road he describes leads is the paradigm of the gift.

---

77 Cf. ibid., 212.

78 Paul Ricoeur, "Love and Justice," in *Paul Ricoeur: The Hermeneutics of Action*, ed. Richard Kearney, trans. David Pellauer (London; Thousand Oaks; New Delhi: Sage Publications, 1996), 23–39.

79 Cf. Paul Ricoeur, *The Course of Recognition*, trans. David Pellauer (Cambridge, Massachusetts: Harvard University Press, 2005), 216–46.

80 Cf. Luc Boltanski, *Love and Justice as Competences: Three Essays on the Sociology of Action* (Cambridge: Polity Press, 2012).

In fact, Ricoeur himself affirms that his considerations are based, to a great extent, on the discussion of Marcel Mauss' comprehensive study on the exchange of gifts in some archaic societies such as the Maori in New Zealand.[81]

By offering a significant contribution towards the establishment of what he calls "states of peace," Ricoeur does take a crucial step forward in the "(dis)course of recognition." However, this text cannot be read but in the light of his earlier essay which is just as much inspiring. The core thesis of Ricoeur's proposal is that alone the idea of agape may be able to break as much the circle of violence and vengeance as the paradigm of justice which pervades our daily life (in terms of equal distribution – *justitia distributiva*). For love "knows nothing of comparison and calculation."[82]

Ricoeur's critique of Hegel's model is put in the form of a question: "Does not the claim for affective, juridical, and social recognition, through its militant, conflictual style, end up as an indefinite demand, a kind of 'bad infinity'?" Ricoeur's major preoccupation concerns here the negative feeling that goes along with the lack of recognition and necessarily leads to what he calls "unhappy consciousness." Besides remaining in an "interminable" struggle, this "temptation" manifests itself "as either an incurable sense of victimization or the indefatigable postulation of unattainable ideals."[83] The underlying assumption of this critique is that a state in which all individuals of a given society would feel fully recognized in all their dimensions can never be reached. Ricoeur's skepticism over this approach is perfectly legitimate, as it questions the possibility of a society remaining constantly in the state of fight. Ricoeur makes it clear that his intention is in no way to criticize the struggle for recognition as such, but, rather, to show the limits of approaching the issue of mutual recognition predominantly in juridical terms, as has been done in *Philosophy of Right*.[84]

---

81 Marcel Mauss, *The Gift: Forms and Functions of Exchange in Archaic Societies* (New York: Norton, 1967).
82 Cf. Ricoeur, *The Course of Recognition*, 220.
83 Ibid., 218.
84 Ibid.

Ricoeur himself acknowledges a valid objection against the notion of agape in the discourse of recognition, conceding that agape "[...] seems to refute in advance the idea of mutual recognition, inasmuch as the generous practice of gift giving, at least in its 'pure' form, neither requires nor expects a gift in return."[85] On the other hand, is it not sensible to hold it in reserve, in order to contrast it with an understanding of recognition based on the "[...] logic of reciprocity that tends to wipe out the interpersonal features [...]," as opposed to what Ricoeur calls the logic of mutuality.[86]

Consequently, Ricoeur as well deems the command to love one's neighbor, whose extreme form is the love of enemy, as overwhelming, hyperethical. As such it is not easy to justify it rationally. Instead, it should be considered from "a broader economy of the gift."[87] To explicate this economy of the gift, Ricoeur avails himself of two Christian theological categories: at one extreme of human life one is faced with the reality of creation, at the other extreme with justification. Both of them are experienced as a free gifts. On the one hand, the predicative good (Hebr.: to*b*) characterizes the original state of all things in Creation. We were created as good. This original state was given us as a gift.[88] Obviously, creation is not conceived here as "[...] a first event within a series of subsequent events, but as a qualifier (*Vorzeichen*) that enables, so to speak, every moment of history to begin anew." Despite our daily experience of chaos and evil, "good" is the qualifier of the world and the present time.[89] At the other extreme is the final end. But here again "God appears as the source of *unknown* possibilities."[90] God is experienced as the one in whom one can put one's hope, as future, as free pardon and safe harbor, which is

---

85 Ibid., 219.
86 Ibid.
87 Ricoeur, "Love and Justice," 32.
88 Ibid., 33.
89 Knut Wenzel, "Menschwerdung im Horizont der Welt: Bildungshandeln in schöpfungstheologischer Resonanz," in *"... und nichts Menschliches ist mir fremd": Theologische Grenzgänge*, ed. Ottmar John and Magnus Striet, Ratio fidei 41 (Regensburg: Friedrich Pustet, 2010), 182f.
90 Ricoeur, "Love and Justice," 33 (emphasis in original).

a gift as well. Therefore, Ricoeur describes human existence as being placed "between" creation and *eschaton*, and thereby marked by an experience of gift.

As a result, the hyperethical love command does not follow the maxim "*do ut des*" (I give so that you will give), but the evangelical one, "You received without charge, give without charge" (Mt 10:8). It does not follow the principle of equivalence, but that of superabundance. It should be reminded, however, that the commandment to love does not go against the principle of justice, as seen above (pp. 160–165). Rather, it just brings it to perfection. For whenever the golden rule (principle of justice) is misinterpreted and misused, ordinary ethics must be suspended (Kierkegaard) and give room to hyperethics so that the balance may be restored and new states of peace may be achieved in society.[91]

The Potential of Love for Cognition

Most of the features of love that have been explored so far are more related to the domain of intersubjective relations. This is, for sure, the area of human experience in which love plays a more evident role. However, there is a very long tradition, though a little neglected nowadays, which in Western philosophy and theology can be traced back to as early as Plato, and has been nurtured over centuries by important thinkers of different areas of knowledge. This tradition ascribes to love a fundamental role in the process of human cognition. Plato, Augustine, Thomas Aquinas, Meister Eckhart, Søren Kierkegaard, Blaise Pascal, Ludwig Feuerbach and Max Scheler are just a few representative names.[92] More than getting to know each of these theories separately, what is of interest in this section is their relevance for the topic under discussion.

Moreover, the assumption that love plays such a great role in

---

91 Ibid., 37.
92 For a short overview, cf. Udo Kern, *Liebe als Erkenntnis und Konstruktion von Wirklichkeit: "Erinnerung" an ein stets aktuales Erkenntnispotential* (Berlin; New York: Gruyter, 2001), 9–22.

acquiring knowledge appears to be important not only for the issue of interreligious dialogue but for theology itself, as it concerns its scientificity as an academic discipline. The intuition behind this assumption is that reason alone cannot grasp reality as a whole. Affirming this does not imply that love and reason are as far from each other as it is often believed. For Pascal, for instance, both are "but one thing."[93] According to Max Scheler, the fierce opposition between love and reason has historical reasons and is to be traced back to the Enlightenment.[94] Since then, the "modern bourgeois judgment" that has prevailed in the West has been the proposition that "love makes one blind" and that, therefore, "all true knowledge of the world can rest only on *holding back* the emotions and simultaneously ignoring the differences in value of the objects known."[95] This move should, in turn, be understood in the context of the Enlightenment's critique of religion, which set European societies towards the process of secularization. What justified the urgency of so radical a rupture with religion and tradition was the supposed irrationality of religion and the alleged role it played in the "nasty, brutish and long-lasting religious wars of the early modern era [in the aftermath of Protestantism] that left European societies in ruin."[96]

---

93 "We have unaptly taken away the name of reason from love and have opposed them to each other without good foundations, for love and reason are but the same thing. [...] Let us not therefore exclude reason from love, since they are inseparable. The poets were not right in painting love blind; we must take off his bandage and restore to him henceforth the enjoyment of his eyes." Blaise Pascal, *Blaise Pascal: Thoughts, Letters, and Minor Works*, ed. Charles W. Eliot (New York: Cosimo, 2007), 425.

94 Cf. Max Scheler, "Love and Knowledge," in *On Feeling, Knowing, and Valuing: Selected Writings*, ed. and trans. Harold J. Bershady (Chicago: University of Chicago Press, 1992), 147; the original text was published in Max Scheler, "Liebe und Erkenntnis," in *Gesammelte Werke*, ed. Maria Scheler, vol. 6, 14 vols. (Bern: Francke, 1963), 77–98. In the subsequent references, the page numbers of both editions will be given, separated by slashes.

95 Scheler, "Love and Knowledge," 147/77 (italics in original).

96 José Casanova, "Public Religions Revisited," in *Religion: Beyond a Concept*, ed. Hent Vries (New York: Fordham University Press, 2008), 109.

Just as there was an endeavor in the course of the Enlightenment to banish the fanaticism of religion from the public sphere, there was another one, just as radical, to secure knowledge against the harmful influence of passions, feelings, love and any other human dimension other than rationality. In the context of that move, the enormous potential of love unfortunately became lost. Max Scheler was, for sure, a great critic of that stance, among several others.[97] He discovers in the Augustinian cognition theory an alternative to the "reductive mindset of the positive sciences and to a degree, American pragmatism," according to which the human being is nothing but *homo faber*.[98] For Scheler, human beings are more than pragmatic beings in that they are capable of not only *using* the things of the world, but also of knowing, through philosophy, their essential purpose and value. Therefore, he defines philosophy as a "loving act of participation by the core of the human being in the essence of all things."[99] This view reaffirms Augustine's proposition *(res) tantum cognoscitur, quantum diligitur* and vice versa *quantum diligitur,*

---

97 Charles Taylor, who has been similarly engaged in "overcoming" this epistemological view, points to four thinkers as the most important critics of epistemology: Hegel, Heidegger, Merleau-Ponty and Wittgenstein (p. 8). His own position tends to go in line with the Heideggerian and Merleau-Pontyan critique of Kant (p. 18), and his vote is for a view of the subject as an engaged one, rather than separate from the world, thereby resolutely opposing any theories building on the disengaged self, on instrumental reason and on atomism. Cf. Charles Taylor, "Overcoming Epistemology," in *Philosophical Arguments* (Cambridge, Massachusetts: Harvard University Press, 1995), 1–19; for a critique of the Enlightenment in the sense of Horkheimer/Adorno's Dialektik der Aufklärung related to the topic of love, see, further, Kern, *Liebe als Erkenntnis und Konstruktion von Wirklichkeit*, 2–8; Bernhard Welte, *Dialektik der Liebe: Gedanken zur Phänomenologie der Liebe und zur christlichen Nächstenliebe im technologischen Zeitalter* (Frankfurt am Main: Knecht, 1973), 88.
98 Zachary Davis and Anthony Steinbock, "Max Scheler," *The Stanford Encyclopedia of Philosophy*, accessed May 5, 2015, http://plato.stanford.edu/archives/sum2014/entries/scheler/.
99 Max Scheler, "Vom Wesen der Philosophie und der moralischen Bedingung des philosophischen Erkennens," in *Gesammelte Werke*, ed. Maria Scheler, vol. 5 (Bern: Francke, 1954), 68; translation by Davis and Steinbock, "Max Scheler."

tantum cognoscitur.[100] The reason for such a proportional relation between love and knowledge is that love functions, for Augustine, alongside willing and representing, "*equally* as a *third* original *source* of unity for all consciousness."[101] However, though being equal to knowledge [*Erkenntnis*], willing [*Wollen*], and striving [*Streben*], love takes primacy over them. That is to say that love "precedes" them inasmuch as it is, simultaneously, "the primacy of taking an interest [...] and the primacy of an act over other acts, such as perceiving, representing, remembering, and thinking [...]."[102] Being so, the relation between knowing and willing is, therefore, not much different from Thomas Aquinas,'[103] inasmuch as he also deems love to be the "primary act of the will" which pervades and inspires all subsequent acts and choices of the will.[104]

Now, Max Scheler observes that, up to this point, there is not much of a difference between Augustine's and Plato's cognition theories. Love (*eros*) is for Plato, too, the guide, the *methodos* (μέθοδος) to knowledge. Only by considering Augustine's teachings of creation and revelation does one realize its *metaphysical-ontic* significance. Whereas for Plato knowledge is a process whereby one progresses from ignorance, i.e., lack of knowledge, to "more" knowledge, Augustine conceives it as an event by which the "knowing subject" is opened up to know that which is other than him/her and the world reveals itself to the knowing subject.[105] Accordingly, even a simple perception of any object existing in the world may not be reduced to a mere act of the knowing subject. This act ought to simultaneously comprise as much the openness of the knowing subject, who is led

---

100 That is, one knows something (only) to the extent to which one loves it. For Augustine's epistemology, see Scheler, "Love and Knowledge"; Kern, *Liebe als Erkenntnis und Konstruktion von Wirklichkeit*, 11.
101 Scheler, "Love and Knowledge," 161/94.
102 Ibid.
103 Cf. ibid., 162/94.
104 Cf. Josef Pieper, Über die Liebe (München: Kösel, 1972), 42. "Primus [...] motus voluntatis et cujuslibet appetitivae virtutis est amor (STh I, 20, 1)"; "Omnis actus appetitivae virtutis ex amore seu dilectione derivatur (STh I, 60 prolog)."
105 Cf. Scheler, "Love and Knowledge," 164/97.

by love, as the self-giving, the self-revealing disposition of the world. "An image is a consequence of a 'question' asked with 'love' [as it were] that the world answers and in so doing reveals itself. In this revelation the world *comes to its full existence and value.*"[106] In that sense, knowledge may be indeed conceived of as an act of love, considering that "[...] all subjective understanding and choice of the contents of the world are founded by the directions of interest and love; all known things first come to their full value in self-revelation."[107] Therefore, Augustine, alongside the Augustinian tradition through Malebranche and Pascal, was, in the opinion of Scheler, the first one who developed, on a philosophical basis, though not so thoroughly, "the conceptual understanding of the basic Christian experience of the relation of love to knowledge [...]."[108]

In the process of cognition, phenomenology plays, for Scheler, a fundamental role, as it is the way through which one encounters the world just as it is. On that account, phenomenology is more of an attitude than a method[109] and knowledge may be best understood as a *Seinsverhältnis*, that is, an ontological relation, "a relation wherein a being 'participates' in what another being is in itself."[110] Max Scheler is not able to find any name other than love to describe this intrinsic tendency in being to come out of one's shell in order to participate in another being.[111] Thus, he also maintains the primacy of love over knowledge and will, as "[l]ove is that which opens the human being up to the world, to that which is other."[112]

It should have become clear that from a perspective such as this,

---

106   Ibid.
107   Ibid.
108   Ibid., 161/94.
109   Cf. Davis and Steinbock, "Max Scheler."
110   Cf. Max Scheler, "Erkenntnis und Arbeit," in *Gesammelte Werke*, ed. Maria Scheler, vol. 8 (Bern: Francke, 1960), 203; translation by Davis and Steinbock, "Max Scheler": "Es [das Wissen] ist das Verhältnis des *Teilhabens* eines Seienden am *S*osein eines anderen Seienden, durch das in diesem Soseienden keinerlei Veränderung mitgesetzt wird."
111   Cf. Scheler, "Erkenntnis und Arbeit," 204.
112   Davis and Steinbock, "Max Scheler."

the aim and purpose of knowledge is not to control reality, as empiricists like F. Bacon had asserted, but to participate in it. Through knowledge, one enters into communion with, becomes committed to reality, instead of being separate from it.[113] Actually, this is, in the opinion of Moltmann, what the Hebrew word for knowledge entails. Knowing is "[...] an act of love, not one of mastery."[114] That close relation between love and knowledge by means of the Hebrew radical ידע (jd') is attested to, for example, by some of the connotations of its profane meaning. For ידע connotes, among other meanings, to meet or to get to know someone (or something) practically, emotionally and volitionally. It means to care for someone, to be concerned, and even to know someone carnally, that is, to have sexual relationships. To know something or someone involves, in the Jewish world, all of one's senses.[115]

In the act of knowing, the heart (לֵב / leḇ) is a privileged organ. It is as much the place where one deepens that which has been perceived by the senses as the chamber in which one makes one's own decisions on the basis of what has been perceived (cf. Ex 7:23; 9:21), thereby entailing one's own judgment as well as one's responsibility in the face of that which was perceived (cf. Jos 14:7).[116] Now, as the heart is the place where one retreats in order to repent and where one's deepest desire to remain faithful to the covenant remains vivid, it is assigned great importance by the prophetic tradition, too. In the context of the proclamation of the messianic Kingdom (Isa 11:2,9; 33:6; 53:11; Jer 31:34; 24:6; 9:23; Hos 2:22), and the denunciation of whatever is against it, the idea of דַּעַת (daʿaṯ), the knowledge (of God), gains a special significance. Even though such knowledge is believed to be given by the Lord in the last days (cf. Hos 2:21f.), the idea of דַּעַת (knowledge) implies that one should seek out the Lord as

---

113 Cf. Jürgen Moltmann, "Theology of Mystical Experience," *Scottish Journal of Theology* 32, no. 6 (1979): 504.
114 Ibid.
115 Cf. G. Johannes Botterweck, "ידע (jada')," ed. G. Johannes Botterweck and Helmer Ringgren, *Theologisches Wörterbuch zum Alten Testament* (Stuttgart: Kohlhammer, 1982), 490–94.
116 Cf. ibid., 492f.

much as he/she can. This may be achieved by means of a certain religious and moral conduct that demands one's wholeness: one's heart, intellect, will, practice and so on.

It was already pointed out above[117] that the synoptic gospels were not as "faithful" as the LXX in their translation of Deut 6:5. Whereas the words of the original Hebrew text are לֵבָב (heart), נֶפֶשׁ (soul/life) and מְאֹד (force), which, in turn, had been translated, in the LXX, respectively, as καρδία (heart), ψυχή (soul/life) and δύναμις (force), Mark substitutes δύναμις with the words διάνοια (reason, intellect) and ἰσχύς (strength), and so does Luke. Whilst the explanation given above for that matter of fact had been the Hellenistic context of the addressees, one could think, at this juncture, bearing in mind what has been just said about the Hebrew epistemic approach, whether the evangelists had the impression that the Greek word καρδία could not convey the whole range of meanings of the Hebrew word לֵבָב, particularly as its cognitive and rational dimension are concerned.

By equally drawing on the Hebrew understanding of knowledge (ידע/*jd'*), Udo Kern makes an attempt to define what the specific contribution of love in knowing could be. He defines love as being the *mater cognitionis cognoscendi*, that is, "the transcendental precondition of the knower's cognition" and, simultaneously, as an *actio cognitionis* itself, i.e., an act of cognition. As a consequence, love is to be understood as a teacher who teaches knowledge, while, at the same time, learning itself from that knowledge it teaches.[118] If that is so, "[k]nowledge changes the one who knows, not that which is known."[119] Thus, what knowledge most promotes is self-knowledge and a greater communion with reality.

Nevertheless, beyond this essential element of love, Kern claims that love enables one to know the real as it is, too. "Love surrenders itself to that which is there in reality and does away with any attempt to repress it through either past, present, or future representations of it."[120] To that extent, it is the object of knowledge, not the knowing

---

117 Cf. above p. 114.
118 Kern, *Liebe als Erkenntnis und Konstruktion von Wirklichkeit*, 15.
119 Moltmann, "Theology of Mystical Experience," 503f.
120 Kern, *Liebe als Erkenntnis und Konstruktion von Wirklichkeit*, 18.

subject, which determines the content of knowledge. The knowing subject owns, through love, a *receptive* role. Love ensures, as it were, that justice be made to the object of knowledge. What makes up the epistemic potential of love is, therefore, for Kern, its "rigorous epistemic topicality."[121] For love can only perceive and know what is there right now. As a consequence, the process of cognition "is driven by love towards the topicality of this process."[122]

Love and the Edification of Reality

Thinking of the epistemic potential of love in terms of its *receptive* character as described above is undoubtedly one of love's most valuable contributions to the acquisition of knowledge. To this epistemic aspect of love, Udo Kern adds one more, to which he assigns a *productive* character on account of its ontic relevance. Two elements are to be taken into account in that: a) in consequence of the primacy of the topicality of reality over any other representation of it, there is, firstly, a new *perception* of reality; b) in addition to that, however, love enables, secondly, the "edification of reality."[123] What is meant by this further aspect of love shall be briefly unfolded in the present section.

Bearing in mind the cognitive aspect of love as presented in the previous section, what will be at issue in this section is a further, subtle distinction between knowledge and love made by Paul in 1Cor 8:1b: "Knowledge puffs up, but love builds up."[124] Obviously, it

---

121   Ibid., 19.
122   Ibid.
123   Cf. ibid., 18f.
124   The wider context of this verse is the edification of the ἐκκλησία (the local church of Corinth), a subject which Paul unfolds in the subsequent chapters (9 and 10). But besides this, he addresses, in chapter 8, another issue that was causing divisions in the community of Corinth. Paul wants to exhort the group of "the stronger," those who, on account of their knowledge (γνῶσις) of the nonexistence of idols, were confident enough to eat the food dedicated to those gods, not to scandalize "the weaker" (1Cor 8:9, πρόσκομμα γένηται τοῖς ἀσθενέσιν), who could not square

is not about despising the value of knowledge as such, but about another essential aspect of love: its constructive character for one's experience of "being-in-the-world," be it individually, dialogically, socially or universally.[125] Thus, love will be considered once more as much in its relation to knowledge as to reality, though the emphasis being now put rather on the "edification of reality."

Apart from the philosophical discussion around the universals that the terms "construction" or "constitution" of reality may evoke, what is at stake here is love's capability to edify, to build up and to exalt what has been apprehended by the knowing subject. For the sake of clarification, one can say that whereas the *receptive* character of love has more to do with the aspect of *recognition* of the real such as it is *in itself*, its *productive* character basically concerns the constructions of reality that occur through love's creative and original potential. Kern reminds us, though, that those constructions are not the real itself, but "vehicles of love," as it were, in order to approach reality.[126]

Such an edifying aspect of love was worked out by Kierkegaard quite extensively in his *Works of Love*.[127] The question that intrigues him therein is the metaphoric, or spiritual, meaning of the words *build up* or *edify* (Greek: οἰκοδομέω; Danish: *opbygge*), just as they are attested to by the Holy Scriptures. For him, the basic point on

---

those practices with their faith in Jesus Christ. On the one hand, Paul is aware that "the strong" had good theological reasons to proceed so, and that they could allow themselves to do so in their freedom gained from Christ (Gal 5:1). On the other hand, he also knows that, as long as "the weak" were not able to answer for those practices themselves, there would be "no use" (1Cor 10:23) in either encouraging them to do the same as the "stronger" or scandalizing them through their behavior. For more details on the context of this text and the relation between γνῶσις and ἀγάπη, see Thomas Söding, *Das Liebesgebot bei Paulus: die Mahnung zur Agape im Rahmen der paulinischen Ethik* (Münster: Aschendorff, 1995), 102–19.

125 Cf. Kern, *Liebe als Erkenntnis und Konstruktion von Wirklichkeit*, 218.
126 Cf. ibid., 219.
127 Cf. Søren Kierkegaard, *Works of Love: Some Christian Reflections in the Form of Discourses*, trans. Howard and Edna Hong (New York: Harper and Row, 1962), pt. 2, esp. ch. 1: "Love Builds Up."

which everything else depends is the particle *up* of the phrasal verb *build up*. "For to *build up* means to build from the ground up."[128] Thus, even grammatically, it is impossible to build up, unless there is a ground. One can only build up *on* something. Now, if it is said that (only) love builds up, the next question to be answered concerns this ground itself, from which love can build up. In that regard, Kierkegaard's assumption is that, on the spiritual plane, love is the ground of everything, and that one can only build up if one *presupposes* that love is already present in the other person or object, even if, to all appearances, the opposite seems to be the case.

> To build up means to presuppose love; to be loving means to presuppose love; only love builds up. For to build up means to draw forth something from the ground up, but, spiritually, love is the ground of everything. No man can bestow the ground of love in another man's heart; nevertheless, love is the ground, and one can build up only from the ground up; therefore one can build up only by presupposing love.[129]

Alone, the confident presupposition that, ultimately, it is love which is at work, not the subject, may enable someone to act in the right way, almost regardless of what he/she does or does not do. Kierkegaard is confident enough to say: "[...] do everything in love, whereby the very same thing is expressed. One man may do the very opposite of what another does; but if each one does the opposite out of love, the opposites build up."[130] In view of Kierkegaard's approach to love, one can therefore say that one's *deeds* do not count as much as the *attitude* with which one does something. For Arne Grøn, this may be described as a new way of *seeing* in ethics.[131] In his view, what concerns Kierkegaard most in *Works of Love* is not so much

---

128 Ibid., 201.
129 Ibid., 212.
130 Ibid., 202.
131 Cf. Arne Grøn, "Kierkegaards 'zweite' Ethik," trans. Schmid Hermann, *Kierkegaard Studies, Yearbook*, 1998, 366; for more details on Kierkegaard's ethics of vision, see also Arne Grøn, "The Dialectic of Recognition in Works of Love," *Kierkegaard Studies, Yearbook*, 1998, 147–57.

what one should morally do as it is *how* one should do that which he/she does. On that account, the term "second ethics" is preferred, as it describes a moral consciousness which goes much beyond general or first ethics. By introducing such a "religious dimension" into ethics, ethical issues are given a radical turn and ethics is essentially transformed.[132]

This is elucidated more precisely by Kierkegaard when he defines what (Christian) mercifulness consists in, and, especially, when he deals with the love of neighbor. By distinguishing between (Christian) mercifulness and beneficence, he affirms that "[...] *to be able* to be merciful is a far greater perfection than to have money and consequently *to be able* to give."[133] Accordingly, it does not matter whether one gives hundreds of thousands to the poor or just a halfpenny. "Mercifulness is *how* it is given."[134] It has to do with the spirit and the attitude with which someone gives or does something. Hence, Kierkegaard can say that "mercifulness [is] a *work* of love even if it can give nothing and is able to do nothing."[135] As a concrete example, Kierkegaard thinks about the right mindset one ought to have when practicing love of neighbor.[136] By drawing the due consequences from Jesus' words as to the guest list one should have in mind when giving a banquet (cf. Lk 14:12-13), everything depends, for him, on the way one *sees* "the poor, the crippled, the lame and the blind." "He who feeds the poor but yet is not victorious over his own mind in such a way that he calls this feeding a feast sees in the poor and unimportant only the poor and unimportant. He who gives a *feast* sees in the poor and unimportant his neighbors

---

132   Cf. Grøn, "Kierkegaards 'zweite' Ethik," 366f.
133   Kierkegaard, *Works of Love*, 294.
134   Ibid., 302.
135   This is the title of seventh chapter of the second part.
136   For an overview of Kierkegaard's stance on the love of neighbor, see Pia Søltoft, "Den Nächsten zu kennen heißt der Nächste werden: Über Ethik, Intersubjektivität und Gegenseitigkeit," in *Ethik der Liebe: Studien zu Kierkegaards "Taten der Liebe,"* ed. Ingolf U. Dalferth (Tübingen: Mohr Siebeck, 2002), 89–109; Antony Aumann, "Self-Love and Neighbor-Love in Kierkegaard's Ethics," *Kierkegaard Studies, Yearbook*, 2013, 197–216.

[…]."¹³⁷ On that account, seeing properly may be said to be a core element in Kierkegaard's ethics, insofar as "[t]he possibility of seeing without seeing or seeing wrongly indicates the ethical significance of vision" and enables, to that extent, a dialectic of recognition.¹³⁸ It is by means of such proper seeing that the other, the self, and reality can be fully appreciated and recognized in its uniqueness, given that, through love, one sees, apart from human limitations and imperfections, in the same manner as God, inasmuch as it is God himself that acts in love.

For Kierkegaard, human beings do have a role to play in the edification of reality, though a secondary one, as a mere servant. However, as compared with Augustine's theology, on which Kierkegaard also draws for certain issues, this is surely a different approach. In his view, "human beings can be genuine agents of love,"¹³⁹ though not subjects of it. Claudia Welz sums it up as follows: "In the performance of love, God and human beings are co-workers; the origin and effect of love, however, lies beyond the human action and ability."¹⁴⁰

> Suppose that a lover did succeed in building up love in another person. When the building stands, the lover stands aside and humbly says, 'Indeed, I presupposed this all the time.' Alas, the lover has no merit at all. The building does not stand as a monument to the craft of the builder or, like the pupil, as a reminder of the teacher's instruction. The lover has indeed done nothing; he has only presupposed that love was fundamentally present.¹⁴¹

One of the benefits of his approach is that, by so arguing, Kierkegaard succeeds in tackling the delicate question of works and grace. What is more, the subject is thereby relieved of the ambitious pretension to changing reality or to determining its purpose and ultimate meaning, while affirming, at the same time, his/her responsibility

---

137 Kierkegaard, *Works of Love*, 92, italics in original.
138 Grøn, "The Dialectic of Recognition in Works of Love," 157.
139 Cf. Jeanrond, *Theology of Love*, 108.
140 Claudia Welz, *Love's Transcendence and the Problem of Theodicy* (Tübingen: Mohr Siebeck, 2008), 155; see also Jeanrond, *Theology of Love*, 112.
141 Kierkegaard, *Works of Love*, 206.

in the world as God's "co-worker."[142] This possibility is conceded to every human being, without exception, and irrespective of one's individual abilities, as long as he/she takes and preserves the above described attitude.

> Building up is not at all, then, an exclusive superiority based on individual *talents*, such as brains, beauty, artistic talent, and the like (such a view would be a love-less and contentious error!). Rather it is just the opposite: every person, through his life, his conduct, through his behaviour in common things, through his relationship with his fellows, through his language, his expression, should and can build up, and every person would do this if love were actually in him.[143]

On the other hand, the price of Kierkegaard's approach is a strict separation between human love and God's love (Christian love).[144] Human beings can never come to know, by themselves, what true love is about, unless they become Christians and live by faith. Human love is not able to build up, only Christian love can. Moreover, human love plays neither an epistemological nor an ontic role, particularly in one's relation to God, but even in the relation to one's neighbor or to reality.

The difficulty, today, with such theories based on Augustinian theology is, chiefly, to accept that love has been in effect "*poured out within our hearts through the Holy Spirit*" (cf. Rom 5:5) and operates within us. Albeit being in line with Pauline theology, such an approach views human beings, basically, as instruments of God, and refuses to acknowledge elements such as human freedom, human agency and, particularly, several human capabilities entrusted to human beings in Creation. Characteristic examples of

---

142 Kierkegaard's expression "co-workers" is based on 1Cor 3:9. Cf. ibid., 74.
143 Ibid., 202 (emphasis in original).
144 Cf. Jeanrond, *Theology of Love*, 105. Along with Kierkegaard, Jeanrond groups three other Protestant theologians who, in a similar way, work out a theology of love based on the strong opposition between *eros* and *agápe* by equating them, respectively, with human love and divine one. Their names are Anders Nygren, Karl Barth and Eberhard Jüngel.

such approaches is the classical work on love by the Protestant theologian Anders Nygren. More problematic, however, in the opinion of J. Pieper is the division made by such authors between the "natural" man and the Christian. The question posed by Pieper is then who the subject of agape is, given that the "natural" person is not capable of it. The answer, for Nygren, is God. One of his famous quotes in that regard is: "He who abides in love is no longer a mere man, but a god [...] for God Himself is in him and does such things as no man nor creature can do. [...] He has nothing of his own to give. He is merely the tube, the channel, through which God's love flows."[145]

Atheistic Love?

In the face of this criticism, the question then arises whether love ought not to be "freed" from the influence of God or from metaphysical predeterminations, in order to be genuinely human. Such an approach to love was worked out by the philosopher and critic of religion Ludwig Feuerbach. As a matter of fact, many of Scheler's concerns were of interest to him just as much, despite, obviously, the difference of their contexts and the divergence of their philosophical thought. Nonetheless, love plays a major role in Feuerbach's philosophy too, particularly as related to cognition, to the need of valuing reality *in itself*, rather than from the observer's standpoint, and to human existence. One of his great achievements was, to that extent, to have "disembedded" love from the divine sphere, while preserving, however, at the same time, its ontic relevance. As Richard McGhee sees it, this is a deliberate result of the method used by Feuerbach throughout his entire philosophy, since his early works, the method of inversion, "whereby he turns predicates into subjects and vice versa." Applied to his ontology, the outcome is that "the absolute Being is reduced to the consciousness of an individual

---

145 Anders Nygren, *Agape and Eros*, trans. Philip S. Watson (Philadelphia: Westminster Press, 1953), 735. Actually, Nygren is quoting Luther here. Nevertheless, this is his line of thought. For a critique of Nygren's approach, see: Pieper, Über die Liebe, 96–105; Jeanrond, *Theology of Love*, 113–20.

human [...]."[146] What renders this new ontology possible is, for Feuerbach, human love. Not only access to reality and true knowledge is mediated through love, but to true existence as well. "Truth does not exist in thought, nor in cognition confined to itself. *Truth is only the totality of man's life and being.*"[147] Moreover, owing to his profound influence on Western thought,[148] especial mention being made of his critique of both idealism and religion, his considerations on the role of love in human life could certainly offer significant insights to the present investigation.

Feuerbach's greatest disagreement with idealism, and, particularly, with Hegelian philosophy, is that it remains a *theology*, rather than being a *philosophy*. This is so, because the thinking subject is dissolved in the absolute Spirit. The absolute, however, is abstract and unreal. At first, Feuerbach actually believed Hegel's philosophy to have succeeded in solving the enigma of human consciousness, but then he realized that his theory was only possible "at the expense of the 'unreality' of the sensuous reality."[149] Therefore, he argues, in his writings "*Vorläufige Thesen zur Reformation der Philosophie*" and "*Grundsätze der Philosophie der Zukunft*," for a new philosophy, whose primary task ought to be to incorporate in its *Text* whatever may be *opposed* to philosophy, whatever is different from thinking, or, more precisely, the very *antithesis* of philosophy. "This unphilosophical, absolutely *antischolastic* essence in us, distinguished from thinking, is the principle of *sensualism*."[150]

---

146 Richard D. McGhee, "Introduction to 'Principles of the Philosophy of the Future' by Ludwig Feuerbach," in *World Philosophers and Their Works*, ed. John K. Roth, vol. 1, 3 vols. (Pasadena, Calif: Salem Press, 2000).
147 Ludwig Feuerbach, "Grundsätze der Philosophie der Zukunft (1843)," in *Kleinere Schriften*, ed. Werner Schuffenhauer, vol. 2, Gesammelte Werke 9 (Berlin: Akademie, 1970), 338 (§ 60), translation by Zawar Hanfi (§ 58), op. cit.
148 Marx, Nietzsche, Buber, Freud are just a few names that could be mentioned among many thinkers influenced by the ideas of Feuerbach.
149 Cf. Josef Winiger, *Ludwig Feuerbach: Denker der Menschlichkeit* (Darmstadt: Lambert Schneider, 2011), 171.
150 Ludwig Feuerbach, "Vorläufige Thesen zur Reformation der Philosophie (1842)," in *Kleinere Schriften*, ed. Werner Schuffenhauer, vol. 2, Gesammelte Werke

In that way, sensuousness is ascribed a central role in philosophical reflection and other cognition processes alike. "*Taken in its reality* or regarded as *real*, the real is the object of the senses – the *sensuous*. Truth, reality, and sensuousness are one and the same thing."[151] By including sensuousness into philosophy, Feuerbach wanted to recover the wholeness of the human being in consciousness, which can be attained, as he conceives it, solely through the unity between *head* and *heart*.

> The essential tools or organs of philosophy are the *head*, the source of activity, of freedom, of metaphysical infinity, and of idealism, and the *heart*, the source of suffering, of finitude, of need, of sensualism. Theoretically expressed, these philosophical tools are *thinking* and *intuition*. For *thinking* is the *need* of the *head, intuition* or *sense* the *need* of the *heart*. Thinking is the principle of the school, of the system; intuition, the *principle of life*. In intuition I am *determined* by an object, in thinking I *determine* the object. In thinking I am an *I*, in intuition a *not-I*. True, objective thought, the true and objective philosophy, is generated only from thinking's *negation*, from *being determined* by an object, from *passion*, the source of all desire and need. The intuition yields simply the essence *immediately identical with existence*. Thinking yields the essence *mediated* by its *distinction* and its *separation* from existence. Therefore, only where the existence unites with the essence, the intuition with the thinking, the passivity with the activity [...], is there alone *life* and *truth*.[152]

---

9 (Berlin: Akademie, 1970), 254, italics in original.
151 Feuerbach, "Grundsätze der Philosophie der Zukunft (1843)," 316 (§ 32); translation from Ludwig Feuerbach, "Principles of Philosophy of the Future," trans. Zawar Hanfi, *Marxists Internet Archive*, accessed May 17, 2015, https://www.marxists.org/reference/archive/feuerbach/works/future/ (§ 32). The divergence of paragraph numbers is accounted for by different editions of this writing.
152 Feuerbach, "Vorläufige Thesen zur Reformation der Philosophie (1842)," 254; translation from Ludwig Feuerbach, "Provisional Theses for the Reformation of Philosophy," in *The Young Hegelians, an Anthology*, ed. Lawrence S. Stepelevich, trans. Daniel O. Dahlstrom (Cambridge: Cambridge University Press, 1983), 164.

As a result, knowledge, for Feuerbach, begins not in the thinking subject, but whenever "my own activity – when I proceed from the standpoint of thought – experiences the activity of another being as a *limit* or boundary to itself."[153] The object of thinking is not a thought, an idea, but an *alter ego* – a You. The *alter ego* does not remain indifferent to this act; it responds to the subject and has an effect on it, to the point that the other may be said to be the key to "the mystery of perception, of feeling, of love."[154] And alone love, understood as passion, "is the distinctive mark of existence" (318, § 34/§ 33).[155]

> Love is not only objectively but also subjectively the criterion of being, the criterion of truth and reality. *Where there is no love there is also no truth.* And only he who *loves something* is also something – to *be nothing* and to *love nothing* is one and the same thing. The more one is, the more one loves, and vice versa.[156]

Nonetheless, Feuerbach's new philosophy deliberately rejects any theory of cognition, at least as understood by his contemporaries.[157] "Only those determinations are productive of *real* knowledge which *determine the object by the object itself,* that is, *by its own individual* determinations but *not* those that are *general,* as for example the logico-metaphysical determinations that, being applicable to *all objects without distinction, determine no abject.*"[158] The new philosophy has, therefore, according to Feuerbach, an *epistemological principle*. What he ascribes the status of *subject* to is "[...] *not the ego, not the absolute – i.e.,* abstract spirit, *in short, not reason for itself alone*

---

153 Feuerbach, "Grundsätze der Philosophie der Zukunft (1843)," 316 (§ 33), translation by Zawar Hanfi (§ 32), op. cit.
154 Cf. Winiger, *Ludwig Feuerbach*, 181.
155 Feuerbach, "Grundsätze der Philosophie der Zukunft (1843)," 318 (§ 34), translation by Zawar Hanfi (§ 33), op. cit.
156 Ibid., 319 (§ 36), translation by Zawar Hanfi (§ 35), op. cit., italics in original.
157 Cf. Winiger, *Ludwig Feuerbach*, 182.
158 Feuerbach, "Grundsätze der Philosophie der Zukunft (1843)," 332 (§ 50), translation by Zawar Hanfi (§ 49), op. cit.

– *but* the *real* and the *whole being of man. Man* alone is the *reality, the subject of reason*. It is man who thinks, not the ego, not reason. [...] *man is the measure of reason.*"[159]

Bruno Kern is, therefore, right to indicate the relatedness of love to both truth and reality as one of Feuerbach's greatest contributions to philosophical thought. The consequence he draws from Feuerbach's philosophy is that "settling on love and its constructions," can never go along with any attempt whatsoever "to cover up, to repress, or to flee from reality." True love does not have any fear to avoid reality, only pseudolove has. It is pseudolove, in his view, that seeks to create "romantic refuges," in which love and reality appear to be utterly alien to each other.[160]

As a result, one could then say that it is through the potential of love that the real can be known, valued, constructed and edified to the greatest possible extent to human beings. Any cognition theory based on rational thinking alone is not able to either grasp reality in its wholeness and complexity or to construct and build it up properly.

Love as Relationship

Despite the flaws and deficiencies of Feuerbach's philosophy, the great Jewish philosopher Martin Buber was deeply influenced by his thought. By making use of the words of the Protestant theologian Karl Heim, Buber describes his discovery of the *Thou*,[161] which he owes greatly to Feuerbach, as "the Copernican revolution," as something "just as rich in consequences as the idealist discovery of the I." In the following sentence of that text, Buber recognizes himself Feuerbach's influence on his thought by saying that in his youth he

---

159 Ibid., 333 (§ 51), translation by Zawar Hanfi (§ 50), op. cit.
160 Cf. Kern, *Liebe als Erkenntnis und Konstruktion von Wirklichkeit*, 220.
161 The paragraph Martin Buber quotes to illustrate it is the following: "The single man *in isolation* possesses in himself the *essence* of man neither as a *moral* nor as a *thinking* being. The *essence* of man is contained only in the community, in the *unity of man with man* – a unity, however, that rests on the *reality* of the *distinction* between 'I' and 'You'" (Feuerbach, "Principles of Philosophy of the Future," § 59).

"was given a decisive impetus by Feuerbach."[162] In fact, the principle of love in Feuerbach's new philosophy opens up a completely new field in philosophy which Buber refers to as the sphere of the "between" (man and man)[163] and certainly constitutes the core of his dialogic philosophy. Buber is deeply convinced that alone this concept of the "between," insofar as it is not an auxiliary construction, "but the real place and bearer of what happens between men," is able to overcome both individualism and collectivism and show the way towards the genuine human being in its wholeness as well as to the establishment of genuine communities.[164]

Being so, the relational character of love could be brought forward to counterbalance the seemingly one-sided nature of agape. Not without good reasons, the German philosopher of religion Bernhard Welte, although admitting that it is impossible to offer an exhaustive definition of love, is deeply convinced that what characterizes love most precisely is its relationality. What is most specific to love is the very fact that "it connects a loving I to a loved you."[165] It does not matter to which extent or under which conditions this relationship develops. What matters is that there is indeed a relationship between two or more persons. Therefore, claiming that one loves humanity in general is, at the first, merely empty rhetoric. In order to be truthful, the great ideal of love must be realized in concrete, real relationships. Already Augustine had drawn attention to the fact that to love is a "transitive verb" and, as such, demands always both a subject and an object. One must always specify whom or what one loves.[166]

By making a similar effort towards identifying the *essential* traits of love, Josef Pieper dares a definition, too. He conceives of love primarily as *Gutheißen,* as approving of, appreciating.[167] *Gut-heißen*

---

162 Martin Buber, "What Is Man?," in *Between Man and Man*, trans. Ronald Gregor Smith (New York: Collier Books, 1985), 148. This article was first published in 1938 in German under the title: "Was ist der Mensch?"
163 Cf. ibid., 203.
164 Ibid., 204f.
165 Cf. Welte, *Dialektik der Liebe*, 14; 16–18.
166 Augustine, *De Trinitate* VIII, 11, apud Jeanrond, *Theology of Love*, 3.
167 Cf. Pieper, Über die Liebe, 38f.

is, firstly, to be taken quite literally. It means as much as to say to someone, "How *good* that you are there, that you exist." However, he warns that what is at stake here is not just a statement, a word. This unconditional approval of someone is rather to be thought of as an expression of the will, which would result in a phrase such as, "I want you to exist!" To love is, therefore, a mode of willing. Not, however, in an all too active sense, as willing (something) is very often understood, i.e., as doing or even changing something, but, first and foremost, in terms of a consent to that which is already there. This entails, by its turn, the premise that the other, in itself, as he/she really is, is fundamentally good. In the words of Maurice Blondel, to love someone would mean "to let be."[168] This is definitively a powerful sentence, as it presupposes that the other is "all right" just as he/she is and must be given room and freedom to develop his/her own potentialities.

A significant contribution to understanding love as a relationship has been made by the theologian Vincent Brümmer. His basic criticism was that, within Christian tradition, "[l]ove has generally been taken to be an attitude of one person towards another, rather than as a relation between persons."[169] The alternative proposed by him is to think about love as a "purposive commitment" taken on within a relationship between subjects that causes them to take mutual actions and attitudes towards each other.[170] The gain of his proposal for the discussion is that the category of attitude is not just given up, but rendered a bit more "flexible." What is given up by that is a static view that there is the one Christian understanding and attitude of love which must apply to every Christian or, still worse, to every human being.

Therefore, in line with Brümmer, Jeanrond holds that a

---

168 *"L'amour est par excellence ce quit fait être"* (Maurice Blondel, *Exigences philosophiques du christianisme* [Paris: Presses universitaires de France, 1950], 241). It is quite difficult to preserve the full meaning of this sentence by translating it into other languages in which the verb to do/make does not allow similar constructions.
169 Vincent Brümmer, *The Model of Love: A Study in Philosophical Theology* (Cambridge: Cambridge University Press, 1993), 33.
170 Ibid., 153; see also Jeanrond, *Theology of Love*, 21.

contemporary theology of love can no longer separate eros and agape, set the one over against the other, or even exclude one of them. In contrast to the theologies of Soren Kierkegaard, Anders Nygren, Karl Barth and Eberhard Jüngel,[171] he also argues against a definition of love in terms of an attitude such as mercy, compassion, altruism, solidarity, sympathy and so forth. One can develop and cultivate such attitudes, but love, as he sees it, goes much beyond it. It desires to shape relationships, it desires community, it has to do with dynamics, creativity, self-knowledge and self-growth.[172]

Outcome

This chapter was basically concerned with the relevance of the concept of love for the contemporary theological discourse, along with its extensive range of meanings and areas of influence in human life. Theologically, this concept seems to be indispensable for any contemporary soteriology. This view might have been shaken by the fashion in which Luhmann conceives the function of love in societal life, namely, simply as a symbolically generalized communication medium whose role is to regulate intimate relationships in complex societies. However, Ricoeur's approach (pp. 189–192) has ascribed a much more significant role to love in social dynamics and Badiou's (pp. 172–177) in subjective processes. Particular attention should be devoted to the epistemic value of love, which can guide not only theological research, but also interreligious encounters.

To be sure, the specific connotation of love as agape has, at different points, experienced strong criticism. Notwithstanding, it remains questionable whether a hermeneutic elucidation of the Jesuanic idea of salvation, as it is pursued here, can be carried out without the principal meaning of the New Testament notion of agape, which is self-surrender, self-abnegation, solidary commitment to the other and to the edification of reality. As Ricoeur demonstrates, even at a philosophical and sociological level of reflection, it is

---

171 Cf. Jeanrond, *Theology of Love*, chap. 5.
172 Ibid., 254.

impossible to ignore or give up such a valuable "competence" of human beings. Therefore, despite the considerable controversy surrounding the idea of agape, it still seems indispensable for a proper comprehension of what the New Testament idea of salvation was intended to convey. The criticism expressed by Brümmer and Jeanrond (pp. 209–212) according to which the Christian idea of agape has contributed to a depreciation of other dimensions of human love such as corporeality, sexuality, reciprocity etc. is perfectly legitimate and can therefore be taken as complementary to or as an important corrective to agape, rather than as a vote against it.

8

When Christian Faith and Human Agency Become One

As was seen in the previous chapter, love permeates all dimensions of human life. It possesses an integrative power, a mediating character, one could say. In the present chapter, it is precisely such a mediating role that has to be examined in more detail. For the thesis suggested above (Part II) with its basis on Lk 10:25-37 according to which God's salvation can and must be mediated through the human being has to be now made plausible philosophically as well as theologically. Only thus can the close relation between God, creation, the human being and salvation be at best grasped.

By proceeding in this manner, we may succeed in rediscovering the *Sitz im Leben* of the suspicious, discredited word "salvation" so that the good news contained in this idea may regain its liberating character and significance in human life. This attempt will be carried out with the aid of the modern concept of freedom. At the same time, even if the correlation with the intellectual concept of human freedom turns to be successful, it must be inquired about the feasibility of religious practice and conveyance of salvation in a secular environment.

Finally, as was pointed out in chapter 1, the last methodical step of theological hermeneutic work consists in the attempt to translate the "original" message of Jesus into a language that can be comprehensible to believers and non-believers alike. Obviously, this chapter shall not be seeking to translate the Christian concept of salvation *as* love, given that those concepts are in effect distinct and refer, ultimately, to different realities. However, given the mutual referenciality between them, the manner in which they are related shall be subjected to closer scrutiny.

Embedding Love in the Modern Discourse on Freedom

Citizens living in Western societies, particularly in urban areas, find it nowadays extremely difficult to derive any meaning for their existences from words like "salvation" or "redemption," which have become foreign to modern life. In fact, Kant's new epistemological approach undermined the solid foundations of the two-story building of scholastic theology (natural vs. supernatural world), thereby assigning philosophy and theology with new tasks altogether. Furthermore, the notion of salvation was precisely the focus of the major critique of the "masters of suspicion"[1] whereby religion was equated with ideology. "Critique of Religion was above all critique of soteriology."[2] According to those views, it was because of faith in salvation in a possible afterlife that people, when facing daily challenges, would try to seek comfort and passively wait for God's intervention, instead of responsibly taking their own lives into their hands and acting proactively.[3]

Yet the idea of salvation shapes, in different fashions and shades, the discourse and the promises of most religions. On that account, it could possibly offer a hermeneutic key to an important anthropological reality that might have been neglected over the last centuries, not least because of the aforementioned critique of religion. Also, even though the semantic fields of the terms love, salvation and freedom may overlap at certain points, their relation is not one of identity or equivalence, but referentiality. Their correlation is by no means self-evident, though, and therefore deserves closer examination. Moreover, if the Christian concept of salvation is to be submitted to

---

1 That is, Marx, Nietzsche and Freud; cf. P. Ricoeur, *Freud and Philosophy*, 1970.
2 Thomas Pröpper, *Erlösungsglaube und Freiheitsgeschichte: Eine Skizze zur Soteriologie*, 3rd ed. (München: Kösel, 1991), 21.
3 Ibid.

a thorough revision in consequence of the new issues arising from the theological discussion on secularization and interreligious dialogue, new hermeneutic, experimental attempts of "translation" of this term must be ventured and all possible interconnections with it must be sought and explored. Hence, this section shall be devoted to the consideration of those relations. Taking account of the fact that many approaches, especially in consequence of the Enlightenment, have seen a possibility of "translation" for the Church's conventional concept of salvation in the idea of freedom or liberation,[4] the concept of freedom shall serve both as pivotal point for the analysis and as a link to the modern philosophical debate on it.

The Modern Age and the Idea of Freedom

No one can cast doubt upon the fact that the legacy left by the Enlightenment to Western societies was very large. Any attempt to give a comprehensive account of the history or development of the concept of freedom in the course of modernity would go far beyond the scope and aim of the present investigation. Nonetheless, the modern philosophical discussion revolving around the idea of freedom could provide this research with a helpful hint in its quest of an anthropological and existential discourse to which the notion of salvation could find a link and unfold. For the purposes of this work, particular mention should be made to the independence of philosophy in relation to theology (thereby overcoming the medieval axiom *philosophia ancilla theologiae*), the reformulation of the concept of religion and, above all, the so-called anthropological turn, which completely inverted the perspective from which all reality was to be perceived, described and thought about.

Thus, one of the great pursuits and, to a certain extent, achievements of the Enlightenment was "the emergence from one's self-incurred immaturity" (Kant), i.e., the possibility of reaching adulthood, of setting humankind free from ignorance and all sorts of

---

4 For a brief overview, see Hans Kessler, *Erlösung als Befreiung* (Düsseldorf: Patmos, 1972).

illusion, in a word, of attaining one's own autonomy as an individual. It was a deliberate effort to break with tradition as well as with any kind of heteronomous principle, law or authority. The basic assumption behind the whole project of the Enlightenment and modernity was that only after overcoming ignorance, foreign laws, mythological explanations etc. by means of knowledge, progress and technology can human beings, in the exercise of their freedom and autonomy, achieve ultimate *fulfillment*. As a result, the prime focus of philosophy and some theologies was shifted to that of freedom or liberation.

> The philosophy of modernity – especially that of Kant, Fichte, Schelling, and Kierkegaard – alongside its ever more critical analysis of human finite freedom and the contingency of reason in its attempt to grasp the totality of the real can be understood in terms of a debate on the very ground of that freedom.[5]

In line with that tradition of thought, there are contemporary theologians who still try to find a possible linkage between the concepts of salvation, freedom and even God. The Catholic theologian Schupp sees, for instance, in the overall semantic fields of the words "freedom" and "future" a possibility of understanding God as he has revealed himself in the person of Jesus. For him, the "function" of the word "God" in any theological discourse contains at once an element of criticism and one of hope. Accordingly, the idea of freedom would meet the former criterion, in that it introduces a critical moment of all human discourses on God and the notion of future the latter one, in that it introduces the aspect of the openendedness of history and the world. If that is so, far from being objects of theological work, "freedom" and "future" constitute the very "formal-methodological principle" that enables every theological discourse to be conceived within a framework that includes, simultaneously, critique of the

---

5 Helmut Peukert, *Wissenschaftstheorie – Handlungstheorie – fundamentale Theologie: Analysen zu Ansatz und Status theologischer Theoriebildung* (Frankfurt am Main: Suhrkamp, 2009), 389f.; see also Thomas Pröpper, *Evangelium und freie Vernunft: Konturen einer theologischen Hermeneutik* (Freiburg im Breisgau: Herder, 2001), 72–92.

present reality and eschatology.⁶ Likewise, the Catholic theologian Hermann Stinglhammer, after examining Hans Urs von Balthasar's entire work, does not hesitate to affirm that, in accordance with his thread of thought, freedom is indeed "a soteriological assertion."⁷ For "freedom builds up a framework of understanding whereby the question of God's salvation towards today's man can be understandably and reasonably posed within its current problematic."⁸

But even to the present day, one of the most remarkable efforts to find this linkage between the concept of freedom, as conceived in the tradition of the Enlightenment, and the theological discourse on salvation certainly was Thomas Pröpper's – at least in the German-speaking world – whose doctoral dissertation⁹ was indeed a landmark for that approach. He understands his theology of salvation in terms of a theology of freedom and is deeply convinced that theology can only remain faithful to its most original message insofar as its discourse is marked by the issues revolving around the idea of freedom. For God manifested himself as love which can only occur in unconditional freedom. In addition, Christian history of salvation can only be understood in terms of history of freedom and liberation.¹⁰ For him, no epoch in the entire history of Christianity has leveled criticism at the conventional understanding of salvation in so fierce a manner as the Enlightenment did, which was the precondition to finding new ways of access to the originality of Christian revelation in Jesus Christ.

---

6   Franz Schupp, *Auf dem Weg zu einer kritischen Theologie* (Freiburg im Breisgau; Basel; Wien: Herder, 1974), 144.
7   Hermann Stinglhammer, *Freiheit in der Hingabe: trinitarische Freiheitslehre bei Hans Urs von Balthasar: ein Beitrag zur Rezeption der Theodramatik* (Würzburg: Echter, 1997), 2. Originally published in: *Handbuch theologischer Grundbegriffe*, edited by Heinrich Fries, vol. 1, p. 399.
8   Philipp Schäffer, *Rationalität in der Theologie vor dem Forum der Vernunft* apud Stinglhammer. *Freiheit in der Hingabe*, 2
9   Pröpper, *Erlösungsglaube und Freiheitsgeschichte*, submitted in 1986.
10 Ibid., 12.

The Practice of Agape as a Possibility of Real Freedom

In view of such a close connection between freedom and salvation, the question that arises from chapter 4 is whether the modern human being still needs or longs for something like salvation, as understood and preached by Jesus, or whether the discourse of freedom alone suffices. After all, we have come to an age in which "fullness may be attained exclusively 'within' the limits of human life"[11] and in which religious discourse is faced with great skepticism, an age in which the afterworld, transcendence and the metaphysical do not seem to be of any significance.

Taking account of such a problematic, the Catholic theologian Schillebeeckx expressed on different occasions a certain degree of skepticism in that respect. He opens his book *Church: The Human Story of God* by delivering rather a disappointing report of the modern times and with a very provocative question, "Who or what brings human beings salvation and liberation?" Is it science, is it knowledge, is it technology? No, he says. Instead,

> [...] to our detriment and shame, we have had to learn how this arbitrary, unrestrained self-fulfilment in the West has failed to bring men and women either personal or socio-political salvation. [...] At present the project of the total liberation of human beings by human beings seems to be the greatest threat to all humankind. Nowadays 'Western modernity' is again calling in a special way for salvation and liberation: for redemption precisely from those dark powers which modern men and women have themselves called to life.[12]

Schillebeeckx did appreciate philosophical and theological endeavors based on hermeneutic methods to interpret the contents of faith in terms of human categories. But he was equally aware of the fact that some approaches that emerged in the context of or as a

---

11   Charles Taylor, *A Secular Age* (Cambridge, Massachusetts; London: The Belknap Press of Harvard University Press, 2007), 15.
12   Edward Schillebeeckx, *Church: The Human Story of God*, The Collected Works of Edward Schillebeeckx 10 (London: Bloomsbury, 2014), 1.

response to modern philosophy failed to achieve their objective. As a consequence, it is noticeable how loud the cry for salvation and liberation in the Western world is. Similarly and with good reasons, the Protestant theologian Ebeling as well raises the question, "[...] whether the cause for the fact that the word 'God' has become empty and void could not lie in the weakening of the belief in salvation."[13]

Karl Rahner, too, was aware of both the advantages and shortcomings of idealist philosophy. He concedes that the idea of freedom "discovered" in modernity was liberating and very promising. At the same time, however, he doubts that it can bring complete fulfillment.

> The free man experiences himself in his very freedom as someone condemned to freedom, as someone who freely inaugurates the uncontrollable [*das Unverfügbare*]. He may still be intoxicated [*berauscht*] to some extent with the emancipation which he has won for himself *vis-à-vis* a *nature* which was impinging directly upon him and threatening him. He will soon notice, however, and experience more and more – and the wise have already had this experience even today – that his creative freedom experiences *itself* as a freedom which is disposed and dares to advance into the immeasurable darkness. Yet to whom should man confide this disposed being, from whom is he to accept it, where can he know his daring freedom to be safe, this freedom which falls into obscurity?[14]

Rahner is correct when he points to the demanding, burdensome and even frightening character of freedom. Indeed this was one of the central issues of existential philosophy and, besides leveling criticism at idealism, it touches on a complex area of modern life: what to "do" with one's freedom? On the other hand, Rahner's philosophical understanding of freedom was, for Pröpper, all too influenced by the Thomistic metaphysic theory of cognition, which impeded him

---

13 Gerhard Ebeling, "Das Verständnis von Heil in säkularisierter Zeit," in *Wort und Glaube*, vol. 3 (Tübingen: Mohr, 1975), 352f.
14 Karl Rahner, "The Man of Today and Religion," in *Theological Investigations*, trans. Karl-H. Kruger and Boniface Kruger, vol. 6 (Darton: Longman & Todd, 1969), 14 (emphasis in original).

from seeing and noticing the "formal unconditionality of freedom."[15] Therefore, precisely in order to avoid such "misunderstandings," Pröpper points out the limits of any approach that tries to explicate freedom as an end to be pursued. Rather, he argues for a conception of freedom as a formal, unconditional principle that enables human autonomy and self-determination. This principle can neither be shown objectively nor justified metaphysically. Yet, if it wills to be human, it must hold as the unconditional principle on the basis of which all thinking along with all its (material) contents can be determined. On that account, it can also serve as "philosophical principle of theological hermeneutics."[16]

Now, if freedom is to be understood as the most basic principle of both human subjectivity and intersubjectivity, insofar as the recognition and respect of the other's freedom is the immediate consequence of the recognition of the subject's freedom, it seems not appropriate to conceive human existence metaphysically or to simply justify human ethics deontologically, as this way of proceeding violates the primacy of freedom. Rather, formal, unconditional freedom functions as the highest judgment criterion of the subject for real existence and as principle of every ethical norm. As a consequence, no ethical norm can be derived from a principle other than freedom, and ethical judgment is completely entrusted to the subject's capability of judging based on this supreme criterion. Thus, the subject's situational awareness assumes crucial significance, and each concrete situation has its own weight in the process of subjective judgment.[17]

Owing to the human condition, however, not always are all freedoms mutually recognized. One very often sees situations in which the freedom of others is not recognized and even violated. One has oneself the experience of not being recognized in one's freedom. But for Pröpper, it is precisely in such circumstances that the subject, by remaining faithful to that supreme principle and nevertheless recognizing the other, discovers what the idea of freedom indeed means,

---

15   Pröpper, *Evangelium und freie Vernunft: Konturen einer theologischen Hermeneutik*, 16f.
16   Ibid., 15.
17   Ibid., 63.

namely, *unconditional* freedom. Therefore, the renouncement of any conditions in interpersonal relationships together with the concern and commitment so that the other, every other, be and become free are, for Pröpper, the essential features in which the ethical idea of solidarity can be grounded.[18] The principle of freedom is thereby embedded in the human category of history, and the idea of solidarity, in a similar manner as in some approaches of political theology,[19] emerges as the core of the Judeo-Christian heritage of thought.

Both Peukert and Pröpper base their theories on Kant's theory of morality which already contains in its essence this element of solidarity, though, obviously, not bearing this name. For Langthaler, Kant's efforts to interconnect purpose (*Zweck*) and duty (*Pflicht*) could be understood as "[...] a sensitivity for the possible endangerment of 'humanness and solidarity' in protest 'against appalling injustice.'"[20] For whenever someone fulfills one's duty in terms of promoting the freedom of the other, one is doing much more than just "benevolent duty"; one is at once fulfilling the very purpose of promoting the happiness of others. Moreover, according to Kant, no good deed towards others can simply count as an act of benevolence. For when someone helps a person in need, that deed is not completely gratuitous. One is just giving back what the society as a whole has taken away from her, what belongs to her as a right.[21]

---

18 Pröpper follows here especially Peukert's theory of solidarity. Cf. ibid., 61–63; see especially Peukert, *Wissenschaftstheorie – Handlungstheorie – fundamentale Theologie*, chap. 10.

19 See also Johann Baptist Metz, ed., *Compassion – Weltprogramm des Christentums: soziale Verantwortung lernen* (Freiburg im Breisgau: Herder, 2000); Johann Baptist Metz, *Memoria passionis: ein provozierendes Gedächtnis in pluralistischer Gesellschaft*, 4th ed. (Freiburg im Breisgau: Herder, 2011).

20 Rudolf Langthaler, "'Ich bin ein Mensch. Alles, was Menschen widerfährt, das trifft auch mich' (Terenz – Kant – Peukert): Motive der kantischen Tugendlehre und Ethiktheologie als philosophischer Hintergrund der fundamentalen Theologie von Helmut Peukert," in *"… und nichts Menschliches ist mir fremd": Theologische Grenzgänge*, ed. Ottmar John and Magnus Striet (Regensburg: Friedrich Pustet, 2010), 87; see especially Kant, Refl. 6997, in AA XIX, 222.

21 Ibid., 88; for that, see especially Kant, AA XXVII.1, 416.

At this juncture, one can notice strong resemblances to that reality to which the New Testament refers as agape. Furthermore, the idea of solidarity contains in itself not only the essential features of agape, but also those of the love of neighbor, at least as it was spelled out by Jesus in the parable of the Good Samaritan. At the same time, two questions arise as to the relation between freedom, solidarity and love. Firstly, whether solidarity and agape mean, ultimately, the same and, secondly, whether the correlation between freedom and the biblical notion of love is just a causal one, in that the formal principle of freedom enables solidarity and love, as Pröpper suggests, or whether there are other elements that must be taken into consideration.

The first question is to be answered with yes, although, of course, the idea of solidarity does not exhaust that of agape. Yet, just as agape, in the context of the New Testament, went beyond the conventional value of philanthropy or the oriental ethics of mercy, so did the idea of solidarity in these days. By so doing, it is able to convey in a "neutral" language the contents of a "religious word," a feature that renders it extremely topical. For that reason, the idea of solidarity can facilitate the comprehension of the New Testamental notion of agape and, to a more limited extent, that of salvation.

The second question is a little more complex. To be sure, there can be no true love, unless one's freedom can be presupposed. However, the reduction of freedom to a formal principle seems to fail to recognize an important element of the New Testamental message of love: that the practice of love is a liberating practice as well. If that is correct, freedom is not just a prerequisite for love, but a consequence, too. If the parable of the Good Samaritan is once again taken as example, all three characters of the story were *formally* free to show compassion towards the half-dead man, but only one of them did. Precisely because he practiced love towards that fallen man, he proved to be or to become free from the conventions of his society according to which he should have acted otherwise, given that Samaritans did not relate to Jews and vice versa. The example set by Jesus in his public life confirms that. It was his "universal" love for each and every person that enabled him to overcome all sorts of boundaries and conventions. The healing of the Syrophoenician woman's daughter, as seen above (p. 104ff), is a very illustrative example. But also his fellowship at the table with tax collectors, sinners and outcasts, and his physical contact with lepers and sinners are further instances that offer clear evidence for the claim that his desire to love made him free to do whatever was necessary to express it, irrespective of the social, ethical and religious barriers and conventions.

Therefore, one can say that, albeit being enabled by the *formal* principle of freedom, the New Testamental notion of agape brings about *real*, effective, liberating freedom. Neither is the "monologic self-referentiality"[22] of the subject entirely broken solely through formal freedom nor is one's opening to the neighbor completely realized. Rather than the belief that one must first become free in order to be capable of loving, as has been normally assumed traditionally and even in some contemporary psychological, philosophical and theological theories, Jesus' message of love seems to suggest that it is the logic of love that frees the subject from solipsism and egocentric illusions.

However, this minor criticism of Pröpper's theory based on the concept of love cannot be equated to contemporary approaches such as Pope's which are based on the concept of love as well, though with the purpose of undermining any theology at the basis of which are the modern ideas of subjectivity, consciousness and volition. Pope's main point is that the Thomistic notion of nature is missing in contemporary Catholic ethics and theology. For Thomas places love in nature itself, by combining nature with biology. Love is not only settled in subjectivity, but also in nature. "Human love was understood by Thomas to be rooted in human generic nature, that is, as a passion rooted in the sensitive appetite and involving somatic aspects of the person."[23] By so arguing, Pope seeks to trace the origin of love (agape/*caritas*) to human nature which, in turn, was created by God to "order" life in the world.

> The *ordo amoris* is the natural basis of the *ordo caritatis*. The former naturally begins with the first principle of creation and orders all other beings

---

22 A phrase by Knut Wenzel, *Sakramentales Selbst: der Mensch als Zeichen des Heils* (Freiburg im Breisgau; Basel; Wien: Herder, 2003), 338.

23 Stephen J. Pope, *The Evolution of Altruism and the Ordering of Love* (Washington, DC: Georgetown University Press, 1995), 68.

according to the ways in which they are 'before' or 'after' one another in relation to God. Thomas understood natural love to share the orderly nature of the created world, as evidently intended by its author (STh I.60.1ad, 3).[24]

Admittedly, embedding love in the order of being, that is, in human nature, is a more compelling argument than linking it to one's (formal) freedom. However, it is doubtful whether one can work meaningfully with the concept of nature for this purpose in a secular, post-metaphysic age. Moreover, in face of the message of Jesus and Christian revelation, to do away with the idea of freedom at the base of a contemporary theory of love appears to be highly problematic. Therefore, it seems more appropriate to opt for an understanding of love based on the idea of freedom rather than on the nature of metaphysics. At the same time, though, a closer examination of the message of Jesus has shown that freedom lies not only in the origin of the practice of love, given that the performance of the latter can bring about real freedom as well. The human being is, therefore, not preprogrammed by God to love and to maintain a certain social order predetermined by him as well. Just as the practice of love and solidarity can only occur in unconditional freedom, it is love that enables a true opening of the subject to the other and allows the possibility of freedom from old patterns of behavior, beliefs, prejudices etc.

The Unity between Love of God and Love of Neighbor

The aspect that still remains to be dealt with is whether or not there is any direct connection between "religious" and "secular" love or, in a more theological language, between love of God and love of neighbor. Given that the twofold commandment of love was made into one in the message of the New Testament, how does one "commence" to love? With love of neighbor or with love of God? An illuminating insight with regard to that question was given by Karl Rahner, who determinedly affirmed an inextricable unity between them, in that love of neighbor is understood, both in the Scripture

---

24 Ibid., 59.

and Christian tradition, *as* love of God.²⁵ Still, the question remains why then the Scripture concentrates "[...] the whole Christian relationship to God in the love of our neighbour [...]."²⁶ In addition, how should the word "commandment" here be properly interpreted: Is it just an external order given by God, is it the "proof" of our love of God or does it mean something beyond it?

In line with Christian tradition, especially by following Scholastic theology, Rahner affirms that the love of neighbor is not merely "preparation, effect, fruit and touchstone" of the love of God, but is itself an *act* of that love of God.

> The tradition of the schools in Catholic theology has already held fast for a long time and this unanimously to the fact that the specific Christian love of neighbour is both in potency and in act a moment of the infused supernatural theological virtue of *caritas* by which we love God in his Spirit for his own sake and in direct community with him. [...] [A]n act within that total believing and hoping surrender of man to God which we call love and which alone justifies man, i.e. hands him over to God, because, being supported by the loving self-communication of God in the uncreated grace of the Holy Spirit, it really unites man with God, not as He is recognised by us but as He is in Himself in His absolute divinity.²⁷

For Rahner, the very fact *that* the human being is at all able to love, *that* the human being is *a priori* inclined to this act must find its wellspring in supernatural grace and thereby constitute part of the theological virtue of *caritas*. If that is correct, love of neighbor cannot be conceived merely as an "external," heteronomous commandment. In his view, love of neighbor is not just a moral act among others, but a human act par excellence, "[...] the basis and sum total of the moral as such."²⁸ Even more, in this act of love for

---

25 See particularly Karl Rahner, "Reflections on the Unity of the Love of Neighbour and the Love of God," in *Theological Investigations*, trans. Karl-H. Kruger and Boniface Kruger, vol. 6 (Darton: Longman & Todd, 1969), 234–37.
26 Ibid., 235.
27 Ibid., 236 (emphasis in original).
28 Ibid., 240.

the other Thou, "[...] the original unity of what is human and what is the totality of man's experience is collected together and achieved [...]."²⁹ Obviously, "achieved" (*vollzogen*) is employed here not in the sense of an accomplishment of a planned task or a goal, as it were a usual activity. As Wenzel observes, the love of neighbor is not an accomplishment – perhaps even a meritorious one – of the subject "who benevolently dispenses the love that springs from the inexhaustible sources of its self-consciousness." Rather, the act of love entails "breaking the monologic self-referentiality, opening to the neighbor."³⁰ The act of love reveals, thus, the subject's necessary referentiality to and dependency on the other.

That openness to the Thou and communication between human beings, whose culmination is love, is conceived by Rahner from the perspective of his metaphysical theory of knowledge. Accordingly, in the process of human communication, "[...] the *a posteriori* object is the necessary mediation of the knowing subject to itself [...]."³¹ As a consequence, without the mediated communication with a human *Thou*, the self can neither "be one with oneself" (*bei sich sein*), i.e., attain deep and true knowledge of itself, nor can it express or realize itself through its freedom and self-disposal. Being so, "[...] the essential *a priori* openness to the other human being which must be undertaken freely belongs as such to the *a priori* and most basic constitution of man and is an essential inner moment of his (knowing and willing) transcendentality."³² Precisely because of its volitional and cognitional character, the love of neighbor enables, thereby, the human being to "attain the whole of reality given to us in categories" and experience God by grace, even if unconsciously or unreflectedly.³³

---

29 Ibid., 243.
30 Wenzel, *Sakramentales Selbst*, 338.
31 Rahner, "Reflections on the Unity of the Love of Neighbour and the Love of God," 240; for Rahner's metaphysical theory of cognition, see Karl Rahner, *Hearer of the Word: Laying the Foundation for a Philosophy of Religion*, ed. Andrew Tallon, trans. Joseph Donceel (New York: Continuum, 1994).
32 Rahner, "Reflections on the Unity of the Love of Neighbour and the Love of God," 241.
33 Ibid., 246.

By conceiving love not merely as a moral act, but as an ontological one, Rahner succeeds in embedding it in the totality of human experience and in making it the key of access to the self, to reality and to God. Obviously, the love of neighbor does not exhaust all the dimensions (prayer, sacraments etc.) of the love of God, but it is definitely the primary act of the love of God. This amounts to saying that, if a person loves her neighbor truly and unconditionally, she may grasp what the nature and essence of God is, at least as Christians understand it, and definitely performs an act of love of and service to God, whether conscious of it or not.

The Secular World: A Conducive Environment to the Praxis of Love

The context in which we live differs radically from that in which Thomas Aquinas wrote his *Summa Theologica*. He could work with Christian categories to develop his metaphysics, theory of knowledge, theory of human nature etc., which is no longer feasible for contemporary theologians, especially when working from an interreligious or intercultural perspective. Moreover, not only do the different interpretations of reality, as they are transmitted by the various religious traditions, constitute a problem for modern individuals, but also the sphere of the religious as such. Talal Asad describes the radical inversion that theological discourses have experienced since the advent of the modern age and the process of secularization as follows.

> In fact the historical process of secularization effects a remarkable ideological inversion. [...] For at one time 'the secular' was a part of a theological discourse (*saeculum*). [...] In the discourse of modernity 'the secular' presents itself as the ground from which theological discourse was generated (as a form of false consciousness) and from which it gradually emancipated itself in its march to freedom.[34]

As a consequence, it is no wonder that the discourse of modernity

---

34 Talal Asad, *Formations of the Secular: Christianity, Islam, Modernity* (Stanford, California: Stanford University Press, 2008), 192.

had the pretension to encompass all facets of reality. One can indeed say with Charles Taylor that "[…] we have moved from a world in which the place of fullness was understood as unproblematically outside of or 'beyond' human life, to a conflicted age in which this construal is challenged by others which place it (in a wide range of different ways) 'within' human life."[35] Needless to say, from a theological or religious point of view, this is not without problems, as this pretension puts in question the very possibility and raison d'être of religious discourses in Western modern societies. In recent years, however, many scholars diagnose not only an increasing search for religious experiences of various kinds, but also a different sensitivity as to the import of religion for a sound society.[36] This, in turn, implies that, far from being but a private affair in the life of individuals, religions can perform a constructive role in any society.[37] If that is correct, not only can the thesis of the "decline of religion" be disclaimed, but also that of the "privatization of religions." Yet, conversely, one must inquire about the feasibility of religious practice in a secular environment.

There should be no doubt about the real possibility of piety, experience of God and even attainment of knowledge of God outside the limits of the church or in the secular world. Karl Rahner expounded it in several of his writings that God's grace, by virtue of his universal salvific will, enables it in ways that are unknown to us.[38] He goes so far as to say that, in a world where religious language is no longer

---

35   Taylor, *A Secular Age*, 15.
36   José Casanova, "Public Religions Revisited," in *Religion: Beyond a Concept*, ed. Hent Vries (New York: Fordham University Press, 2008), 101; Jürgen Habermas, *Glauben und Wissen*, Friedenspreis des Deutschen Buchhandels (Frankfurt am Main: Suhrkamp, 2001), 21; see also Hans Joas and Klaus Wiegandt, eds., *Säkularisierung und die Weltreligionen* (Frankfurt am Main: Fischer Taschenbuch, 2007); David Martin, *On Secularization: Towards a Revised General Theory* (Aldershot: Ashgate, 2005).
37   See especially José Casanova and Hans Joas, *Religion und die umstrittene Moderne* (Stuttgart: Kohlhammer, 2010).
38   See particularly Karl Rahner, "Kirchliche und außerkirchliche Religiosität," in *Schriften zur Theologie*, vol. 12 (Zürich; Einsiedeln; Köln: Benziger, 1975), 582–98.

predominant, authentic experiences of God can even dispense with important words such as "God" or "salvation." Moreover, every epoch has its own particular catchwords that embody the spirit of their time.[39]

Precisely on that account, the Danish theologian Troels Nørager sees in a secularized environment as much a chance for believers to "innovate" their practices as one to "update" the understanding of God. Beyond doubt, this is a difficult move, but absolutely necessary. He describes this change as follows:

> Thus, gradually from the eighteenth century onward we have come to think of power and justice as prerogatives of the political realm, and we can learn from contemporary political philosophy how the legitimate functions of power and justice are secured by a constitutional, liberal democracy. This development has fundamentally altered the whole agenda of theology. Whereas at the time of Luther and Calvin theologians could confidently proclaim God as the sovereign ruler of both kingdoms, today we must acknowledge that on the level of society God has been reduced to symbolic references in the residues of civil religion.[40]

By seeking more appropriate fashions of spelling out what the Christian idea of God comprises, he observes that "[...] the overall process of Western secularization [...] has left us in a situation where love stands out as the fundamental category of God-talk."[41] This being the case, just as the process of secularization has caused believers of all traditions to rethink the vocabulary of their "God-talk," so they, too, are urged to reconsider the mode of expression of their faith in a world that may not understand such language anymore.

If that is correct, the process of secularization ought to be regarded positively by Christians. Without regard to Gogarten's thesis as to whether secularization may in fact be said to be an inherent

---

39 Rahner, "Reflections on the Unity of the Love of Neighbour and the Love of God," 248.

40 Troels Nørager, "Difficult but Necessary: Conditions of a Contemporary Theology of Love," *Dialog* 50, no. 1 (2011): 47.

41 Ibid., 48.

and legitimate development of Christianity,[42] what seems important to emphasize is that the challenges posed by secularization are beneficial to religious life and must be faced up to with seriousness and creativity.

The Complex Relation between Religion and Identity in a Secularized World
To recognize and affirm positively the value of secularity has profound consequences for the believer. The first important issue which one has to seriously face and cope with is one's identity. In the view of Charles Taylor, whereas in early societies individuals derived their identity from the socio-political-religious system in which they were "embedded," modern identities seem to have gone through a process of disembedding. In pre-modern societies, individuals would define themselves as belonging to this tribe or as being subjects of that king "since time out of mind." Modern citizens, by contrast, regard "[...] all as coming together to form a political entity, to which we all relate in the same way, as equal members."[43] As Taylor puts it, the subject has gradually become "buffered" with regard to his/her environment, which meant abandoning the condition of being "porous," i.e., vulnerable. Ingredients such as ethnicity, religion, social class etc. ended up no longer being absolute categories for the definition of one's identity. The modern individual has achieved independence of them to such an extent as to acquire autonomy to assemble his/her own identity according to his/her imaginary.

In the course of that gradual process of disembedding, a very promising way of dealing with religious identity and, by extension, religious difference was political secularism. To this end, secular states and modern ideologies like nationalism have made every effort to persuade their citizens that their identity is and was given them "since time out of mind" by X nation which speaks Y language and has W and Z values so that citizenship could become the primary

---

42 Friedrich Gogarten, *Verhängnis und Hoffnung der Neuzeit: die Säkularisierung als theologisches Problem*, 2nd ed. (Stuttgart: Vorwerk, 1958), 12.
43 Charles Taylor, "The Future of the Religious Past," in *Religion: Beyond a Concept*, ed. Hent Vries (New York: Fordham University Press, 2008), 192.

principle of identity. In that fashion, the idea of citizenship had to and did

> [...] transcend the different identities built on class, gender, and religion, replacing conflicting perspectives by unifying experience. In an important sense, this transcendent mediation *is* secularism. Secularism is not simply an intellectual answer to a question about enduring social peace and toleration. It is an enactment by which a *political medium* (representation of citizenship) redefines and transcends particular and differentiating practices of the self that are articulated through class, gender, and religion.[44]

Applied to the topic of interreligious dialogue this would amount to saying that the solution adopted by political secularism to the conflicts created by religious difference was to ignore them or to act as though they would not play any relevant role in society. To be sure, European societies had to learn a bitter lesson in the course of the denominational wars of the 16th and 17th centuries, the most painful of which having been the Thirty Years' War (1618–1648).[45] In that context, the suppression of religious identity might have indeed brought about peace, tolerance and, in a sense, an experience of liberation.

However, as seen earlier in this chapter, the factor religion can neither be downplayed as irrational or the like nor be constrained to a private affair. To simply ignore this fundamental aspect of both human life and a sound society cannot be accepted as a satisfactory answer to the problem of religious identity and difference.[46] Even the establishment of democracy cannot be seen as a sustainable solution

---

44 Asad, *Formations of the Secular*, 5 (emphasis in original).
45 Cf. José Casanova, "Public Religions Revisited," in *Religion: Beyond a Concept*, ed. Hent Vries (New York: Fordham University Press, 2008), 109f.
46 In his book *Identity and Violence*, Amartya Sen also shows how political secularism and the principle of tolerance cannot suffice as a solution to the issue of identity and how other models of integration of religious difference were possible in Indian or other Asian societies even before the Enlightenment (cf. Amartya Kumar Sen, *Identity and Violence: The Illusion of Destiny* [New York: W.W. Norton & Co., 2006], 49–55).

to this problem, as it raised new issues that can in the end cause deep divisions between the different groupings constituting a given society. Taylor observes that, insofar as in the age of democracy to be in the majority is a decisive factor, democracy does underlie identity struggles, considering that, in the end, it concerns the "political identity of the state." This particularly affects religious minorities, as they are commonly underrepresented and must really struggle to maintain their identities. The questions that arise out of that struggle can be put in the following terms: "[...] can I/we 'identify with' this state? Do we see ourselves as reflected there? Can we see ourselves as part of the people this state is meant to reflect/promote?"[47]

As a consequence, each grouping tends to see the other as a threat to its own or to the nation's political identity, a sufficient reason for the conflicts between them to intensify. For Assmann, the touchstone to test how respectfully a society treats the minorities existing in it is the use (or not) of coercion to assimilate or, in worse cases, to convert. Such a demand shows the impossibility of recognition of the others such as they are or, alternatively, of a translation of the values present in the predominant religion. As a reaction against such a menace of being dominated and swallowed up by the hegemonic culture, minority groups or religions tend to vigorously defy it. That is construed by Assmann "[...] as an 'immune reaction' of the cultural system, a tendency to build up a deliberate 'counter-identity' against the dominating system."[48] In consequence of such struggle for survival, minority religions frequently go through a process of transformation and renewal, so that their identity may either be reinforced or formed anew. But again, what lies behind the claims of either of those ends, that is, minorities or hegemonic powers, including the different forms of modern nationalisms, is ultimately "a need for difference," for the recognition of one's self-worth and dignity.[49]

---

47   Taylor, "The Future of the Religious Past," 234.
48   Jan Assmann, "Translating Gods: Religion as a Factor of Cultural (Un)Translatability," in *Religion: Beyond a Concept*, ed. Hent Vries (New York: Fordham University Press, 2008), 142.
49   Taylor, "The Future of the Religious Past," 235.

Unconditional Recognition
That being the case, it is impossible to dissociate the question of identity from that of recognition. Indeed, Taylor argues "[...] that identities in the modern world are more and more formed in this direct relation to others, in a space of recognition."[50] For no human identity can be thought to be purely inwardly formed. Someone's identity always requires the recognition of the other, either in the mode of approval or rejection. Hence the decisive importance of interaction between the various groups. For (enemy) stereotypes can only resist in the absence of interaction, dialogue and encounter. In fact, in order to perpetuate stereotypes, the less interaction the better. Since it is questionable whether the state is able or willing to mediate such interactions or to find forms of mutual recognition between the various groups of which its society is comprised, it is important that churches, institutional religions and ordinary believers develop new initiatives to this purpose. For, in the last analysis, not only does the society as a whole benefit from it, as the probability of conflicts and violence tends to be reduced, but every individual, too.

The Dynamics of Recognition. Following Hegel's and Mead's theories of recognition, the social philosopher Axel Honneth describes the interconnectedness between recognition and self as follows:

> The connection between the experience of recognition and one's relation-to-self stems from the intersubjective structure of personal identity. The only way in which individuals are constituted as persons is by learning to refer to themselves, from the perspective of an approving or encouraging other, as being with certain positive traits and abilities. The scope of such traits – and hence the extent of one's positive relation-to-self – increases with each new form of recognition that individuals are able to apply to

---

50 Ibid., 236; for a more detailed study on that subject, see Charles Taylor, "The Politics of Recognition," in *Multiculturalism: Examining the Politics of Recognition*, ed. Amy Gutmann (Princeton: Princeton University Press, 1992), 25–73; in addition, the book *Multiculturalism: Examining the Politics of Recognition*, ed. Amy Gutmann (Princeton: Princeton University Press, 1992) offers a few comments on and criticisms of Taylor's essay.

themselves as subjects. In this way, the prospect of basic self-confidence is inherent in the experience of love; the prospect of self-respect, in the experience of legal recognition; and finally, the prospect of self-esteem, in the experience of solidarity.[51]

Both Hegel and Mead are aware that legal recognition does not suffice for human beings to feel fully recognized in their identities. Hegel and Mead propose, respectively, ethical life and the division of labor as further stages in which every individual can be recognized for his/her particular traits and abilities. Even so, there seems to be a gap that cannot be filled by any institutional instance. Precisely when a determined group feels oppressed and fights for its recognition or equal rights, Honneth observes that an extremely crucial human component comes into play, namely, solidarity. By solidarity he means all sorts of interactions of mutual support among (groups of) subjects in a given society who share a common value, have similar traits and struggle for due recognition.[52]

On the other hand, as in the case of love or forgiveness, solidarity cannot be commanded or guaranteed by the state or law either. As was seen above (p. 224), it can only come forth from one's unconditional freedom. This, in turn, makes the dynamics of identity extremely vulnerable, as the full recognition of any identity ultimately depends on human love and solidarity, which cannot be planned or assured. This being the case, one can indeed say with Paul Ricoeur that the struggle for mutual recognition can only reach "states of peace," that is, moments of reconsideration, reconciliation and mutual recognition, within the logic of love (agape), within the paradigm of the gift.[53]

Obviously, this is not an easy way to go. Ricoeur's choice of the word "course" (*chemin*) implies indeed that this is a path that must be pursued by the subject. This course marks the passage from the *reconnaissance* as identification (Kant), whereby the subject aims at

---

51 Axel Honneth, *The Struggle for Recognition: The Moral Grammar of Social Conflicts* (Cambridge, Massachusetts: MIT Press, 1996), 173.
52 Ibid., 128f.
53 Paul Ricoeur, *The Course of Recognition*, trans. David Pellauer (Cambridge, Massachusetts: Harvard University Press, 2005), 220.

the mastering of meaning, to the *reconnaissance mutuelle* (Hegel), the mutual recognition, by which the subject puts him- or herself under the "tutelage of a relationship of reciprocity," in passing through the *reconnaissance de soi* (Bergson), the self-recognition amidst the variety of capacities that enable "one's ability to act, one's agency."[54]

Recognition through Love. In view of Ricoeur's description of the "course of recognition," two aspects of his theory seem to be of relevance to this section and deserve closer scrutiny. The first one concerns the role of love in this process and the second the element of human agency. As far as love is concerned, it should be noted that whereas Hegel ascribes it a significant role, particularly in the early stages of human life – love is predominantly understood in terms of sexual, marital, and family love – and at the beginning of the course of recognition, that is, as a necessary precondition for participation in the public life,[55] Ricoeur sees in love, understood in terms of agape, the only possibility of attaining the mutual recognition intended by Hegel. Ricoeur regards the struggle for recognition, as conceived by Hegel, as perfectly legitimate and necessary for individual as well as social life. Even the violence that may break out from such fights must be regarded as natural. However, since the process of formation of identity is a very dynamic one and the human being constantly needs "newer" forms of recognition which can often be linked to experiences of violence and vengeance, Hegel's proposal does not provide a satisfactory solution. For Ricoeur, as long as the experiences of violence and vengeance rest at the root of any struggle for recognition, the ordinary, legal procedures fail in their purpose of putting an end to any dispute. This can be accomplished only through

---

54 The whole book is devoted to the explanation of this course. Yet, a short summary of his project is provided in ibid., 248.

55 "[...] [F]or every subject, the experience of being loved constitutes a necessary precondition for participation in the public life of a community. [...] Only the feeling of having the particular nature of one's urges fundamentally recognized and affirmed can allow one to develop the degree of basic self-confidence that renders one capable of participating, with equal rights, in political will-formation" (Hegel, Jena Lectures on the Philosophy of Spirit, apud Honneth, *The Struggle for Recognition*, 38).

love. For even if the demands of the other person, in her struggle for recognition, appear to be unjustified, love is *capable* of recognizing them, inasmuch as it knows nothing of comparison and justifications are foreign to it. "In moving beyond comparison, agape cares for 'the person one sees.'"[56] The real needs of the other are given highest priority. Precisely because one cannot always understand the other or his/her needs through empathy, love believes him/her and gives what is being asked. For love is for-*give*-ness, in spite of the other being guilty or in the wrong. Thus, the greatest gain of Ricoeur's inclusion of agape in the course of recognition is that love is de facto the only "competence" of human beings capable of *recognizing* the real needs of the other, even if they do not sound plausible or justifiable in the eyes of the subject. Obviously, love proceeds that way without, at the same time, infringing on the competence of justice.[57]

A similar effort to incorporate that essential ingredient of recognition is made by Honneth in his theory of intersubjectivity.[58] To this end, he avails himself of the Kantian category of respect (*Achtung*) contained in his "*Groundwork of the Metaphysic of Morals.*" To clearly illustrate what is implied in Kant's idea of *Achtung*, which in German can mean at once attention, respect, esteem and even reverence, Honneth uses opposite words such as blindness or insensitivity. Accordingly, to fully recognize someone means to perceive others in their otherness and to allow them to emerge from their condition of *invisibility*. Under the term invisibility, he subsumes all those social, cultural or religious barriers that may prevent us from seeing others as they actually are and, even worse, that cause us to look through them as though they were not there despite their physical presence.[59] Honneth observes that such a phenomenon can occur in every society and most individuals may not even realize it. For him, Kant's idea of

---

56 Ricoeur, *The Course of Recognition*, 221.
57 As for the relation between love and justice, see above pp. 160–165.
58 Axel Honneth, "Unsichtbarkeit: Über die moralische Epistemologie von 'Anerkennung,'" in *Unsichtbarkeit: Stationen einer Theorie der Intersubjektivität* (Frankfurt am Main: Suhrkamp, 2003), 10–27.
59 Ibid., 10. Honneth borrows this figure of speech from a famous novel by Ralph Ellison entitled *Invisible Man* (1952).

Achtung, by contrast, offers a valuable insight for overcoming such patterns of behavior. Besides, Honneth maintains that such an attitude towards others has a profound effect not only on the person or group who is respected and recognized, but also on the subject of that action, since she/he is transformed, too, by performing it. After all, in the view of Honneth, the idea of *Achtung* allows the subject the possibility of disruption of self-love and tendencies towards selfishness.[60] Obviously, such respect for the other as well as for his/her needs does not eliminate the asymmetry between the seeing subject and the visible other. This gap between both cannot be completely bridged, so that the other remains, for the subject, a mystery. Ricoeur sums up the process of mutual recognition as being at once "a struggle against the misrecognition of others" and "a struggle for recognition of oneself by others."[61] For that reason, what is at stake, for Ricoeur, is not as much the *cognition* of the protagonists of the process of recognition as it is the exchange of gifts and values that takes place *between* them through which *recognition* can be expressed and made visible.[62]

(Self-)Recognition through One's Agency. The second question posed above, based on Ricoeur's theory of recognition, concerns the agency of the subject as a key of access to self-recognition. Following Nietzsche, Ricoeur doubts that the Cartesian *cogito* along with its long tradition in the philosophy of subjectivity offers an adequate model to attain self-knowledge and self-consciousness, which are the essential elements for the question of identity.[63] Accordingly, he regards the idea of an immediate self-givenness, self-disclosure or self-transparency with a degree of skepticism. By contrast, he sees in self-attestation and testimony much more reliable means of access to

---

60 Ibid., 21f; see also Ulrich Dehn, "In die Sichtbarkeit treten: Phasen und Koordinaten des interreligiösen Dialogs," *Zeitschrift für Missionswissenschaft* 37, no. 1 (2011): 43f.

61 Ricoeur, *The Course of Recognition*, 258.

62 Ibid., 262f.

63 Paul Ricoeur, *Oneself as Another*, reprint (Chicago: University of Chicago Press, 1995), 11ff.

self-consciousness. Whereas the *epistēmē* of the *cogito* claims immediate certainty, irrespective of the recognition or refusal of another, the attestation of the subject requires gestures of recognition of the other and is dependent on trust.[64] Therefore the truth of the subject, its identity, cannot be verified with the aid of the tools and epistemological methods of science. One's identity can only be attested to. Attestation "[...] is fundamentally attestation *of* self."[65] Therefore, the identity of the subject has to be "discovered" through words and deeds performed by it, through its own testimony. Self-knowledge and self-consciousness can thus be attained through mediations, be it through words and deeds, be it through the re-action of others in the face of one's self-attestation.

Elsewhere, Ricoeur claims, similarly, that "[...] there is no self-understanding that is not *mediated* by signs, symbols, and texts; in the last resort understanding coincides with the interpretation given to these mediating terms."[66] Insofar as self-attestation is nothing but "hermeneutics of the self,"[67] self-consciousness and identity are to be understood as a hermeneutic process. Such intricate aspects of (religious) identity have been worked out in more detail by Marianne Moyaert, with particular attention being devoted precisely to the question of interreligious encounters.[68] In her view, the tension between sameness and otherness, inherent to identity processes, can

---

64 Knut Wenzel, *Glaube in Vermittlung: theologische Hermeneutik nach Paul Ricoeur* (Freiburg im Breisgau; Basel; Wien: Herder, 2008), 196; Ricoeur, *Oneself as Another*, 21f.

65 Ricoeur, *Oneself as Another*, 22 (emphasis in original).

66 Paul Ricoeur, "On Interpretation," in *From Text to Action*, trans. Kathleen Blamey, Essays in Hermeneutics 2 (Evanston: Northwestern University Press, 1991), 15.

67 Ricoeur, *Oneself as Another*, 21.

68 Marianne Moyaert, *In Response to the Religious Other: Ricoeur and the Fragility of Interreligious Encounters* (Lanham, Md.: Lexington Books, 2014), chap. 4; as far as the relation between religious identity and otherness is concerned, see a number of insightful essays recently published in Ulrich Schmiedel and James M. Matarazzo Jr., eds., *Dynamics of Difference: Christianity and Alterity*, A Festschrift for Werner G. Jeanrond (New York: Bloomsbury T&T Clark, 2014).

in fact be reduced by a sort of "narrative identity" whereby such mediations certainly play a decisive role.

> Self-understanding implies mediation and hermeneutical detours. The self is refigured by conversing with 'others,' and that conversation is defined broadly: it includes both dialogue with real others (the *face-à-face*) and the reading and studying of written sources (great literature, stories from different wisdom traditions, poetry, and philosophy, for instance).[69]

Following this line of thought, (inter)religious encounters are an opportunity to attest to one's religion's truth by means of narratives. Due to certain circumstances or depending on the interlocutor, one's narrative may change in its "details." The same event or experience may be told in several fashions. "It is always possible to revise a recounted story which takes account of other events, or even which organizes the recounted events differently."[70] What remains is one's commitment to the absolute, transcendent Thou, despite all contingency, which, in the last resort, can only be attested to, never "proved true."

Interestingly, Wenzel sees in Ricoeur's theory of consciousness a very close link to the Hebrew notion of truth (אֱמֶת, *emeth*). Based on a study by Hans von Soden, he maintains that truth, in the Old Testament, rather than being the equivalence between intellect and thing, consists in the "*self-attestation of an agent over time.*"[71] *Emeth* has more to do with faithfulness and reliability than it has to do with epistemic knowledge. Accordingly, for a Hebrew, truth is more of an ethical concept than an epistemic one. Thus, what reveals the truthfulness or the actual identity of a person are her words and deeds that

---

69 Moyaert, *In Response to the Religious Other*, 100.
70 Paul Ricoeur, "Reflections on a New Ethos for Europe," in *Paul Ricoeur: The Hermeneutics of Action*, ed. Richard Kearney, trans. David Pellauer (London; Thousand Oaks; New Delhi: Sage Publications, 1996), 6; see also Moyaert, *In Response to the Religious Other*, 100.
71 Wenzel, *Glaube in Vermittlung*, 187.

are uttered and performed over time. It is, in a word, her consistent agency.[72]

Now, if that is correct, if the question of identity ought to really be understood in terms of testimony and a hermeneutics of the self, then there should be no doubt that a secular, plural world is a conducive environment to a process of that kind. As has been shown, neither political secularism nor a confessional state prove to promote the shaping of one's or a group's identity. Whereas the former denies and combats an essential dimension of human life, the latter tends to become ideological and to develop forms of oppression, especially of minorities. By contrast, a secular, plural society provides individuals with favorable conditions for innumerable forms of exchange, dialogue and practices. The other is not automatically regarded as the same as me, as is normally the case in a uniform society, but as another. Due to such interactions and personal forms of self-attestation, expressions like *the* Christian identity or *the* Christian practice may become matter of discussion and be given closer consideration. This does not mean proclaiming the dictatorship of individuality over the churches, communities or institutional religions. On the contrary, individuals are formed in a community of faith, in a social environment. But they can give what they received in return through a personal, unique contribution of theirs. In that way, each religious tradition gains new shapes and their precious treasures are creatively reinterpreted.

Not without good reasons does Felix Wilfred argue for the term "becoming Christians" instead of "being Christians." This holds all the more true in a plural context as is India. According to him, it is an illusion to conceive Christian identity as something static and already pre-established. He prefers speaking of Christian identity as a project by which one is in continuous growth and a dialectical relationship

---

72 This example illustrates the useful distinction that is made, in Ricoeurian jargon, between *idem* (sameness) and *ipse* (selfhood) identity. Accordingly, *idem* identities, which are essentialist by nature, insofar as they focus on stability and essence, are rather inclined towards ideology, whereas *ipse* identities take account of elements such as freedom and commitment despite changes and uncertainties (cf. Moyaert, *In Response to the Religious Other*, 97–99).

with others.⁷³ In those interactions, the element of testimony plays a decisive role, since the question of identity or even an interreligious dialogue cannot be reduced to an exchange of information.⁷⁴ Therefore, Phan maintains that interreligious dialogue must encompass not only theological debates but also other elements such as worship and practical engagement in common projects or causes.⁷⁵ At times, encoded acts, that is, deeds that reflect something intended by the author as a form of testimony, have more weight than words or a profession of faith. For an explicit declaration of faith can have, in a secular environment, the opposite effect, since the other may feel threatened or hurt in his/her own identity. At times, expressing one's own faith and love through genuine deeds exerts a more profound impact in societal life and evangelizes (brings the Good News) more persuasively.

On the other hand, living in a secular world means to be exposed to the risk that determined groups or individuals may isolate themselves and treat others or the world with contempt. They tend to avoid interrelations and have an exclusive understanding of truth. It is not always easy to find a balance. In the view of Kessler, however, if believers, especially Christians, truly live in an attitude of repentance and focused on the foundational experience of their religion, they will certainly find orientation to see and meet others with the due dignity and respect they deserve.⁷⁶ After all, one is not in the world to preserve one's identity as it were an unchangeable kernel or to impose it on others. Instead, the shaping of identity has been suggested as a hermeneutic process whereby individuals exchange testimonies of their selves in mutual recognition, which is ultimately the fruit of love.

---

73 Felix Wilfred, "Interreligiös Christ werden," *Concilium* 47, no. 2 (2011): 154f.

74 Catherine Cornille, "Das Zeugnis und seine Bedeutung im interreligiösen Dialog," *Concilium* 47, no. 1 (2011): 51.

75 Peter C. Phan, *Being Religious Interreligiously: Asian Perspectives on Interfaith Dialogue* (Maryknoll, N.Y.: Orbis Books, 2004).

76 Hans Kessler, *Den verborgenen Gott suchen: Gottesglaube in einer von Naturwissenschaften und Religionskonflikten geprägten Welt* (Paderborn; München; Wien; Zürich: Schöningh, 2006), 259.

The Motif of the Likeness of God
Having set out some of the benefits of a secular environment for the shaping of one's own identity for interreligious encounters and even for religious practice, one may ask whether, beyond such external, favorable conditions, there are also relevant theological reasons to treat secularity in so positive a manner. In his remarkable endeavor to produce a theology of secularity, Wenzel proposes the theologoumenon of the image and likeness of God (cf. Gn 1:26-28) as being the most genuine biblical motif as well as justification for a secular theology. This text lays, for him, the foundation for the full recognition of the autonomy of the freedom of human beings. "If the word of the likeness of God is to be really taken seriously, then what should be heard from it is the affirmation of an original and autonomous freedom rather than of a derived and heteronomous one, one that constitutes the subjectivity of human beings."[77] Indeed, if the human being is conceived of as a "derived and theonomous" freedom, it cannot be said to be the likeness of the "underivable God." This does not imply that man and woman were created as self-contained beings who are, from the most original moment of their existence, closed to and independent of God. For attitudes such as gratefulness are also genuine stages within one's personal journey towards the realization of one's freedom.[78] On the contrary, what it affirms is human freedom as a gift of God (grace) and as a condition for a free relationship of love between Creator and creature.

> God recognized the reality of creation in human beings as a truly autonomous reality, as something unconditionally affirmed and loved by him. He recognizes the human being as a creature who can relate to, address, and fulfill him/herself, a creature who is free. The theological idea of the creation of a free creature can be solely conceived of as basis for a founding relation of recognition.[79]

77 Knut Wenzel, "Gott in der Stadt: Zu einer Theologie der Säkularität," in *Aufbruch in die Urbanität: theologische Reflexion kirchlichen Handelns in der Stadt*, ed. Michael Sievernich and Knut Wenzel, Quaestiones disputatae 252 (Freiburg im Breisgau: Herder, 2013), 377.
78 Ibid.
79 Knut Wenzel, "Liebe als Gerechtigkeit: Zu einem Kernaspekt des christlichen Gottesverständnisses," in *Prekär: Gottes Gerechtigkeit und die Moral der Men-*

To think about God's relationship towards human beings as unconditional recognition implies, in turn, to recognize the subjectivity of every person, which includes her freedom and autonomy. Such an affirmation has a revealing character, as God reveals himself as someone who "does justice" to the human being. In fact, God is the righteous. The radical consequence and the most visible sign of this truth is the incarnation. God wants to communicate with human beings "as a human being." Human nature, human condition, human materiality in the form of body could not be recognized by God to a higher degree than it was through the incarnation.[80]

Such autonomy, however, does not apply exclusively to human beings. The whole creation is accorded this status, too. Therefore, in Wenzel's opinion the Second Vatican Council's formulation of the "autonomy of earthly affairs" (cf. GS 36: *terrenarum rerum autonomia*) should be regarded as a genuine interpretation of the autonomy of freedom of the whole creation, as told in the Book of Genesis, chapter 1. The text of *Gaudium et spes* itself says that the claim

> [...] that created things and societies themselves enjoy their own laws and values [...] is merely required by modern man, but harmonizes also with the will of the Creator. For by the very circumstance of their having been created, all things are endowed with their own stability, truth, goodness, proper laws and order. [GS 36] [...] [T]he rightful autonomy of the creature, and particularly of man is not withdrawn, but is rather re-established in its own dignity and strengthened in it. [GS 41].

Now, if such "rightful autonomy" of the whole creation is to be taken seriously, the relation between Church and (profane) world has to be reconsidered anew. To this end, the first step to be taken,

---

schen, ed. Klaus Bieberstein and Hanspeter Schmitt (Luzern: Exodus, 2008), 157f.; see also Knut Wenzel, "Menschwerdung im Horizont der Welt: Bildungshandeln in schöpfungstheologischer Resonanz," in *"... und nichts Menschliches ist mir fremd": Theologische Grenzgänge*, ed. Ottmar John and Magnus Striet, Ratio fidei 41 (Regensburg: Friedrich Pustet, 2010), 179–83. Tertullian, for instance, recognizes in the freedom of human beings their likeness of God (cf. *Adv. Marc.* II,5)

80   Cf. Wenzel, "Liebe als Gerechtigkeit," 158.

according to Rahner, is to overcome a certain misleading "integralism" that is still deeply rooted in the minds of many Christians owing to historical reasons and developments.[81] For such integralism represents neither the original experience of Christianity nor does it help to understand the world in its genuine plurality. Hence the legitimacy of secularization as a positive phenomenon as well as a form of challenge for the Church in face of such erroneous views that have been established throughout history.

Therefore, the "inherent plurality of the world" must be recognized and accepted as it is. For today's world is not "essentially" different from that of the Scripture. Jesus' world was surely as plural as today's and he nevertheless accepted and loved it so much as to lay down his own life for it (cf. Jn 3:16; 15:13).[82] So, the problem, for Rahner, cannot reside in the plurality of the world. He goes so far as to say that, in reality, this plurality is just a reflection of the inner plurality of the human being. If that is correct, the best concept to properly comprehend what such plurality means, a concept which is deeply rooted in the Christian tradition of thought, is that of *concupiscence*. Rahner warns, however, that one should not be too hasty in judging it negatively. According to the Council of Trent, concupiscence as such is not *already* sin. This concept is rather an attempt to take account of an "[...] inner pluralism of the human being in all his/her dimensions and drives [...] which can never be adequately and radically integrated in the *one* choice of freedom (either for or against God)."[83] That is the reason why there can be no theory, doctrine, ideology, scientific discipline, religion etc. that can completely and adequately integrate such plurality (hence the idea of integralism above).

Rahner is aware that it is extremely difficult to endure one's impotence in the face of such a pluralism. It is de facto an "agonal" experience, a struggle with oneself on ethical and epistemological planes alike. At the same time, even the Council of Trent declares that this

---

81 Karl Rahner, "Theologische Reflexionen zur Säkularisation," in *Schriften zur Theologie*, vol. 8 (Einsiedeln; Zürich; Köln: Benziger, 1967), 640.

82 Ibid., 666.

83 Ibid., 660f. (emphasis in original).

fight does not turn out to be any easier if one refuses to accept it. To deny the reality of concupiscence would amount to deny the most fundamental constitution of both the world and the human being. One does not gain anything in proceeding that way. Quite the contrary, one becomes even more vulnerable to its dynamics and power. By contrast, a proper attitude would be to accept, be aware of, and endure it vigorously (*viriliter*), while at the same time believing that God alone can and will integrate and redeem the world and human beings in the end of time. Ultimately, such an inner pluralism must be regarded as intended by God in the act of creation and can hardly be dissociated from what has been referred above as "autonomy of earthly affairs."

Bearing that in mind, Rahner argues for a redefinition of the role of the Church *within* today's world. Obviously, the Church can neither rule the world, nor can she prescribe what it has to do or be like. In the face of the pluralism of the world, the role of the Church cannot primarily be an integralistic, a doctrinal or a juridical one. Rahner holds the view that the mission of the Church can best be grasped as a prophetic or a pastoral one. The qualifier *prophetic* should not be (mis)understood in apocalyptic terms, in the sense of condemnation of the world, as though the Church would be outside of or separate from it. Being within the world, the Church can be a prophetic *sign* of God's presence, love, and salvation and can certainly offer a unique and indispensable contribution to the intricate questions of meaning and orientation.

Hence, disregarding tendentious and ideological distortions of the concept of secularity, which are particularly manifest in most forms of political secularism, the idea of secularity seems to contain important thoughts of Christian theology such as the unconditional freedom and autonomy of every person, the autonomy of earthly affairs, and the inner pluralism of both the world and the human being. Granted, the idea of secularity does not exhaust and may not even explicitly render the motif of the enormous dignity accorded to the human being conveyed through the biblical assertion of the "likeness of God." Yet it assures the framework conditions required for further reflection and deeper consideration.

Sacramental Love

In the face of the current context, which is marked by the talk of the end of metaphysics and the age of secularity, Rahner holds that the understanding and the practice of love, as testified in the gospel, acquires more significance than ever in the entire history of Christianity. Since, for Rahner, love is the only human act capable of bringing the realities of faith, hope and charity, which constitute the very essence of Christianity, into a unity, yet without abandoning the sphere of human experience, which renders it comprehensible to every person, "[...] then love could be the valid topical word for today which calls the whole of Christianity in the man of tomorrow into the concreteness of life and out of that depth into which God (and not ourselves) has immersed it by his offer of grace, the grace which He is Himself."[84] In this quote, one can notice very clearly that it is the grace poured into our hearts, which is fruit and consequence of God's unconditional and undeserved love of us, either consciously or not, that prompts us "into the concreteness of life." It is no mystery that, in the course of one's existence, one is daily confronted with circumstances demanding decisions and actions which must be squared with one's deepest conscience and one's very self. In many cases, the subject feels overwhelmed by the fact that it has to make a decision with regard to those circumstances. Precisely in those cases, love is the gift of God that helps one see the "concreteness of life" and find the right standard to judge. Yet, it is the subject who bears responsibility for its own acts towards others or their needs. One has to decide to love. One can always act with indifference or solidarity, respect or contempt, hate or love.

In a secular society, one must be equally able to answer for one's acts and decisions as in a theocratic society or whichever one. Still, there is a fundamental difference between both. In a secular or plural society, the sources from which the one derives the criteria for one's decisions and actions is not given, predetermined or uniform. For, in such societies, one is demanded to be accountable for one's actions, and not for one's beliefs or one's motives for actions. This obviously

---

84 Rahner, "Reflections on the Unity of the Love of Neighbour and the Love of God," 233.

has advantages and disadvantages. On the one hand, every subject enjoys complete autonomy in its quest of meaning from which its will derives the power and the motives to carry out its project of life. On the other, though, precisely because of the inner pluralism that dwells within every person and can be understood, as seen in the previous section, as concupiscence, it may be at times extremely overwhelming to remain faithful to the one choice of one's freedom for God (Rahner), when the external environment fosters such inner dynamics and deliberately evades the task of offering orientation in the void left by the age of fragmentation of meaning.

This being the state of affairs, the exercise of religious life has become much more demanding in the course of modernity and secularization, perhaps all too demanding. Hence the decisive importance of the "sources of the self" (Taylor), one's inner life. In order to carry out one's project of life and achieve the desired coherence between inner and outer life, one has to first come to terms with one's inwardness, with one's fragmentation and make one's fundamental choice. However, it is hard to believe that someone will be capable of unconditionally making use of one's freedom to make such a decision if one is not in tune with oneself and innerly composed, if one does not possess a sound degree of self-esteem, self-love and self-confidence. They are nurtured by the experience of being loved and constitute a solid foundation for inner freedom and for taking the courage to make such choice. For, in a secular society, one cannot be obliged to love, to show solidarity towards others or to lead a religious life, but one *can* do it all by reason of that choice. So being, a Christian can love "anonymously," as it were, that is, without having to profess publicly the reasons why one acts in that determined manner, though perfectly knowing in one's innermost self why one does. It is precisely this feature enabled by love that confers to human existence such an overall consistency and coherence as to render human fulfillment possible and worth striving for. If that is so, one can truly affirm with Rahner that "[a]ctive love [is] the illuminating situation of modern man's existence."[85] However paradoxical this may sound, the "commandment of love," one could say with Rahner, not least because of

---

85 Ibid., 232.

the element of absolute commitment implied in it, can and does overcome the helplessness caused by concupiscence and brings about in the subject a provisional, yet sufficient integration of life, insofar as it is sustained by the hope that God can and will integrate and redeem everything completely in due time.

Thus, genuine love gives rise to a radically new society of human beings on earth. "[I]t allows the Kingdom of God to begin [and spread] in secret and is the miracle of the birth of eternity."[86] It must be noted, however, that true love of neighbor cannot be equated to help and assistance, be it material, psychological or spiritual. The help that emanates from love "[...] is not merely an organised effort and effect of socio-political organization [...]."[87] Since organized efforts towards the needs of citizens can just as well be performed without real love, the function of promoting real love of neighbor cannot be fulfilled by secular societies, but only by such a "new society" which is united by the bond of love. As Schillebeeckx put it,

> Essentially and substantially salvation is *love*, but not in such a way that everything else is merely the *presupposition* for salvation. Love is not sheer inwardness; the corporeal and the social elements enter into the substance of love in the mode of corporeality and society. However, the corporeal element, structures, never constitute salvation [...].[88]

If that is correct, love is in fact capable of integrating the various dimensions of human beings, the inner ones and the outer alike, without however confusing them with salvation, as they are but "expressions" of a greater reality existing beyond them. Although those concrete signs of love and salvation can certainly be read and interpreted as such, there is, nevertheless, nothing beyond a mutual, significant referentiality, which is not the same as essential identity. Accordingly, they refer to each other without being reduced to or

---

86 Ibid., 231.
87 Ibid.
88 Edward Schillebeeckx, *Christ: The Christian Experience in the Modern World*, ed. Robert J. Schreiter, The Collected Works of Edward Schillebeeckx 7 (London: Bloomsbury, 2014), 740f. italics in original.

equated with each other. Still, Rahner ascribes to the genuine act of love a decisive role within God's salvific plan. He dares postulate the thesis that

> [...] wherever man posits a positively moral act in the full exercise of his free self-disposal, this act is a positive supernatural salvific act in the actual economy of salvation even when its *a posteriori* object and the explicitly given *a posteriori* motive do not spring tangibly from the positive revelation of God's Word but are in this sense 'natural.' [...] [W]herever there is an absolutely moral commitment of a positive kind in the world and within the present economy of salvation, there takes place also a saving event, faith, hope and charity, an act of divinising grace, and thus *caritas* is exercised in this [...].[89]

It follows, for Rahner, that between a moral act, as described above, and a salvific act there can be at most a logical, but not real distinction. This is also one of the thoughts that liberation theology tried to make clear in various fashions. Just as there is no "real" distinction between profane history and history of salvation, there can be no actual difference between God's act of salvation and human, ethical acts, albeit, obviously, the former cannot be reduced to the latter. Or else, Ellacuría asks, how can God's salvific act of the delivery of Israel from Egyptian slavery be understood without the leadership and commitment of Moses?[90]

The consequences of this train of thought are far-reaching. If an ethical act, squared with one's conscience, can be referred to as "a positive supernatural salvific act in the actual economy of salvation even when its *a posteriori* object and the explicitly given *a posteriori* motive do not spring tangibly from the positive revelation of God's Word," then each ethical, answerable act must be entitled, at least in theory, to "convey" salvation. The gap between intention

---

89 Rahner, "Reflections on the Unity of the Love of Neighbour and the Love of God," 239.
90 Ignacio Ellacuría, "Historicidad de la salvación cristiana," in *Mysterium liberationis: Conceptos fundamentales de la teología de la liberación*, ed. Ignacio Ellacuría and Jon Sobrino, vol. 1 (Madrid: Editorial Trotta, 1990), 337–39.

and effect is here particularly manifest.⁹¹ It does not allow the subject to plan, organize or produce salvation, even though salvation can be conveyed through or inferred from determined acts of the subject or events of history.

Therefore, considering the peculiar feature of love of not being "just *any* one of the moral acts among many others," but "the basis and sum total of the moral as such,"⁹² thereby acquiring a special status among other moral acts, one could refer to it as a "sacramental act." For such love is not simply an "external practice," "[...] but an expression of one's freedom for another freedom in the concrete situations of life." Thus, such symbolic praxis "[...] follows Jesus' situational proclamation which was endorsed by the unity between word and conduct, and corresponds to the historical constitution of human freedom."⁹³ The threshold between symbolic and sacramental is not easy to define. However, the word "sacramental" seems to convey in a clearer manner than symbolic the salvific character that can be attached to the act of love of neighbor, without taking away from God the merit and origin of salvation.

To start with, the very word "sacrament" bears its original, etymological connotation, one related to "mystery." In fact, the equivalent word in the Orthodox Church is μυστήριον (*mysterion*), and supports this argument. Love is, first and foremost, a mystery to human beings. Why else should one love? What are the rational reasons for such an act? Whence does the drive to love come? Who is the author of an act of love?

Secondly, every sacrament requires a valid matter and form, which, in this case, is the very act of love. At this juncture, the problems begin to arise. Can there be an explicit form for this sacrament? What can be defined as an act of love? From experience, one knows that at times love cannot be reduced to a particular action. Sometimes it is just standing at someone's bedside, speechless and hoping for his/her recovery or for the alleviation of pain. Sometimes it is just

---

91 For more on that matter, see above p. 157ff and below p. 253ff.
92 Rahner, "Reflections on the Unity of the Love of Neighbour and the Love of God," 239.
93 Pröpper, *Erlösungsglaube und Freiheitsgeschichte*, 221.

a loving, encouraging attitude towards someone, without "concrete" deeds. Sometimes it is a lifelong commitment, as in the case of a marriage or a family. In spite of those difficulties, though, one can hold on to the general formulation that any human act of genuine love is the condition or the matter of such sacramental act. Far most important than the identification of the precise act is what the act of love essentially consists in, namely, an absolute commitment, care, and service towards the other without reserves of any kind. Just as in a sacrament God wants to give his love, him himself as a gift (grace), so too does the subject in its act of love. For the subject of love, the good, the well-being, the "salvation" of the loved person matters much more than its own. Genuine love is always a gift, unmerited care.

Thirdly, the gap between the intention and motives behind an act of love and its "real" effects is attested to and supported by the Catholic doctrine of "*ex opere operato*" (from the work worked) according to which the sacraments work independently of the intention of the person who performs them. This feature of a sacrament safeguards God's original authorship of the work or gift of salvation that is realized in and through the sacrament. Similarly, since the act of love refers to the grace and love of God present in our hearts, which is the condition of possibility of all human genuine love, the authorship of the act of love cannot be ascribed alone to the person who performs it.

Finally, it must be made clear that this endeavor to understand the human mystery of love from the perspective of the Christian notion of sacraments is not motivated by the intention of instituting another sacrament *among* the established ones, which, ultimately, is not even feasible due to the difficulties pointed out above. Instead, the first reason was to draw attention to the mystery-related character of love as well as to the especial dignity of this act in human existence or in Christian life. The second intention was to make a determined effort to discover new possibilities for religious life *within* the challenging context of secularity or, in some cases, secularism. To this end, understanding love as a sacrament, that is, as a visible act that refers to an invisible, mysterious reality that is ultimately a gift, grace, salvation may shed new light on the reality of salvation, which constitutes the purpose of the present investigation. What this view makes particularly clear is that salvation is neither an act in the performance of which the human being does not participate nor is it a monopoly of Christians by reason of their explicit belief in Christ and his mediating role. Salvation is rather a much broader reality that occurs everywhere and beyond the limits of the Church, a reality which, in theory, can be conveyed by each person through genuine love and committed moral life.

Does Love Ensure Salvation?

It might have become clear that so far the interconnectedness between love and salvation has been primarily understood as care for the salvation of the other. Little has been said about the effects of the act of love on its subject or perhaps about the "benefits" that it can bring. In other words, does love just *convey* salvation to the loved person or does it exert any kind of influence on the salvation of the subject of love as well? To start with, brief mention must be made of the millenary controversy over the interrelation between works and grace, faith and love. Although particular attention started being devoted to this issue in dogmatic reflection after the famous dispute between Augustine and Pelagius in the fifth century, which reached its climax in the 16th century with the spreading of the Reformation and the definitions of the Council of Trent, one might say that this predicament has accompanied Christianity from its very outset and extends unresolved to the present day. The substantial disagreements between Jewish and Hellenistic Christians in the early church briefly described above[94] support this assertion. This is indeed a very delicate issue and cannot be exhaustively treated here. But a few thoughts regarding the significance of love for faith and justification shall be formulated in the following.

Throughout this work, the reader may have become aware of the enormous difficulty of defining love comprehensively. Yet, conceiving it just in terms of works would fail to grasp its essential nature.

---

94 See especially chapter 2 (p. 32ff).

Perhaps the concept of self-justification, i.e., the idea that certainly creates the most serious predicaments, could help us throw light on this issue. The idea of self-justification is an expression of the natural desire of human beings to do, to effect something, to bring something about. In the age of *homo faber*, this is all the more so. This implies, of course, an essentially optimistic view of both human beings and their capability for doing good. But even if that is the case, what the notion of love ultimately means cannot simply amount to activities or achievements. Admittedly, in order to be authentic, love must bring forth works and concrete deeds, nevertheless none of them can encompass all that is implied in the word "love." Irrespective of whether love is meant as an attitude, as an emotion or as a relationship, it surpasses the category of works. True love does not wish to achieve anything. It simply wants to love.

Yet, even assuming that a lover wished to achieve something through his/her "works of love," no sensible person can deny that there is a large gap between intention, act and producibility, of effects, an aspect that has been mentioned a few times in the course of the work. As a consequence, even if a believer construes his/her ethical life as a form of "pleasing" God, of fostering one's relationship with him, one cannot expect it to produce the intended effect, if the freedom of the beloved is really respected and if the relationship is indeed built up on true love. The response of the beloved to one's acts or attitude must always be a free one. God's response to our life is, therefore, always grace, free response, love. As a consequence, if salvation is conceived of as being a free act of God, it must primarily be an act of grace, gratuitous. Salvation can never be produced, be it through one's acts, be it even through one's love. Salvation is always an act of grace.

Still, in the opinion of Karl Rahner, love does perform a decisive role in the "totality of the process of justification." For faith alone "[…] is not indeed the whole of man's grace-supported attitude towards God and hence cannot by itself constitute the process of justification."[95]

---

[95] Karl Rahner, "The 'Commandment' of Love in Relation to the Other Commandments," in *Theological Investigations*, trans. Karl-H. Kruger, vol. 5 (Darton: Longman & Todd, 1966), 457.

Furthermore, faith concerns solely the relationship of the person with God. However, the reality of human life involves several other dimensions and relations which can be covered by love. Therefore, even for Paul, faith and hope are subordinate to charity (1Cor 13:13) which is the "highest law" of Christian existence,[96] the sum total of "the whole of the Law" (Gal 5:14), the fulfillment of the Law (Rom 13:10). In addition, one's acceptance or response to justifying grace has to occur, for Rahner, by an act "[...] which is the actualization of the possibilities given by the grace of justification." For him, there must be a correspondence, a coherence between the accepted gift of divine grace and the very act of accepting it. And he has no doubts that the act of love, given its nature, performs it more appropriately than the act of faith.[97] Accordingly, to lead a life in love would be a "sacramental" (reflective) expression of that which one has received in faith by virtue of grace, namely, love. It goes without saying that such a conception of justification can only work if conceived of in terms of a relationship with God, be it conscious or unconscious.

At the same time, Rahner is aware of the fact that throughout the entire Christian tradition there has been no other name to describe the *beginning* of a "justified life" other than *fides* (faith). Accordingly, there is nothing necessarily wrong in preaching that "everything is faith." If someone found ultimate significance in the act whereby everything begins, in the act of faith, one may find completion as well. From that perspective, even love would be seen as an act of faith, "a believing love."[98] All depends on where the main emphasis is laid.

Although the above is correct, there are nevertheless theologians, especially some engaged in the (bilateral) dialogue with Judaism, who have urged a reconsideration of the Christian idea of "the works of the Law" and even of the Christian (mis)interpretation of the Jewish understanding of Law. To that effect, the Protestant theologian

---

96 For more details, see Oda Wischmeyer, *Der höchste Weg: das 13. Kapitel des 1. Korintherbriefes*, Studien zum Neuen Testament 13 (Gütersloh: Gütersloher Verlagshaus Mohn, 1981).
97 Rahner, "The 'Commandment' of Love," 457.
98 Ibid., 458f. (emphasis added).

Friedrich-Wilhelm Marquardt fiercely criticizes the Joint Declaration between Catholics and Protestants on the Doctrine of Justification[99] for perpetuating mistaken views in that regard. For him, Catholics and Protestants came indeed to an agreement on the issue of justification, however "at the expense of the truth of the Old Testament and Judaism alike." In his view, by equating the Law with a "path to salvation," which is with certainty a purely Christian category, this declaration fails to grasp the core of the Jewish understanding of Law. Contrary to that, the Law is understood and lived in Judaism "in the sense of the biblical and Jewish idea of a continuous validation (*Bewährung*) of the salvation of the covenant through the observance of the Law."[100] Here again the Jewish understanding of Law presupposes a living relationship between God and the Jewish people initiated through the covenant and maintained through the observance of the Law.

Curiously enough, Marquardt avails himself of Barth's theology of justification to support his argumentation. According to him, the Law does not play any role for Christians in Barth's theory. What matters is the new life in Christ. On the contrary, Barth sees in the idea of the Jewish Law the same function being fulfilled as Christ for Christians. The Law is "the power of the new life rescued from the Flood and from slavery" and can therefore be recognized as implied in or coinciding with the Christ whom Christians proclaim.[101] Therefore, he too holds that the reliability of the Christian proclamation

---

99   Lutheran World Federation and Catholic Church, "Joint Declaration on the Doctrine of Justification," The Official Website of the Vatican, 1999, http://www.vatican.va/roman_curia/pontifical_councils/chrstuni/documents/rc_pc_chrstuni_doc_31101999_cath-luth-joint-declaration_ en.html.

100   Friedrich-Wilhelm Marquardt, "Vom Rechtfertigungsgeschehen zu einer Evangelischen Halacha," in *Die Lehre von der Rechtfertigung des Gottlosen im kulturellen Kontext der Gegenwart: Beiträge im Horizont des christlich-jüdischen Gesprächs*, ed. Hans Martin Dober and Dagmar Mensink, Hohenheimer Protokolle 57 (Stuttgart: Akademie der Diözese Rottenburg-Stuttgart, 2002), 43.

101   Ibid., 50. In Marquardt's words, "[...] in der Anerkennung der Einheit und Selbigkeit des uns verkündigten Christus mit der in ihm auch uns Nichtjuden verkündigten Tora."

of the new life gained through Christ must be validated (*Bewährung*) through "good works," so that faith may indeed work through love (cf. Gal 5:6).[102]

Viewed from the perspective of love such "good works," such "works of love" are neither proof, as it were, which the subject has to provide someone with nor are they part of a course of action designed in the context of a strategic plan in order to obtain approval, social recognition or a reward on the day of final judgment. Rather, they are "spontaneous" consequences of an attentive existence that sees reality with the eyes of love that dwells within it. No matter whether one is a believer or not, if one is driven by love, one desires to and indeed shall yield fruits of love, shall express it concretely. As Schillebeeckx sees it, the distinction between inwardness and outwardness is a merely dualistic category that hinders us from seeing reality properly. There can be neither true freedom nor true love solely in one's heart, in one's inwardness. "Of ourselves we are only a possibility for freedom, and this freedom is still a vacuum; it has no content." This void can only be filled in the encounter with other free persons. Love can be complete only if it is expressed.[103] As for the question whether acts of love shall bring any benefit to their performer in a possible afterlife, this cannot be assured on account of God's unconditional freedom and may even be of little relevance. What matters is rather that one is transformed by them already in this existence and that one has discovered the adequate relation to both the Creator and the other creatures, an experience that can provide meaning and ultimate fulfillment.

This brief problematization has served the sole purpose of bringing forward a few elements for further consideration with respect to these delicate and complex issues. Since this work is particularly concerned with a reconsideration of Christian contents of faith from an interreligious perspective, these observations may provoke further critical thinking not only to understand others more appropriately, but especially to value them and to increase one's awareness of the critical issues of each tradition as well as

---

102 Ibid., 45.
103 Schillebeeckx, *Christ*, 808f.

of ways of partaking in the dialogue as free as possible from preconceptions and prejudices about others influenced by one's own tradition.

Outcome

On a theological level, especially as far as the concept of salvation is concerned, the idea of agape takes account of two basic ideas: the unbridgeable asymmetry inherent to intersubjective relationships and the character of unconditional freedom (give without expecting anything in return). This, however, must be properly understood. The fashion in which Jesus' words about self-abnegation (Lk 9:23) have been construed down the centuries must be submitted to more rigorous scrutiny, too, given that some interpretations miss a central point of the commandment to love: "You shall love God [...] and your neighbor *as yourself.*" Admittedly, agape implies the renunciation of basic human needs, including legitimate ones such as the right of revenge, but it does not mean in any way disapproving of self-love. Although nothing specific about it is said in the Scripture, this chapter has indirectly pointed out a few aspects. It would be misleading, for instance, to regard self-love as a precondition for love of neighbor, as though love would consist of "consecutive" acts (first self-love, then love of neighbor, then love of God, etc.). Instead, as has been seen, the relation of proportionality implied in the preposition "as" seems to suggest a process of simultaneousness. It is by loving others, including God, and by being loved by others that one can experience recognition and (self-)esteem which, in turn, empower the subject to love as well. Simultaneously, the more one makes the experience of a constructive self-love, the more one realizes how much one has already received, often gratuitously, and what one has become over the years. Such an experience of gratefulness, which is an inherent moment of self-love, can prompt one to pass on whatever one has received (Mt 10:8) in the form of love.

Also, it is delusive to assume that self-love or self-esteem is fostered by the praises of others in reaction to one's deeds and achievements.

Such self-love is built on an illusion, as it stands on too fragile a foundation. By contrast, genuine, constructive self-love appears to spring from the aforementioned attitude of existential gratitude in the face of one's createdness. This attitude was given expression in Psalm 8 in a unique fashion: "I look up at your heavens, shaped by your fingers, at the moon and the stars you set firm: what are human beings that you spare a thought for them, or the child of Adam that you care for him?" (Ps 8:3f.). Indeed, it is in the awareness that one has been created in the image and likeness of God that one discovers one's unconditional freedom and autonomy (cf. above p. 243ff; Gn 1:27). The correct equation of such an autonomy conferred to human beings, though, far from being arbitrariness is responsibility for the whole creation (Ps 8:6; Gn 1:26), which lays the foundation for the principle of universal solidarity and, by extension, universal love of neighbor.

Thus conceived, (human) love can serve as an appropriate idea to render into a comprehensible language what the synoptic gospels, particularly Luke's, tried to convey by means of the notion of salvation. Obviously, love and salvation do not coincide. However, their mutual referenciality in the message of Jesus seems to suggest that one cannot be fully grasped in the absence of the other. Still, one can say that all salvation is a consequence of love, or else God cannot be referred to as love (1Jn 4:8). Conversely, even though one cannot claim with the same confidence that every act of love is already a sign of (God's) salvation, one can nevertheless say that the experience of both loving and being loved redeems, frees. One is freed by love from all sorts of barriers, conventions, standards, etc. People learn all the time from love stories or maybe from their own experience that because of love someone becomes capable of even something believed to be impossible; one can overcome what appears unsurmountable. For love has an inherent potential for criticism of the established and for the creation of the new, for cognition and for the construction of reality. It is a mystery and a source of transformation.

Therefore, although what enables and empowers one to love is in fact one's *formal* unconditional freedom, it is through the practice of love of neighbor that one can *really* become free. In the act of love, the subject is not only liberated from the alienation in which it is entangled,[104] but it discovers what it is capable of, its true identity. Human agency becomes, thus, not only the means through which love becomes concrete and thereby complete, but the key of access to one's true identity. Whereas the latter, a movement of the subject inwards, can be referred to as a process of hermeneutics of the self, the former, a movement outwards, is a symbolic form of expression of the subject. It is precisely because of this feature of human agency that love can gain particular significance for (Christian) religious practice in the current secular age. For love can thus be a form of proclamation of the good news, of confession of faith, of evangelization in the form of quiet deeds.

By loving one's neighbor, one is bearing witness to what God is like, to how God acts himself. One is making every effort to become perfect as the heavenly Father is perfect. In the act of love of neighbor, one passes on what one has received in one's relation with God. By reason of such symbolic character of human agency, one can therefore speak of a sacramental act of love, that is, a mode of expressing in a visible act a believed, invisible reality, which confers to love a character of mystery. By practicing love of neighbor, everyone is thus entitled, at least formally, to mediate God's salvation in the world so that the Kingdom of God may continue to silently grow in every corner of the earth.

---

104 Rudolf Schnackenburg, "Die Forderung der Liebe in der Verkündigung und im Verhalten Jesu," in *Prinzip Liebe: Perspektiven der Theologie*, ed. Eugen Biser (Freiburg im Breisgau; Basel; Wien: Herder, 1975), 99–100.

9

By Way of Conclusion

The present work has dealt with the real feasibility of interreligious encounters from a Christian perspective. This concern entails, in its turn, a further question, which is prior to and more fundamental than that, namely, the theological justification for such a practice. It concerns, essentially, the question why Christians should at all engage in interreligious dialogue, if they sincerely believe that the plenitude of revelation as well as salvation come exclusively in and through the person of Jesus Christ. One could ask further, how can other religions convey salvation, if, for Christians, Jesus Christ is the only mediator of salvation between God and humankind?

Notwithstanding the fact that most of the Theology-of-Religions discourse has predominantly revolved around the latter question over the past decades, our study has shown that this so-called Western soteriological fixation does constitute a major stumbling block to genuine interreligious dialogues (see above chapter 1). For what is at issue here is not just the overemphasis on salvation on the basis of Christian theology, but also, and especially, a fairly narrow understanding of Christian salvation itself. In the first place, conventional soteriologies appear to be underlain by a fairly hypostatized concept of salvation, as though it was a "thing" that can be granted to some and rejected to others based on the fulfillment of determined criteria. Secondly, human beings are reduced to their religious affiliation, which says very little about their actual identity and nothing really precise about their true beliefs.

As was shown in our analysis, among the factors that most contributed towards the portrayed scenario in Theology of Religions was the dominant influence exerted on this discourse by the well-established typology of exclusivism, inclusivism, pluralism (and particularism). Albeit recognizing its significance for the mentioned discourse, particularly as far as one's efforts to systematically approach religious plurality are concerned, I have argued that the practice of interreligious dialogue cannot be theoretically underpinned by this typology. For even inclusivism – a category that could be squared with Catholic teachings – does not offer any satisfactory explanation either for the *fact* that people do seek to encounter other believers along with their religions or for the motive that *drives* someone towards otherness. After all, inclusivists believe that, in reality, everything they "need" in terms of salvation and truth can be found in their own tradition. In the second place, precisely on account of such an attitude of "having" already everything, others cannot be fully recognized as they actually are, since they are judged with the same measure that inclusivists have. Finally, the hypostatized concept of salvation with which the typology operates does not take sufficient account of elements such as God's unmerited grace and human agency, which are of cardinal importance in Christian tradition.

Rethinking Universal Salvation in the Light of Agape

"Love, and you shall live." Freely translated, and interpreted, this is the answer given by Jesus in Lk 10:28 to the question, "Master, what must I do to inherit eternal life?" But this is, fundamentally, also the answer at which we have arrived at the end of this investigation to both the questions posed above. It should be noted, though, that this answer is by no means self-evident, neither is it meant as a stopgap solution to those complex predicaments. This realization results, rather, from the observation that the soteriological status ascribed to love in Lk 10:25-37 is extremely high (cf. chapters 4 and 5). This being the case, every Christian soteriology is to be evaluated in the light of agape. More importantly, an agape-based soteriology brings clearly to the fore the aforementioned interplay between God's unmerited grace and human action. Thus, the parable of the Good Samaritan, precisely in the fashion in which it was embedded in the

Gospel of Luke, was proposed as an "exemplary solution" to the predicaments of "religious" difference and salvation (chapter 4). For this parable, together with its foreword, comprise the two essential elements of Christian faith: on the one side, its theoretical, cognitive, revelatory feature (Lk 10:25-28); on the other side, its practical, ethical, performative dimension (Lk 10:30-37). As it seems, in Luke's understanding, the New Testament notion of *agape* not only combines both of these elements, but is also their very condition of possibility.

By means of agape, Christians can express their innermost identity as well as the true identity (name) of their God. Therefore, one can refer to love as being a sacramental act whose authorship may be said to be shared between God and human beings. Considering that an act of unconditional love is not as "natural" as, for instance, a (re)action of revenge, but can nevertheless be performed by the subject in its freedom, it contains an element of mystery[1] which can be said to be caused by God's grace. Furthermore, since the authorship of an act of genuine love cannot be fully imputed to the subject alone, owing to its aforesaid character of mystery, and since it in fact conveys God's salvation, assuming that salvation is always a consequence of love, the nature of an act of love corresponds to that of a sacrament. An act of genuine love is, therefore, one in which the inner profession of faith and the outer agency attain such a unity and coherence as to enable existential meaning and fulfillment. Yet God's love precedes every act of love. Just as God's unconditional love accompanies Jesus, as a human being, right from the very beginning of his public life, the most clear expression of which were the words pronounced at his baptism, so, too, is the entire life of a Christian sustained by God's love. Thus, the affirmation that stands at the beginning of every existence is the same that stood at the beginning

---

1 Considering that the Medieval disputation between Franciscan and Dominican friars, whose leading exponents were Thomas Aquinas and Duns Scotus, regarding the origin of love, that is, whether or not love precedes the will and the intellect, whether love should be rather subordinated to the will or to the intellect, and other questions related to that would go too far afield, suffice it to qualify it as a mystery whose precise origin is far from being certain or self-evident.

of Jesus' (public) life: "σὺ εἶ ὁ υἱός μου ὁ ἀγαπητός [/ἡ θυγάτηρ μου ἡ αγαπητή], ἐν σοὶ εὐδόκησα" (you are my beloved son/daughter, my favor rests on you).[2] The power of this assurance is definitely a source of strength and sustainment throughout every human being's life journey, which cannot be described otherwise as grace.

From this perspective, the Christian traditional concepts of grace and salvation are freed from an all too hypostatized understanding, as mentioned above. As opposed to that, I suggest that grace and salvation are not primarily *what* God gives us, but the very fact *that* he at all gives us something gratuitously and unmeritedly, in spite of guilt and human failure. Obviously, such care for and devotion to human beings on the part of God does not remain without consequences, this "does not return to him before having yielded fruit" (cf. Isa 55:11). The unconditional trust given as a gift to human beings in the act of creation and constantly renewed in the world through his caring Providence, which, again, is consequence of his love, triggers a gradual process in human beings by which they can come to self-consciousness and be directed to the fundamental purpose of their existence. This is surely a liberating experience. It is a dynamic process whereby one allows to be changed by Reality (God) to such an extent that one becomes one with oneself, and that one's performative agency becomes a symbolic attestation of this new, true identity (cf. Gal 2:20).[3]

The very fact *that* God has made it manifest and in fact loves us is grace and salvation. But this can only be referred to as grace or salvation because it is unexpected, unmerited, illogical, if one likes. And whenever someone acts likewise, that is, whenever someone loves beyond merits and expectations, one refreshes, endorses this assertion. The act of love of neighbor performed by human beings is the proof that God's unconditional love and, consequently, God's salvific will, is not solely a great ideal, but also a reality. It is because human beings are capable of communicating this love through words

---

2 Mk 1:11 par; see also a connection to Isa 42:1.
3 For a similar view on it, see, for instance, Monika Renz, *Erlösung aus Prägung: Botschaft und Leben Jesu als Überwindung der menschlichen Angst-, Begehrens- und Machtstruktur* (Paderborn: Junfermann, 2008).

and deeds that the affirmation of God's salvation is made feasible and credible.

At the same time, it must be observed that this love, in order to be genuine and authentic, has to be an expression of one's love towards one's neighbor "*over and above all social mediation.*"⁴ Seen from a sociological perspective, such love can neither be predicted nor planned. Precisely because this love has to be free from all social conventions, measures and standards, it is always innovative, unexpected, and unprecedented. It is grounded in the paradigm of the gift and driven by the logic of abundance. Instead of letting himself be occupied by a social role or just following a religious code of conduct, the Samaritan man, in the parable, thanks to his vitality and spontaneity, which are proper to human beings, allowed himself to be moved (σπλαγχνίζομαι) by the presence of the other. It is precisely this availability for an encounter that allows the subject the possibility of both divesting itself of all prejudices and perceiving, seeing the other in his/her otherness.⁵

The radical consequence of this observation is that the practice of the love of neighbor is not necessarily bound to any social mediation nor to any particular religious tradition. The ultimate source from which one draws the required power to love is one's heart, the wellspring of vitality and humanness. This does not amount to devaluing the importance of religions or institutional churches nor does it mean shifting the debate surrounding the predicament of salvation from the level of religions exclusively to that of individuals. Religions and their adherents stand in a relation of mutual interdependence. On the one hand, religions and churches are a perennial "sacrament of salvation in the world" and constantly thematize,

---

4 Paul Ricoeur, "The Socius and the Neighbor," in *History and Truth*, trans. Charles A. Kelbley (Evanston, Illinois: Northwestern University Press, 1965), 101 (emphasis in original).

5 Ulrich Dehn, "In die Sichtbarkeit treten: Phasen und Koordinaten des interreligiösen Dialogs," *Zeitschrift für Missionswissenschaft* 37, no. 1 (2011): 43f.; see also Axel Honneth, "Unsichtbarkeit: Über die moralische Epistemologie von 'Anerkennung,'" in *Unsichtbarkeit: Stationen einer Theorie der Intersubjektivität* (Frankfurt am Main: Suhrkamp, 2003), 10–27.

remind individuals of and refer them to the absolute, to "the salvation from God."⁶ On the other, they are made up by individuals who continually reinterpret and renew them. What cannot happen, though, according to Rahner, is to conceive of the relation between individuals and their respective religions in so separate a fashion as to consider the latter just as an outward circumstance of the former. For "[…] it is quite unthinkable that man, being what he is, could actually achieve this relationship to God – which he must have and which if he is to be saved, is and must be made possible for him by God – in an absolutely private interior reality and this outside of the actual religious bodies which offer themselves to him in the environment in which he lives."⁷

Despite this close interdependence, however, the text of the Final Judgment (Mt 25:31-46; see above p. 100ff) seems to direct attention to the fact that the subject is not granted access to the true meaning and significance of the act of love of neighbor during its earthly existence, not even through the variety of answers to the question of meaning offered by religions. In a sense, the text of the Final Judgment makes religious traditions relative, inasmuch as the practice of solidarity and love of neighbor are performed independently of a direct, objective correspondence to external prescriptions. After all, those who were judged *"did not know"* the criteria for their judgment, although they might have *sensed* it in consonance with their conscience (σπλαγχνίζομαι). Thus, the ultimate significance of the practice of love "[…] does not depend on *any criterion immanent to history* and cannot be definitely recognized by the actors themselves but will be discovered on the last day […]."⁸

Consequently, the criteria for God's salvation or God's judgment cannot be one's (explicit) profession of faith or one's membership in a

---

6 Edward Schillebeeckx, *Church: The Human Story of God*, The Collected Works of Edward Schillebeeckx 10 (London: Bloomsbury, 2014), 13.

7 Karl Rahner, "Christianity and the Non-Christian Religions," in *Theological Investigations*, vol. 5 (Darton: Longman & Todd, 1966), 128.

8 Ricoeur, "The Socius and the Neighbor," 101 (emphasis in original); see also Knut Wenzel, *Glaube in Vermittlung: theologische Hermeneutik nach Paul Ricoeur* (Freiburg im Breisgau; Basel; Wien: Herder, 2008), 133.

By Way of Conclusion

determined religious tradition. In a sense, those criteria are *hidden* to us.[9] In the last resort, not even religion is transparent enough to that mystery. For religion is not an end in itself. As was seen just above in Rahner's quote, it serves its purpose insofar as it conducts the subject to that living relationship with God in which God can make the subject a living being.[10] But in order to make room for God, religion must naturally recede into the background. For God's love can be experienced, in great measure, *thanks to* religions, but also *despite* them. Obviously, an approach of this kind opens up new possibilities as much for religious people living in a secular environment as for secular or atheistic individuals. Whereas the former are given the opportunity to live out their faith sacramentally, rather than confessionally, the latter enjoy greater freedom to search for meaning in their lives beyond the realm of religion. Nonetheless, chapter 8 has equally shown that affirming this cannot imply, at the same time, the retreat or exclusion of religion from the public sphere.

Thus, the basic distinction between Christians and non-Christians employed by the typology of exclusivism, inclusivism and pluralism as a parameter for soteriological considerations must be deemed as problematic and misleading. After all, the purpose which the parable of the Final Judgment appears to serve is to suggest an inversion in the understanding of God's salvation. Instead of conceiving it exclusively in a vertical manner, the parable proposes a horizontal model. Whilst in the former salvation is conceived of as coming directly from God in consequence of the fulfillment of determined established prescriptions, in the latter the (co)responsibility of human beings in caring for others and for the world seems to be asked in the form of attentive,

---

9   Cf. Ricoeur, "The Socius and the Neighbor," 100 (emphasis in original).

10 Needless to say, I conceive religion here from a Christian perspective and informed by the Western tradition of thought. Furthermore, I concede that there are religions in which such a living relationship with God is unconceivable. Yet, I would argue that even in those religions, one's contact to transcendence, to the absolute, the Real, can be said to have an existential impact on one's life in terms of becoming more aware, more compassionate, more submissive to God, more human, in a word, becoming freer and more living, rather than remaining captive to sin, ignorance, and illusion.

respectful, creative commitment. As was seen above (chapters 4 and 5), such deep commitment can be ensured by agape in the form of observance of the love of neighbor commandment.

Agape, Truth and Justice

Now, by turning the focus of our attention back to the theological justification of interreligious dialogue, I suggest that such absolute commitment to and deep respect for the other – a core element of Jesus' life and proclamation, which was preserved and handed down by the New Testament authors by means of the concept of *agape* – is to constitute the solid foundation on which a Christian theology of interreligious dialogue can build, and develop. Thus, the Jesuanic message of love of neighbor can assure the required recognition for a true encounter between Christians and believers of other religions or even non-believers. Such unconditional recognition is the result of both the character of asymmetry and the logic of the paradigm of the gift contained in the idea of agape. Thanks to its asymmetrical, even one-sided granting of unconditional recognition to the other, the idea of agape makes possible a first indispensable step, namely, that of "seeing" the other, and then approaching him/her.[11] Now, to affirm the importance of such asymmetry of agape does not mean doing away with the relational character of a relationship of mutual recognition. Rather, it is an

---

11 Properly understood, such a movement towards the other is in line with Pope Francis' constant demand concerning the Church's missionary activity: the call to a "new missionary 'going forth'" (*Evangelii gaudium*, n. 20–24), as opposed to an attitude of self-enclosedness and isolationism. To be sure, the adjective "missionary" is not to be understood here as an effort to persuade others or to do proselytism. Still, the qualifier "missionary" reminds us, in this context, of two important elements of dialogue: (a) that dialogue does not consist only in hearing the other, but also in saying something. In other words, Christians definitely have something to say, good news to announce. (b) that Christians are called upon to "take the first step [...] take the initiative, go out to others [...]" (n. 24), instead of remaining in their comfort zone (n. 21).

unconditional vote of trust in the other that can, thereafter, either be reciprocated positively or not. At the same time, it implies that, even if other religions or non-Christian believers do not recognize Christians in the same proportion (asymmetry), a Christian is bound to recognize them unconditionally on account of his/her commitment to the person and message of Jesus of Nazareth, that is, the normative, foundational event of his/her faith.

Nevertheless, the Jesuanic message of love of neighbor is by no means just an "external" normative commandment for Christians. Rather, it constitutes a unique possibility, inasmuch as a respectful, face-to-face encounter may help Christians find or better understand their own identity through the detour of the other. Since the neighbor is a valuable mediation for one's self-transcendence, this command enables and sustains hermeneutic processes of self-consciousness. Love is the capacity to endure difference whilst constantly questioning and reformulating one's own identity in the face of the other. If that is correct, an act of agape can never be construed as an act of hegemonic thinking.[12] For agape is always the "outward" expression of one's willingness to *become a neighbor* to someone else. Although willingness may not be the most appropriate word to describe such an inner urge, considering that there is a long Christian tradition of thought that affirms the primacy of love over knowledge and will, agape can certainly be said to comprise an inner drive towards otherness. This drive involves, among other aspects, an important cognitive moment. Therefore, whilst affirming the normative character of agape in the face of otherness (chapter 5), the present study has also consistently shown the fundamental role played by love in the process of human cognition. For love is inhabited by a desire to *do justice* to the other's radical otherness, a desire to participate "in the essence of all things."[13]

---

12 Cf. Marianne Moyaert, "Christianity as the Measure of Religion? Materializing the Theology of Religions," in *Twenty-First Century Theologies of Religions: Retrospection and Future Prospects*, ed. Elizabeth J. Harris, Paul Hedges, and Shanthikumar Hettiarachchi, Currents of Encounter 54 (Leiden; Boston: Brill; Rodopi, 2016), 241–44.

13 Max Scheler, "Vom Wesen der Philosophie und der moralischen Bedingung des

The subject of love does not content itself with the realization *that* the other is different from itself. It also wants to know both *why* the other is not the same as itself and why *it* is not like the other. As a consequence, agape can be indicated as the theological justification for interreligious dialogue, at its deepest level. Otherwise, if dialogue is not sustained by agape's inextricable interconnection to truth (knowledge) and justice, it can hardly go beyond the level of information exchange. But as was seen above in chapter 7, based on Kierkegaard's interpretation of 1Cor 8:1b, knowledge (γνῶσις) can edify (reality) only insofar as it is based on love, the ground of reality. For knowledge can be used as much for liberation as for domination. But if the knowing subject is led by love, neither can knowledge nor the other nor reality be misused. For agape is always intent on doing justice to every other.

Therefore, as against certain theories of love which depict it as ever seeking harmony, union, and even fusion, I would argue that love, instead, enables us to endure difference, pluralism, disagreement and even dissent, without, at the same time, damning the other or seeking segregation. Love truly seeks the other, it takes the initiative, but neither with the primary purpose of changing the other, nor with that of being changed by the other. On the contrary, to love essentially consists in *ex*-isting in the face of the other, in overcoming indifference and self-enclosedness and turning one's existence to one's neighbor without any reason or merit on his/her part. Gratuitously, freely, in response to a greater love. Grace.

---

philosophischen Erkennens," in *Gesammelte Werke*, ed. Maria Scheler, vol. 5 (Bern: Francke, 1954), 68.

BIBLIOGRAPHY

Alonso, Pablo. *The Woman Who Changed Jesus: Crossing Boundaries in Mk 7:24-30*. Biblical Tools and Studies 11. Leuven; Paris; Walpole: Peeters, 2011.

Amaladoss, Michael. *Beyond Inculturation: Can the Many Be One?* Reprinted. Delhi: Vidyajyoti Education Welfare Society, 2005.

———. *Making All Things New: Dialogue, Pluralism, and Evangelization in Asia*. Maryknoll, N.Y.: Orbis Books, 1990.

———. "Religiões: Violência ou Diálogo?" *Perspectiva Teológica* 34, no. 93 (2002): 179–96.

———. *Walking Together: The Practice of Interreligious Dialogue*. Amand: Gujarat Sahitya Prakash, 1992.

Anderson, Benedict R. O'G. *Imagined Communities: Reflections on the Origin and Spread of Nationalism*. London: Verso, 1983.

Ansorge, Dirk. *Gerechtigkeit und Barmherzigkeit Gottes: die Dramatik von Vergebung und Versöhnung in bibeltheologischer, theologiegeschichtlicher und philosophiegeschichtlicher Perspektive*. Freiburg im Breisgau; Basel; Wien: Herder, 2009.

Arendt, Hannah. *Love and Saint Augustine*. Edited by Joanna Vecchiarelli Scott and Judith Chelius Stark. Chicago: University of Chicago Press, 1996.

Arens, Edmund. *Christopraxis: Grundzüge theologischer Handlungstheorie*. Quaestiones disputatae 139. Freiburg im Breisgau; Basel; Wien: Herder, 1992.

Asad, Talal. *Formations of the Secular: Christianity, Islam, Modernity*. Stanford: Stanford University Press, 2008.

———. *Genealogies of Religion: Discipline and Reasons of Power in Christianity and Islam*. Baltimore: Johns Hopkins University Press, 1993.

———. "Reading a Modern Classic: W. C. Smith's 'The Meaning and End of Religion.'" *History of Religions* 40, no. 3 (2001): 205–22.

Assmann, Jan. *Herrschaft und Heil: politische Theologie in Altägypten, Israel und Europa*. München: C. Hanser, 2000.

———. "Translating Gods: Religion as a Factor of Cultural (Un)Translatability." In *Religion: Beyond a Concept*, edited by Hent Vries, 139–49. New York: Fordham University Press, 2008.

Assmann, Jan, Bernd Janowski, and Michael Welker. "Richten und Retten: Zur Aktualität der altorientalischen und biblischen Gerechtigkeitskonzeption." In *Die rettende Gerechtigkeit*, edited by Bernd Janowski, 220–46. Beiträge zur Theologie des Alten Testaments 2. Neukirchen-Vluyn: Neukirchener, 1999.

Augenstein, Jörg. *Das Liebesgebot im Johannesevangelium und in den Johannesbriefen*. Beiträge zur Wissenschaft vom Alten und Neuen Testament 134. Stuttgart: Kohlhammer, 1993.

Aumann, Antony. "Self-Love and Neighbor-Love in Kierkegaard's Ethics." *Kierkegaard Studies, Yearbook*, 2013, 197–216. doi:10.1515/kier.2013.2013.1.197.

Badiou, Alain. *Being and Event*. Translated by Oliver Feltham. London; New York: Continuum, 2007.

———. *In Praise of Love*. London: Serpent's Tail, 2012.

———. *Paulus: die Begründung des Universalismus*. Translated by Heinz Jatho. München: Sequenzia, 2002.

———. *Saint Paul: The Foundation of Universalism*. Translated by Ray Brassier. Stanford: Stanford University Press, 1997.

Balthasar, Hans Urs von. *Theodramatik*. 4 vols. Einsiedeln: Johannes, 1973.

Barthes, Roland. *Fragmente einer Sprache der Liebe*. 6th ed. Frankfurt am Main: Suhrkamp, 1988.

Barth, Karl. *Die kirchliche Dogmatik*. 4th ed. 4 vols. Zürich: Theologischer Verlag, n.d.

Batlogg, Andreas R. *Die Mysterien des Lebens Jesu bei Karl Rahner: Zugang zum Christusglauben*. Innsbrucker theologische Studien 58. Innsbruck: Tyrolia, 2001.

———. "Wieviel Jesus braucht die Fundamentaltheologie: Zur Relevanz des (unterschätzten) Lebens Jesu – eine Problemanzeige." In *Was den Glauben in Bewegung bringt: Fundamentaltheologie in der Spur Jesu Christi*, edited by Andreas R. Batlogg, Mariano Delgado, and Roman A. Siebenrock, 402–22. Festschrift für Karl H. Neufeld. Freiburg im Breisgau; Basel; Wien: Herder, 2004.

Bauer, Christian. "Optionen des Konzils?: Umrisse einer konstellativen Hermeneutik des Zweiten Vatikanums." *Zeitschrift für katholische Theologie* 134, no. 2 (2012): 141–62.

Bauer, Walter. *Griechisch-deutsches Wörterbuch zu den Schriften des Neuen Testaments und der frühchristlichen Literatur*. Edited by Kurt Aland. 6th ed. Berlin: de Gruyter, 1988.

———. *Orthodoxy and Heresy in Earliest Christianity*. Edited by Gerhard Krodel and Robert A. Kraft. Philadelphia: Fortress Press, 1971.

———. *Rechtgläubigkeit und Ketzerei im ältesten Christentum.* Edited by Georg Strecker. 2nd ed. Beiträge zur historischen Theologie 10. Tübingen: Mohr Siebeck, 1964.

Bauman, Zygmunt. *Liquid Love: On the Frailty of Human Bonds.* Cambridge: Polity Press, 2004.

Beck, Ulrich, and Elisabeth Beck-Gernsheim. *Das ganz normale Chaos der Liebe.* Frankfurt am Main: Suhrkamp, 2005.

Beinert, Wolfgang. "Das Christentum und die Religionen." *Stimmen der Zeit* 229, no. 4 (2011): 229–38.

Beirer, Georg. *Selbst werden in Liebe: Eine Begründung christlicher Ethik im interdisziplinären Dialog.* St. Ottilien: EOS, 1988.

Ben-Chorin, Shalom. *Jüdische Ethik anhand der patristischen Perikopen: Jerusalemer Vorlesungen.* Tübingen: Moh, 1983.

Bernhard, Casper. "Liebe." Edited by Hermann Krings. *Handbuch philosophischer Grundbegriffe.* Studienausgabe. München, 1993.

Bernhardt, Reinhold, and Perry Schmidt-Leukel. *Kriterien interreligiöser Urteilsbildung.* Zürich: Theologischer Verlag Zürich, 2005.

Bernhardt, Reinhold, and Klaus von Stosch, eds. *Komparative Theologie: interreligiöse Vergleiche als Weg der Religionstheologie.* Beiträge zu einer Theologie der Religionen 7. Zürich: Theologischer Verlag Zürich, 2009.

Beutler, Johannes. "Gesetz und Gebot in Evanglium und Briefen des Johannes." In *Neue Studien zu den johanneischen Schriften,* 11–24. Bonner Biblische Beiträge 167. Göttingen: Bonn University Press, 2012.

Beyer, Gerald J. "Karl Rahner on the Radical Unity of the Love of God and Neighbour." *Irish Theological Quarterly* 68, no. 3 (2003): 251–80. doi:10.1177/002114000306800304.

Bible. *The New Jerusalem Bible.* London: Darton, Longman and Todd, 1985.

Bieberstein, Klaus, and Hanspeter Schmitt, eds. *Prekär: Gottes Gerechtigkeit und die Moral der Menschen – im Gespräch mit Volker Eid.* Luzern: Edition Exodus, 2008.

Binder, Hermann. "Das Gleichnis vom Barmherzigen Samariter." *Theologische Zeitschrift* 15 (1959): 176–94.

Bjerg, Ole. "Die Welt als Wille und System. Oder: Eine Schopenhauerische Kritik der Systemtheorie Luhmanns." *Zeitschrift für Soziologie* 34, no. 3 (2005): 223–35.

Blondel, Maurice. *Exigences philosophiques du christianisme.* Paris: Presses universitaires de France, 1950.

Boff, Clodovis. "Epistemología y método de la teología de la liberación." In *Mysterium liberationis: Conceptos fundamentales de la teología de la liberación*, edited by Ignacio Ellacuría and Jon Sobrino, 1:79–113. Madrid: Editorial Trotta, 1990.

Boltanski, Luc. *Love and Justice as Competences: Three Essays on the Sociology of Action*. Cambridge: Polity Press, 2012.

Bornhäuser, Karl. *Studien zum Sondergut des Lukas*. Gütersloh: Bertelsmann, 1934.

Bornkamm, Günther. "Das Doppelgebot der Liebe." In *Geschichte und Glaube*. Beiträge zur evangelischen Theologie 48. München: Kaiser, 1968.

Bosch, David. *Transforming Mission: Paradigm Shifts in Theology of Mission*. Maryknoll, N.Y.: Orbis Books, 1991.

Botterweck, G. Johannes. "ידע (jada')." Edited by G. Johannes Botterweck and Helmer Ringgren. *Theologisches Wörterbuch zum Alten Testament*. Stuttgart: Kohlhammer, 1982.

Bouwman, Gijs. "Σαμάρεια." *Exegetisches Wörterbuch zum Neuen Testament*. Stuttgart; Berlin; Köln: Kohlhammer, 1992.

Bovon, François. *Das Evangelium nach Lukas*. Vol. III/1. Evangelisch-Katholischer Kommentar zum Neuen Testament. Zürich: Benziger, 1986.

———. *Das Evangelium nach Lukas*. Vol. III/2. Evangelisch-Katholischer Kommentar zum Neuen Testament. Zürich: Benziger, 1996.

———. *Luke the Theologian*. 2nd ed. Waco: Baylor University Press, 2006.

———. *Studies in Early Christianity*. Wissenschaftliche Untersuchungen zum Neuen Testament 161. Tübingen: Mohr Siebeck, 2003.

Boyarin, Daniel. *Border Lines: The Partition of Judaeo-Christianity*. Philadelphia: University of Pennsylvania Press, 2004.

Broadhead, Edwin K. *Jewish Ways of Following Jesus: Redrawing the Religious Map of Antiquity*. Wissenschaftliche Untersuchungen zum Neuen Testament 266. Tübingen: Mohr Siebeck, 2010.

Brocher, Tobias. *Von der Schwierigkeit zu lieben*. 2nd ed. Maßstäbe des Menschlichen 8. Stuttgart: Kreuz, 1976.

Brox, Norbert. *Der Glaube als Weg und als Zeugnis: Nach biblischen und altchristlichen Zeugnissen*. Ostfildern: Matthias-Grünewald, 2010.

———. *Kirchengeschichte des Altertums*. Leitfaden Theologie 8. Düsseldorf: Patmos-Verlag, 1983.

Brück, Michael von, and Jürgen Werbick, eds. *Der einzige Weg zum Heil?: die Herausforderung des christlichen Absolutheitsanspruchs durch pluralistische Religionstheologien*. Quaestiones disputatae 143. Freiburg im Breisgau; Basel; Wien: Herder, 1993.

Brümmer, Vincent. *The Model of Love: A Study in Philosophical Theology.* Cambridge: Cambridge University Press, 1993.

Bryant, Herschel Odell. *Spirit Christology in the Christian Tradition: From the Patristic Period to the Rise of Pentecostalism in the Twentieth Century.* Cleveland: CPT Press, 2014.

Buber, Martin. "What Is Man?" In *Between Man and Man*, translated by Ronald Gregor Smith, 118–205. New York: Collier Books, 1985.

Bullivant, Stephen. *The Salvation of Atheists and Catholic Dogmatic Theology.* Oxford Theological Monographs. Oxford: Oxford University Press, 2012.

Bultmann, Rudolf. "Das christliche Gebot der Nächstenliebe." In *Glauben und Verstehen*, by Rudolf Bultmann, 229–44, 3rd ed. Tübingen: Mohr, 1958.

———. *Die Geschichte der synoptischen Tradition.* 10th ed. (first published in 1921). Göttingen: Vandenhoeck & Ruprecht, 1995.

———. *Geschichte und Eschatologie.* 2nd ed. Tübingen: Mohr, 1964.

Burchard, Christoph, and Dieter Sänger. *Studien zur Theologie, Sprache und Umwelt des Neuen Testaments.* Wissenschaftliche Untersuchungen zum Neuen Testament 107. Tübingen: Mohr Siebeck, 1998.

Burggraeve, Roger. "Alterity Makes the Difference: Ethical and Metaphysical Conditions for an Authentic Interreligious Dialogue and Learning." In *Interreligious Learning*, edited by Didier Pollefeyt, 231–56. Leuven: Peeters, 2007.

Casanova, José. "Public Religions Revisited." In *Religion: Beyond a Concept*, edited by Hent Vries, 101–19. New York: Fordham University Press, 2008.

Casanova, José, and Hans Joas. *Religion und die umstrittene Moderne.* Stuttgart: Kohlhammer, 2010.

Casper, Bernhard. *Das dialogische Denken: Franz Rosenzweig, Ferdinand Ebner und Martin Buber.* Freiburg im Breisgau: Alber, 2002.

Chia, Edmund Kee-Fook. *Edward Schillebeeckx and Interreligious Dialogue: Perspectives from Asian Theology.* Eugene, Oregon: Wipf and Stock Publishers, 2012.

Christian, Paul. *Jesus und seine geringsten Brüder: Mt 25,31-46 redaktionsgeschichtlich untersucht.* Leipzig: St. Benno, 1975.

Clooney, Francis X. *Comparative Theology: Deep Learning across Religious Borders.* Hoboken, NJ: John Wiley & Sons, 2010.

Comte-Sponville, André. *Liebe: Eine kleine Philosophie.* Zürich: Diogenes, 2014.

Conzelmann, Hans. *Die Mitte der Zeit: Studien zur Theologie des Lukas.* Beiträge zur historischen Theologie 17. Tübingen: Mohr, 1954.

Cornille, Catherine. "Conditions for Inter-Religious Dialogue." In *The Wiley-Blackwell Companion to Inter-Religious Dialogue*, edited by Catherine Cornille, 20–33. The Wiley-Blackwell Companions to Religion. Chichester: Wiley-Blackwell, 2013.

———. "Das Zeugnis und seine Bedeutung im interreligiösen Dialog." *Concilium* 47, no. 1 (2011): 49–58.

———. "Empathy and Inter-Religious Imagination." *Religion and the Arts* 12, no. 1 (2008): 102–17. doi:10.1163/156852908X270944.

———. *The Im-Possibility of Interreligious Dialogue*. New York: Crossroad, 2008.

Dalferth, Ingolf U. *Ethik der Liebe: Studien zu Kierkegaards "Taten der Liebe."* Religion in Philosophy and Theology 4. Tübingen: Mohr Siebeck, 2002.

Dalferth, Ingolf U., and Heiko Schulz, eds. *Religion und Konflikt: Grundlagen und Fallanalysen*. Research in Contemporary Religion 8. Göttingen: Vandenhoeck & Ruprecht, 2011.

Daniélou, Jean. *A History of Early Christian Doctrine before the Council of Nicaea*. Translated by John Austin Baker. Vol. 1. 3 vols. London: Darton, Longman & Todd, 1964.

Danz, Christian. *Einführung in die Theologie der Religionen*. Wien: Lit Verlag, 2005.

Davidson, Scott. "Linguistic Hospitality: The Task of Translation in Ricoeur and Levinas." *Analecta Hermeneutica* 4 (2012).

Davis, Zachary, and Anthony Steinbock. "Max Scheler." *The Stanford Encyclopedia of Philosophy*. Accessed May 5, 2015. http://plato.stanford.edu/archives/sum2014/entries/scheler/.

D'Costa, Gavin. "The Impossibility of a Pluralist View of Religions." *Religious Studies* 32, no. 2 (1996): 223–32. doi:10.1017/S0034412500024240.

———. *The Meeting of Religions and the Trinity*. Maryknoll, N.Y.: Orbis Books, 2000.

Dehn, Ulrich, ed. *Handbuch Dialog der Religionen: Christliche Quellen zur Religionstheologie und zum interreligiösen Dialog*. Frankfurt am Main: Lembeck, 2008.

Dihle, Albrecht. *Die goldene Regel: Eine Einführung in die Geschichte der antiken und frühchristlichen Vulgärethik*. Göttingen: Vandenhoeck & Ruprecht, 1962.

Dillmann, Rainer, and César Mora Paz. *Das Lukas-Evangelium: ein Kommentar für die Praxis*. Stuttgart: Katholisches Bibelwerk, 2000.

Dirks, Walter. *Die Samariter und der Mann aus Samaria: vom Umgang mit der Barmherzigkeit*. Freiburg im Breisgau: Labertus, 1985.

Dober, Hans Martin, and Dagmar Mensink, eds. *Die Lehre von der Rechtfertigung des Gottlosen im kulturellen Kontext der Gegenwart: Beiträge im Horizont des christlich-jüdischen Gesprächs*. Hohenheimer Protokolle 57. Stuttgart: Akademie der Diözese Rottenburg-Stuttgart, 2002.

Dömer, Michael. *Das Heil Gottes: Studien zur Theologie des lukanischen Doppelwerkes*. Bonner biblische Beiträge 51. Köln; Bonn: Hanstein, 1978.

Drury, John. *Tradition and Design in Luke's Gospel: A Study in Early Christian Historiography*. Atlanta: John Knox Press, 1976.

Dupuis, Jacques. *Christianity and the Religions: From Confrontation to Dialogue*. Maryknoll, N.Y.: Orbis Books, 2002.

———. *Towards a Christian Theology of Religious Pluralism*. Maryknoll, N.Y.: Orbis Books, 1997.

Durrwell, Francois-Xavier. *Jésus, fils de Dieu dans l'Esprit Saint*. Paris: Desclée, 1997.

Ebeling, Gerhard. "Das Verständnis von Heil in säkularisierter Zeit." In *Wort und Glaube*, 3:349–61. Tübingen: Mohr, 1975.

Ebersohn, Michael. *Das Nächstenliebegebot in der synoptischen Tradition*. Marburger theologische Studien 37. Marburg: Elwert, 1993.

Eckey, Wilfried. *Das Lukasevangelium: unter Berücksichtigung seiner Parallelen*. Vol. 1. 2 vols. Neukirchen-Vluyn: Neukirchener, 2004.

Eicher, Peter. *Die anthropologische Wende: Karl Rahners philosophischer Weg vom Wesen des Menschen zur personalen Existenz*. Freiburg, Switzerland: Universitätsverlag, 1970.

Ellacuría, Ignacio. "Historicidad de la salvación cristiana." In *Mysterium liberationis: Conceptos fundamentales de la teología de la liberación*, edited by Ignacio Ellacuría and Jon Sobrino, 1:323–72. Madrid: Editorial Trotta, 1990.

Esler, Philip F. "Jesus and the Reduction of Intergroup Conflict: The Parable of the Good Samaritan in the Light of Social Identity Theory." *Biblical Interpretation* 8, no. 4 (2000): 325–57. doi:10.1163/156851500750118953.

Evangelische Kirche in Deutschland. *Für uns gestorben: Die Bedeutung von Leiden und Sterben Jesu Christi*. Orientierungshilfen. Gütersloh: Gütersloher Verlagshaus, 2015. Accessed April 4, 2015. http://www.ekd.de/download/fuer_unsgestorben2015.pdf.

Fabris, Adriano. *I paradossi dell'amore: Fra grecità, ebraismo e cristianesimo*. Brescia: Morcelliana, 2000.

Federation of Asian Bishops' Conferences. Office of Evangelization. "Evangelisation and Inculturation." Pauline Publications, 2001.

Feil, Ernst. *Religio*. 4 vols. Göttingen: Vandenhoeck & Ruprecht, 1986.

———. *Streitfall "Religion": Diskussionen zur Bestimmung und Abgrenzung des Religionsbegriffs*. Münster: Lit, 2000.

Feine, Paul. *Eine vorkanonische Überlieferung des Lukas in Evangelium und Apostelgeschichte: eine Untersuchung*. Gotha: F. A. Perthes, 1891.

Feuerbach, Ludwig. "Grundsätze der Philosophie der Zukunft (1843)." In *Kleinere Schriften*, edited by Werner Schuffenhauer, 2:264–341. Gesammelte Werke 9. Berlin: Akademie, 1970.

———. "Principles of Philosophy of the Future." Translated by Zawar Hanfi. *Marxists Internet Archive*. Accessed May 17, 2015. https://www.marxists.org/reference/archive/feuer bach/works/future/.

———. "Provisional Theses for the Reformation of Philosophy." In *The Young Hegelians, an Anthology*, edited by Lawrence S. Stepelevich, translated by Daniel O. Dahlstrom. Cambridge: Cambridge University Press, 1983.

———. *The Essence of Christianity*. Translated by Marian Evans. 2nd ed. London: Kegan Paul, Trench, Trübner, 1890.

———. "Vorläufige Thesen zur Reformation der Philosophie (1842)." In *Kleinere Schriften*, edited by Werner Schuffenhauer, 2:243–63. Gesammelte Werke 9. Berlin: Akademie, 1970.

Fink, Renate. *Die Botschaft des heilenden Handelns Jesu: Untersuchung der dreizehn exemplarischen Berichte von Jesu heilendem Handeln im Markusevangelium*. Salzburger Theologische Studien 15. Innsbruck; Wien: Tyrolia, 2000.

Fitzmyer, Joseph A. *The Gospel According to Luke*. Vol. 1. 2 vols. The Anchor Bible 28. New York: Doubleday, 1981.

———. *The Gospel According to Luke*. Vol. 2. 2 vols. The Anchor Bible 28A. New York: Doubleday, 1985.

Fletcher, Jeannine Hill. "As Long as We Wonder: Possibilities in the Impossibility of Interreligious Dialogue." *Theological Studies* 68, no. 3 (September 1, 2007): 531–54. doi:10.1177/004056390706800303.

Fredericks, James L. "Das Selbst vergessen: Buddhistische Reflexionen zur Trinität." In *Komparative Theologie: Interreligiöse Vergleiche als Weg der Religionstheologie*, edited by Reinhold Bernhardt and Klaus von Stosch, 203–23. Beiträge zu einer Theologie der Religionen 7. Zürich: Theologischer Verlag Zürich, 2009.

Friedrich, Johannes. *Gott im Bruder?: Eine methodenkritische Untersuchung von Redaktion, Überlieferung und Traditionen in Mt 25,31-46*. Stuttgart: Calwer, 1977.

Fromm, Erich. *The Art of Loving*. London: Unwin, 1982.

Fuchs, Peter. *Das System selbst: Eine Studie zur Frage: wer liebt wen, wenn jemand sagt: "Ich liebe dich!"?* Weilerswist: Velbrück, 2010.

———. *Liebe, Sex und solche Sachen: Zur Konstruktion moderner Intimsysteme.* Konstanz: Universitätsverlag, 2003.

Gadamer, Hans-Georg. *Wahrheit und Methode: Grundzüge einer philosophischen Hermeneutik.* 4th ed. Tübingen: Mohr, 1975.

Ganoczy, Alexandre. "Liebe als Prinzip der Theologie." In *Prinzip Liebe: Perspektiven der Theologie*, edited by Eugen Biser, 36–58. Freiburg im Breisgau; Basel; Wien: Herder, 1975.

Gerhardsson, Birger. *The Shema in the New Testament: Deut 6:4-5 in Significant Passages.* Lund: Novapress, 1996.

Gerlitz, Peter, Horst Seebaß, Reinhard Neudecker, Oda Wischmeyer, Pierre Maraval, Tuomo Mannermaa, Günter Meckenstock, Hermann Ringeling, and Georg Scherer. "Liebe." *Theologische Realenzyklopädie.* Berlin; New York: Walter de Gruyter, 1991.

Gertler, Thomas. *Jesus Christus – die Antwort der Kirche auf die Frage nach dem Menschsein: Eine Untersuchung zu Funktion und Inhalt der Christologie im ersten Teil der Pastoralkonstitution "Gaudium et Spes" des Zweiten Vatikanischen Konzils.* Leipzig: St. Benno, 1986.

Glöckner, Richard. *Die Verkündigung des Heils beim Evangelisten Lukas.* Mainz: Matthias-Grünewald, 1976.

Gnilka, Joachim. *Das Evangelium nach Markus.* Vol. II/1. Evangelisch-Katholischer Kommentar zum Neuen Testament. Zürich; Einsiedeln; Köln: Benziger, 1978.

———. *Das Evangelium nach Markus.* Vol. II/2. Evangelisch-Katholischer Kommentar zum Neuen Testament. Zürich; Einsiedeln; Köln: Benziger, 1979.

Gogarten, Friedrich. *Verhängnis und Hoffnung der Neuzeit: die Säkularisierung als theologisches Problem.* 2nd ed. Stuttgart: Vorwerk, 1958.

Gradl, Hans-Georg. *Zwischen Arm und Reich: das lukanische Doppelwerk in leserorientierter und textpragmatischer Perspektive.* Forschung zur Bibel 107. Würzburg: Echter, 2005.

Gregory, Eric. *Politics and the Order of Love: An Augustinian Ethic of Democratic Citizenship.* Chicago: University of Chicago Press, 2008.

Greshake, Gisbert. *Erlöst in einer unerlösten Welt?* Mainz: Matthias-Grünewald, 1987.

———. *Gottes Heil, Glück des Menschen: theologische Perspektiven.* Freiburg im Breisgau: Herder, 1983.

Grilli, Massimo. "Schlussbeobachtungen." In *Handle danach und du wirst leben: Reichtum und Solidarität im Werk des Lukas*, edited by Cordula Langner. Stuttgart: Katholisches Bibelwerk, 2010.

Grøn, Arne. "Kierkegaards 'zweite' Ethik." Translated by Schmid Hermann. *Kierkegaard Studies, Yearbook*, 1998, 358–68. doi:10.1515/9783110244007.358.

———. "The Dialectic of Recognition in Works of Love." *Kierkegaard Studies, Yearbook*, 1998, 147–57. doi:10.1515/9783110244007.147.

Groß, Walter. "Gott als gewalttätiger Geschichtslenker im AT?: Eine Problemanzeige." *Theologische Quartalschrift* 191, no. 4 (2011): 291–303.

———. "YHWH und die Religionen der Nicht-Israeliten." *Theologische Quartalschrift* 169, no. 1 (1989): 34–44.

Guanzini, Isabella. *Il giovane Hegel e Paolo: L'amore fra politica e messianismo*. Filosofia: ricerche. Milano: Vita e Pensiero, 2013.

Gutiérrez, Gustavo. *A Theology of Liberation: History, Politics, and Salvation*. Edited and translated by Caridad Inda and John Eagleson. Revised version of the original English translation [reprint]. London: SCM Press, 2010.

———. "The Task and Content of Liberation Theology." In *The Cambridge Companion to Liberation Theology*, edited by Christopher Rowland, 19–38. Cambridge; New York: Cambridge University Press, 1999.

Habermas, Jürgen. "Exkurs zu Luhmanns systemtheoretischer Aneignung der subjektphilosophischen Erbmasse." In *Der philosophische Diskurs der Moderne*, edited by Jürgen Habermas, 426–45. Frankfurt am Main: Suhrkamp, 1985.

———. *Glauben und Wissen*. Friedenspreis des Deutschen Buchhandels. Frankfurt am Main: Suhrkamp, 2001.

———. "Vorpolitische Grundlagen des demokratischen Rechtsstaates." In *Dialektik der Säkularisierung: Über Vernunft und Religion*, edited by Jürgen Habermas, Joseph Ratzinger, and Florian Schuller, 4th ed. Freiburg im Breisgau: Herder, 2006.

Haker, Hille. "Neue Erwägungen zu Solidarität und Gerechtigkeit." *Concilium* 50, no. 1 (2014): 7–18.

Häring, Hermann. *Hans Küng: Grenzen durchbrechen*. Mainz: Matthias-Grünewald, 1998.

Harris, Elizabeth J., ed. *Twenty-First-Century Theologies of Religions: Retrospection and Future Prospects*. Currents of Encounter 54. Leiden; Boston: Brill; Rodopi, 2016.

Hengel, Martin. "Zur Wirkungsgeschichte von Jes 53 in vorchristlicher Zeit." In *Der leidende Gottesknecht: Jesaja 53 und seine Wirkungsgeschichte*, edited by Bernd Janowski and Peter Stuhlmacher, 49–91. Forschungen zum Alten Testament 14. Tübingen: J.C.B. Mohr, 1996.

Hengel, Martin, and Anna Maria Schwemer. *Geschichte des frühen Christentums*. Vol. 1. Tübingen: Mohr Siebeck, 2007.

Hick, John. *An Interpretation of Religion: Human Responses to the Transcendent.* New Haven: Yale University Press, 1989.

———. "The Non-Absoluteness of Christianity." In *The Myth of Christian Uniqueness: Toward a Pluralistic Theology of Religions,* edited by John Hick and Paul F. Knitter, 16–36. Maryknoll, N.Y.: Orbis Books, 1987.

Hick, John, and Paul F. Knitter, eds. *The Myth of Christian Uniqueness: Toward a Pluralistic Theology of Religions.* Faith Meets Faith Series. Maryknoll, N.Y.: Orbis Books, 1987.

Hilberath, Bernd Jochen. *Begegnen statt importieren: Zum Verhältnis von Religion und Kultur.* Ostfildern: Matthias-Grünewald, 2011.

Honneth, Axel. *Das Recht der Freiheit: Grundriß einer demokratischen Sittlichkeit.* Berlin: Suhrkamp, 2011.

———. *The Struggle for Recognition: The Moral Grammar of Social Conflicts.* Cambridge, Massachusetts: MIT Press, 1996.

———. "Unsichtbarkeit: Über die moralische Epistemologie von 'Anerkennung.'" In *Unsichtbarkeit: Stationen einer Theorie der Intersubjektivität,* 10–27. Frankfurt am Main: Suhrkamp, 2003.

Hünermann, Peter. "Die methodologische Herausforderung der Dogmatik durch die Wiederentdeckung der theologischen Relevanz des Judentums." In *Methodische Erneuerung der Theologie: Konsequenzen der wiederentdeckten jüdisch-christlichen Gemeinsamkeiten,* edited by Peter Hünermann and Thomas Söding. Quaestiones disputatae 200. Freiburg im Breisgau; Basel; Wien: Herder, 2003.

———. "Theologischer Kommentar zur dogmatischen Konstitution über die Kirche (Lumen Gentium)." In *Herders theologischer Kommentar zum Zweiten Vatikanischen Konzil,* edited by Peter Hünermann and Bernd Jochen Hilberath, 2:263–582. Freiburg im Breisgau: Herder, 2004.

Huntington, Samuel P. *The Clash of Civilizations and the Remaking of World Order.* New York: Simon & Schuster, 1996.

Hurst, Lincoln Douglas. *The Glory of Christ in the New Testament: Studies in Christology – in Memory of George Bradford Caird.* Oxford: Clarendon Press, 1987.

Imbach, Josef. *Daß der Mensch ganz sei: Vom Leid, vom Heil und vom ewigen Leben in Judentum, Christentum und Islam.* Düsseldorf: Patmos, 1991.

International Theological Commission. "Christianity and the World Religions." Libreria Editrice Vaticana, 1997.

———. "Select Questions on the Theology of God the Redeemer." Libreria Editrice Vaticana, 1995.

Jackson-McCabe, Matt. "What's in a Name? The Problem of 'Jewish Christianity.'" In *Jewish Christianity Reconsidered: Rethinking Ancients Groups and Texts*, edited by Matt Jackson-McCabe, 7–38. Minneapolis: Fortress Press, 2007.

Jacobs-Vandegeer, Christiaan. "Method, Meaning, and the Theologies of Religions." *Irish Theological Quarterly* 80, no. 1 (2015): 30–55. doi:10.1177/0021140014552162.

Jacoby, Norbert. "pístis di' energouménē (Gal 5,6b): Versuch einer Interpretation." *Theologie und Philosophie* 89, no. 3 (2014): 407–18.

Janowski, Bernd. "Der barmherzige Richter: Zur Einheit von Gerechtigkeit und Barmherzigkeit im Gottesbild des Alten Orients und des Alten Testaments." In *Der Gott des Lebens*, edited by Bernd Janowski, 75–133. Beiträge zur Theologie des Alten Testaments 3. Neukirchen-Vluyn: Neukirchener, 2003.

———. "Der eine Gott der beiden Testamente: Grundfragen einer biblischen Theologie." In *Die rettende Gerechtigkeit*, edited by Bernd Janowski, 249–84. Beiträge zur Theologie des Alten Testaments 2. Neukirchen-Vluyn: Neukirchener, 1999.

Jeanrond, Werner G. *A Theology of Love*. London: T & T Clark, 2010.

———. "Hermeneutics and Christian Praxis: Some Reflections on the History of Hermeneutics." *Literature and Theology* 2, no. 2 (1988): 174–88. doi:10.1093/litthe/2.2.174.

———. "Interkulturalität und Interreligiosität: Die Notwendigkeit einer Hermeneutik der Liebe." In *Kontextualität und Universalität: Die Vielfalt der Glaubenskontexte und der Universalitätsanspruch des Evangeliums*, edited by Thomas Schreijäck and Knut Wenzel, 156–73. Kohlhammer, 2012.

———. "Subjectivity and Objectivity in Theological Hermeneutics: The Potential of Love for Interfaith Encounter." *Al-Bayan: Journal of Qur'an and Hadith Studies* 11, no. 2 (2013): 71–91. doi:10.11136/jqh.1311.02.05.

———. *Text and Interpretation as Categories of Theological Thinking*. Translated by Thomas J. Wilson. New York: Crossroad, 1988.

Jeremias, Joachim. *Das Problem des historischen Jesus*. Calwer Hefte zur Förderung biblischen Glaubens und christlichen Lebens 32. Stuttgart: Calwer, 1960.

———. *Die Gleichnisse Jesu*. 11th ed. (first published in 1947). Göttingen: Vandenhoeck & Ruprecht, 1998.

———. *Jesus und seine Botschaft*. Stuttgart: Calwer, 1976.

———. *Neutestamentliche Theologie*. 3rd ed. Vol. 1. Gütersloh: Mohn, 1979.

———. "Σαμάρεια." *Theologisches Wörterbuch zum Neuen Testament*. Stuttgart: Kohlhammer, 1964.

Joas, Hans. *Braucht der Mensch Religion?: Über Erfahrungen der Selbsttranszendenz*. Freiburg im Breisgau: Herder, 2004.

———. *Glaube als Option: Zukunftsmöglichkeiten des Christentums*. Freiburg im Breisgau: Herder, 2012.

Joas, Hans, and Klaus Wiegandt, eds. *Säkularisierung und die Weltreligionen*. Frankfurt am Main: Fischer Taschenbuch, 2007.

John, Ottmar, and Matthias Möhring-Hesse, eds. *Heil – Gerechtigkeit – Wahrheit*. Theologie: Forschung und Wissenschaft 22. Berlin: Lit, 2006.

John, Ottmar, and Magnus Striet, eds. *"... und nichts Menschliches ist mir fremd": theologische Grenzgänge*. Ratio fidei 41. Regensburg: Pustet, 2010.

Jonkers, Peter. "Religiöse Wahrheit im Horizont des gesellschaftlichen Pluralismus." *Theologie und Philosophie* 89, no. 3 (2014): 384–406.

Jossa, Giorgio. *Jews or Christians?: The Followers of Jesus in Search of Their Own Identity*. Wissenschaftliche Untersuchungen zum Neuen Testament 202. Tübingen: Mohr Siebeck, 2006.

Jüngel, Eberhard. *Gott als Geheimnis der Welt: Zur Begründung der Theologie des Gekreuzigten im Streit zwischen Theismus und Atheismus*. 7th ed. Tübingen: Mohr, 2001.

Kant, Immanuel. *Religion within the Limits of Reason Alone*. Translated by Theodore Meyer Greene and Hoyt H. Hudson. New York: Harper & Row, 1960.

Kappes, Clemens. "Freiheit und Erlösung: Überlegungen zu den Grundlagen der Soteriologie in den Entwürfen von Hans Urs von Balthasar, Karl Rahner und Jürgen Moltmann." Westfälische Wilhelms-Universität, 1986.

Kapsch, Edda. *Verstehen des Anderen*. Fremdverstehen im Anschluss an Husserl, Gadamer und Derrida. Berlin: Parodos, 2007.

Kasper, Walter. *Jesus der Christus*. Gesammelte Schriften 3. Freiburg im Breisgau; Basel; Wien: Herder, 2007.

Kearney, Richard. "Introduction: Ricoeur's Philosophy of Translation." In *On Translation*, by Paul Ricoeur, vii–xx. London: Routledge, 2006.

———, ed. *Paul Ricoeur: The Hermeneutics of Action*. London; Thousand Oaks; New Delhi: Sage Publications, 1996.

Kern, Udo. *Liebe als Erkenntnis und Konstruktion von Wirklichkeit: "Erinnerung" an ein stets aktuales Erkenntnispotential*. Berlin; New York: Gruyter, 2001.

Kessler, Hans. "Christologie." In *Handbuch der Dogmatik*, edited by Theodor Schneider, 3rd ed., 1:241–442. Düsseldorf: Patmos, 2006.

———. *Den verborgenen Gott suchen: Gottesglaube in einer von Naturwissenschaften und Religionskonflikten geprägten Welt*. Paderborn; München; Wien; Zürich: Schöningh, 2006.

———. *Erlösung als Befreiung*. Düsseldorf: Patmos, 1972.

Kierkegaard, Søren. *Works of Love: Some Christian Reflections in the Form of Discourses*. Translated by Howard and Edna Hong. New York: Harper and Row, 1962.

Kirchschläger, Peter G. "Nächstenliebe – das Leitprinzip christlicher Moraltheologie." *Zeitschrift für katholische Theologie* 137, no. 2 (2015): 170–92.

Klassen, William. "Love (NT and Early Jewish)." Edited by David Noel Freedman. *The Anchor Bible Dictionary*. New York: Doubleday, 1992.

Klauck, Hans-Josef. *Der erste Johannesbrief*. Evangelisch-Katholischer Kommentar zum Neuen Testament 23/1. Zürich; Neukirchen-Vluyn: Benziger; Neukirchener, 1991.

Klein, Hans. *Barmherzigkeit gegenüber den Elenden und Geächteten: Studien zur Botschaft des lukanischen Sondergutes*. Biblisch-theologische Studien 10. Neukirchen-Vluyn: Neukirchener Verlag, 1987.

Klinger, Elmar. *Christentum innerhalb und außerhalb der Kirche*. Quaestiones disputatae 73. Freiburg im Breisgau: Herder, 1976.

Knapp, Markus. *Die Vernunft des Glaubens: Eine Einführung in die Fundamentaltheologie*. Freiburg im Breisgau: Herder, 2009.

———. *Verantwortetes Christsein heute: Theologie zwischen Metaphysik und Postmoderne*. Freiburg im Breisgau: Herder, 2006.

Knauber, Bernt. *Liebe und Sein: Die Agape als fundamentalontologische Kategorie*. Berlin: Walter de Gruyter, 2006.

Knauer, Peter. "Christus 'in' den Religionen: Interiorismus." *Freiburger Zeitschrift für Philosophie und Theologie* 51 (2004): 237–52.

Knitter, Paul F. *Horizonte der Befreiung: Auf dem Weg zu einer pluralistischen Theologie der Religionen*. Edited by Bernd Jaspert. Freiburg im Breisgau; Basel; Wien: Bonifatius; Lembeck, 1997.

———. *Introducing Theologies of Religions*. Maryknoll, N.Y.: Orbis Books, 2002.

———. *No Other Name?: A Critical Survey of Christian Attitudes toward the World Religions*. American Society of Missiology Series 7. London: SCM Press, 1985.

Koch, Kurt. "Theologische Fragen und Perspektiven im christlich-jüdischen Dialog." October 30, 2011. Katholisch-Theologische Fakultät der Universität Bonn. *Die Kirchen und das Judentum*. Accessed July 12, 2014. http://www.nostra-aetate.uni-bonn.de/kirchliche-dokumente/online-publikation-die-kirchen-und-das-judentum/i.-katholische-verlautbarungen-1/dokumente/theologische-fragen-und-perspektiven-im-christlich-juedischen-dialog.

Konradt, Matthias. "Menschen- oder Bruderliebe?: Beobachtungen zum Liebesgebot in den Testamenten der Zwölf Patriarchen." *Zeitschrift für die neutestamentliche Wissenschaft* 88, no. 3–4 (1997): 296–310.

Körner, Christoph. *(K)ein Heil außerhalb der Kirche?: Überlegungen zur theologischen Bedeutung religiöser Pluralität.* Forum Religion & Sozialkultur 21. Berlin: Lit, 2006.

Körner, Felix. *Kirche im Angesicht des Islam: Theologie des interreligiösen Zeugnisses.* Stuttgart: Kohlhammer, 2008.

———. "Offen in Wahrheit und Liebe: Evangelii Gaudium und der katholisch-muslimische Dialog." *CIBEDO-Beiträge*, no. 1 (2014): 4–13.

Krebs, Angelika. "Liebe." Edited by Petra Kolmer and Armin G. Wildfeuer. *Neues Handbuch philosophischer Grundbegriffe.* Freiburg im Breisgau: Karl Alber, 2011.

Küng, Hans. *Christ sein.* München: Piper, 1974.

———. *Projekt Weltethos.* München: Piper, 1990.

Kuschel, Karl-Josef, ed. *Christentum und nichtchristliche Religionen: theologische Modelle im 20. Jahrhundert.* WB-Forum 91. Darmstadt: Wissenschaftliche Buchgesellschaft, 1994.

———. *Leben ist Brückenschlagen: Vordenker des interreligiösen Dialogs.* Ostfildern: Patmos, 2011.

———. *Martin Buber – seine Herausforderung an das Christentum.* Gütersloh: Gütersloher Verlagshaus, 2015.

Ladaria, Luis Ferer. "Amore di Dio e del Prossimo: Aspetti teologici e spirituali." *Gregorianum* 91, no. 2 (2010): 219–39.

Lanczkowski, Günter, Jürgen Lebram, Karlheinz Müller, August Strobel, Karl-Heinz Schwarte, Robert Konrad, and Gottfried Seebaß. "Apokalyptik/Apokalypsen." *Theologische Realenzyklopädie.* Berlin; New York: Walter de Gruyter, 1995.

Lanczkowski, Günter, Adrian Schenker, Edvin Larsson, Martin Seils, and Edvin Larsson. "Heil und Erlösung." *Theologische Realenzyklopädie.* Berlin; New York: Walter de Gruyter, 1986.

Langner, Cordula, ed. *Handle danach und du wirst leben: Reichtum und Solidarität im Werk des Lukas.* Stuttgart: Katholisches Bibelwerk, 2010.

Langthaler, Rudolf. "'Ich bin ein Mensch. Alles, was Menschen widerfährt, das trifft auch mich' (Terenz – Kant – Peukert): Motive der kantischen Tugendlehre und Ethiktheologie als philosophischer Hintergrund der fundamentalen Theologie von Helmut Peukert." In *"… und nichts Menschliches ist mir fremd": Theologische Grenzgänge*, edited by Ottmar John and Magnus Striet, 76–111. Ratio fidei 41. Regensburg: Friedrich Pustet, 2010.

Le Boulluec, Alain. *La notion d'hérésie dans la littérature grecque IIe-IIIe siècles.* Paris: Études Augustiniennes, 1985.

Lehmann, Karl. *Das Christentum – eine Religion unter anderen?: Zum interreligiösen Dialog aus katholischer Perspektive*. Eröffnungsreferat bei der Herbst-Vollversammlung der Deutschen Bischofskonferenz in Fulda, 23 September 2002. Bonn: Sekretariat der deutschen Bischofskonferenz, 2002.

———. "Kriterien des interreligiösen Dialogs." *Stimmen der Zeit* 227, no. 9 (2009): 579–95.

Leutzsch, Martin. "Nächstenliebe als Antisemitismus?: Zu einem Problem der christlich-jüdischen Beziehung." In *Eine Grenze hast Du gesetzt / Edna Brocke zum 60. Geburtstag*, edited by Ekkehard Stegemann and Klaus Wengst, 77–95. Judentum und Christentum 13. Stuttgart: Kohlhammer, 2003.

Limbeck, Meinrad. "Die Religionen im Neuen Testament." *Theologische Quartalschrift* 169, no. 1 (1989): 44–56.

Lindbeck, George. "The Gospel's Uniqueness: Election and Untranslatability." *Modern Theology* 13, no. 4 (1997): 423–50. doi:10.1111/1468-0025.00047.

Löffler, Alexander. "Religiöser Atheismus?: Die Herausforderung des Buddhismus." *Religionsunterricht heute* 43, no. 1 (2015): 18–21.

Lohfink, Gerhard. *Jesus of Nazareth: What He Wanted, Who He Was*. Collegeville, Minnesota: Liturgical Press, 2012.

Lohfink, Norbert. "Das Hauptgebot." In *Das Siegeslied am Schilfmeer: christliche Auseinandersetzungen mit dem Alten Testament*, edited by Norbert Lohfink, 129–50. Frankfurt am Main: Knecht, 1965.

———. "Heil als Befreiung in Israel." In *Erlösung und Emanzipation*, edited by Leo Scheffczyk. Freiburg im Breisgau: Herder, 1973.

Loisy, Alfred. *L'Évangile et l'Église*. Paris: A. Picard et fils, 1902.

Long, J. Bruce. "Love." *The Encyclopedia of Religion*. New York: Macmillan, n.d.

Losinger, Anton. *The Anthropological Turn: The Human Orientation of Karl Rahner*. New York: Fordham University Press, 2000.

Löwith, Karl. *Weltgeschichte und Heilsgeschehen: die theologischen Voraussetzungen der Geschichtsphilosophie*. Urban-Bücher 2. Stuttgart: Kohlhammer, 1953.

Luckmann, Thomas. *Die unsichtbare Religion*. 2nd ed. Suhrkamp-Taschenbuch Wissenschaft. Frankfurt am Main: Suhrkamp, 1993.

Luhmann, Niklas. "Einführende Bemerkungen zu einer Theorie symbolisch generalisierter Kommunikationsmedien." In *Soziologische Aufklärung*, 2:170–92. Köln; Opladen: Westdeutscher, 1970.

———. "Liebe als Passion (1969)." In *Liebe: Eine Übung*, edited by André Kieserling, 9–91. Frankfurt am Main: Suhrkamp, 2008.

———. *Liebe als Passion: Zur Codierung von Intimität.* 6th ed. Frankfurt am Main: Suhrkamp, 1992.

———. *Social Systems.* Stanford: Stanford University Press, 1995.

———. *Soziale Systeme: Grundriß einer allgemeinen Theorie.* Frankfurt am Main: Suhrkamp, 1984.

———. "Soziologie als Theorie sozialer Systeme." In *Soziologische Aufklärung*, 1:113–36. Köln; Opladen: Westdeutscher, 1970.

Luomanen, Petri. *Recovering Jewish-Christian Sects and Gospels.* Leiden; Boston: Brill, 2012.

Lutheran World Federation and Catholic Church. "Joint Declaration on the Doctrine of Justification." 1999. *The Official Website of the Vatican.* Accessed June 1, 2015. http://www.vatican.va/roman_curia/pontifical_councils/chrstuni/documents/rc_pc_chrstuni_doc_31101999_cath-luth-joint-declaration_en.html.

Luz, Ulrich. "Das Evangelium nach Matthäus." *Evangelisch-Katholischer Kommentar zum Neuen Testament.* Zürich; Neukirchen-Vluyn: Benziger; Neukirchener, 1997.

———. *Studies in Matthew.* Grand Rapids, Cambridge: Eerdmans, 2005.

Manson, Thomas Walter. *The Sayings of Jesus as Recorded in the Gospels according to St. Matthew and St. Luke Arranged with Introduction and Commentary.* London: SCM Press, 1950.

Marquardt, Friedrich-Wilhelm. "Vom Rechtfertigungsgeschehen zu einer Evangelischen Halacha." In *Die Lehre von der Rechtfertigung des Gottlosen im kulturellen Kontext der Gegenwart: Beiträge im Horizont des christlich-jüdischen Gesprächs*, edited by Hans Martin Dober and Dagmar Mensink, 43–75. Hohenheimer Protokolle 57. Stuttgart: Akademie der Diözese Rottenburg-Stuttgart, 2002.

Marshall, I. Howard. *Luke: Historian and Theologian.* Grand Rapids: Zondervan, 1970.

———. *The Gospel of Luke: A Commentary on the Greek Text.* The New International Greek Testament Commentary. Grand Rapids: Eerdmans, 1978.

Martin, David. *On Secularization: Towards a Revised General Theory.* Aldershot: Ashgate, 2005.

Masuzawa, Tomoko. *The Invention of World Religions: Or, How European Universalism Was Preserved in the Language of Pluralism.* Chicago: University of Chicago Press, 2005.

Mathys, Hans-Peter. "Goldene Regel (I. Judentum)." *Theologische Realenzyklopädie.* Berlin: de Gruyter, 1992.

———. *Liebe deinen Nächsten wie dich selbst: Untersuchungen zum alttestamentlichen Gebot der Nächstenliebe (Lev 19,18)*. Orbis biblicus et orientalis 71. Freiburg, Switzerland; Göttingen: Universitätsverlag; Vandenhoeck & Ruprecht, 1986.

Mauss, Marcel. *The Gift: Forms and Functions of Exchange in Archaic Societies*. New York: Norton, 1967.

McGhee, Richard D. "Introduction to 'Principles of the Philosophy of the Future' by Ludwig Feuerbach." In *World Philosophers and Their Works*, edited by John K. Roth, Vol. 1. Salem Press, 2000.

Meeks, Wayne A. *The Origins of Christian Morality: The First Two Centuries*. New Haven: Yale University Press, 1993.

Meisinger, Hubert. *Liebesgebot und Altruismusforschung: Ein exegetischer Beitrag zum Dialog zwischen Theologie und Naturwissenschaft*. Freiburg, Switzerland: Universitätsverlag, 1996.

Merklein, Helmut. *Die Gottesherrschaft als Handlungsprinzip*. Untersuchungen zur Ethik Jesu 34. Würzburg: Echter, 1978.

———. *Jesu Botschaft von der Gottesherrschaft: Eine Skizze*. Stuttgarter Bibelstudien 111. Stuttgart: Katholisches Bibelwerk, 1983.

Mette, Norbert, and Hermann Steinkamp, eds. *Sozialwissenschaften und praktische Theologie*. Leitfaden Theologie 11. Düsseldorf: Patmos, 1983.

Metz, Johann Baptist, ed. *Compassion – Weltprogramm des Christentums: soziale Verantwortung lernen*. Freiburg im Breisgau: Herder, 2000.

———. *Memoria passionis: ein provozierendes Gedächtnis in pluralistischer Gesellschaft*. 4th ed. Freiburg im Breisgau: Herder, 2011.

Meuffels, Hans Otmar. *Theologie der Liebe in postmoderner Zeit*. Würzburg: Echter, 2001.

Möller, Joseph. "Freiheit und Erlösung: Eine Reflexion zur Freiheitsgeschichte der Neuzeit." *Theologische Quartalschrift* 162 (1982): 275–88.

Moltmann, Jürgen. "Christsein, Menschsein und das Reich Gottes: Ein Gespräch mit Karl Rahner." *Stimmen der Zeit* 203, no. 9 (1985): 619–31.

———. "Theology of Mystical Experience." *Scottish Journal of Theology* 32, no. 6 (1979): 501–20. doi:10.1017/S0036930600044434.

Moyaert, Marianne. "Recent Developments in the Theology of Interreligious Dialogue: From Soteriological Openness to Hermeneutical Openness." *Modern Theology* 28, no. 1 (2012): 25–52. doi:10.1111/j.1468-0025.2011.01724.x.

———. *In Response to the Religious Other: Ricoeur and the Fragility of Interreligious Encounters*. Lanham, Md.: Lexington Books, 2014.

———. "Christianity as the Measure of Religion? Materializing the Theology of Religions." In *Twenty-First-Century Theologies of Religions: Retrospection and Future Prospects*, edited by Elizabeth J. Harris, Paul Hedges, and Shanthikumar Hettiarachchi, 239–66. Currents of Encounter 54. Leiden; Boston: Brill; Rodopi, 2016.

Moyaert, Marianne, and Didier Pollefeyt, eds. *Never Revoked: Nostra Aetate as Ongoing Challenge for Jewish-Christian Dialogue*. Louvain Theological & Pastoral Monographs 40. Leuven: Peeters, 2010.

Mühling, Markus. *Gott ist Liebe: Studien zum Verständnis der Liebe als Modell des trinitarischen Redens von Gott*. Marburg: Elwert, 2000.

Müller, Harro, and Larson Powell. "Luhmann's Systems Theory as a Theory of Modernity." *New German Critique*, no. 61 (1994): 39–54. doi:10.2307/488620.

Müller, Karlheinz. "Apokalyptik." *Lexikon für Theologie und Kirche*. Freiburg im Breisgau; Basel; Wien: Herder, 2006.

———. "Apokalyptik/Apokapypsen (III. Die Jüdische Apokalyptik. Anfänge und Merkmale)." *Theologische Realenzyklopädie*. Berlin; New York: Walter de Gruyter, 1995.

Mussner, Franz. *Was hat Jesus Neues in die Welt gebracht?* Stuttgart: Katholisches Bibelwerk, 2001.

Nestle, Eberhard, Erwin Nestle, Barbara Aland, Kurt Aland, and Holger Strutwolf, eds. *Novum Testamentum Graece: Greek-English New Testament*. 28th ed. Stuttgart: Deutsche Bibelgesellschaft, 2013.

Neufeld, Karl H. "Joseph Maréchal und Karl Rahner: Vom Umgang mit Thomas von Aquin." *Zeitschrift für katholische Theologie* 137, no. 2 (2015): 127–40.

Neumann, Nils. *Armut und Reichtum im Lukasevangelium und in der kynischen Philosophie*. Stuttgarter Bibelstudien 220. Stuttgart: Katholisches Bibelwerk, 2010.

Neville, Robert Cummings. "Philosophische Grundlagen und Methoden der Komparativen Theologie." In *Komparative Theologie: Interreligiöse Vergleiche als Weg der Religionstheologie*, edited by Reinhold Bernhardt and Klaus von Stosch, 35–54. Beiträge zu einer Theologie der Religionen 7. Zürich: Theologischer Verlag Zürich, 2009.

Newman, Paul W. *A Spirit Christology: Recovering the Biblical Paradigm of Christian Faith*. Lanham, MD: University Press of America, 1987.

Nissen, Andreas. *Gott und der Nächste im antiken Judentum: Untersuchungen zum Doppelgebot der Liebe*. Wissenschaftliche Untersuchungen zum Neuen Testament 15. Tübingen: Mohr, 1974.

Nitsche, Bernhard. *Gott – Welt – Mensch: Raimon Panikkars Gottesdenken – Paradigma für eine Theologie in interreligiöser Perspektive*. Zürich: Theologischer Verlag Zürich, 2008.

Nolan, Albert. *Jesus before Christianity*. 8th ed. Maryknoll, N.Y.: Orbis Books, 1985.

Nørager, Troels. "Difficult but Necessary: Conditions of a Contemporary Theology of Love." *Dialog* 50, no. 1 (2011): 47–52. doi:10.1111/j.1540-6385.2010.00580.x.

Nussbaum, Martha Craven. *Political Emotions: Why Love Matters for Justice*. Cambridge, Massachusetts: The Belknap Press of Harvard University Press, 2013.

Nygren, Anders. *Agape and Eros*. Philadelphia: Westminster Press, 1953.

O'Collins, Gerald. "Jacques Dupuis's Contributions to Interreligious Dialogue." *Theological Studies* 64, no. 2 (2003): 388–97.

———. *Salvation for All: God's Other Peoples*. Oxford: Oxford University Press, 2008.

———. *The Second Vatican Council on Other Religions*. Oxford: Oxford University Press, 2013.

O'Dwyer, Kathleen. *The Possibility of Love: An Interdisciplinary Analysis*. Newcastle upon Tyne, UK: Cambridge Scholars Publishing, 2009.

Otto, Eckart. *Theologische Ethik des Alten Testaments*. Theologische Wissenschaft 3,2. Stuttgart: Kohlhammer, 1994.

Outka, Gene. *Agape: An Ethical Analysis*. New Haven; London: Yale University Press, 1972.

Paffenroth, Kim. *The Story of Jesus according to L*. Journal for the Study of the New Testament 147. Sheffield: Sheffield Academic Press, 1997.

Paget, James Carleton. *Jews, Christians and Jewish Christians in Antiquity*. Wissenschaftliche Untersuchungen zum Neuen Testament 251. Tübingen: Mohr Siebeck, 2010.

Panikkar, Raimon. *The Intrareligious Dialogue*. Rev. ed. New York: Paulist Press, 1999.

———. *The Unknown Christ of Hinduism*. London: Darton, Longman & Todd, 1964.

Pannenberg, Wolfhart. "Die Religionen als Thema der Theologie: Die Relevanz der Religionen für das Selbstverständnis der Theologie." *Theologische Quartalschrift* 169, no. 2 (1989): 99–110.

———. *Wissenschaftstheorie und Theologie*. Frankfurt am Main: Suhrkamp, 1977.

Pascal, Blaise. *Blaise Pascal: Thoughts, Letters, and Minor Works*. Edited by Charles W. Eliot. New York: Cosimo, 2007.

Peck, M. Scott. *The Road Less Traveled: A New Psychology of Love, Traditional Values and Spiritual Growth*. London: Rider, 1978.

Perrin, Norman. *Jesus and the Language of the Kingdom: Symbol and Metaphor in New Testament Interpretation*. Philadelphia: Fortress Press, 1976.

———. *The Kingdom of God in the Teaching of Jesus*. London: SCM Press, 1963.

Pesch, Otto Hermann. *Das Zweite Vatikanische Konzil: 1962-1965: Vorgeschichte, Verlauf, Ergebnisse, Nachgeschichte*. Würzburg: Echter, 1993.

———. "Der junge Mann aus Nazaret – Retter aller Menschen?" In *Jesus von Nazareth*, edited by Jürgen Thomassen, 102–30. Würzburg: Echter, 1993.

———. *Frei sein aus Gnade: Theologische Anthropologie*. Freiburg im Breisgau: Herder, 1983.

Pesch, Otto Hermann, and Albrecht Peters. *Einführung in die Lehre von Gnade und Rechtfertigung*. Darmstadt: Wissenschaftliche Buchgesellschaft, 1981.

Petzke, Gerd. *Das Sondergut des Evangeliums nach Lukas*. Zürcher Werkkommentare zur Bibel. Zürich: Theologischer Verlag, 1990.

Peukert, Helmut. "Bildung als Wahrnehmung des Anderen: Der Dialog im Bildungsdenken der Moderne." In *Dialog zwischen den Kulturen: Erziehungshistorische und religionspägogische Gesichtspunkte interkultureller Bildung*, edited by Ingrid Lohmann and Wolfram Weiße. Waxmann Verlag, 1994.

———. "Kommunikative Freiheit und asolut befreiende Freiheit: Bemerkungen zu Karl Rahners These über die Einheit von Nächsten- und Gottesliebe." In *Wagnis Theologie: Erfahrungen mit der Theologie Karl Rahners*, edited by Herbert Vorgrimler, 274–83. Freiburg im Breisgau: Herder, 1979.

———. "Kontingenzerfahrung und Identitätsfindung: Bemerkungen zu einer Theorie der Religion und zur Analytik religiös dimensionierter Lernprozesse." In *Erfahrung, Glaube und Moral*, edited by J. Blank and G. Hasenhüttl, 76–102. Düsseldorf: Patmos, 1982.

———. "Nachwort zur dritten Auflage 2009: Fundamentale Theologie im interdisziplinären Gespräch entwickeln." In *Wissenschaftstheorie – Handlungstheorie – fundamentale Theologie: Analysen zu Ansatz und Status theologischer Theoriebildung*, by Helmut Peukert, 357–400. Frankfurt am Main: Suhrkamp, 2009.

———. *Wissenschaftstheorie – Handlungstheorie – fundamentale Theologie: Analysen zu Ansatz und Status theologischer Theoriebildung*. Frankfurt am Main: Suhrkamp, 2009.

Phan, Peter C. *Being Religious Interreligiously: Asian Perspectives on Interfaith Dialogue*. Maryknoll, N.Y.: Orbis Books, 2004.

Philipp, Thomas. "Christliche Identität im 21. Jahrhundert." *Zeitschrift für katholische Theologie* 133 (2011): 175–90.

Pieper, Josef. *Über die Liebe*. München: Kösel, 1972.

Pixley, Jorge. "¿Nos ayuda la Biblia en el diálogo interreligioso?" *Revista Latino Americana de Teología* 375. Accessed June 16, 2015. http://servicioskoinonia.org/relat/375.htm.

Pollefeyt, Didier. "Interreligious Dialogue beyond Absolutism, Relativism and Particularism: A Catholic Approach to Religious Diversity." In *Encountering the Stranger: A Jewish-Christian-Muslim Trialogue*, edited by Leonard Grob and John K. Roth, 245–59. Seattle: University of Washington Press, 2012.

Pontifical Council for Interreligious Dialogue and Congregation for Evangelization of Peoples. "Dialogue and Proclamation: Reflection and Orientations on Interreligious Dialogue and the Proclamation of the Gospel of Jesus Christ." Libreria Editrice Vaticana, May 19, 1991.

Pope, Stephen J. *The Evolution of Altruism and the Ordering of Love.* Washington, DC: Georgetown University Press, 1995.

Popkes, Enno Edzard. *Die Theologie der Liebe Gottes in den johanneischen Schriften: Zur Semantik der Liebe und zum Motivkreis des Dualismus.* Wissenschaftliche Untersuchungen zum Neuen Testament 2. Reihe 197. Tübingen: Mohr Siebeck, 2005.

Pröpper, Thomas. *Erlösungsglaube und Freiheitsgeschichte: Eine Skizze zur Soteriologie.* 3rd ed. München: Kösel, 1991.

———. *Evangelium und freie Vernunft: Konturen einer theologischen Hermeneutik.* Freiburg im Breisgau: Herder, 2001.

———. *Theologische Anthropologie.* 2 vols. Freiburg im Breisgau: Herder, 2011.

Race, Alan. *Christians and Religious Pluralism: Patterns in the Christian Theology of Religions.* Maryknoll, N.Y.: Orbis Books, 1983.

Radl, Walter. *Das Evangelium nach Lukas: Kommentar.* Vol. 1. 2 vols. Freiburg im Breisgau; Basel; Wien: Herder, 2003.

Rahner, Karl. "Anonymer und expliziter Glaube." In *Schriften zur Theologie,* 12:76–84. Zürich; Einsiedeln; Köln: Benziger, 1975.

———. "Anonymes Christentum und Missionsauftrag der Kirche." In *Schriften zur Theologie,* 9:498–515. Zürich; Einsiedeln; Köln: Benziger, 1970.

———. "Atheismus und implizites Christentum." In *Schriften zur Theologie,* 8:187–212. Zürich; Einsiedeln; Köln: Benziger, 1967.

———. "Bemerkungen zum Problem des 'anonymen Christen.'" In *Schriften zur Theologie,* 10:531–46. Zürich; Einsiedeln; Köln: Benziger, 1972.

———. "Bemerkungen zur Bedeutung der Geschichte Jesu für die katholische Dogmatik." In *Schriften zur Theologie,* 10:215–26. Zürich; Einsiedeln; Köln: Benziger, 1972.

———. "Christianity and the Non-Christian Religions." In *Theological Investigations*, 5:115–34. London: Darton, Longman & Todd, 1966.

———. "Das Christentum und die nichtchristlichen Religionen." In *Schriften zur Theologie*, 5:136–58. Zürich; Einsiedeln; Köln: Benziger, 1962.

———. "Das 'Gebot' der Liebe unter den anderen Geboten." In *Schriften zur Theologie*, Vol. 6. Zürich; Einsiedeln; Köln: Benziger, 1965.

———. "Der eine Jesus Christus und die Universalität des Heils." In *Schriften zur Theologie*, 12:250–82. Zürich; Einsiedeln; Köln: Benziger, 1975.

———. "Der eine Mittler und die Vielfalt der Vermittlungen." In *Schriften zur Theologie*, 8:218–335. Einsiedeln; Zürich; Köln: Benziger, 1967.

———. "Die anonymen Christen." In *Schriften zur Theologie*, 6:545–54. Zürich; Einsiedeln; Köln: Benziger, 1965.

———. "Die bleibende Bedeutung des II. Vatikanischen Konzils." In *Schriften zur Theologie*, 14:303–18. Zürich; Einsiedeln; Köln: Benziger, 1980.

———. "Gnade als Mitte menschlicher Existenz: Ein Gespräch mit und über Karl Rahner aus Anlaß seines 70. Geburtstages." *Herder Korrespondenz* 28, no. 2 (1974): 77–92.

———. *Grundkurs des Glaubens: Einführung in den Begriff des Christentums*. Freiburg im Breisgau; Basel; Wien: Herder, 1976.

———. *Hearer of the Word: Laying the Foundation for a Philosophy of Religion*. Edited by Andrew Tallon. Translated by Joseph Donceel. New York: Continuum, 1994.

———. "Jesu Gottgeheimnis – Grund seiner radikalen Nächstenliebe." In *Unsere Hoffnung: Predigtmodelle zu einem Bekenntnis des Glaubens in dieser Zeit*, edited by Peter Düsterfeld and Helmuth Rolfes, 36–39. Mainz: Matthias Grünewald, 1976.

———. "Kirche und Atheismus." In *Schriften zur Theologie*, 15:139–51. Zürich; Einsiedeln; Köln: Benziger, 1983.

———. "Kirchliche und außerkirchliche Religiosität." In *Schriften zur Theologie*, 12:582–98. Zürich; Einsiedeln; Köln: Benziger, 1975.

———. "Liebe." Edited by Karl Rahner. *Sacramentum mundi: Theologisches Lexikon für die Praxis*. Freiburg im Breisgau: Herder, n.d.

———. "Natur und Gnade." In *Schriften zur Theologie*, 4:209–36. Zürich; Einsiedeln; Köln: Benziger, 1960.

———. "Profangeschichte und Heilsgeschichte." In *Schriften zur Theologie*, 15:11–23. Zürich; Einsiedeln; Köln: Benziger, 1983.

———. "Reflections on the Unity of the Love of Neighbour and the Love of God." In *Theological Investigations*, translated by Karl-H. Kruger and Boniface Kruger, 6:231–49. London: Darton, Longman & Todd, 1969.

———. "The 'Commandment' of Love in Relation to the Other Commandments." In *Theological Investigations*, translated by Karl-H. Kruger, 5:439–59. London: Darton, Longman & Todd, 1966.

———. "The Man of Today and Religion." In *Theological Investigations*, translated by Karl-H. Kruger and Boniface Kruger, 6:3–20. London: Darton, Longman & Todd, 1969.

———. "Theologische Reflexionen zur Säkularisation." In *Schriften zur Theologie*, 8:637–66. Einsiedeln; Zürich; Köln: Benziger, 1967.

———. "Über das Verhältnis von Natur und Gnade." In *Schriften zur Theologie*, 1:323–46. Zürich; Einsiedeln; Köln: Benziger, 1954.

———. "Über die Einheit von Nächsten- und Gottesliebe." In *Schriften zur Theologie*, 6:277–98. Zürich; Einsiedeln; Köln: Benziger, 1965.

———. "Über die Heilsbedeutung der nichtchristlichen Religionen." In *Schriften zur Theologie*, 13:341–50. Zürich; Einsiedeln; Köln: Benziger, 1978.

———. "Weltgeschichte und Heilsgeschichte." In *Schriften zur Theologie*, 5:115–35. Zürich; Einsiedeln; Köln: Benziger, 1962.

———. *Wer ist dein Bruder?* Freiburg im Breisgau: Herder, 1981.

———. "What Is a Dogmatic Statement?" In *Theological Investigations*, 5:42–66. Darton: Longman & Todd, 1966.

———. "Zur scholastischen Begrifflichkeit der ungeschaffenen Gnade." In *Schriften zur Theologie*, 1:347–76. Zürich; Einsiedeln; Köln: Benziger, 1954.

Rainer, Michael J., ed. *"Dominus Iesus": anstössige Wahrheit oder anstössige Kirche?: Dokumente, Hintergründe, Standpunkte und Folgerungen*. Wissenschaftliche Paperbacks 9. Münster: Lit, 2001.

Rashi. *Perush Rashi 'al Ha-Torah [= Rashi: The Torah – with Rashi's Commentary]*. Edited by Yisrael Isser Zvi Herczeg, Yaakov Petroff, and Yosef Kamenetzky. 2nd ed. Vol. 3. 5 vols. The ArtScroll Series. Brooklyn: Mesorah Publications, 1999.

Ratzinger, Joseph. "Der christliche Glaube und die Weltreligionen." In *Gott in Welt: Festgabe für Karl Rahner*, edited by Herbert Vorgrimler and Johannes Baptist Metz, 2:287–305. Freiburg im Breisgau: Herder, 1964.

Reinmuth, Eckart. *Paulus: Gott neu denken*. Leipzig: Evangelische Verlagsanstalt, 2004.

Renz, Andreas. *Die katholische Kirche und der interreligiöse Dialog: 50 Jahre "Nostra aetate" – Entstehung, Rezeption, Wirkung*. Stuttgart: Kohlhammer, 2013.

Renz, Monika. *Erlösung aus Prägung: Botschaft und Leben Jesu als Überwindung der menschlichen Angst-, Begehrens- und Machtstruktur*. Paderborn: Junfermann, 2008.

Riches, John. *Jesus and the Transformation of Judaism*. London: Darton, 1980.

Ricoeur, Paul. *Geschichte und Wahrheit*. Translated by Romain Leick. München: List, 1974.

———. *History and Truth*. Translated by Charles A. Kelbley. Evanston: Northwestern University Press, 1965.

———. "Love and Justice." In *Paul Ricoeur: The Hermeneutics of Action*, edited by Richard Kearney, translated by David Pellauer, 23–39. London; Thousand Oaks; New Delhi: Sage Publications, 1996.

———. *Memory, History, Forgetting*. Chicago: University of Chicago Press, 2004.

———. *Oneself as Another*. Reprint. Chicago: University of Chicago Press, 1995.

———. "On Interpretation." In *From Text to Action*, translated by Kathleen Blamey, 1–20. Essays in Hermeneutics 2. Evanston: Northwestern University Press, 1991.

———. *On Translation*. Translated by Eileen Brennan. London: Routledge, 2006.

———. "Philosophy and Religious Language." *The Journal of Religion* 54, no. 1 (1974): 71–85.

———. *The Course of Recognition*. Translated by David Pellauer. Cambridge, Massachusetts: Harvard University Press, 2005.

———. "The Socius and the Neighbor." In *History and Truth*, translated by Charles A. Kelbley, 98–109. Evanston: Northwestern University Press, 1965.

Rose, Miriam. *Fides caritate formata: das Verhältnis von Glaube und Liebe in der Summa Theologiae des Thomas von Aquin*. Forschungen zur systematischen und ökumenischen Theologie 112. Göttingen: Vandenhoeck & Ruprecht, 2007.

Rowland, Christopher, ed. *The Cambridge Companion to Liberation Theology*. Cambridge Companions to Religion. Cambridge; New York: Cambridge University Press, 1999.

Sajak, Clauß Peter. *Das Fremde als Gabe begreifen: Auf dem Weg zu einer Didaktik der Religionen aus katholischer Perspektive*. Münster u.a: Lit, 2005.

Sakenfeld, Katharine Doob. "Love (OT)." In *The Anchor Bible Dictionary*, edited by David Noel Freedman, 4:375–81. New York: Doubleday, 1992.

Sander, Hans-Joachim. "Der eine Gott der Juden, Christen und Muslime und seine Heterotopien der Macht – der unmögliche Lebensraum des religiösen Dialogs." In *Weltkirche und Weltreligionen: Die Brisanz des Zweiten Vatikanischen Konzils 40 Jahre nach Nostra aetate*, edited by Josef Sinkovits and Ulrich Winkler, 45–66. Innsbruck; Wien: Tyrolia, 2007.

———. "Theologischer Kommentar zur Pastoralkonstitution über die Kirche in der Welt von heute (Gaudium et Spes)." In *Herders theologischer Kommentar zum Zweiten Vatikanischen Konzil*, edited by Peter Hünermann and Bernd Jochen Hilberath, 4:581–886. Freiburg im Breisgau: Herder, 2005.

Schambeck, Mirjam. "Interreligiöse Kompetenz – nötig wie nie: Eine Konzeptualisierung in praktischer Absicht." *CIBEDO-Beiträge*, no. 2 (2015).

Scheffczyk, Leo, ed. *Erlösung und Emanzipation*. Quaestiones disputatae 61. Freiburg im Breisgau; Basel; Wien: Herder, 1973.

Scheler, Max. "Erkenntnis und Arbeit." In *Gesammelte Werke*, edited by Maria Scheler, 8:191–382. Bern: Francke, 1960.

———. "Liebe und Erkenntnis." In *Gesammelte Werke*, edited by Maria Scheler, 6:77–98. Bern: Francke, 1963.

———. "Love and Knowledge." In *On Feeling, Knowing, and Valuing: Selected Writings*, edited and translated by Harold J. Bershady, 147–65. Chicago: University of Chicago Press, 1992.

———. "Ordo amoris." In *Schriften aus dem Nachlass*, edited by Maria Scheler, 1:345–76. Gesammelte Werke 10. Bern: Francke, 1957.

———. "Ordo Amoris." In *Selected Philosophical Essays*, translated by David R. Lachterman, 98–135. Evanston: Northwestern University Press, 1992.

———. "Vom Wesen der Philosophie und der moralischen Bedingung des philosophischen Erkennens." In *Gesammelte Werke*, edited by Maria Scheler, 5:61–99. Bern: Francke, 1954.

Schillebeeckx, Edward. *Christ: The Christian Experience in the Modern World*. Edited by Robert J. Schreiter. The Collected Works of Edward Schillebeeckx 7. London: Bloomsbury, 2014.

———. *Christus und die Christen: die Geschichte einer neuen Lebenspraxis*. Freiburg im Breisgau: Herder, 1977.

———. *Church: The Human Story of God*. The Collected Works of Edward Schillebeeckx 10. London: Bloomsbury, 2014.

———. *Jesus, an Experiment in Christology*. The Collected Works of Edward Schillebeeckx 6. London: Bloomsbury, 2014.

———. *Jesus: die Geschichte von einem Lebenden*. 3rd ed. Freiburg im Breisgau; Basel; Wien: Herder, 1975.

Schlegel, Friedrich. *Von der wahren Liebe Gottes und dem falschen Mystizismus [1819]*. Kritische Friedrich-Schlegel-Ausgabe, VIII. Paderborn; Zürich, 1975.

Schlette, Heinz Robert. *Die Religionen als Thema der Theologie: Überlegungen zu einer "Theologie der Religionen."* Quaestiones disputatae 22. Freiburg im Breisgau; Basel; Wien: Herder, 1964.

Schlette, Heinz Robert, and Eberhard Rolinck. *Humanismus statt Religion?: Grundzüge einer neuen Solidarität*. Düsseldorf: Patmos, 1970.

Schmidt-Leukel, Perry. *Gott ohne Grenzen: eine christliche und pluralistische Theologie der Religionen*. Gütersloh: Gütersloher Verlagshaus, 2005.

Schmiedel, Ulrich, and James M. Matarazzo Jr., eds. *Dynamics of Difference: Christianity and Alterity*. A Festschrift for Werner G. Jeanrond. New York: Bloomsbury T&T Clark, 2014.

Schnackenburg, Rudolf. *Das Johannesevangelium*. Vol. 3. 3 vols. Herders theologischer Kommentar zum Neuen Testament 4. Freiburg im Breisgau; Basel; Wien: Herder, 1975.

———. "Die Forderung der Liebe in der Verkündigung und im Verhalten Jesu." In *Prinzip Liebe: Perspektiven der Theologie*, edited by Eugen Biser. Freiburg im Breisgau; Basel; Wien: Herder, 1975.

Schneider, Gerhard. *Das Evangelium nach Lukas*. Ökumenischer Taschenbuchkommentar zum Neuen Testament 3. Würzburg: Gütersloher Verlagshaus Mohn; Echter-Verlag, 1977.

———. *Lukas, Theologe der Heilsgeschichte: Aufsätze zum lukanischen Doppelwerk*. Bonner biblische Beiträge 59. Königstein/Ts; Bonn: Hanstein, 1985.

———. "Ἀγάπη." *Exegetisches Wörterbuch zum Neuen Testament*. Stuttgart; Berlin; Köln: Kohlhammer, 1980.

Schnelle, Udo. *Theologie des Neuen Testaments*. Stuttgart: Vandenhoeck & Ruprecht, 2007.

Scholtissek, Klaus. "'Eine größere Liebe als diese hat niemand, als wenn einer sein Leben hingibt für seine Freunde' (Joh 15,13): Die hellenistische Freundschaftsethik und das Johannesevangelium." In *Kontexte des Johannesevangeliums: das vierte Evangelium in religions- und traditionsgeschichtlicher Perspektive*, edited by Jörg Frey and Udo Schnelle, 413–39. Wissenschaftliche Untersuchungen zum Neuen Testament 175. Tübingen: Mohr Siebeck, 2004.

Schröter, Jens. "Gerechtigkeit als Thema biblischer Theologie: Ein neutestamentliches Votum." In *Gerechtigkeit als Thema biblischer Theologie*, edited by Markus Witte and Jens Schröter, 45–73. Antrittsvorlesung, 24. Juni 2010, Humboldt-Universität zu Berlin, Theologische Fakultät. Berlin: Humboldt Universität, 2011.

Schupp, Franz. *Auf dem Weg zu einer kritischen Theologie*. Freiburg im Breisgau; Basel; Wien: Herder, 1974.

———. *Schöpfung und Sünde: von der Verheißung einer wahren und gerechten Welt, vom Versagen der Menschen und vom Widerstand gegen die Zerstörung*. Düsseldorf: Patmos, 1990.

Schürmann, Heinz. *Das Lukasevangelium*. Vol. III/2. Herders theologischer Kommentar zum Neuen Testament. Freiburg im Breisgau; Basel; Wien: Herder, 1994.

———. "Eschatologie und Liebesdienst in der Verkündigung Jesu." In *Kaufet die Zeit aus: Beiträge zu einer christlichen Eschatologie*, edited by Hermann Kirchhoff, 39–71. Festgabe für Professor Dr. Theoderich Kampmann. Paderborn: Schöningh, 1959.

———. *Gottes Reich, Jesu Geschick: Jesu ureigener Tod im Licht seiner Basileia-Verkündigung*. Freiburg im Breisgau; Basel; Wien: Herder, 1983.

Schüssler Fiorenza, Elisabeth. *Zu ihrem Gedächtnis...: Eine feministisch-theologische Rekonstruktion der christlichen Ursprünge*. München: Kaiser, 1988.

Schwager, Raymund. *Jesus im Heilsdrama: Entwurf einer biblischen Erlösungslehre*. Innsbrucker theologische Studien 29. Innsbruck; Wien: Tyrolia, 1990.

Schweizer, Eduard. *Das Evangelium nach Lukas*. 19th ed. Göttingen: Vandenhoeck & Ruprecht, 1986.

Schwerdtfeger, Nikolaus. *Gnade und Welt: zum Grundgefüge von Karl Rahners Theorie der "anonymen Christen."* Freiburger theologische Studien 123. Freiburg im Breisgau: Herder, 1982.

Scullion, John J. "Righteousness (OT)." *The Anchor Bible Dictionary*. New York: Doubleday, 1992.

Seckler, Max. "Theologein. Eine Grundidee in dreifacher Ausgestaltung: Zur Theorie der Theologie und zur Kritik der monokausalen Theologiebegründung." *Theologische Quartalschrift* 163 (1983): 241–64.

———. "Theologie der Religionen mit Fragezeichen." *Theologische Quartalschrift* 166, no. 3 (1986): 164–84.

Sedmak, Clemens. "Der Glaube ist praktisch – über die Erkennbarkeit der Orthodoxie." *Zeitschrift für katholische Theologie* 137, no. 1 (2015): 86–103.

———. *Die politische Kraft der Liebe: Christsein und die europäische Situation*. Innsbruck: Tyrolia, 2007.

———. *Theologie in nachtheologischer Zeit*. Mainz: Matthias-Grünewald, 2003.

Sellin, Gerhard. "Lukas als Gleichniserzähler: die Erzählung vom barmherzigen Samariter (Lk 10 25-37)." *Zeitschrift für die neutestamentliche Wissenschaft und die Kunde der älteren Kirche* 65, no. 3–4 (1974): 166–89.

Sellner, Hans Jörg. *Das Heil Gottes: Studien zur Soteriologie des lukanischen Doppelwerks*. Beihefte zur Zeitschrift für die neutestamentliche Wissenschaft und die Kunde der älteren Kirche 152. Berlin: De Gruyter, 2007.

Sen, Amartya Kumar. *Development as Freedom*. New York: Knopf, 1999.

———. *Identity and Violence: The Illusion of Destiny*. New York: W.W. Norton & Co., 2006.

———. *The Idea of Justice*. London: Allen Lane, 2009.

Sequeri, Pierangelo. *L'umano alla prova: soggetto, identità, limite. Filosofia: ricerche*. Milano: Vita e Pensiero, 2002.

———. *Sensibili allo spirito: umanesimo religioso e ordine degli affetti*. Milan: Glossa, 2001.

Siebenrock, Roman A. "Theologischer Kommentar zur Erklärung über die Haltung der Kirche zu den nichtchristlichen Religionen (Nostra aetate)." In *Herders theologischer Kommentar zum Zweiten Vatikanischen Konzil*, edited by Peter Hünermann and Bernd Jochen Hilberath, 3:591–693. Freiburg im Breisgau: Herder, 2005.

Siegwalt, Gérard. "Das II. Vaticanum: zwischen Katholizismus und Katholizität: von einer Theologie der Abgrenzung zu einer Theologie der Rekapitulation." *Concilium* 48, no. 3 (2012): 286–95.

Sievernich, Michael, and Knut Wenzel. *Aufbruch in die Urbanität: theologische Reflexion kirchlichen Handelns in der Stadt*. Freiburg im Breisgau: Herder, 2013.

Sitzler-Osing, Dorothea, Rolf P. Knierim, Stefan Schreiner, Richard Schenk, Christine Axt-Piscalar, and Wilhelm Gräb. "Sünde." *Theologische Realenzyklopädie*. Berlin; New York: Walter de Gruyter, 2001.

Smith, Wilfred Cantwell. *The Meaning and End of Religion: A New Approach to the Religious Traditions of Mankind*. New York: Mentor Books, 1962.

Sobrino, Jon. *Christ the Liberator: A View from the Victims*. Maryknoll, N.Y.: Orbis Books, 2001.

———. "El conocimiento teológico en la teología europea y latinoamericana." In *Liberación y cautiverio: debates en torno al método de la teología en América Latina*, edited by Comité Organizador, 177–207. Encuentro Latinoamericano de Teología. México, 1975.

———. *No Salvation outside the Poor: Prophetic-Utopian Essays*. Maryknoll, N.Y.: Orbis Books, 2008.

———. "Teología en un mundo sufriente: la teología de la liberación como 'intellectus amoris.'" *Revista Latinoamericana de Teología* 15, no. 3 (1988): 243–66.

Sobrino, Jon, and Ignacio Ellacuría, eds. *Systematic Theology: Perpspectives from Liberation Theology – Readings from Mysterium Liberationis*. Maryknoll, N.Y.: Orbis Books, 1996.

Söding, Thomas. *Das Liebesgebot bei Paulus: die Mahnung zur Agape im Rahmen der paulinischen Ethik*. Münster: Aschendorff, 1995.

———. *Die Trias Glaube, Hoffnung, Liebe bei Paulus: Eine exegetische Studie.* Stuttgart: Katholisches Bibelwerk, 1992.

———. "'... die Wurzel trägt dich' (Röm 11,18): Methodische und hermeneutische Konsequenzen des jüdisch-christlichen Dialoges in der neutestamentlichen Exegese." In *Methodische Erneuerung der Theologie: Konsequenzen der wiederentdeckten jüdisch-christlichen Gemeinsamkeiten,* edited by Peter Hünermann and Thomas Söding, 35–70. Quaestiones disputatae 200. Freiburg im Breisgau; Basel; Wien: Herder, 2003.

Solov′ev, Vladimir S. *Der Sinn der Liebe.* Translated by Elke Kirsten. Philosophische Bibliothek 373. Hamburg: Meiner, 1985.

Søltoft, Pia. "Den Nächsten zu kennen heißt der Nächste werden: Über Ethik, Intersubjektivität und Gegenseitigkeit." In *Ethik der Liebe: Studien zu Kierkegaards "Taten der Liebe,"* edited by Ingolf U. Dalferth, 89–109. Mohr Siebeck, 2002.

Splett, Jörg. *Konturen der Freiheit: Zum christlichen Sprechen vom Menschen.* Frankfurt am Main: J. Knecht, 1974.

Steiner, George. *After Babel: Aspects of Language and Translation.* Oxford; New York: Oxford University Press, 1998.

Steyn, Gert J. "Soteriological Perspectives in Luke's Gospel." In *Salvation in the New Testament: Perspectives on Soteriology,* edited by Jan Gabriel van der Watt, 67–99. Supplements to Novum Testamentum 121. Leiden: Brill, 2005.

Stinglhammer, Hermann. *Freiheit in der Hingabe: trinitarische Freiheitslehre bei Hans Urs von Balthasar: ein Beitrag zur Rezeption der Theodramatik.* Bonner dogmatische Studien 24. Würzburg: Echter, 1997.

Stosch, Klaus von. "Komparative Theologie als Hauptaufgabe der Theologie der Zukunft." In *Komparative Theologie: Interreligiöse Vergleiche als Weg der Religionstheologie,* edited by Reinhold Bernhardt and Klaus von Stosch, 15–33. Beiträge zu einer Theologie der Religionen 7. Zürich: Theologischer Verlag Zürich, 2009.

———. *Komparative Theologie als Wegweiser in der Welt der Religionen.* Beiträge zur Komparativen Theologie 6. Paderborn: Schöningh, 2012.

Strack, Hermann L., and Paul Billerbeck. *Kommentar zum Neuen Testament aus Talmud und Midrasch.* 2nd ed. Vol. 4 (Exkurse). 4 vols. München: C. H. Beck'sche, 1956.

Strecker, Georg. "Zum Problem des Judenchristentums." In *Rechtgläubigkeit und Ketzerei im ältesten Christentum,* by Walter Bauer, 243–87, 2nd ed. Beiträge zur historischen Theologie 10. Tübingen: Mohr Siebeck, 1964.

Striet, Magnus. "Keine Erlösung ohne Gerechtigkeit: Zugleich ein Plädoyer für die mosaische Differenz." In *Heil – Gerechtigkeit – Wahrheit,* edited by Ottmar John and Matthias Möhring-Hesse, 63–78. Theologie: Forschung und Wissenschaft 22. Berlin: Lit, 2006.

———. "Kommunikative Vernunft und Theodizee: Versuch einer Perspektive." In *"... und nichts Menschliches ist mir fremd": Theologische Grenzgänge*, edited by Ottmar John and Magnus Striet, 247–64. Ratio fidei 41. Regensburg: Friedrich Pustet, 2010.

Striet, Magnus, and Jan-Heiner Tück, eds. *Erlösung auf Golgota?: Der Opfertod Jesu im Streit der Interpretationen*. Theologie kontrovers. Freiburg im Breisgau: Herder, 2012.

Ström, Ake V., Erich Zenger, Louis Jacobs, Andreas Lindemann, Rudolf Mau, Michael Beintker, and Christian Walther. "Herrschaft Gottes/Reich Gottes." *Theologische Realenzyklopädie*. Berlin; New York: Walter de Gruyter, 1986.

Taylor, Charles. *A Secular Age*. Cambridge, Massachusetts; London: The Belknap Press of Harvard University Press, 2007.

———. *Multiculturalism: Examining the Politics of Recognition*. Edited by Amy Gutmann. Princeton: Princeton University Press, 1992.

———. "Overcoming Epistemology." In *Philosophical Arguments*, 1–19. Cambridge, Massachusetts: Harvard University Press, 1995.

———. *Philosophical Arguments*. Cambridge, Massachusetts: Harvard University Press, 1995.

———. *The Ethics of Authenticity*. Cambridge, Massachusetts: Harvard University Press, 1992.

———. "The Future of the Religious Past." In *Religion: Beyond a Concept*, edited by Hent Vries, 178–244. New York: Fordham University Press, 2008.

———. "The Politics of Recognition." In *Multiculturalism: Examining the Politics of Recognition*, edited by Amy Gutmann, 25–73. Princeton: Princeton University Press, 1992.

———. *Varieties of Religion Today: William James Revisited*. Cambridge, Massachusetts: Harvard University Press, 2002.

Theißen, Gerd. *Die Jesusbewegung: Sozialgeschichte einer Revolution der Werte*. Gütersloh: Gütersloher Verlagshaus, 2004.

———. *Die Religion der ersten Christen: Eine Theorie des Urchristentums*. 3rd ed. Gütersloh: Kaiser, 2003.

———. "Urchristlicher Liebeskommunismus." In *Texts and Contexts: Biblical Texts in Their Textual and Situational Contexts – Essays in Honor of Lars Hartman*, edited by Tord Fornberg. Oslo: Scandinavian University Press, 1995.

Theißen, Gerd, and Dagmar Winter. *The Quest for the Plausible Jesus: The Question of Criteria*. Translated by M. Eugene Boring. Louisville: Westminster John Knox Press, 2002.

Theobald, Christoph. *Le christianisme comme style: Une manière de faire de la théologie en postmodernité*. Paris: Les Éditions du Cerf, 2007.

Tillich, Paul. *Love, Power, and Justice: Ontological Analyses and Ethical Applications*. Reprint. London: Oxford University Press, 1968.

———. *My Search for Absolutes*. New York: Simon and Schuster, 1967.

Tracy, David. *Plurality and Ambiguity: Hermeneutics, Religion, Hope*. San Francisco: Harper and Row, 1989.

Uelmen, Amelia J. "Reconciling Evangelization and Dialogue through Love of Neighbor." *Villanova Law Review* 52, no. 2 (2007): 303–30.

Vechtel, Klaus. "Musste Jesus für uns leiden? Soteriologie und Gottesbild." *Theologie und Philosophie* 89, no. 3 (2014): 341–59.

Verweyen, Hansjürgen. *Gottes letztes Wort: Grundriß der Fundamentaltheologie*. 3rd ed. Regensburg: Pustet, 2000.

———. *Ist Gott die Liebe?: Spurensuche in Bibel und Tradition*. Regensburg: Pustet, 2014.

Vigil, José María. "Escritos sobre Pluralismo: Cruzando la teología de la liberación con la teología del pluralismo religioso." Libros Digitales Koinonia, 2012. Accessed November 21, 2014. http://www.servicioskoinonia.org/LibrosDigitales/LDK/Vigil-EscritosSobre Pluralismo.pdf.

———, ed. "O atual debate da Teologia do Pluralismo Depois da Dominus Iesus." Libros Digitales Koinonia, 2005. Accessed November 21, 2014. http://www.servici oskoinonia.org/Libros Digitales/LDK/LDK1port.pdf.

Voegelin, Eric. *Ordnung und Geschichte*. Edited by Friedhelm Hartenstein. Vol. 2: Israel und die Offenbarung: die Geburt der Geschichte. 10 vols. Paderborn: Fink, 2005.

Vries, Hent, ed. *Religion: Beyond a Concept*. New York: Fordham University Press, 2008.

Vuola, Elina. *Limits of Liberation: Praxis as Method of Latin American Liberation Theology and Feminist Theology*. Helsinki: Suomalainen Tiedeakatemia, 1997.

Wall, John. "The Economy of the Gift: Paul Ricoeur's Significance for Theological Ethics." *Journal of Religious Ethics* 29, no. 2 (2001): 235–60. doi:10.1111/0384-9694.00079.

Watt, Jan Gabriel van der, ed. *Salvation in the New Testament: Perspectives on Soteriology*. Supplements to Novum Testamentum 121. Leiden: Brill, 2005.

Davies, W. D., and Dale, Allison C. "The Gospel According to Saint Matthew." *The International Critical Commentary*. Edinburgh: T&T Clark, 1997.

Weber, Max. *Gesammelte Aufsätze zur Religionssoziologie*. Vol. 1. 3 vols. Tübingen: Mohr, 1922.

Weder, Hans. "Das neue Gebot: Eine Überlegung zum Liebesgebot in Johannes 13." In *Studien zu Matthäus und Johannes / Festschrift für Jean Zumstein*, edited by Andreas Dettwiler and Uta Poplutz, 188–205. Abhandlungen zur Theologie des Alten und Neuen Testaments 97. Zürich: Theologischer Verlag Zürich, 2009.

Weiss, Bernhard. *Die Quellen der synoptischen Überlieferung*. Leipzig: J.C. Hinrichs, 1908.

———. *Die Quellen des Lukasevangeliums*. Stuttgart; Berlin: Cotta, 1907.

Weiße, Wolfram, ed. *Religiöse Differenz als Chance?: Positionen, Kontroversen, Perspektiven*. Münster; New York; München; Berlin: Waxmann, 2010.

Welte, Bernhard. *Dialektik der Liebe: Gedanken zur Phänomenologie der Liebe und zur christlichen Nächstenliebe im technologischen Zeitalter*. Frankfurt am Main: Knecht, 1973.

Welz, Claudia. "The Self as a Site of Conflicts." In *Religion und Konflikt: Grundlagen und Fallanalysen*, edited by Ingolf U. Dalferth and Heiko Schulz, 137–67. Göttingen: Vandenhoeck & Ruprecht, 2011.

Wenzel, Knut. *Das Zweite Vatikanische Konzil: Eine Einführung*. Freiburg im Breisgau; Basel; Wien: Herder, 2014.

———. *Glaube in Vermittlung: theologische Hermeneutik nach Paul Ricoeur*. Freiburg im Breisgau; Basel; Wien: Herder, 2008.

———. "Gott in der Moderne." In *Moderne Religion: Theologische und religionsphilosophische Reaktionen auf Jürgen Habermas*, edited by Knut Wenzel and Thomas M. Schmidt, 347–76. Freiburg im Breisgau: Herder, 2009.

———. "Gott in der Stadt: Zu einer Theologie der Säkularität." In *Aufbruch in die Urbanität: theologische Reflexion kirchlichen Handelns in der Stadt*, edited by Michael Sievernich and Knut Wenzel, 330–89. Quaestiones disputatae 252. Freiburg im Breisgau: Herder, 2013.

———. *Kleine Geschichte des Zweiten Vatikanischen Konzils*. Freiburg im Breisgau: Herder, 2005.

———. "Kritik – Imagination – Offenbarung: Zur theologischen Hermeneutik nach Paul Ricoeur (1913–2005)." *Theologie und Philosophie* 88, no. 4 (2013): 560–74.

———. "Liebe als Gerechtigkeit: Zu einem Kernaspekt des christlichen Gottesverständnisses." In *Prekär: Gottes Gerechtigkeit und die Moral der Menschen*, edited by Klaus Bieberstein and Hanspeter Schmitt, 150–59. Luzern: Exodus, 2008.

———. "Menschwerdung im Horizont der Welt: Bildungshandeln in schöpfungstheologischer Resonanz." In *"... und nichts Menschliches ist mir fremd": Theologische Grenzgänge*, edited by Ottmar John and Magnus Striet, 175–96. Ratio fidei 41. Regensburg: Friedrich Pustet, 2010.

———. *Sakramentales Selbst: der Mensch als Zeichen des Heils*. Freiburg im Breisgau; Basel; Wien: Herder, 2003.

———. "Theologische Implikationen säkularer Philosophie?: vom 'Kampf um Anerkennung' zur Anerkennung unbedingten Anerkanntseins." *Theologie und Philosophie* 86, no. 2 (2011): 182–200.

Wenzel, Knut, and Thomas M. Schmidt, eds. *Moderne Religion?* Freiburg im Breisgau; Basel; Wien: Herder, 2009.

Werbick, Jürgen. *Den Glauben verantworten: eine Fundamentaltheologie*. 3rd ed. Freiburg im Breisgau; Basel; Wien: Herder, 2005.

———. *Einführung in die theologische Wissenschaftslehre*. Freiburg im Breisgau; Basel; Wien: Herder, 2010.

Weß, Paul. "Wie in säkularer Sprache von Gott reden?: Ein Beitrag zu der von Jürgen Habermas verlangten Übersetzung." *Stimmen der Zeit* 231, no. 1 (2013): 3–13.

Whitehead, Philip. "Rethinking the Typology from a Biblical Perspective: Paul, Adam, and the Theology of Religions." In *Twenty-First-Century Theologies of Religions: Retrospection and Future Prospects*, edited by Elizabeth J. Harris, Paul Hedges, and Shanthikumar Hettiarachchi, 93–108. Currents of Encounter 54. Leiden; Boston: Brill; Rodopi, 2016.

Wiederkehr, Dietrich. "Die ganze Erlösung: Dimensionen des Heils." *Theologische Quartalschrift* 162 (1982): 329–41.

———. *Glaube an Erlösung*. Freiburg im Breisgau: Herder Verlag, 1976.

Wilfred, Felix. "Interreligiös Christ werden." *Concilium* 47, no. 2 (2011): 153–61.

Winiger, Josef. *Ludwig Feuerbach: Denker der Menschlichkeit*. Darmstadt: Lambert Schneider, 2011.

Wink, Walter. *Verwandlung der Mächte: Eine Theologie der Gewaltfreiheit*. Regensburg: Pustet, 2014.

Wischmeyer, Oda. "1 Korinther 13. Das Hohelied der Liebe zwischen Emotion und Ethos." *Deuterocanonical and Cognate Literature*, Yearbook 2011: Emotions from Ben Sira to Paul, no. 1 (2012): 343–60. doi:10.1515/dcly.2012.2011.1.343.

———. "Das alte und das neue Gebot: Ein Beitrag zur Intertextualität der johanneischen Schriften." In *Studien zu Matthäus und Johannes / Festschrift für Jean Zumstein*, edited by Andreas Dettwiler and Uta Poplutz, 207–20. Abhandlungen zur Theologie des Alten und Neuen Testaments 97. Zürich: Theologischer Verlag Zürich, 2009.

———. "Das Gebot der Nächstenliebe bei Paulus: Eine traditionsgeschichtliche Untersuchung." *Biblische Zeitschrift* 30, no. 2 (1986): 161–87.

———. *Der höchste Weg: das 13. Kapitel des 1. Korintherbriefes*. Studien zum Neuen Testament 13. Gütersloh: Gütersloher Verlagshaus Mohn, 1981.

———. "Traditionsgeschichtliche Untersuchung der paulinischen Aussagen über die Liebe (ἀγάπη)." *Zeitschrift für die Neutestamentliche Wissenschaft und die Kunde der Älteren Kirche* 74, no. 3–4 (1983): 222–36. doi:10.1515/zntw.1983.74.3-4.222.

Wißmann, Hans, Rudolf Smend, Benjamin Uffenheimer, Günter Klein, Gerhard May, Robert E. Lerner, Ulrich Asendorf, and Carl Heinz Ratschow. "Eschatologie." *Theologische Realenzyklopädie*. Berlin; New York: Walter de Gruyter, 1982.

Witte, Markus. *Gerechtigkeit*. Themen der Theologie 6. Tübingen: Mohr Siebeck, 2012.

Wohlleben, Ekkehard. *Die Kirchen und die Religionen: Perspektiven einer ökumenischen Religionstheologie*. Göttingen: Vandenhoeck & Ruprecht, 2004.

Wolter, Michael. *Das Lukasevangelium*. Handbuch zum Neuen Testament 5. Tübingen: Mohr Siebeck, 2008.

Yong, Amos. *The Missiological Spirit: Christian Mission Theology in the Third Millennium Global Context*. Cambridge: Clarke, 2015.

———. "The Spirit of Hospitality: Pentecostal Perspectives toward a Performative Theology of Interreligious Encounter." *Missiology: An International Review* 35, no. 1 (2007): 55–73. doi:10.1177/009182960703500105.

———. *The Spirit Poured out on All Flesh: Pentecostalism and the Possibility of Global Theology*. Grand Rapids: Baker Academic, 2005.

Young, Pamela Dickey. "Rahner's Searching Christology." *New Blackfriars* 68, no. 809 (1987): 437–43.

Zimmermann, Ruben, and Detlev Dormeyer, eds. *Kompendium der Gleichnisse Jesu*. Gütersloh: Gütersloher Verlagshaus, 2007.

Žižek, Slavoj. *Sehr innig und nicht zu rasch: zwei Essays über sexuelle Differenz als philosophische Kategorie*. Wien: Turia und Kant, 1999.

———. *The Fragile Absolute: Or, Why Is the Christian Legacy Worth Fighting For?* London; New York: Verso, 2000.

INDEX OF NAMES

Abraham, patriarch, 12, 44, 45, 52, 79, 92, 94
Adorno, Th. W., 194
Agamben, G., 144, 172
Alonso, P., 104-106
Ansorge, D., ix, 85, 148, 150, 151, 153, 154
Aquinas, Th., 185, 192, 195, 228, 263
Asad, T., 228, 232
Assmann, J., 148-150, 153, 233
Augenstein, J., 134
Augustine, 67, 192, 194-196, 203, 210, 253

Bacon, F., 197
Badiou, A., 144, 172-177
Balthasar, H. U. v., 54, 218
Barth, K., 56, 163, 204, 212, 256
Batlogg, A., 15, 16, 25, 26, 38
Bauer, W., 33-36, 51, 65-67
Ben-Chorin, Sh., 73
Berger, K., 34, 35
Beutler, J., 133
Biser, E., 103, 260
Boltanski, L., 189
Bornkamm, G., 34, 121
Bosch, D., 71
Botterweck, G. J., 197
Boulluec, A., 35
Bouwman, G., 90
Bovon, F., 52, 53, 62-65, 74-76, 92, 93, 97, 99, 108, 110, 111, 119, 121
Boyarin, D., 35, 65, 67
Broadhead, E. K., 65, 82
Brümmer, V., 211, 213
Buber, M., 67, 206, 209, 210
Bultmann, R., 47, 49, 59, 120, 121
Burggraeve, R., 9

Casanova, J., 193, 229, 232
Christian, P., 102
Clooney, F. X., 7
Conzelmann, H., 75, 98
Cornille, C., 7, 10, 242

Daniélou, J., 82, 85, 88
Davis, Z., 194, 196
D'Costa, G., 9
Dehn, U., 238, 265
Delgado, M., 16, 25
Dihle, A., 119
Dirks, W., 110
Drury, J., 21

Ebeling, G., 220
Ebersohn, M., 111-113, 115-117, 119, 120, 124-127
Eckey, W., 52, 61-63
Eckhart, Meister, 192
Ellacuría, I., 49, 250
Esler, Ph., 155

Feine, P., 78, 79
Feuerbach, L., 192, 205-210
Fichte, J. G., 217
Fink, R., 105, 106
Finkelde, D., 144
Fitzmyer, J., 52, 57, 59
Francis, Pope, 268
Fredericks, J. L., 7
Freud, S., 206, 215
Friedrich, J., 101, 102

Gadamer, H.-G., 77, 78
Gewiess, J., 97
Girard, R., 54
Gnilka, J., 105, 113, 114, 120, 122, 126
Gogarten, F., 230, 231
Gradl, H.-G., 95, 96

Grilli, M., 96
Grøn, A., 201, 202, 203
Habermas, J., 229

Harnack, A. v., 117
Harris, E. J., 4, 6, 13, 269
Hedges, P., 4, 6, 13, 269
Hegel, G. W. F., 189, 190, 194, 206, 234-236
Heidegger, M., 194
Hengel, M., 26, 43, 51, 53, 57
Hettiarachchi, S., 4, 6, 13, 269
Hilberath, B. J., 16
Honneth, A., 234-238, 265
Horkheimer, M., 194
Hünermann, P., 16, 27
Huntington, S. P., 4

Jackson-McCabe, M., 82, 87, 88
Janowski, B., 148-152
Jeanrond, W. G., 3, 121, 129-131, 163, 164, 171, 172, 203-205, 210-213, 239
Jeremias, J., 41, 42, 62, 73, 75, 90, 91, 98, 100, 103, 104, 111, 126, 128
Joas, H., 229
John the Baptist, 41-45, 50, 52, 57, 59, 60-62, 64, 69, 94
John, Gospel and Letters, 20, 85, 86, 90, 96, 102, 104, 129, 130, 132, 134, 144, 156
John, O., 191, 222, 244
Jossa, G., 82
Jülicher, A., 92, 94
Jüngel, E., 163, 204, 212

Kant, I., 194, 215-217, 222, 235, 237
Kern, U., 192, 194, 195, 198, 199, 200, 209
Kessler, H., 216, 242
Kierkegaard, S., 157, 158, 163, 192, 200-204, 212, 217, 270
Kirchschläger, P., 159
Klassen, W., 156

Klauck, H.-J., 129-131
Klein, H., 73, 79-81, 83-87, 89, 91-95
Köstenberger, A., 33
Krebs, A., 156
Kruger, M. J., 33
Küng, H., 4
Kuschel, K.-J., 67

Langthaler, R., 222
Lehmann, K., 3
Lindbeck, G., 6, 11
Lohfink, G., 48, 68
Löwith, K., 14, 50
Luhmann, N., 177-188, 212
Luke, the Evangelist, ix, 11, 13, 15, 20, 21, 38, 53, 54, 56-64, 70, 71-74, 76-80, 83-85, 87, 90, 92, 93, 95-97, 99, 100, 103, 107, 108, 110, 111, 113, 118, 121, 122, 127, 128, 144, 145, 198, 259, 263
Luomanen, P., 82
Luz, U., 116-118, 120, 122, 123, 126

Manson, Th. W., 74
Marcion of Sinope, 67, 148
Mark, the Evangelist, 20, 26, 53, 57, 81, 85-87, 90, 93, 104-106, 110-115, 118, 198
Marquardt, F.-W., 256
Marshall, I. H., 62, 64, 97
Martin, D., 229
Marx, K., 206, 215
Mathys, H.-P., 116, 119, 124-126
Matthew, the Evangelist, 20, 53, 54, 56, 57, 61, 62, 81, 85, 90, 100, 102, 105, 110, 111-113, 115, 116, 122, 123
Mauss, M., 190
McGhee, R., 205, 206
Mead, G. H., 235
Meeks, W. A., 58
Merklein, H., 41, 44, 50, 51, 54, 55
Merleau-Ponty, M., 194
Metz, J. B., 222

Index of Names

Moltmann, J., 197, 198
Moyaert, M., 4, 10, 14, 239-241, 269
Müller, H., 179
Müller, K., 45-47

Neumann, N., 58, 59, 95, 97
Nietzsche, F., 206, 215, 238
Nørager, T., 230
Nygren, A., 163, 204, 205, 212

Otto, E., 85, 154

Paffenroth, K., 51, 52, 73, 77, 79-81, 84, 86, 87, 89, 93
Paget, J. C., 82, 87, 88
Pascal, B., 192, 193, 196
Paul, the Apostle, 12-14, 21, 44, 46, 51, 58, 66, 67, 72, 74, 83, 85, 94, 102, 104, 119, 122, 123, 128, 133, 135, 136-145, 155, 164, 172, 173-176, 199, 200, 204, 255
Petzke, G., 73, 78, 86, 118
Peukert, H., 22, 48, 49, 217, 222
Phan, P. C., 242
Pieper, J., 195, 205, 210
Plato, 156, 163, 192, 195
Pollefeyt, D., 6, 9
Pope, S., 224
Popkes, E. E., 129-133
Powell, L., 179
Pröpper, Th., 162, 170, 215, 217, 218, 220-224, 251

Race, A., 5, 6
Radl, W., 60-64
Rahner, K., 15, 25, 26, 37, 38, 49, 158, 159, 220, 225-230, 245-248, 250, 251, 254, 255, 266, 267
Renz, M., 264
Ricoeur, P., 21, 22, 154, 160, 161, 189-192, 212, 215, 235-241, 265-267
Rose, M., 135
Rotterdam, E., 26

Scheler, M., 192-197, 205, 270
Schelling, F. W. J., 217
Schillebeeckx, E., 26-32, 37, 48, 49, 157-159, 219, 249, 257, 266
Schlegel, F., 161
Schmidt, K. L., 26
Schmithals, W., 74
Schnackenburg, R., 103, 122, 134, 260
Schneider, G., 74, 78, 85
Schnelle, U., 129, 135, 136, 141, 157
Scholtissek, K., 134, 135
Schupp, F., 14, 20, 21, 31, 50, 217, 218
Schürmann, H., 59, 73, 74, 77, 101, 103, 110, 111, 120, 122, 124, 126
Schwager, R., 36, 37, 54, 55, 91, 148
Schweizer, E., 74
Schwemer, A. M., 26, 43, 51, 53, 57
Scotus, D., 263
Scullion, J., 149
Sellin, G., 75
Sen, A. K., 4, 232
Siebenrock, R., 16-18, 25
Sievernich, M., 243
Slenczka, N., 152
Sobrino, J., 49, 250
Söding, Th., 27, 135-144, 200
Søltoft, P., 202
Steinbock, A., 194, 196
Steiner, G., 22
Steyn, G. J., 20
Stinglhammer, H., 218
Stosch, K., 7
Strecker, G., 33, 65, 66
Striet, M., 191, 222, 244

Taylor, Ch., 7-9, 194, 219, 229, 231, 233, 234, 248
Theißen, G., 155, 156
Tillich, P., 163-165

Verweyen, H., 27, 68, 69, 171
Voegelin, E., 50

Weiss, B., 78, 79
Welker, M., 148-150
Wellhausen, J., 26
Welz, C., 203
Wenzel, K., ix, x, 3, 16, 148, 154, 161, 191, 224, 227, 239, 240, 243, 244, 266
Whitehead, Ph., 12, 13
Wiefel, W., 74
Wiegandt, K., 229
Wilfred, F., 241, 242
Winiger, J., 206, 208
Wischmeyer, O., 132-134, 136-142, 255
Wittgenstein, L., 194
Wolter, M., 20, 118, 119, 121
Wrede, W., 26
Yong, A., 71
Young, P., 158
Žižek, S., 144, 172

www.ingramcontent.com/pod-product-compliance
Lightning Source LLC
Chambersburg PA
CBHW020753020526
44116CB00028B/126